SMALL PLACES, LARGE ISSUES

Anthropology, Culture and Society

Series Editors:
Dr Richard A. Wilson, University of Sussex
Professor Thomas Hylland Eriksen, University of Oslo

SMALL PLACES, LARGE ISSUES

An Introduction to Social and Cultural Anthropology

Thomas Hylland Eriksen

Pluto Press

LONDON • STERLING, VIRGINIA

First published 1995 by
PLUTO PRESS
345 Archway Road, London N6 5AA
and 22883 Quicksilver Drive,
Sterling, VA20166–2012, USA

ISBN 0 7453 0952 6 (hbk)

A catalogue record for this book is available from
the British Library and the Library of Congress

Fourth impression 1998

Produced for Pluto Press by
Chase Production Services, Chadlington, OX73LN
Printed in the EC by
The Cromwell Press, Trowbridge, England

CONTENTS

PREFACE

To write an introductory textbook feels like trying to juggle too many balls at once – or, to use another metaphor, trying to kill as many birds as possible with as few stones as possible. In working with various versions of this book (a different edition has been published in Norwegian), it has repeatedly struck me what an incredibly diverse discipline this is. The comments and suggestions I have received from sympathetic readers and referees have been extremely useful, but I am afraid it has been impossible to take every good suggestion into account. The book is bulky enough as it is, and it was necessary to make a number of difficult decisions.

Readers who are not completely new to anthropology may notice that the main theoretical framework of the book is that of European and particularly British (and Scandinavian) anthropology, but the influence of French structuralism and American symbolic anthropology should also be obvious. I have prepared my own translations when quoting work written in languages other than English.

The most controversial thing I have done is probably to give 'classic' anthropological research a prominent place in several of the chapters, although recent developments are of course also dealt with. The main reason for this decision is simply that it is a great advantage to know at least the outline of the classic studies in order to understand later trends and debates.

The general movement, both at the theoretical and at the empirical level, is from simple to more and more complex models and sociocultural environments. The book is intended as a companion volume to ethnographic monographs, which remain an absolutely indispensable part of an anthropologist's early training, notwithstanding the capsule reviews a textbook is capable of providing.

My aim with this book is to teach undergraduates both something about the subject-matter of social anthropology and something about an anthropological way of thinking. It is my conviction that the comparative study of society and culture is a fundamental intellectual activity with a very powerful existential and political potential. Through the study of different societies, we learn something essential not only about the world, but also about ourselves. In Kirsten Hastrup's words, what anthropologists do amounts to making the familiar exotic and the exotic familiar. Therefore comparisons with 'Western' society are an underlying problematic throughout, even when the topic is Melanesian gift-giving, Malagasy ritual or Nuer politics. In fact, the whole book may perhaps be read as a series of lessons in comparative thinking.

Writing this book was a labour of love but also one of frustration and occasional despair. I am therefore sincerely grateful to Richard Wilson, Tim Ingold and my numerous Scandinavian colleagues and critics of the Norwegian edition of the book, for their encouragement and many suggestions. This printing also benefits from Margaret E. Kenna's useful comments. Although it would be hypocrisy on my part to claim that my undergraduate students at the University of Oslo have taught me a great deal of anthropology, they have taught me most of what I know about the teaching of anthropology. So they too are accomplices in this. But as usual in this kind of society, the responsibility rests with myself alone.

Thomas Hylland Eriksen
Oslo,
Summer 1995

1 SOCIAL ANTHROPOLOGY: COMPARISON AND CONTEXT

Anthropology is philosophy with the people in.
                              —*Tim Ingold*

This book is an invitation to a journey which, in the author's opinion, is one of the most rewarding a human being can embark on – and it is definitely one of the longest. It will bring the reader from the damp rainforests of the Amazon to the cold semi-desert of the Arctic; from the skyscrapers of Manhattan to mud huts in the Sahel; from villages in the New Guinea highlands to cities in modern Africa.

It is a long journey in a different sense too. Social and cultural anthropology has the whole of human society as its field of interest, and tries to understand the connections between the various aspects of our existence. When, for example, we study the traditional economic system of the Tiv of central Nigeria, we simultaneously try to find out how their economy is connected with other aspects of their society; otherwise it becomes incomprehensible to anthropologists. If we do not know that the Tiv traditionally cannot buy and sell land, and that they have customarily not used money as a means of payment, it will be plainly impossible to understand how they themselves see their situation and how they responded to the economic changes imposed on their society during colonialism.

Anthropology tries to account for the social and cultural variation in the world, but a crucial part of the anthropological project also consists in conceptualising and understanding similarities between social systems and human relationships. As one of the foremost anthropologists of the twentieth century, Claude Lévi-Strauss, has expressed it: 'Anthropology has humanity as its object of research, but unlike the other human sciences, it tries to grasp its object through its most diverse manifestations' (1983, p. 49). Put in another way: anthropology is about how different people can be, but it also tries to find out in what sense it can be said that all humans have something in common.

Another prominent anthropologist, Clifford Geertz, has expressed a similar view in an essay which essentially deals with the differences between humans and animals:

If we want to discover what man amounts to, we can only find it in what men are: and what men are, above all other things, is various. It is in understanding that variousness – its range, its nature, its basis, and its implications – that we shall come to construct a concept of human nature that, more than a statistical shadow and less than a primitivist dream, has both substance and truth. (Geertz 1973, p. 52)

Although anthropologists have wide-ranging and frequently highly specialised interests, they all share a common concern in trying to understand both connections *within* societies and connections *between* societies. As will become clearer as we proceed on this journey through the subject-matter and theories of social and cultural anthropology, there is a multitude of ways in which to approach these problems. Whether one is interested in understanding why and how the Azande of Central Africa believe in witches, why there is greater social inequality in Brazil than in Sweden, how the inhabitants of Mauritius avoid violent ethnic conflict, or what has happened to the traditional way of life of the Inuits (Eskimos) in recent years, frequently one or several anthropologists have carried out research and written on the issue. Whether one is interested in the study of religion, child-raising, political power, economic life or the relationship between men and women, one may go to the professional anthropological literature for inspiration and knowledge.

The discipline is also concerned with accounting for the interrelationships between different aspects of human existence, and usually anthropologists investigate these interrelationships taking as their point of departure a detailed study of local life in a particular society or a delineated social environment. One may therefore say that anthropology asks large questions, while at the same time it draws many of its insights from small places.

It has been common to regard its traditional focus on small-scale non-industrial societies as a distinguishing feature of anthropology, compared with other subjects dealing with culture and society. However, because of changes in the world and in the discipline itself, this is no longer an accurate description. Practically any social system can be studied anthropologically and contemporary anthropological research displays an enormous range, empirically as well as thematically.

Before moving on to a closer look at the distinguishing features of anthropology, we shall make a brief excursion into its history. Like the other social sciences, modern anthropology is a fairly recent discipline. It emerged in its present shape during the twentieth century, but it has important forerunners in the historiography, geography, travel writing, philosophy and jurisprudence of earlier times.

Theories of Primitive Society

There are many possible ways of writing the history of anthropology. If one looks closely enough, it would be possible to find the roots of the subject in the classic Greek historian Herodotos (c. 484–420 BC) or in the geographer

Strabo (c. 64–32 BC). Both were significant pioneers regarding ethnographic description; they wrote detailed narratives about foreign peoples. The writings of both deal with foreigners whose customs, languages and peculiarities they describe in as detailed a fashion as possible, frequently without passing moral judgement. Herodotos would probably have been sympathetic to the contemporary anthropological view that every society must be understood on its own terms. Both of them related critically to their sources, and held that one could only be certain about an alleged fact if one had observed it oneself. In this sense, they could be described as social scientists *avant la lettre*.

An historical account of the growth of modern anthropology might also begin with the eighteenth-century philosophers David Hume and Immanuel Kant. Hume, one of the most famous British empiricists (along with Locke and Berkeley), argued that experience was the only trustworthy source of valid knowledge; he would later become an important source of inspiration for empirical social science, whose pioneers did not trust thought and speculation, but would rather travel into the social world itself in order to obtain first-hand experience through the senses (empirical means, literally, 'based on experience'). Kant, who tried to refute some of Hume's doctrines, argued that people had certain shared innate faculties, which were assumed to be embedded in their mode of thought. In other words, he held that humans were born with certain 'formulas' for thinking; from this idea, it follows that people all over the world would think in roughly the same way. Related notions about universal mental traits have formed an important focus for discussion in modern anthropology.

Most histories of anthropology begin neither with Herodotos nor with Kant, but rather with scholars working in the mid-nineteenth century. Frequently, the foundations of modern anthropology are traced to Henry Maine's *Ancient Law* (1861) and Lewis Henry Morgan's books, including *Ancient Society* (1877). Both of these authors developed theories of 'primitive society' which were to wield influence far into the twentieth century. Maine, who had worked in India, proposed a distinction between status and contract societies, a conceptual pair which is reminiscent of many later distinctions between 'modern' and 'traditional' societies. In status-based or traditional societies, Maine argued, kinship was usually crucial in determining one's position in society; in contract-based societies, on the contrary, it would rather be the individual achievements of persons that provided them with their positions.

Morgan's most important contribution to early anthropology was doubtless his theory of social evolution. He distinguished between three main phases in the evolution of societies: savagery, barbarism and civilisation. In the condition of savagery, humans subsisted through hunting and gathering; during barbarism, agriculture and animal husbandry existed; while humans who had reached the level of civilisation had developed literacy and the state.

Morgan's developmental scheme was only one of many evolutionist theories in the nineteenth century. The most famous, and arguably most complex, is Karl Marx's theory on social development through class struggle (see Chapter 9). Although Marx was clearly a more significant thinker than Morgan, the latter was particularly important in the early development of anthropology because of his interest in non-industrial societies and his use of ethnographic sources.

Evolutionism and Diffusionism

A characteristic of the anthropology of the nineteenth century was the belief in social evolution – the idea that human societies developed in a particular direction – and the related notion that European societies were the end-product of a long developmental chain which began with 'savagery'. This idea was typical of the Victorian age, dominated by an optimistic belief in technological progress and, simultaneously, European colonialism, which was frequently justified with reference to what Kipling wrote of as 'the white man's burden'; the alleged duty of the European to 'civilise the savages'. Charles Darwin's theory of evolution, first presented in *On the Origin of Species by Means of Natural Selection* (1859), was also a powerful influence on intellectual life in the second half of the nineteenth century. Darwin's supporter Herbert Spencer developed Social Darwinism, which held that human societies evolve roughly in the same way as animal species adapt and develop, through competition between individuals and 'the survival of the fittest'.

Another important anthropological current in the nineteenth century, with its focal point in Germany, was diffusionism, a doctrine about the geographical dissemination of cultural traits. Whereas evolutionists would argue that every society has an intrinsic potential for change, a diffusionist would rather try to show that the development of specific cultural traits is usually caused by influence from the outside. Although there were frequent arguments between the two, diffusionism is not in principle incompatible with evolutionism: it was, and is, possible to favour both. Within anthropology, diffusionism became unfashionable when, around the time of the First World War, people began to study single societies in great detail without trying to explain their historical development. However, a theoretical direction reminiscent of diffusionism is returning in the 1990s, under the label of globalisation theory (see Chapter 18), which is an attempt to understand and account for the ways in which modern mass communications, migration, global capitalism and other 'global' phenomena affect local conditions everywhere in the world.

With British late-nineteenth and early-twentieth century scholars like Edward Tylor, James Frazer and W.H.R. Rivers, we approach modern social anthropology. Tylor wrote on a multitude of topics, and thanks to his definition of culture, dating from 1871, his place in any history of anthropology is secure. This famous definition reads: 'Culture or Civilization, taken in its widest ethnographic sense, is that complex whole which includes knowledge, belief, art, morals, custom, and any other capabilities and habits acquired by man as a member of society' (Tylor 1968 [1871]). This early definition of culture is still seen as useful by many anthropologists.

Tylor's student Frazer wrote the twelve-volume study *The Golden Bough* (1890), which is a massive book even in a heavily abridged version (Frazer 1974 [1922]). This work is a wide-ranging comparative study of religion and rituals, and contains a wealth of ethnographic details from every corner of the world. Both Tylor and Frazer were evolutionists, and Frazer's main theoretical project consisted in demonstrating how thought had developed from the magical via the religious to the scientific.

Neither Tylor nor Frazer conducted detailed field studies, although Tylor spent several years in Mexico and wrote a book there. A famous anecdote tells of a dinner party where William James, the pragmatist philosopher, asked Frazer whether he had ever become acquainted with any of those savages he wrote so much about. Frazer allegedly replied, in a shocked tone of voice, 'Heaven forbid!' (Evans-Pritchard 1962).

The situation was different with W.H.R. Rivers and his collaborators, who included A.R. Haddon and Charles Seligman. Rather than depending on the frequently unreliable material collected by missionaries and explorers, they carried out field research themselves. Rivers and his colleagues took part in an important expedition to the Torres Strait (between New Guinea and Australia) in 1898, which many regard as the last important precursor of the modern anthropological field study.

The Emergence of Modern Anthropology

Franz Boas and Bronislaw Malinowski are often regarded as the first modern anthropologists. Boas was of German origin, but moved to the US in the 1880s to study American Indians. He did thorough field research himself among Inuits and several Indian peoples, and nearly single-handedly founded American cultural anthropology. Several famous anthropologists, including Alfred Kroeber, Ruth Benedict and Margaret Mead, were students of Boas. His influence was profound in many fields, but his most important single contribution may have been the doctrine of cultural relativism, the idea that every culture must be understood according to its own logic and that it is therefore analytically misleading to try to arrange cultures on an evolutionary ladder. Cultural relativism is still indispensable as a methodological tool, and is treated in greater detail later.

Malinowski was a Pole, but he emigrated to Britain in 1910. His most important work was the meticulous recording of social life in the Trobriand Islands off New Guinea. His fieldwork there lasted for more than two years between 1915 and 1918, and this kind of work, where he had close and enduring contact with the local community, would become an ideal to follow for later generations of anthropologists. Malinowski emphasised

---

Franz Boas (1859–1941), born in Minden, Westphalia (in present-day Germany), was educated as a geographer in his native Germany but became an anthropologist after participating in Arctic expeditions in 1883–4. Later he moved to the United States and eventually became an American citizen. Boas is the unrivalled paternal figure of American cultural anthropology. He carried out fieldwork among Inuits (Eskimos) as well as North American Indians; his numerous writings span five decades, and he may rightfully be called the founder of modern American anthropology. Indeed, his four main fields of interest – ethnology, linguistics, archaeology and physical anthropology – remain the basis of American anthropology.

Reacting against the grand evolutionary schemes of Tylor and other European anthropologists, Boas took an early stance in favour of what has since come to be known as historical particularism; the view that the evolution of each society (or culture) has to be understood in relation to its own proper dynamics. In this, Boas also differed from British social anthropologists, whose advocacy of detailed fieldwork he nonetheless shared. Unlike Radcliffe-Brown and to a lesser extent Malinowski, he emphasised cultural variation and the uniqueness of each culture in the sense that he tended to reject general explanatory frameworks, although it could also be argued that Boas, like his British colleagues, searched for patterns and cross-cultural uniformities, perhaps particularly at the psychological level. Boas was perhaps the earliest anthropologist to formulate the principles of cultural relativism, and his insistence on the meticulous collection of empirical data was due not only to his scientific views but also to the realisation that cultural change quickly obliterated what he saw as unique cultures, particularly in North America. As far back as *The Mind of Primitive Man* (1911), Boas argued that anthropology ought to be engaged on behalf of threatened indigenous populations.

---

the importance of studying the interrelationships of various aspects of society, and therefore held that long field studies were absolutely necessary. Notably, he stressed, it was important to talk the language fluently. Malinowski's monograph *Argonauts of the Western Pacific* (1922) became an instant classic through its thorough and systematic ethnographic descriptions and its persuasive demonstrations of the necessity of studying any social or cultural phenomenon in its full context.

One of Malinowski's contemporaries, who was also important in the development of social anthropology, was A.R. Radcliffe-Brown. He was profoundly inspired by the writings of the great French sociologist Emile Durkheim on social integration. Durkheim, who wrote important studies about the division of labour in 'primitive' societies and about religion and totemism (see Chapters 13 and 14), saw society as an organic whole where the constituent parts, which could be conceptualised as individuals or social institutions, fulfilled particular functions; that is to say, their most important role consisted in their contribution to the stability of society. Radcliffe-Brown applied Durkheim's social theory to his own as well as others' ethnographic material from 'primitive' societies. He stressed the importance of studying

societies as they were, rather than engaging in 'conjectural history' as the earlier generation of anthropologists had been inclined to. Indeed, both Malinowski and Radcliffe-Brown were positively hostile towards cultural history.

Radcliffe-Brown is regarded as the founder of structural-functionalism in anthropology. This is a doctrine about the ways in which the various institutions of a society contribute to its stability. Malinowski was no structural-functionalist, although he described himself as a functionalist. Whereas Radcliffe-Brown and his followers regarded individuals and their actions as 'side-effects' of society, whose deepest meaning consisted in contributing to social integration, Malinowski was instead inclined to argue that society existed to satisfy the needs of the individuals. The contrast between these leading characters in early modern anthropology can be traced up to this very day: some anthropologists tend to regard society as an unintended consequence of the actions of individuals, whereas others tend to regard persons largely as products of their society.

Alfred Reginald Radcliffe-Brown (1881–1955) founded 'the British school' of anthropology. He taught at several universities, from Cape Town to Chicago, and played a decisive role in the spread and development of the subject between the wars. Radcliffe-Brown was strongly influenced by Durkheim's social theory, which he applied and developed in his own empirical analyses, notably *The Andaman Islanders* (1922) and *The Social Organization of Australian Tribes* (1931). In these books, as well as in *Structure and Function in Primitive Society* (1952), he developed structural-functionalism in social anthropology: the doctrine of how societies are integrated, and how social institutions reinforce each other and contribute to the maintenance of society.

Radcliffe-Brown's scientific ideals were taken from natural science, and he hoped to develop 'general laws of society' comparable in precision to those of physics and chemistry. This programme has been abandoned by most anthropologists – as has structural-functionalism in its pure form – but many of the questions raised by contemporary anthropologists, particularly in Europe, were originally posed by Radcliffe-Brown.

Many other important influences on contemporary anthropological thought could be mentioned. Durkheim and his French sociological school have been immensely influential on anthropology. His nephew, Marcel Mauss, wrote, among other things, a very important essay on gifts and social life, *Essai sur le don* (*The Gift*, 1954 [1925]; see Chapter 11). Lucien Lévy-Bruhl, a contemporary of Mauss, wrote books about different modes of thought, starting a long and complex debate concerning whether 'primitives' think in a radically different fashion from 'moderns' (see Chapter 14). Ferdinand de Saussure, a linguist, must also be mentioned in this context. His work on the structure of language inspired one of the most magnificent anthropological projects of this century, namely Claude Lévi-Strauss's structuralism (Chapters 7 and 14).

Sigmund Freud's psychoanalytical theories have also been influential, particularly in American anthropology. Finally, classic German sociology, from Marx, Ferdinand Tönnies, Max Weber and others, continues to exert a strong influence on contemporary social anthropological thinking. In later chapters, we return to several of the topics introduced by these great social theorists.

Different Traditions of Anthropology

Anthropology is a large and diversified subject, which is practised somewhat differently in different countries, although it retains its distinctive character everywhere. Since the Second World War, the core areas have been Great Britain, the US, France and Australia. British anthropology, which is generally spoken of as *social* anthropology and which also enjoys a strong position in Scandinavia and India, emphasises the study of social processes and is thus close to sociology. The British social anthropologist Edmund Leach (1982) once characterised his subject as a 'comparative micro-sociology'. In the US, we tend instead to speak of *cultural* anthropology, and in general the sociological underpinning characteristic of the British tradition has been less prominent there. Instead, linguistics and prehistory have informed American anthropology in different ways. Several important specialisations, such as cultural ecology, linguistic anthropology and various approaches in psychological and interpretive or hermeneutic anthropology, were developed in the US.

French anthropology in the postwar period has been strongly associated with structuralism (see Chapter 7), notably with the names of Claude Lévi-Strauss, Louis Dumont and the structural Marxist Maurice Godelier. In South America, Italy and the Iberian peninsula, and partly in Belgium and the Netherlands, the French orientation is strong.

These and other regional variations should not be exaggerated. Despite certain historical (and present) differences between the professional traditions of different countries, there is little doubt that the discipline is one – although it has many specialisations and encompasses many divergent strands of thought. In this book, cultural and social anthropology are not generally distinguished between, but it should nonetheless be noted that the point of departure is that of social anthropology. For example, the presentation of basic theoretical concepts (Chapters 3–5) draws extensively on sociological theory. The perspective of this book is also strongly comparative in that each example or case described is compared, explicitly or implicitly, to other phenomena in other societies.

An Outline of the Subject

What, then, is anthropology? Let us begin with the etymology of the concept. It is a compound of two Greek words, 'anthropos' and 'logos', which can be translated as 'human' and 'reason', respectively. So anthropology means 'reason about humans' or 'knowledge about humans'. Social anthropology would then mean knowledge about humans in societies. Such a definition would, of course, cover the other social sciences as well as anthropology, but it may still be useful as a beginning.

The word 'culture', which is also crucial to the discipline, originates from the Latin 'colere', which means to cultivate. (The word 'colony' has the same origin.) Cultural anthropology thus means 'knowledge about cultivated humans'; that is, knowledge about those aspects of humanity which are not natural, but which are related to that which is acquired.

'Culture' has been described as one of the two or three most complicated words in the English language (Williams 1981, p. 87). In the early 1950s, Clyde Kluckhohn and Alfred Kroeber (1952) presented 161 different definitions of culture. It would not be possible to consider the majority of these definitions here; besides, many of them were – fortunately – quite similar. Let us therefore, as a preliminary conceptualisation of culture, define it as those abilities, notions and forms of behaviour persons have acquired as members of society. A definition of this kind, which is indebted to both Tylor and Geertz (although the latter stresses meaning rather than behaviour), is the most common one among anthropologists.

Culture nevertheless carries with it a basic ambiguity. On the one hand, every human is equally cultural; in this sense, the term refers to a basic *similarity* within humanity. On the other hand, people have acquired different abilities, notions, etc., and are thereby *different* because of culture. Culture refers, in other words, both to basic similarities and to systematic differences between humans.

The relationship between culture and society can be described in the following way. Culture refers to the acquired, cognitive and symbolic aspects of existence, whereas society refers to the social organisation of human life, patterns of interaction and power relationships. The implications of this analytical distinction, which may seem bewildering, will eventually be evident.

A short definition of anthropology may read thus: 'Anthropology is the comparative study of cultural and social life. Its most important method is participant observation, which consists in lengthy fieldwork in a particular social setting.' The discipline thus compares aspects of different societies, and continuously searches for interesting dimensions for comparison. If, say, one chooses to write a monograph about a people in the New Guinea highlands, one will always choose to describe it with at least some concepts (such as kinship, gender and power) that render it comparable with aspects of other societies.

Further, the discipline emphasises the importance of fieldwork, which is a thorough close-up study of a particular social and cultural environment, where the researcher is normally required to spend a year or more.

Clearly, anthropology has many features in common with other social sciences and humanities. Indeed, a difficult question consists in deciding whether it is a science or one of the humanities. Do we search for general laws, as the natural scientists do, or do we instead try to understand and interpret different societies? E.E. Evans-Pritchard in Britain and Alfred Kroeber in the US, leading anthropologists in their day, both argued around 1950 that anthropology had more in common with history than with the natural sciences. Although their view, considered something of a heresy at the time, has become commonplace since, there are still some anthropologists who feel that the subject should aim at scientific rigour similar to that of the natural sciences.

Some of the implications of this divergence in views will be discussed in later chapters. A few important defining features of anthropology are nevertheless common to all practitioners of the subject: it is comparative and empirical; its most important method is fieldwork; and it has a truly global focus in that it does not single out one region, or one kind of society, as being more important than others. Unlike sociology proper, anthropology does not concentrate its attention on the industrialised world; unlike philosophy, it stresses the importance of empirical research; unlike history, it studies society as it is being enacted; and unlike linguistics, it stresses the social and cultural context of speech when looking at language. To be sure, there are great overlaps with other sciences and disciplines, and there is a lot to be learnt from them, yet anthropology has its distinctive character as an intellectual discipline trying simultaneously to account for actual cultural variation in the world and to develop a theoretical perspective on culture and society.

Before moving on to field method and the process of inquiry in the next chapter, there follows an outline of a few further central characteristics of anthropology.

Ethnocentrism

A society or a culture, it was remarked earlier, must be understood on its own terms. In saying this, we warn against the application of a shared, universal scale to be used in the evaluation of every society. Such a scale, which is often used, could be defined as longevity, gross national product (GNP), democratic rights, literacy rates, etc. Until quite recently, it was common in European society to rank non-Europeans according to the ratio of their population which was admitted into the Christian church. Such a ranking of peoples is utterly irrelevant to anthropology. In order to pass judgement on the quality of life in a foreign society, we must first try to understand that society from the inside; otherwise our judgement has a very limited intellectual interest. What is conceived of as 'the good life' in the society in which we live may not appear attractive at all if it is seen from a different vantage-point. In order to understand people's lives, it is therefore necessary to try to grasp the totality of their experiential world; and in order to succeed in this project, it is inadequate to look at selected 'variables'. Obviously, a concept such as 'annual income' is absurd in a society where neither money nor wagework is common.

This kind of argument may be read as a warning against ethnocentrism. This term (from Greek 'ethnos', meaning 'a people') means evaluating other people from one's own vantage-point and describing them in one's own terms. One's own 'ethnos', including one's cultural values, is literally placed at the centre. Other peoples would, within this frame of thought, necessarily appear as inferior imitations of oneself. If the Nuer of the Sudan are unable to get a mortgage to buy a house, they thus appear to have a less perfect society than ourselves. If the Kwakiutl Indians of the west coast of North America lack electricity, they seem to have a less fulfilling life than we do. If the Kachin of upper Burma reject conversion to Christianity, they are less civilised than we are, and if the San ('Bushmen') of the Kalahari are illiterate, they appear less intelligent than us. Such points of view express an ethnocentric attitude which fails to allow other peoples to be different from ourselves on their own terms and can be a serious obstacle to understanding. Rather than comparing strangers with our own society and placing ourselves on top of an imaginary pyramid, anthropology calls for an understanding of different societies as they appear *from the inside*. Anthropology cannot provide an answer to a question of which societies are better than others, simply because the discipline does not ask it. If asked what is the good life, the anthropologist will have to answer that every society has its own definition(s) of it.

Moreover, an ethnocentric bias, which may be less easy to detect than moralistic judgements, may shape the very concepts we use in describing and classifying the world. For example, it has been argued that it may be inappropriate to speak of politics and kinship when referring to societies which themselves lack concepts of 'politics' and 'kinship'. Politics, perhaps, belongs to the ethnographer's society and not to the society under study. We return to this fundamental problem later.

Cultural relativism is sometimes posited as the opposite of ethnocentrism. This is the doctrine that societies or cultures are qualitatively different and have their own unique inner logic, and that it is therefore scientifically absurd to rank them on a scale. If one places a San group, say, at the bottom of a ladder where the variables are, say, literacy and annual income, this ladder is irrelevant to them if it turns out that the San do not place a high priority on money and books. It should also be evident that one cannot, within a cultural relativist framework, argue that a society with many cars is 'better' than one with fewer, or that the ratio of cinemas to population is a useful indicator of the quality of life.

Cultural relativism is an indispensable and unquestionable theoretical premiss and methodological rule-of-thumb in our attempts to understand alien societies in an as unprejudiced way as possible. As an ethical principle, however, it is probably impossible in practice, since it seems to indicate that everything is as good as everything else, provided it makes sense in a particular society. It may ultimately lead to nihilism. For this reason, it

Before the Second World War, 'negro caravans' were popular in European cities. Africans were displayed in the same way that wild animals are exhibited in zoos. This photo depicts a 'negro village' in Christiania (now Oslo) in 1914. To what extent has the general European view of 'exotic peoples' changed since that time? (Photo courtesy of Oslo Ethnographic Museum)

may be timely to stress that many anthropologists are impeccable cultural relativists in their daily work, while they have definite, frequently dogmatic notions about right and wrong in their private lives.

Cultural relativism cannot, when all is said and done, be posited simply as the opposite of ethnocentrism, the simple reason being that it does not in itself contain a moral principle. The principle of cultural relativism in anthropology is a methodological one – it helps us investigate and compare societies without relating them to an intellectually irrelevant moral scale; but this does not logically imply that there is no difference between right and wrong. Finally, we should be aware that many anthropologists wish to discover general, shared aspects of humanity or human societies. There is no necessary contradiction between a project of this kind and a cultural relativist approach, even if universalism – doctrines emphasising the similarities between humans – is frequently seen as the opposite of cultural relativism. One may well be a relativist at a certain level of anthropological analysis, yet simultaneously argue that a particular underlying pattern is common to all societies or persons. Many would indeed claim that this is what anthropology is about: to discover both the uniqueness of each social and cultural setting *and* the ways in which humanity is one.

Suggestions for Further Reading

E.E. Evans-Pritchard: *Social Anthropology*. Glencoe: Free Press 1951.
Clifford Geertz: The Uses of Diversity. In *Assessing Cultural Anthropology*, ed. Robert Borofsky. New York: McGraw-Hill 1994.
Adam Kuper: *Anthropology and Anthropologists: The Modern British School*. London: Routledge & Kegan Paul 1983.

2 FIELDWORK AND INTERPRETATION

Theory without data is empty, but data without theory are blind.
                                                            —C. Wright Mills

Fieldwork

Anthropology distinguishes itself from the other social sciences through the great emphasis put on fieldwork as the most important source of new knowledge about society and culture. A field study may last for between a few months to two years or longer, and it aims at developing as intimate an understanding as possible of the phenomena investigated. Although there are differences in field methods between different anthropological schools, it is generally agreed that the anthropologist ought to stay in the field long enough for his or her presence to be considered more or less 'natural' by the permanent residents, although he or she will always to some extent remain a stranger.

Many anthropologists involuntarily take on the role of the clown when in the field. They speak strangely with a flawed grammar; they ask surprising and sometimes tactless questions, and tend to break many rules regarding how things ought to be done. Such a role can be an excellent starting-point for fieldwork, even when it is not chosen: through discovering how the locals react to one's own behaviour, one obtains an early hint about their way of thinking. We are all perceived more or less as clowns in unfamiliar surroundings; there are so many rules of conduct in any society that one will necessarily break some of them when one tries to take part in social life in an alien society. In Britain, for example, it is considered uncultured to wear white socks with a dark suit; still, it happens that people who are not fully conversant with the local dress code do so. In the field, anthropologists have been known to commit much more serious mistakes than this.

A different, and sometimes more problematic, role of the field anthropologist can be the expert role. Many fieldworkers are treated with great deference and respect by their hosts, are spoken to in extremely polite ways and so on, and can thus run the risk of never seeing aspects of society which the locals are ashamed of showing to high-ranking strangers.

No matter which role one takes on in the field – most ethnographers are probably partly expert, partly clown – fieldwork is very demanding, both in professional and in human terms. The tidy, systematic and well-rounded texts written by anthropologists are more often than not the end-product of long periods in the field characterised by boredom, illness, personal privations, disappointments and frustration: few anthropologists can state squarely that their fieldwork was a continuously exciting journey of exploration, full of pleasant experiences. In a strange setting, one will usually master the language and the codes for behaviour poorly at the beginning, and one will feel helpless in many situations. Besides, one runs the risk of encountering suspicion and hostility, and it can be profoundly unpleasant for the body to have to cope with an unfamiliar climate, strange food and a different hygienic standard than one is accustomed to. Last but not least, it can be very trying for people with a middle-class 'Western' background (which most anthropologists have) to adapt to societies where being alone is considered a sad condition. Plainly put, in many village settings one is never left alone. This problem, of course, does not exist to the same degree for the growing number of anthropologists who carry out their fieldwork in modern urban settings.

Field Methods

A principal requirement in fieldwork consists of trying to take part in local life as much as possible. Anthropologists also use a variety of specified, formal techniques for the collection of data (see for example, Pelto and Pelto 1970; Ellen 1984). Depending on the kind of fieldwork one is engaged in, structured interviews, statistical sampling and other techniques may be required to varying degrees. Most anthropologists depend on a combination of formal techniques and unstructured participant observation in their fieldwork.

Participant observation refers to the informal field methods which form the basis for most fieldwork, whether or not it is supplemented with other techniques. The aim of this method is to enter as deeply as possibly into the social and cultural field one researches; in practice one becomes, as Evans-Pritchard remarks (1983 [1937], p. 243), a 'doubly marginal' person, in a sense suspended between one's own society and the society under investigation. During participant observation, one tries to immerse oneself into the life of the locals and tries not to be noticed, so that they can carry on with their own lives as usual. In this regard, the issue of hidden versus open observation has been discussed in the anthropological community. Generally, it is agreed that it would be unethical not to inform one's hosts what one's mission consists of. The people explored must have the right to refuse to be subjected to anthropological analyses; in the case of hidden observation, they are deprived of this possibility.

There are many ways of doing fieldwork, and it is impossible to provide a clear recipe for how to carry it out. For one thing, the anthropologist him- or herself is the most important 'scientific instrument' used, investing a great deal of his or her own personality in the process. Another source of variation is the greatly differing settings and topics investigated by anthropologists. The methods must be tailored to fit the requirements of the subject, but it is difficult to be more specific. Evans-Pritchard once recalled his first attempts to learn about fieldwork in the early 1920s (1983 [1937]: 239–54). He had asked a number of renowned anthropologists how to do it and had received various answers. First, he asked the famous Finnish ethnologist Westermarck, who said, 'Don't converse with an informant for more than twenty minutes because if you aren't bored by that time he will be.' Evans-Pritchard comments: 'Very good advice, if somewhat inadequate.' Alfred Haddon said 'that it was really all quite simple; one should always behave as a gentleman'. Evans-Pritchard's teacher, Charles Seligman, 'told me to take ten grams of quinine every night and to keep off women'. Finally, Malinowski himself told the novice 'not to be a bloody fool'. Evans-Pritchard himself emphasises, later in the same account, that facts are themselves meaningless; in other words, 'one must know precisely what one wants to know' and then fashion a suitable methodology from the available techniques. There is – alas – no simple recipe for fieldwork. It is a method where the researcher's most important 'scientific instrument' is him- or herself.

Many anthropological accounts of the process of inquiry, and especially fieldwork, are probably strongly idealised. The expression 'participant observation', a vaguely defined research technique, may serve as a convenient blanket term to conceal both ethical and methodological shortcomings in the actual research process. One problem could, perhaps, be the fact that one develops an antagonistic attitude towards the people one studies. When Malinowski's private diaries were published in 1967, they spurred a long and heated debate. Malinowski, who was and is regarded as an outstanding ethnographer, turned out to have a less than flattering view of his hosts in the Trobriand Islands. His project consisted of understanding the islanders in their own terms, yet he personally regarded them as unwashed savages and frequently, he reports, had to force himself to leave his hut in the morning for fieldwork. The question which has been raised in this context is whether it is possible to carry out good fieldwork among people one has this little respect for. The answer is obviously yes; and as long as one does not molest one's hosts in the field, there can be no rules against negative attitudes on the part of the anthropologist. At the end of the day, the value of participant observation lies in the quality of the empirical data one has collected, not in the number of close friends one has acquired in the field.

Common weaknesses in fieldwork are limited knowledge of the field language, gender bias (see Chapter 8), or the fact that one's chief informants fail to be representative of the society as a whole. Concerning the latter point, it is probably true that anthropologists have tended to pay too much attention to the elite of the community; frequently chiefs, teachers and other atypical individuals are most efficient in offering their services to a visiting anthropologist. Gerald Berreman (1962) once wrote a confessional piece on his own field experiences in North India. He depended on an interpreter, and only after he had been working, rather unsuccessfully, for a while did it become evident that the interpreter was a significant source of distortion in his fieldwork; not because he lied or was inadequate as an interpreter, but because of his position in the caste hierarchy. People did not talk as openly to him as they would to someone like Berreman himself, or to a local with a different caste membership.

Bronislaw Kaspar Malinowski (1884–1942) was born in Krakow, Poland, and settled in Great Britain in 1910, where he established himself as a theoretical anthropologist. During the period 1915–18 he carried out his legendary fieldwork in the Trobriand Islands, and he later published a number of books based on this work, including *Argonauts of the Western Pacific* (1922), *Crime and Custom in Savage Society* (1927) and *The Sexual Life of the Savages in North–western Melanesia* (1929).

Malinowski has made a significant contribution to anthropology,although his theoretical perspectives were controversial from the beginning. His field method, emphasising long-term participant observation, became the standard for later research, and his ethnography was much more detailed than had previously been common. Thematically, he also broke new ground, writing on law, technology, sexuality, exchange and other subjects rarely dealt with in detail earlier.

Malinowski regarded all institutions of a society as intrinsically linked to each other, and stressed that every social or cultural phenomenon ought to be studied in its full context. He also held that inborn human needs were the driving force in the development of social institutions.

Fieldwork does not have to be either capital-intensive or labour-intensive: as a research process it is cheap, since the only scientific instruments involved are the fieldworkers themselves and possibly a few assistants. However, and this is perhaps the main point about fieldwork as a scientific method, it is time-intensive. Ideally, one should stay in the field long enough to be able to see the world as the locals see it. Even if this may be impossible, among other reasons because one cannot entirely get rid of one's own cultural background, it can be a worthwhile aim to pursue. The strength of the anthropologist's knowledge can thus be said to lie in his or her mastery of both the local culture and a different culture (his or her own), and of tools of analysis, making it possible to give an analytical, comparative account of both.

Theory and Data

The relationship between theory and empirical material, or data, is fundamental in all empirical science, including anthropology. No science can rely on theory alone (it then becomes pure mathematics or philosophy), just as it cannot rely on pure facts: in that case, it would be unable to tell us anything interesting. To put it differently, research has an inductive and a deductive dimension. Induction consists of going out there, 'watching and wondering', collecting information about what people say and do. Deduction consists of attempts to account for facts by means of a general hypothesis or theory. Suppose I were to explore the hypothesis that the position of women in society is proportional to their contribution to the economy (see Chapter 8). Working deductively, I would develop an argument showing why this made sense. In the actual research process, however, I would have to shift to an inductive mode, exploring the relationship between the position of women and the economy in a number of existing societies. As soon as I came across one or several societies where there was no apparent relationship between the contribution to the economy and the relative rank of women, I would have to modify my initial hypothesis.

We may envisage the search for this kind of general insight as a zigzag movement between the observation of fact and theoretical reasoning, where new facts modify the theory and (modified) theory accounts for the facts. Each time one shifts from theory to description of empirical process and back, one's insight has become a little bit more accurate.

If one were to reproduce everything one's informants said and to describe everything they did, one would be unable to falsify, or for that matter justify, specific hypotheses. One would literally drown in details without being able to present patterns and regularities. The description of society would be as complex and ambiguous as society itself and therefore superfluous. The anthropological project consists, to a great extent, of imposing ordering patterns and regularities onto the observed material, and we depend on our own theoretical abstractions in order to do so. The challenge lies in saying something significant about culture and social life through these abstractions.

The choice of an accurate topic for investigation therefore is an important part of the preparation for fieldwork. One should, at the very least, know if one is interested in, say, resource management or child-raising before embarking on fieldwork. Otherwise one will end up knowing too little about everything rather than knowing enough about something. Godfrey Lienhardt (1985), borrowing an analogy from Geertz, has compared the relationship between theory and ethnography to an elephant-and-rabbit stew. What is required, says Lienhardt, is one elephant of ethnography and one rabbit of theory. The art, as he sees it, consists of bringing out the flavour of the rabbit.

Anthropology at Home

Anthropology has traditionally distinguished itself from sociology through (i) the great emphasis put on participant observation and fieldwork, and (ii) through studying chiefly non-industrialised societies. Sociology has concentrated on understanding, criticising and administrating modern societies, whereas the historical task of anthropology has been to account for the variations in human existence and, to some extent, to rescue disappearing peoples from oblivion by recording their way of life in writing.

For a number of reasons, fieldwork in the anthropologist's own society or a neighbouring one has become much more common since the early 1960s. First, our discipline today faces a number of new challenges because of historical changes in the world, including the virtual disappearance of 'the tribal world'. It has become impossible to posit sharp distinctions between 'us' (moderns) and 'them' (primitives), not least because modernisation and 'development' have contributed to shrinking spatial distances and have blurred boundaries between cultures which formerly seemed relatively clear. Our 'objects of study' may now be our readers as well. Second, the analyses of tribal societies have inspired researchers to use similar analytical models when dealing with their own society, and have also provided a useful basis for comparison. It is easier to see what is unique to our own society when we have intimate knowledge of other societies than it would otherwise. Third, there are today many researchers competing for scarce resources, and far from everybody is able to raise funding for long-term fieldwork in a remote place. In addition, a number of governments in the Third World are sceptical of anthropologists. As later chapters will reveal, many highly interesting research projects concern 'modern' societies.

One argument sometimes used against fieldwork in one's own society is that the overall aim of the discipline is to account for cultural variation in the world. It therefore seems reasonable that one should study people who seem culturally remote. Another argument is that it is necessary to use our own society as an implicit basis for comparison, something which vanishes when we study our neighbours. On the other hand, thorough field studies of 'modern' societies have revealed that they are far more heterogeneous, in terms of culture and social organisation, than generally assumed.

A general argument in favour of anthropological research 'at home' is that the questions we ask about culture, society and so on are equally relevant anywhere in the world. One of the grand old men of anthropology, Sir Raymond Firth, expressed his own view in a lecture in 1989: 'Since we can explore the anthropological problems anywhere, we might as well go to places where it is comfortable to spend some time' (Firth 1989). For his own part, Firth has done most of his fieldwork in Tikopia, a tropical island in the Pacific. As a matter of fact, today's anthropology encompasses the whole world, including the areas which anthropolo-

Fredrik Barth, who had previously concentrated his research efforts on societies in the Middle East, did fieldwork among the Baktaman of New Guinea in 1968. In a popular account of his field experiences, Barth described his malnourishment among them, stating that he lost ten kg (21 lb) during the fieldwork, but he also grew 10 cm (4 in) around the waist. (Photo courtesy of Scandinavian University Press)

gists call home. Fieldwork at home, like anywhere in the world, depends on the anthropologist's professional skills. In a familiar or semi-familiar setting, one has the advantage of mastering the language and cultural conventions better than in a culturally distant place, but one also tends to take too much for granted. This problem is sometimes called 'homeblindness', and it can, at least to a great extent, be overcome through proper training. The comparative, detailed study of cultural variation which forms the core of the education of an anthropologist enables us to study familiar societies with roughly the same methods and analytical apparatus we would apply to distant societies.

Interpretation and Analysis

When modern anthropology took shape in the early years of the twentieth century, there were still large areas that had hardly been visited by Europeans and were much less subjected to systematic exploration. When

Boas studied Indians on the west coast of North America, when Malinowski lived in the Trobriand Islands, when Bateson visited the Iatmul in New Guinea and when Evans-Pritchard went to live among the Azande, they could only to a limited extent prepare themselves through reading earlier studies of the same people. They knew comparatively little about the sites they were going to. The world has changed quite dramatically since then. There now always exist studies from the region one visits as ethnographer, although it may still be possible to come across smaller groups, for example in the Amazon basin or New Guinea, which have not been studied anthropologically. Frequently, one can learn the language before leaving home, and very often there exists a large specialist literature that it may be necessary to study before embarking on fieldwork.

The classic anthropological monograph dealt with a people's most important institutions, usually taking detailed village fieldwork as its point of departure. It frequently aimed at a comprehensive overview of 'the way of life' of a people, describing the interrelationship between religion, politics, the economy, kinship and so on. For a number of reasons, this model is no longer common. One obvious reason is that most anthropological studies now take place in complex large-scale settings and are not limited to villages. Another is the growing specialisation within the discipline, which has turned many professionals into highly specialised sub-disciplinary experts focusing, say, on medical systems, socialisation, public rituals or political rhetoric in particular societies. A third, related reason is the fact that a wealth of general ethnography has already been carried out on most regions, so it is frequently unnecessary to begin from scratch. When Annette Weiner left for fieldwork in the Trobriand Islands in the 1970s, therefore, she did not need to study every aspect of the Melanesian island society in detail: Malinowski and others had already done so, and she could relate her own work to lacunae or controversial points in earlier analyses of the Trobrianders (Weiner 1988). Her studies deal chiefly with the role of women and gender relations, and they engage in a critical dialogue with earlier work in the area (see Chapters 8 and 11).

In addition, social theory is now being produced from within in many of the societies studied by anthropologists. Sociology, anthropology and other theoretically informed texts are being written by the grandchildren of Radcliffe-Brown's and Kroeber's informants. This implies that today's anthropologist may engage in a dialogue with the society explored to a much greater extent than her predecessors did. It also implies that anthropological studies may affect local communities directly. If someone today writes a monograph on, say, a South African neighbourhood, the book will necessarily influence South African society; it will be read by some of the 'natives', and thus becomes part of the social reality of the informants. This situation has created obvious ethical problems. It would not have occurred to Malinowski or Bateson that their books on Melanesia might have a direct influence on the societies in question (although Malinowski's work is by now well known in the Trobriand Islands): they could write freely without taking such issues into account. This is no longer possible, at least if one's work is published in English or French.

The Ethnographic Present and the Past

Anthropological texts are usually written in the present tense. Many of the most influential monographs were nevertheless written half a century ago or more, and in virtually every case the societies they deal with have changed radically since the original fieldwork took place. Frequently, moreover, fieldwork was carried out during an unusual, not a 'typical', historical period. For example, classic African anthropology was developed during the last phase of French and British colonialism, namely between the First World War and 1960. It has since been pointed out that this period was atypical because it was a time of political stability – which has been absent both before and afterwards in large parts of Africa.

Social anthropology has never tried to replace history. Our analyses have traditionally been focused on social and cultural interrelationships at a particular point in time and, until recently, have rarely emphasised the historical processes which have led up to the present. In the British, American and French traditions, the aim has usually been to account for the workings of a particular society or culture, not to try to explain how it emerged. Boas, Radcliffe-Brown and Malinowski were all critical of the rather speculative forms of cultural history which preceded modern anthropology. However, an appropriate response to the bad cultural history exemplified in much early anthropological writing would not be to discredit history as such, but rather to improve one's historical accuracy.

Although the historical dimension has become more important in recent anthropological work, particularly since the 1980s, most anthropological studies may be described as stills or 'snapshots'. We may use the term 'the ethnographic present' to characterise the literary tense involved. In a certain sense, it can be irrelevant *when* the Nuer, the Trobrianders or the Swat Pathans enact a certain culture or form of social organisation as described in a monograph. The importance of the studies of these peoples does not lie primarily in their historical or genealogical explanatory power, but rather in their contribution to our understanding of differences and similarities of human existence in the widest sense. They contribute to our comparative knowledge of forms of human life. As Kirsten Hastrup argues, the ethnographic present does not imply that timelessness is a feature of other societies, 'but we do stress that ethnographic knowledge transcends the empirical' (1992, p. 128) in that it deepens our understanding of the human condition in general.

There is also a clear methodological advantage involved in the synchronic study of social life. Anthropology may be described as the process whereby one wades into a river and explores it as it flows by, whereas historians are forced to study the dry riverbed. One cannot engage in participant observation of the past.

On the other hand, many anthropologists have followed the lead of Kroeber and Evans-Pritchard in stressing the importance of knowing the history of a society and its contribution to the present. This can be especially rewarding – some would say absolutely necessary – in studies dealing with societies with a written history. Further, the connections between different societies, which are often crucial for the understanding of each society, can only be properly investigated historically (see Wolf 1982). It would be impossible to understand, for example, the industrial revolution in England properly without prior knowledge of the slave trade and the cotton plantations in the United States.

In sum, the ethnographic present and the historical dimension should not be seen as mutually exclusive. The critics of diffusionism, who correctly pointed out the importance of studying societies and cultures as more or less integrated systems, tended to overemphasise the relative isolation and unchanging character of societies. To the extent that historical sources are available, they doubtless make important contributions to the contemporary understanding of single societies.

Writing and Reading Ethnography

Although fieldwork remains the most important method of generating new knowledge in anthropology, the transmission of knowledge within the professional community generally takes place through the writing and reading of texts. Geertz claims in a study of the writings of several prominent practitioners, that the most characteristic activity of anthropologists is writing, and he therefore calls attention to the way in which such texts are produced (Geertz 1988). Far from being neutral and objective descriptions and analyses of customs and cultural systems, anthropological writings are shaped by each author's biography, literary style and rhetoric, as well as by the historical period in which they were written (such as colonialism) and, of course, by the character of the fieldwork. These aspects of the production of anthropological knowledge have often been understated or dismissed as irrelevant to the end-product, the monograph.

The approach to ethnography exemplified in Geertz's book may seem to undermine the authority of these works as sources of knowledge about society and culture, and to reduce them to mere literature. This is not Geertz's aim: he simply wants to provide a context of interpretation enabling the reader to appreciate the full significance of ethnographic texts. For example, he shows how Raymond Firth establishes his ethnographic authority by starting his book on the Tikopia with a lengthy descriptive literary passage 'marshaled with Dickensian exuberance and Conradian fatality' (Geertz 1988, p. 13) to communicate his familiarity with the society he then goes on to describe in strict sociological terms for the following 500 pages. This observation does not mean that Firth's work is invalid, but that a different anthropologist would have written a different book –

in other words, that the anthropologist as author is situated in the field and in his or her own text.

Several anthropologists (or meta-anthropologists) have in recent years followed Geertz's lead in applying techniques from literary criticism to ethnographic writings (see, in particular, Clifford and Marcus 1986; Manganaro 1990), and have suggested that Malinowski's style was indebted to Joseph Conrad, that Evans-Pritchard's representation of Africans was tainted by his colonial background and attitudes, that Ruth Benedict's study of the Japanese, *The Chrysanthemum and the Sword* (Benedict 1974 [1946]), had to be understood in the context of the Second World War and not as a research monograph, and so on. A possible implication of this focus on narrative strategies and implicit agendas is that anthropological studies tend to be persuasive rather than convincing; that they evoke more than they describe; that they are shaped by the author's personal bias, not by the studied society; and that they create a 'suspension of disbelief' in the reader not so much because of the data presented but because of the author's style and rhetoric.

The recent interest in the writing of ethnographic texts does not necessarily lead to a conclusion this radical. Geertz's aim was not to dismiss ethnography as fiction, but rather 'that we shall learn to read with a more percipient eye' (1988, p. 24). Some understanding of literary techniques and the importance of personal and historical contexts in the production of knowledge can in the long run only lead to more accurate comprehension than a naïve reading would. Such insights into the social conditions of the production of knowledge have in the 1980s and 1990s led, particularly in the United States, to a proliferation of 'experimental ethnographies' that try to solve the problem of representing others in novel ways (see Marcus and Fischer 1986; Clifford and Marcus 1986), as well as 'postcolonial ethnographies' that are either written by members of the formerly colonised peoples or by anthropologists explicitly or implicitly arguing against previous understandings of the areas in question, which they see as informed by a colonial way of thinking or at least by exoticism and stereotypes (see, for example, Guha 1989).

The Problem of Translation

When discussing cultural relativism in the last chapter, it was stressed that we would not arrive at a satisfactory understanding of a society if we were to evaluate its achievements in relation to the standards and values of our own society. It therefore becomes a central challenge to connect our analytical concepts to the alien social and cultural world we deal with. The related problems arising from this project are frequently spoken of as the problem of translation. How can we translate an alien way of experiencing the world into our own mode of thought; how can we be certain that we do not misinterpret or distort the society when we try to describe it in our own terms? And how can we be entirely certain that we understand

Human Rights in Anthropological Perspective

In debates over human rights, universalistic and relativistic perspectives may clash. On the one hand, it may be argued that human rights are a universal good which should be promoted worldwide and which should not, therefore, be regarded as the product of a particular kind of society. On the other hand, it may be pointed out that notions of human rights were undoubtedly developed in Europe in modern times, and that the 'universal' Declaration of Human Rights of 1948 is therefore anything but universal, but rather a child of modern European social philosophy. If the latter argument is followed through, it may be seen as an ethnocentric error to claim that our human rights should be enshrined and defended with the same vigour in African and Amazonian societies as in West European ones. Every society must, according to this kind of logic, be understood in its own terms, since every culture contains its own concepts of justice and rights. According to the first, universalistic line of thought, it would nevertheless be inhuman and arrogant to deny tribal peoples and other non-Europeans human rights only because they happen to have a different history from ourselves.

Alison Dundes Renteln (1990) has studied findings from over 100 societies and investigated whether or not universal human rights exist empirically. The answer is, in fact, no. There are enormous variations between societies concerning what is regarded as right and wrong; what kind of punishment is seen as legitimate for offenders; and what is seen as a serious crime and what is not. Some societies traditionally impose the death penalty for witchcraft; others torture thieves; some send murderers to die in electric chairs; still others have no established norm to the effect that 'freedom of speech' is inherently valuable.

Renteln's conclusion is nevertheless that there exists at least one universal principle, namely that of 'lex talionis', or 'an eye for an eye, a tooth for a tooth'. Everywhere there seems to be a rule stating that the punishment for a crime ought to be proportional to the gravity of the crime. Naturally, which acts are seen as more or less amoral varies, as do the methods of punishment. Renteln nonetheless suggests that future refinement of human rights should take some of this variation into account, lest it remains a European or Western principle which is being forced upon others. What she does not discuss, however, is the fact that during the twentieth century the idea of human rights has increasingly been adopted by peoples to whom it was previously alien – a fact which must surely mitigate any relativistic stance towards these principles.

the alien society and culture at all, imbued as we are with our own cultural background, concepts and values? These interrelated problems are fundamental to anthropology, and they are dealt with extensively in Chapter 14. For now, we will keep to an outline of some dimensions of the problem.

Within the discipline of anthropology, it is necessary to use abstract terms such as kinship, social organisation, social control, religion and so on. These terms are necessary for the discipline to be comparative in its scope: how could it be possible to compare, say, the kinship system of the Trobrianders with that of the Yanomamö if we did not have a general concept of kinship? However, the abstract, technical terms used by anthropologists exist only rarely in the societies we study: they form part of our world, not theirs. How, then, can we justify accounting for an alien society in terms which are demonstrably not its own, if the aim of anthropology is to understand societies and cultures from within?

There are several possible solutions to this seeming paradox. A first step could be to distinguish between description and analysis. The descriptive aspect of an anthropological account is usually close to the native conceptualisation of the world, and a major problem lies in translating native concepts into the anthropologist's working language. When describing a social and cultural life-world, the anthropologist will often resort to direct quotations from informants, to give an account of the world as it appears from within. The analysis, on the other hand, will try to connect the society, at a theoretical level, to other societies by describing it in the comparative terms of anthropology. It will, in other words, describe the society with concepts which do not exist in the society itself. What kind of 'kinship system' do the people have? How do they resolve 'conflicts'? What is the 'division of labour between men and women'? What is the role of 'religion and rituals'? How are 'power relations' structured?

The suggested distinction between description and analysis, although helpful, is not absolute. Even the description is necessarily shaped by the anthropologist's selection of facts and own interpretations, and he or she can never become a native. In addition, it would be plainly impossible to include everything in a description, even if one's aim is to provide a comprehensive account of a society and one has a thousand pages at one's disposal.

Emic and Etic

Let us look a little more closely at the relationship between the view from within and the view from the outside. Ethnographic description lies closer, in a sense, to the world as experienced by the informants than the analysis does, as the latter may ultimately aim at general statements about culture and society. This level – life as experienced and described by the members of a society themselves – is sometimes spoken of as the 'emic' level. Its counterpart, the analytical descriptions or explanations of the researcher, is the 'etic' level.

The emic–etic dichotomy was introduced into anthropology by Marvin Harris (1964, 1979), but it was first developed by the linguist Kenneth Pike, who derived the terms from the linguistic distinction between phonetics and phonemics, referring to the objective relationship between sounds and the meaning of sounds, respectively.

The 'native's point of view' is emic, whereas the analytical perspective of the anthropologist is etic. However, even if the anthropologist aims to reproduce reality the way it is perceived by the informants, there are three reasons why the result may never be an emic description: First, we must usually translate between two different languages, and the translation is different from the original. Second, we use a written medium to reproduce oral statements, and the meaning of utterances changes when they are transformed into writing. Third, the anthropologist can never become identical with the people he or she writes about. The only truly emic descriptions possible in anthropology are therefore accounts written by natives in their vernacular.

It is a common assumption that emic perspectives are wrong, whereas the etic perspectives are correct. This is an unfortunate way of framing the issue. The point is not whether the 'natives' or the 'scientists' are correct, but rather that social scientists have specialised interests and that the kinds of insight they aim at are frequently not identical with the interests of their hosts in the field. There are a number of equally correct ways of describing a cultural and social system; one's choice must depend on one's interests. A further misunderstanding regarding the emic–etic distinction amounts to the idea that emic notions are 'concrete' whereas etic notions are 'abstract'. This may be the case, but it is not inherently true. As Geertz (1983) reminds us, many of the studied peoples use highly abstract, or 'experience-distant', concepts such as 'God', 'witchcraft', 'mortgage interest' or 'karma'.

However, a necessary condition for anthropological research to be meaningful at all is that the researcher knows something essential that the native does not know. He or she has the ability to connect a local reality to a comparative conceptual apparatus, enabling a particular society to shed light on other societies and contributing to the growth of our total body of knowledge about social and cultural variation. There are 'strong' and 'weak' programmes in this regard: some anthropologists plainly see themselves as in a way like natural scientists in search of general theories and laws of culture and societies, while others are more strongly concerned with elucidating dimensions of a single society in great detail, doubting the validity of theories with a highly general scope. What all of them have in common is, nevertheless, an interest in the similarities and differences of forms of human existence, and confidence in the ability of anthropology to say something meaningful about it.

Anthropology as Politics

There are anthropologists in a number of professions. Only a minority research and teach at university level. Many are involved in development cooperation, and an even greater number work in public administration. There are also anthropologists working in publishing, in private enterprises, in hospitals and so on. The discipline may in other words be useful in a great variety of professional practices. Here we focus on the production of anthropological knowledge in the most powerful milieux of the profession, namely where the authoritative texts – monographs and articles – are written and evaluated, and where reading lists and curricula are made; in short, where the discipline is being defined.

Anthropology, arising out of a particular kind of social environment, can itself be studied anthropologically. The knowledge offered to students is not developed in a social and cultural vacuum, and theoretical as well as empirical directions are decided through social cooperation, competition, the search for personal prestige and political decisions. Students must, for their part, be socialised (see Chapter 3) into a particular mode of reasoning and style of writing in order to succeed.

Anthropology may, in this way, be regarded as a social and cultural field; and like any social phenomenon, it entails power disparities. This fact is frequently pointed out, and criticised, by students, who form the least powerful group. In the 1970s it was thus commonplace for students all over the Western world to form informal 'countercultural' groups where they analysed and criticised what they saw as an inherent ideological bias in the subject. Notably, they argued that a feminist perspective was lacking, and that traditional anthropology was incapable of coming analytically to terms with coercion and exploitation. In this period, the dominant professional priorities were challenged. Above all, the critics stressed that anthropology, as a human science, is intimately related to society as such and that it is therefore influenced by power interests in society. Some Third World critics claimed that anthropology was simply an extension of the colonial ideology, trying to subjugate non-white peoples by incorporating their way of life into a Western body of knowledge. A related issue was the question of how knowledge advances. Are research environments fundamentally self-critical and ruthless in their impartial search for knowledge (Karl Popper, 1968 [1959]), or are they rather deeply conservative, since every new idea threatens to challenge their own claim to authority (Thomas Kuhn, 1962)?

The radical students, and other critics of the anthropological practice, did contribute to a transformation of the discipline, even if it remains true – perhaps necessarily – that it is being defined by a professional power elite. What is most remarkable about the kind of autocritique referred to is perhaps the willingness to apply insights from social science to one's own situation.

Finally, something must be said about the anthropological production of knowledge as a social process. Although fieldwork is emphasised as the main source of new insights, the production of anthropological understanding mainly takes place at universities and research institutes. The exchange of knowledge between anthropologists occurs at international conferences and through professional journals, doctoral theses and books. Since many anthropologists compete over prestige and power within their professional environment, a rather frenzied rate of publishing can be observed in parts of the international anthropological community. The American maxim 'Publish or perish!' is as valid among anthropologists as in other scientific disciplines. In other words, it may be the case that the 'love of knowledge' programmatically underlying scientific publishing is not necessarily the main motivation for publishing.

Of course, the discipline of anthropology is about understanding social systems and cultural variation, not about the professional careers of individual anthropologists. We should nevertheless keep in mind that this knowledge is not being produced in an ivory tower inhabited by pure vocational spirit; that fallible human beings of flesh and blood are responsible for the advancement of analysis; and that our modes of analysis, claiming universal applicability, should occasionally be applied to ourselves as well as to 'the Others'.

The population explosion which has taken place among anthropologists since the 1960s, perhaps especially evident in anthropological publishing, has made it difficult for any single individual to follow every development within the subject. The number of professional journals and monographs published annually is enormous, and we have also witnessed an increasing specialisation within the discipline. Through the development of a growing number of sub-disciplines, such as regional specialisations, medical anthropology, symbolic anthropology and development anthropology, the subject may seem threatened by fission. In the 1940s it was relatively easy to acquire an overview of the discipline; there were perhaps only 30 or 40 canonical books to relate to. Today the number of relevant studies is enormous, and specialisation is inevitable. However, in this kind of situation it is important to retain a common core of shared concepts and some shared knowledge of culture and social systems if the discipline is to remain one. This book aims at presenting the bulk of this common foundation, which makes it possible for anthropologists everywhere to have informed professional exchanges, even if their specialisations are very different. If we lacked such a shared professional language, we would not have a common discipline, nor would we be able to exchange ideas and experiences across the many specialisations and emerging sub-disciplines.

Suggestions for Further Reading

Gerald Berreman: *Behind Many Masks: Ethnography and Impression Management in a Himalayan Village*. Society for Applied Anthropology: Monograph no. 4, 1962.

Russell H. Bernard: *Research Methods in Anthropology. Qualitative and Quantitative Approaches*. London: Sage 1994.

Roy F. Ellen, ed.: *Ethnographic Research*. London: Academic Press 1984.

3 THE SOCIAL HUMAN

The self is something which has a development; it is not initially there, at birth, but arises in the process of social experience and activity, that is, develops in the given individual as a result of his relations to that process as a whole and to other individuals within that process.

—*George Herbert Mead*

The Social Character of Humanity

The press occasionally reports stories about 'jungle children' who are discovered after allegedly having spent many years in a forest or similar wilderness, isolated from culture and human society. According to such stories – Kipling's novel about Mowgli, *The Jungle Book*, is the most famous one (and one of the few which does not claim authenticity) – these children have been raised by animals, usually monkeys, and are therefore unable to communicate with humans. Normally, 'jungle children' are said to reveal a pattern of acting similar to animal behaviour; they growl, they are terrified of humans and they lack human language, table manners and other capabilities which render the rest of us culturally competent. In all probability, stories of this kind are myths, but they can nevertheless be useful as illustrations of a crucial anthropological insight, namely the fact that human beings are social products. As Michael Carrithers puts it, 'from infancy humans are directed to other human beings as the significant feature of their environment' (1992, p. 57).

What we think of as our human character is not inborn; it must be acquired through learning. The truly human in us, as anthropology sees it, is primarily created through our engagement with the social and cultural world; it is not individual and natural. All behaviour has a social origin; how we dress (for that matter, the mere fact that we dress), how we communicate through language, gestures and facial expressions, what we eat and how we eat – all of these capabilities so self-evident that we tend to think of them as natural, are acquired. Of course, humans are also biological creatures with certain unquestionably innate needs (such as those for nourishment and sleep), but there are always socially created ways of satisfying these needs. It is a biological fact that humans need food to grow and to survive; on the other hand, the food is always prepared and eaten in a culturally determined way, and food habits vary. Ways of cooking, seasoning and mixtures of ingredients which may seem natural to me may seem disgusting to you; and – a topic of great interest to anthropologists – food taboos are nearly ubiquitous but differ from society to society. High-caste Hindus are not supposed to eat meat at all; rule-abiding Jews and Muslims do not eat pork; many Europeans refuse to eat horse meat, and so on. It is also a biological fact that hair grows on our heads, but our ways to relate to this fact are socially and culturally shaped. Whether we let it grow, cut it, shave it, dye it, curl it, straighten it, wash it or comb it depends on the social conventions considered valid in our society.

In order for humans to exist at all, they depend on a number of shared social conventions or implicit rules for behaviour. For example, there is general agreement in Britain that one speaks English and not Japanese, that one buys a ticket upon entering a bus, that one does not wander naked around shopping centres, that one rings the bell before entering one's neighbour's house and so on. Most social conventions of this kind are taken for granted and are therefore frequently perceived as natural. In this way, we may learn something about ourselves by studying other societies, where entirely different conventions are taken for granted. These studies remind us that a wealth of facts about ourselves, considered more or less innate or natural, are actually socially created.

Nature and Society

Figure 3.1 depicts some important dimensions of human existence. The bottom left field presents humanity as a biological species. Typical characteristics of *homo sapiens sapiens* seen through this lens, through its shared biological features, could be its digestive system, its average length and body weight, its reproductive apparatus and its brain volume. Inborn aptitudes common to all humanity, such as the capability for language acquisition, also belong here.

The bottom right field depicts differences between humans which can be accounted for biologically. Some scientists have argued (and some still do) that there are important genetic differences between human populations, that is 'racial differences', which account for some cultural variation. However, it has been shown that only a tiny proportion of the genetic variation in the world is related to what is conventionally thought of as racial variations (Cavalli-Sforza et al. 1994). To begin with, all humans have about 99.8 per cent of their genes in common. Of the remaining 0.2 per cent, 85 per cent can be found within any ethnic group, and 'racial' differences account for only 9 per cent of 0.2 per cent, which is 0.012 per cent difference in genetic material. Finally, quite a bit of this 'racial' variation is unrelated to physical appearance. For example, many human groups when adult lack the enzyme lactase, which is necessary for digesting milk. Following this criterion, North Europeans must be classified together with Arabs and some West African peoples such as the Fulani, while

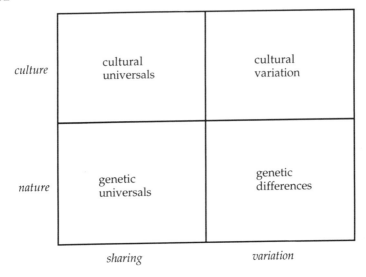

Figure 3.1: A way of conceptualising dimensions of human existence

South Europeans belong with most Africans and East Asians. The classification of humanity into races, based on physical appearance, is arbitrary and scientifically uninteresting. The study of race thus belongs to the anthropology of power and ideology, not to the area of cultural variation.

The top left field of Figure 3.1 refers to the shared cultivated, social dimensions of humanity, that is, the shared characteristics developed by humans through their lives in society; whereas the top right field represents cultural variation. Put together, these dimensions form the core of anthropological research. By demonstrating variations between the human qualities created in different societies, anthropology has shown that there are large areas of human existence which biology cannot account fully for, since the inborn genetic variation between human groups is unable to account for the enormous cultural variation in the world (Harris 1979). There are evident biological limits concerning human potential: for instance, there is probably no society which has taught its members how to fly or to live eternally, or which has dispensed with the need for food and drink. In addition, there are ecological limitations to human potential. Anthropology generally does not see it as its task to account for these limitations, but rather focuses on the social and cultural dimensions, trying to elucidate variations as well as uniformities between discrete forms of human life. The relationship between anthropology and biological accounts of humanity is nevertheless the subject of debate. Some biologists-cum-anthropologists, the sociobiologists, hold that important aspects of human life ultimately have a genetic origin. Others, including most anthropologists, would rather argue that dimensions of existence which seem inborn, such as the differences between the genders, or even aggression and other emotions commonly seen as genetically determined, must be understood as social and cultural products. Evidence for this normally comprises a convincing account of a people where aggression is seemingly absent (as in Howell 1989) or, more generally, where the emotions displayed are radically different from the emotions we know (Rosaldo 1984).

If we regard humanity in general, we may explore both similarities and differences between humans. Most biologists focus on the similarities. In the study of humans as cultural beings, the situation is more complicated. Certainly, anthropology necessarily deals with something all humans have in common, since we have already established that all humans are cultural creatures and relate to social conventions. On the other hand, many anthropologists have also been concerned with accounting for individual variations and with the uniqueness of particular societies.

Gregory Bateson (1904–80) was the son of a famous English geneticist and originally studied to be a biologist. Instead he became an anthropologist (after meeting Alfred Haddon on a train from London to Cambridge), but kept his interest in biology throughout his life. Bateson's first anthropological monograph, *Naven* (1936), was an unorthodox book about a ritual where the Iatmul men of New Guinea pretend, through role play, to be homosexual. Later, Bateson wrote mostly shorter papers on a very wide range of topics, but everything he wrote was characterised by a wish to understand process, communication, and the relationship between ideas and their contexts. Through the 'double-bind theory' of schizophrenia, Bateson exerts great influence on contemporary psychology; he carried out research both into the communication of dolphins and into inmates at mental hospitals, and he was one of the founders of cybernetics. His influence in anthropology has been considerable at the levels of theory and epistemology (theory of knowledge). His main epistemological work, a highly original attempt at a synthesis of humanistic and natural science thought, is *Mind and Nature* (1979). Many of Bateson's most important articles are collected in *Steps to an Ecology of Mind* (1972), and a number of short texts also appear in the posthumously published *A Sacred Unity* (1991).

Concerning the thorny concept of culture, this always refers to something shared, but there are two ways in which it is so. First, culture may refer to something universally shared – a shared quality of all humans is the fact of their culturedness (top left square of Figure 3.1). Second, culture is also used in the meaning of *a* culture (which is thus distinct from other cultures, a word which can be conjugated in the plural; top right square of Figure 3.1). Seen in this perspective, culture is a marker of difference between groups (who are differently cultured, so to speak), and not a marker of human universals. Both of these meanings of culture are commonly used – and sometimes confused.

Language

'Language', the author William Burroughs has famously said, 'is a virus from outer space'. Biologists have argued that although Burroughs is probably wrong, several components of the human speech faculty are related to other evolutionary features which humanity shares with other species. Further, chimpanzees who have been taught the meaning of a limited number of words seem to form abstract concepts representing classes of phenomena such as 'car' and not merely terms for specific objects (Lieberman 1994).

Notwithstanding the similarities with biologically related species, notably the great apes, verbal language is often seen as the main discriminating mark of humanity. No other species uses meaningful sounds in nearly as many ways as humans, and no other species is actually able to speak. In human societies, objects are named and classified, human acts are named, and abstract entities such as spirits and gods are named. The symbolic meaning and verbal form of each phenomenon are conventionalised and perpetuated throughout the speech community, and the interrelationship between concepts and symbols makes up a particular cultural universe within which people think and act. This makes language a cultural universal. On the other hand, people in different parts of the world obviously speak different languages, and in this sense language (in the meaning of *a* language), like culture, can be seen as a concept which describes differences rather than similarities between groups of humans.

However, just as most of the genetic variation in the world can be found within any single group, there is much linguistic and cultural variation within groups as well. Earlier anthropologists, tending to stress the uniformity and integration of traditional societies, have frequently been criticised for overstating the cultural and linguistic uniformity within groups, suggesting that all members of a people share the same basic repertoire of knowledge and world view and are equally linguistically competent. It has nevertheless been well documented that there are important differences in cultural repertoire, skills and indeed world views within even small groups, even if they also share important cultural characteristics, such as a mother tongue.

Culture and Ecology

It is no longer commonplace among professional anthropologists to regard some peoples are 'closer to nature' than others by virtue of their simple technology. It is a dogma in modern social and cultural anthropology that culture is the fundamental human diacritic, shared by all humans, and that it would be nonsense to claim that some peoples 'have more culture' than others. Humans in all societies are equally cultured, although in different ways.

On the other hand, a view which is far from uncommon in modern societies amounts to the idea that people with a simple technology have an intuitive understanding of the processes of nature because they live 'closer to nature' than we do, whereas we moderns, for our part, have 'removed ourselves from nature' by placing a thick layer of alienating filters – computers, concrete buildings, highways and books – between ourselves and nature. Let us consider an example.

The Mbuti pygmies of the Ituri forest in what is today north-eastern Zaïre are hunters and gatherers with a simple technology and a social differentiation based on gender, age and personal qualities (Turnbull 1979 [1961], 1983). They carry out hunting in two different ways: individually, with bow and arrow, and collectively, with nets. Women and children gather edible things, which are abundant. In their own view, any shortage of food is due to laziness.

The Mbuti live in groups numbering about 20 persons and have a classificatory kinship system. Rank is determined according to gender, age and personal authority, and the transition between life-stages is marked by elaborate rites of passage. Weddings are also important rituals and divorce is discouraged. Although non-marital sex occurs, it is negatively sanctioned. Flirtation is subjected to strict rules.

Both men and women appropriate a wide variety of skills necessary for survival. The majority of these are culturally specific; they are not shared by the neighbouring Bantu-speaking peoples, most of whom are agriculturalists. Hunting techniques, the preparation of poison for arrows and techniques for honey-gathering are among the most important male skills. Women have specialised knowledge about the plants in the forest and their uses: which are edible, which have healing qualities and which can be used in basket-weaving.

All men are initiated into a secret cult, the *molimo* cult, which gives them privileged access to higher powers. At important rites, the molimo trumpet is blown and ritual songs are performed.

In short, the lives of the Mbuti are culturally ordered from beginning to end. In this sense, there is no reason to assume that they are 'closer to nature' than people in industrial societies are.

On the other hand, it is clear that the alterations they make to their natural environment are much less significant than those inflicted by people with a different mode of subsistence, be they agriculturalists or industrial peoples. Their population grows very slowly, and they do not alter the fundamental processes of the environment permanently.

From a different perspective, it is also tempting to conclude that the Mbuti are closer to nature than, say, agricultural peoples or people living in Paris. Their religion is characterised by a deep reverence for the forest: after all, they subsist on what the forest 'gives' them, and they worship the spirits of the forest. Among agriculturalists, Claude Meillassoux has written (1967), there is instead a tendency to perceive nature as an enemy. Meillassoux, drawing on Turnbull's ethnography, argues that the Mbuti perceive nature as a *subject* – they harvest its products and see it essentially as a friend – while the neighbouring farmers regard it as an *object* – as something they continuously modify and cultivate, and which they have to protect against natural phenomena such as weeds and baboons.

The Senses

Karl Marx once wrote that the five senses were the product not of nature but of all of world history up to the present. Although Marx did not develop this thought further, he thus foreshadowed a set of problems which have often been overlooked by anthropologists: how does the use of the senses differ cross-culturally, and which methodological problems arise from this variation?

A certain visual bias is evident in many – perhaps most – ethnographic writings. Descriptions of field settings usually concentrate on spatial organisation, buildings, plants and generally what meets the eye. Sounds, tastes and smells are conspicuously absent.

Mary Louise Pratt (1986) thus notes that smells are virtually absent from ethnographic accounts, but there are societies where smell is of paramount importance in ordering the world. Constance Classen (1993) observes that the Ongee of the Andaman Islands live in a world ordered by smell, and links the 'olfactory decline of the West' with the growth of scientific rationalism. Whereas a rose was associated with smell in antiquity and in medieval times, by the eighteenth century its main purpose had become 'to divert the eye and thereby divert the mind' (Classen 1993, p. 27).

In *Sound and Sentiment*, Steven Feld (1982) describes a people in New Guinea, the Kaluli, for whom sound and music are central cosmological categories. The Kaluli classify birds not only according to their appearance but also according to their songs. Indeed, Feld shows how sounds function as a symbolic system of meaning in Kaluli society. Song and music are thus considered highly important among the Kaluli. Speaking more generally, Walter Ong (1969) argues that oral societies, unlike literate ones, tend not to 'picture' the world and thus do not, in a strict sense, have a 'world view', but rather 'cast up actuality in comprehensive auditory terms, such as voice and harmony'. Classen, comparing three oral societies, the Tzotzil of Mexico, the Ongee of the Andaman Islands and the Desana of Colombia, finds that they all have distinct ways of making sense of the world: 'the Tzotzil order the cosmos by heat, the Ongee by smell, and the Desana by colour' (Classen 1993, p. 122). In other words, the visual/aural dichotomy is too simple, but at least it points out the importance of studying the social use of the senses – and of reflecting critically on ethnography's over-reliance on sight and visual metaphors (Salmond 1982).

On the other hand, it must be stressed that the Mbuti, like Bantus or Frenchmen, take great pains to turn their offspring into something different from animals or members of another tribe: the children are to be transformed from their initial, unmoulded state to follow the proper way; they are to become real Mbutis, neither more nor less.

Two Natures and Two Approaches

Anthropology has two main kinds of concepts about nature: external nature, or the ecosystem, and inner nature, or human nature. Both of these concepts represent the opposite of culture. What is cultural is always something other than nature, and culture always implies a transformation, and sometimes a denial, of that which is natural. Claude Lévi-Strauss's axiom that all human societies distinguish between culture and nature is accepted by many anthropologists (but challenged by others). Our non-humanised surroundings may sometimes appear as a major threat to human projects: they may threaten to destroy our crops, kill our livestock and so on. Every cultural project seems to imply a transformation of both external and human nature.

At the same time, culture is intrinsically connected with nature. Many peoples hold that nature furnishes the raw materials culture is based on, and that there is a strong relationship of mutual interdependence between the two. Nature also seems to be stronger and more permanent in character than cultural products, which by comparison appear as fragile, vulnerable and temporary. If one succeeds in presenting a particular social order as 'natural', one has indeed legitimated it.

Nature is often perceived as threatening and difficult to control, yet it is always necessary as the provider of raw materials for cultural products. At the same time it is ambiguous: it is simultaneously a source of legitimation and an opponent. In *After Nature*, Marilyn Strathern (1992) describes a system of kinship and descent which is exceptional in that it tries to replace 'natural' reproduction with (cultural) technologically controlled reproduction (test tubes, insemination, surrogate mothers, etc.). One palpable cultural result is a change in popular conceptions of what is cultural and what is natural. Strathern's book deals with kinship in the English middle class at the end of the twentieth century.

There are two principal ways of approaching the nature–culture relationship. On the one hand, one may study how nature and the nature–culture relationship is conceptualised in different societies; on the other, one may investigate how nature (the environment or inborn characteristics of humans) affects society and culture. Nature thus exists both as cultural representations of nature and as something outside of culture and society, yet influencing the ways in which humans live. As a biological species, we take part in ecosystems and modify them; as cultural beings, we develop concepts about our environment and place ourselves outside it.

Interaction and Actors

Above all, social life consists of action, or interaction: if people ceased to interact, society would no longer exist. It may be useful for our purpose to distinguish the concept of action from the related concept of behaviour: behaviour refers to observable events involving humans or animals, whereas action, the way the concept is used here, implies that actors can reflect on what they do. It calls attention to the intentional (willed, reflexive) aspect of human existence. As far as we know, no other species apart from humanity is able to reflect upon its behaviour intentionally. Karl Marx referred to this fact when, in *Capital*, he compares a human master-builder with a bee (Marx 1906 [1867–94]). The beehive may be more perfectly fashioned and more functional than the house constructed by the builder (at least if he happens to be mediocre), but there is a qualitative difference: the human builder has an image of the house in his consciousness before starting on his work, and we have no reason to suppose that the bee starts from a similar image. It acts directly on pre-programmed 'instincts', and human actors do not.

The notion of agency thus implies that people know that they act, even if they do not necessarily know the consequences of their acts. In other words, it is always possible to do something different from what one is doing at the moment. This indeterminacy in agency makes it difficult to predict human agency; indeed, many social scientists hold that it is in principle impossible.

In anthropology and sociology, an acting person is frequently spoken of as an actor (or agent). This term can also include collective actors and is therefore more encompassing than words like 'person', 'individual' and so on. The state, for example, may be an actor. Further, *corporations* frequently appear as actors in anthropological studies. A corporation is a collective of humans which appears as an acting unit in one or several regards. In many societies, political parties and trade unions are typical actors; in others, kin groups make up corporations (see Chapters 4, 6 and 10). The concept of the corporation must be distinguished from that of the *category*: a category of persons who have something in common at the level of classification without ever functioning as an acting unit.

The concept of agency, or action, can usually be replaced by the concept of interaction. Conceptualising whatever people are up to as interaction calls attention to the reciprocal character of agency, and most acts are not only directed towards other agents, but shaped by the relationship. The smallest entity studied by social anthropologists is not an individual, but a relationship between two. In other words, the mutual relationship between two persons may be seen as the smallest building-block of society.

Statuses and Roles

Concepts such as social convention, interaction, corporations and categories are highly abstract comparative concepts. They are useful in cross-cultural comparison, but rarely form part of the native (or emic) vocabulary. This also holds true for an additional, useful group of concepts which have been developed to describe the various kinds of social relationships engaged in by humans. First, all members of society have certain rights and duties in relation to other members, and there are hardly two individuals who have exactly the same rights and duties. Second, each person has many different rights and duties in relation to different persons and different situations. In order to distinguish analytically between these aspects of social processes, it is customary to speak of social statuses.

A status is a socially defined aspect of a person which defines a social relationship and entails certain rights and duties in relation to others. Each person may have a great number of statuses, such as uncle, dentist, neighbour, customer, friend and so on. The social person is composed of, and defined by, the sum of these statuses. There are also social expectations connected with each status, which contribute to its maintenance through time. The relative importance of each status for the actor varies greatly. Membership of an ethnic or religious group, for example, may be so important to the actor that it affects his or her field of agency in nearly every respect. Other statuses, such as that of grandson in a society where kinship is relatively unimportant, have less importance for the individual – they define the person in a smaller number of situations and are marginal to his or her self-perception.

It can be instructive to distinguish between *ascribed* and *achieved* statuses. Ascribed statuses cannot be opted out of; a seven-year-old boy cannot choose not to be say, a second-grade pupil, a son and a child. Achieved statuses, on the contrary, are acquired by the actor. In modern societies, one's profession is usually considered an achieved status, but in many societies it is clearly ascribed (not chosen). A central notion in classic anthropology and sociology is the view that modern societies are qualitatively different from traditional societies in that many of the social statuses are achieved in the former, whereas most statuses are ascribed in the latter. Ferdinand Tönnies's (1963 [1889]) famous distinction between 'Gemeinschaft' (community) and 'Gesellschaft' (society), as well as Maine's distinction between contract and status societies, relates to this kind of duality. Later research has shown this kind of distinction to be simplistic, but it may still be useful as an analytical starting-point.

A term which is closely related to the concept of status is the concept of role, and the two words are sometimes used as synonyms. In anthropology, however, the role is generally defined as the dynamic aspect of the status, that is, a person's actual behaviour within the limitations set by the status definition. A typical status in a modern society may be 'bus driver'; the role of the bus driver will then be defined by what one actually does as a bus driver.

Being the incumbent of a particular social status directs one's actions in specified ways. A princess, for instance, is expected not to drink beer late at night at seedy joints. A shaman among the Inuits is expected to establish contact with supernatural powers when necessary; a wife in the Trobriand Islands is expected to be sexually monogamous; a worker in a German factory is expected to register for work before 8 a.m. every weekday. When one breaks the rules and expectations connected with the role enactment of a status, other members of society may react by imposing sanctions or different forms of punishment.

Switching between Roles

Thanks to status differentiation and the regular implementation of sanctions, social life has a certain degree of regularity and predictability. However, this predictability is far from total. If it were, social scientists would be outstanding prophets. The social status and its dynamic counterpart, the role, delineate some of the possible scope for the actor, by giving him or her certain rights and duties connected to expectations and possible sanctions. However, the social status of a person never defines his or her entire field of agency. This is partly due to the fact that a status rarely entails exact, detailed rules concerning how to behave in every situation, and also to the fact that the role is never identical with the status. One is, in other words, forced to improvise – for example, there are many, widely different ways of enacting the father role in every society, although the social definition of the status 'father' also entails certain expectations. Every status, however, is ambiguous in the sense that actors have to interpret it before enacting it.

In his major micro-sociological and existentialist work, *Being and Nothingness* (*L'Etre et le néant*), the philosopher Jean-Paul Sartre (1957 [1943]) meticulously describes how actors reflect upon, define and enact statuses in frequently contrived and highly self-conscious ways. One of his most famous examples is the waiter at a Parisian cafe, who cautiously and professionally tries to exude 'waiterness'. By virtue of his gaze, his gestures and his elegant way of balancing a full tray of drinks while he swings, in a seemingly nonchalant way, through the kitchen doors, he gives a clear expression of being a waiter. However, if he were to maintain this role at home with his wife, she would presumably file for a divorce within a few weeks.

In his philosophical descriptions of role enactment, Sartre brings up a topic which has since been pursued by many sociologists and anthropologists. They have focused on the ability of actors to manipulate their statuses and thereby liberate themselves – not from the statuses as such, but from the apparent coercion certain statuses seem to imply. Actors may thus regard their status from a distance; they decide, within limits, which expression they give to it, in order to give their co-actors a certain impression of who they are. Through the study of role enactment, we may thus study aspects of the relationship between freedom and coercion in social life.

One of the most influential elaborations on role enactment and role distance extant in the literature is arguably Erving Goffman's *The Presentation of Self in Everyday Life* (1978 [1959]). The author shows, drawing on a wide variety of examples, how people determinedly use their more or less ascribed statuses and social relationships to pursue their own ends. In his descriptions of social processes, Goffman uses expressions from the theatre. He talks of actors, roles and performances, and distinguishes between the frontstage and the backstage. His point in doing so is that there are situations we master well and feel relatively secure in, as when the (literal) actors, in their backstage dressing-rooms, can 'truly be themselves', make jokes, display their true emotions and feel free from the strict requirements of their roles on stage. In the frontstage area, on the contrary, impression management becomes important: the actor has to be self-

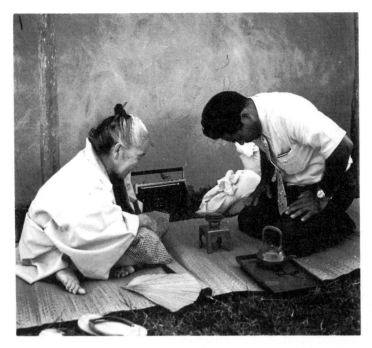

The leader of a village council shows his deference to the eldest village priestess in the Ryukyu Islands, now a part of Japan. Modes of greeting can indicate differences in rank between people, as well as saying something about the social hierarchy of the society in question. (Photo: Arne Røkkum)

consciously aware of the impression he or she makes on others, and tries to shape it in the desired ways. In this kind of situation, as in a formal interview or some other scenario where one feels slightly uncomfortable for lack of complete mastery of the role, one will contrive to appear in a specific way through what Goffman calls impression management.

The notion of impression management has been taken up by Fredrik Barth in his study of the social organisation of a trawler off western Norway (Barth 1966). The boat has a captain, a crew of five to eight fishermen, and a 'netboss'. All of them have a variety of statuses, but in the boat their professional statuses are by far the most important. Each category of actors has specified tasks. The captain's job is to steer the boat and to supervise the others. The 'netboss' is expected to find schools of fish and to order the fishermen to drop the net when he 'feels' that there are large amounts of fish down below. The fishermen, for their part, carry out all the manual work.

With this simple status distribution as his point of departure, Barth describes the role play on the ship. He shows how certain aspects of the statuses are overcommunicated; that is, the actors place great emphasis on presenting these aspects in their impression management. The captain acts as a sturdy man with immense experience and a sound sense of judgement. The fishermen frequently gather on deck, watch the ocean and talk quietly together to display their willingness to do a good job. The netboss, who plays the 'trickster' role, gives the impression of being endowed with great intuitive powers of partly mystical origins; he watches the weather for signs which are invisible to others, wanders restlessly about 'sniffing' for fish, and so on. In this situation, through deliberate over-communication of certain role aspects, all the actors do their best to present themselves as fully competent carriers of their status.

Are we, then, identical with the roles we 'play'? Does social life largely consist of conscious impression management and, ultimately, manipulation? It may be tempting to criticise Goffman and his followers for giving the impression that human life consists of a series of attempts to outsmart and see through the strategies of others, where no act seems authentic or sincere. This kind of criticism, even if it may have some relevance, is largely misplaced. Goffman's main point is the fact that there are social conventions defining everything we do as social creatures. Even to express the most powerful and sincere emotions, one has to follow specific, culturally defined rules prescribing how to express such emotions. Even the most spontaneous of acts must be channelled through a socially defined mode of expression if it is to be comprehensible.

Furthermore, even when one would like to violate the conventions of society there are a limited number of ways of doing so. Generally, criticism of social conventions is fairly common in modern societies. The conventions may then be described as 'straitjackets' or as a 'prison' preventing the true self from emerging. In the 1960s and 1970s a large number of young people in many West European and North American societies rejected what they saw as 'empty routines' in order to live in a more 'natural, authentic' way. They let their hair grow, had extra-marital sex with several partners, rejected cultural practices which led to environmental deterioration and so on. Since then, it has been claimed by critics of these movements that two general social scientific lessons could be drawn from them. First, new social conventions were surprisingly rapidly developed by the long-haired rebels. For example, it was difficult to be accepted in the group unless one obeyed a certain dress code. Second, it has been argued that it turned out that people had little or nothing left in life when they had abandoned all 'empty routines'. In other words, people seemed to depend on social rituals, conventions and routines to relate to, even if they disliked them.

Power and Social Life

A common criticism of role theory is its alleged lack of ability to deal with power relationships in society. For it is clear that social conventions, role expectations and the very distribution of roles and statuses in society contribute to systematic differences in power. Some actors are able to exert considerable power over others; some have very limited control of their own lives, let alone other people's. This dimension of social life is only dealt with indirectly in the work of Goffman and other role theorists.

Power is an elusive and difficult concept. The philosopher Bertrand Russell once said that power is to the social sciences what energy is to physics: it is one of a few extremely central concepts, but it is impossible to define it accurately. Russell is still right to the extent that no definition of power exists which is universally agreed upon. Yet there are obvious and clearly very significant differences between societies regarding power relationships, both in the public and the private spheres.

It can be useful to distinguish between two principal ways of conceptualising power. More generally, society as such may be conceptualised in two chief ways, which are discussed later as the actor perspective and the systemic perspective, respectively (see especially Chapter 5). Society may be envisaged either as the product of intentional, willed agency, or as the totality of institutional structures which condition all agency. If we see power from the actor perspective (Max Weber's view), it may be defined as an aspect of a social relationship, namely the ability to make someone do something they would otherwise not have done. If we look at power from a systemic perspective (as Marx did), it instead becomes crucial to show how power differences embedded in the fabric of society are, in fact, constitutive of those very social relationships. One cannot simply choose not to have a powerless status. On the other hand, one can certainly improve one's relative position, so it could be said that although they must be kept apart for analytical purposes, both perspectives are useful, and most contemporary anthropologists switch between them in their analyses.

The Self

Another criticism which has been levelled against role theory is represented in the view that the self is an integrated whole and that it is artificial to 'chop it up' into separated roles. This may be the case – at least many modern individuals may feel that they are 'integrated persons' – but different social relationships nevertheless require of us that we develop specialised behaviour tailored to fit different situations. Few persons, presumably, behave identically when they are with their grandmother, their professor and their friends, respectively. Since the social person is constituted through his or her social relationships, and since these relations vary in their content, one must necessarily vary one's behaviour somewhat, through some degree of impression management, when confronted with different persons.

Usually this flexibility in social life does not lead to major problems for the individual actor, but quite often one meets conflicting expectations from different persons – which may present a problem when they arise simultaneously. Which status ought one to choose when one is forced to choose between two, mutually exclusive statuses? Most adolescents in contemporary Western societies have presumably experienced this kind of awkward situation when they have unexpectedly met their friends while out with their parents.

Role theory, as exemplified above in Goffman's work, can be a powerful tool for describing social relationships, and its usefulness will be shown further later. We should nevertheless keep in mind that statuses and roles are theoretical abstractions from the ongoing process of social life, and are as such etic terms. Comparative research has indicated that all human groups have a concept of the self or the person (Mauss 1985 [1938], Geertz 1983), but this concept varies in important ways. In European societies, the self is usually conceived of as undivided (as in the word 'in-dividual'), integrated and sovereign – as an independent agent. In many non-Western societies, however, the self may be seen rather as the sum total of the social relationships of the individual. Indeed, as Strathern (1992) has argued in a comparison between the English and Melanesian kinship systems, the typical Melanesian view of the self is, sociologically speaking, the more correct one. In highland societies in New Guinea, a human being is not perceived as a fully-fledged person until he or she has acquired the basic categories of local culture. Personhood is, in other words, acquired gradually from birth onwards as the child becomes increasingly familiar with the shared customs and knowledge of society. In many central African societies we may discern a similar notion, since children who die do not turn into proper ancestral spirits: as their cultural competence is limited, and as they have yet to forge a wide array of social relationships, their personhood is still only partial. Further – to return to Melanesia – a person is not considered dead until all debts are paid and the inheritance has been distributed. Only when all of the social relationships engaged in by the deceased have been formally ended can he or she be considered properly dead. Strathern concludes that Melanesians conceive of persons pretty much as social scientists do, as the sum of their social relationships – unlike the English, who tend to see persons as isolated entities.

The Latin term 'persona', Mauss notes in his celebrated essay on selfhood (1985 [1938]), originally meant 'mask'. He attempts to show that the idea of the 'self' as something distinct from the 'masks' or roles that people took on appeared in Europe only after the spread of Christianity. Among the Zuñi (Pueblo) Indians, he writes, only a limited number of first names existed in each clan, and each incumbent of a particular name was expected to play a specified role in the 'cast-list' of the clan. They were not, in other words, seen as autonomous individuals, but saw themselves as predestined to 'act out … the prefigured totality of the clan' (Mauss 1985 [1938], p. 5).

Public and Private Self

It should at this point be added that the anthropological emphasis on everything public and social does not necessarily mean that nothing private and 'inner' exists. Many writers distinguish between the public and private self (Fitzgerald 1993); the latter being the 'I' as it sees itself from the inside, which is not, of course, available for direct observation by an anthropologist. As Godfrey Lienhardt (1987) has noted, several African peoples talk of identity in a way that is closely related to this distinction of ours. Using the metaphor of the tortoise, they distinguish between the public persona (the tortoise displaying its head and limbs) and the private persona (the tortoise withdrawn in its shell). Although the two levels of personhood are certainly related, it is difficult to reduce one to the other.

If the tools provided by role analysis are universally applicable – can be useful in the study of any society – they provide a mere starting-point if the goal is an understanding of differences as well as similarities between social and cultural systems. It has often been argued by anthropologists that some peoples lack a concept of the private persona (or, as we might put it, of personal identity). At the very least, it is certain that the relationship between private and public aspects of personhood varies greatly between societies. Even in the comparatively culturally homogeneous Western European and North American societies, there are important variations. Many Europeans are shocked at the ease with which North Americans may speak about their private lives to strangers. If we move further afield, the differences become more profound. In Indian society, Louis Dumont (1980) has argued, the individual is entirely subordinated to the collectivity and sees him- or herself not as an independent agent, but as a part of an organic whole.

Personal names may give a clue as to the concept of personhood prevailing in a society. Among the Cuna of Central America, Richard Alford notes (1988), children do not acquire a proper first name until they are about ten years of age. Geertz (1973) has described naming in Java as an extremely bewildering and complex affair to the outsider, where each person has seven different names pertinent in different situations. Compare this to the informality of North American society, where even complete strangers may address each other with a diminutive of their first, or Christian, name (Bill, Bob, Jim, etc.). This kind of cultural difference, which may be significant, may not be evident from mere role analysis, but role analysis can help us in posing the relevant questions about cultural constructions of the self, since it helps in structuring observations of social life which may at first glance seem random and purely improvisational.

Brian Morris (1994) has suggested a threefold distinction between different aspects of personhood. First, a person can be identified as a human being, as 'embodied, conscious and as a social being with language and moral agency' (Morris 1994, p. 11). This kind of notion, he remarks, seems to be universal. Second, the person can be described as a cultural category. This kind of categorisation can be both more and less inclusive than the first. On the one hand, some societies will in many contexts exclude strangers, children and slaves from the rights associated with full personhood; on the other, non-human entities such as ancestral spirits and features of the physical environment may be included. Third, Morris discusses the human person as a self, the 'I as opposed to others', the construal of which exhibits vast cultural variations. Individuals proper, in Dumont's terminology (which I choose to follow), see the origins of their agency as located within the ego, while many societies hold that the causes of human agency may be social, religious or suprahuman.

This chapter has described social life in quite abstract and general terms, largely at the level of interpersonal interaction. The study of the enactment of roles shows how people are free to choose their actions within a socially and culturally defined framework which is by and large given. In the next chapter, we move on to some of the conditions under which people choose their actions; in other words, the main emphasis will be placed on the level of society rather than the level of the person.

Suggestions for Further Reading

Michael Carrithers: *Why Humans Have Cultures*, Chapter 4. Oxford: Oxford
    University Press 1992.
Thomas K. Fitzgerald: *Metaphors of Identity. A Culture–Communication
    Dialogue*. New York: SUNY Press 1993.
Erving Goffman: *The Presentation of Self in Everyday Life*. Harmondsworth:
    Penguin 1978 [1959].
Brian Morris: *Anthropology of the Self*. London: Pluto 1994.

4 LOCAL ORGANISATION

The people who live in any society may be unaware, or only dimly aware, that it has a structure. It is the task of the social anthropologist to reveal it.
—*E.E. Evans-Pritchard*

Anthropology obtains much of its empirical material through studies of local communities. Most classic anthropological analyses are based on detailed descriptions of culture and social organisation in a delineated system, which could be a village or an urban environment. Anthropology has in recent decades developed in a variety of new, specialised directions, and it has become increasingly clear that it is often necessary to consult sources which cannot be obtained through fieldwork (historical sources, statistics, etc.). Still, the holistic study of social life – the exploration of interrelationships between different aspects of a social system through participant observation – remains a central concern.

Two factors could be mentioned as partial explanations for the traditional anthropological stress on studies of small-scale localities. First, local communities are methodologically manageable units which can easily be studied through participant observation. In a village or a local environment, most inhabitants know each other personally; they participate, and reproduce, a social system characterised by face-to-face contact. In this kind of setting, it is possible for the anthropologist to become acquainted with most of the locality's inhabitants in the course of fieldwork. He or she can map out, without insuperable methodological difficulties, which actors find themselves in which relationships to which other actors, and can thus develop a comprehensive picture of the patterns of interaction that make up the local community.

Second, local communities may be studied as though they were self-sustaining. Most of the activities of the inhabitants take place locally, many of their needs are satisfied locally, and the local community is being reproduced – maintained – through a period of time. It is thereby possible, using the methodological tools of anthropology, to study the interrelationships between different social institutions within the framework of local communities.

It must be stressed, however, that in fact virtually no local community is completely self-sustaining and unchanging through time. Furthermore, a large and growing number of anthropologists are concerned with the study of social systems of a staggering scale – nations, cities, regions. However, the methods and logic of inquiry applied to large-scale systems are by and large the same as the methods used in small-scale systems, although they must frequently be supplemented by methods other than participant observation. This chapter draws most of its material from small-scale societies of the kind typical of classic anthropological studies, where basic tenets of the discipline were developed.

The previous chapter concentrated on persons and interpersonal relationships. This chapter, on the contrary, presents different levels of social organisation which it may be useful to distinguish between in anthropological research – whether one's unit of study is a San homestead or a nation-state. Whereas the previous chapter saw social life from the viewpoint of the individual, this chapter sees it from the viewpoint of society. In the next chapter, the relationship between individual and society is dealt with theoretically.

Norms and Social Control

Every social system requires the existence of rules stating what is permitted and what is not. Such rules, whether they are stated openly or are simply followed by tacit consent, are called norms. They are activated in all fields of life; some are extremely important, whereas others have a marginal importance. A key norm in many societies is the rule 'You shall not steal'. A rather less important norm, which is limited in scope to certain environments in modern societies, is 'You shall always wear a tie at work'. Some norms concern all members of society, others concern only small groups, while still others, such as the Declaration of Human Rights, are sometimes considered to be valid for all humanity.

The existence of norms does not imply that there is total agreement on them or total obeisance towards them in any society. For instance, there may very well be a rule about virilocality (that a newly wed couple should move in with the groom's family; see Chapter 6) without it being followed by all members of society.

All norms have in common that they are connected with sanctions. In principle, both positive and negative sanctions exist. A positive sanction involves a reward for following the norms, while a negative one entails punishment for breaching the rules. However, the term sanction is usually used about negative sanctions – mild and severe forms of punishment.

The ability to impose sanctions, whether punishments or rewards, represents a main source of power in all societies. It is therefore important to study the system of norms and sanctions in any social system. The norms reflect the basic values of society, while the kinds of sanctions applied to different norm-breaking activities give an indication of the relative importance of different values and reveal power discrepancies. For example, in some societies sexual unfaithfulness is considered more serious, and is punished more severely, than theft; in other societies, the situation may be the opposite.

The system of sanctions applied when norms are violated can be called social control. Social institutions such as the family, the village council, the police, the judicial system or the school system have social control as one of their appointed tasks: they aim to prevent the violation of social norms, and are endowed with power to apply appropriate punishment when such breaches happen.

One cannot expect all members of society to follow the norms. However, even when they are violated they are important, since they demarcate what is and what is not socially acceptable. Generally, people who violate norms will of course try to do so without being 'found out' and subjected to sanctions. Further, norms change through time as society changes; some vanish, some are replaced by others, others are reinterpreted, and yet others remain but are accorded reduced importance. Blasphemy, for example, is still considered a violation of a norm in many Christian societies, but it is by no means as serious as it was a few hundred years ago. The social power of the church and the symbolic power of Christian dogma have been reduced.

One should keep in mind that although norms and sanctions give a clue as to the basic values and modes of thought and behaviour in a society, they cannot explain fully why people act the way they do. This is due to the obvious fact that people do not always 'follow the rules', but also to the fact that norms, like role scripts, are rarely sufficiently detailed to specify exact instructions as to how to behave. In real life, people always have to improvise and take decisions for themselves, but in doing so, they refer to a culturally learnt system of 'oughts' and 'ought-nots'; that is, norms.

Socialisation

Many anthropologists have studied child-raising, or socialisation, in a comparative perspective. Socialisation is the process whereby one becomes a fully competent member of society – where one acquires the knowledge and abilities required to function as a member of society. In many societies, the family has the main responsibility for socialisation. In societies with a complex division of labour, however, the responsibility is in practice divided between different institutions; for instance, the family, school, leisure clubs, sports associations, television and so on. All societies nevertheless accord the socialisation of children and adolescents great importance. Children do not only have to learn the categories of language, they also have to learn when and how to use it. In addition, they have to acquire thousands of little bits and pieces of knowledge – manners and rules of conduct, whom to respect and whom to worship, and how eventually to manage on their own and lead a good life in accordance with the values of society. Socialisation is the chief way in which cultural categories are transferred from one generation to the next; in other words, it secures a certain cultural continuity.

Many anthropologists who have studied socialisation have emphasised that examination of child-raising may reveal how a society gradually shapes forms of behaviour and thought in its members. It is, obviously, in the formative stages of life that cultural competence is acquired. Among social psychologists and anthropologists in the 1940s, it was a widespread view that the presumedly authoritarian German method of socialisation was an important contributing factor to the Second World War. However, studies of socialisation in 'exotic' societies have been far more widespread in anthropology than comparative studies of 'modern' societies have, and they have chiefly aimed at accounting for the interrelationship between patterns of socialisation and social organisation and culture in general. Some anthropologists have also investigated the possibility of cross-cultural invariants, or constants, in socialisation.

A classic study of socialisation, which also draws parallels with the author's own society, is Margaret Mead's *Coming of Age in Samoa* (Mead 1978 [1928]). In this book, Mead describes how the personality of girls and young women is shaped in a cultural environment very different from our own, in a Polynesian island. Among other things, Mead shows how the girls are socialised into a more relaxed and flexible view of sexuality than those she compares them to, namely middle-class girls in the US. Further, she stresses that the absence of strong individual competition makes it easier for Samoans than for Americans to reconcile themselves with their lives and be at peace with the world. The problems of quotidian life are easy to understand and grasp, and they usually have a simple solution, she says. She also writes that adolescence in Samoa is not characterised by personal crises and confusion:

[Adolescence] represented no period of crisis or stress, but was instead an orderly developing of a set of slowly maturing interests and activities. The girls' minds were perplexed by no conflicts, troubled by no philosophical queries, beset by no remote ambitions. To live as a girl with many lovers as long as possible and then to marry in one's own village, near one's relatives, and to have many children, these were uniform and satisfying ambitions. (Mead 1978 [1928], p. 129)

In her comparison with the North American society she was familiar with, Mead argued that socialisation in Samoa created more harmonious and balanced personalities than the American system was capable of. Her general theoretical (and political) point was that important aspects of the personalities of humans, far from being inborn, are created through the dynamic interplay between individual and society. Since societies are different, they create persons differently.

It needs to be added that Mead's research has met severe criticism from several quarters; it is not the general theoretical framework, but the validity of her substantial findings that has been challenged. Derek Freeman, who did research in Samoa for many years, has probably been her sharpest critic (Freeman 1983). His image of Samoa differs sharply from

Margaret Mead's studies of socialisation and gender roles in Samoa gained widespread attention well beyond the confines of anthropology. In this photo, Mead (left) is dressed as a Samoan. (Photo courtesy of the Royal Anthropological Institute)

the harmonious society presented by Mead, where children are exclusively taught love and friendliness. Freeman presents a picture of a society where the pressure to conform is extremely strong, and where deviants and 'dropouts' of different kinds develop profound personal problems. He shows that the suicide rate is unusually high, and that certain mental disorders are quite widespread among persons who fail to conform.

According to Freeman, anomie is a major problem in Samoa. Anomie, a concept developed by Durkheim, refers to that feeling of alienation which is caused by inability to believe in, or to live up to, the values of society. Such an inability leads to exclusion and may be extremely painful. Durkheim believed that anomie would be most common in urban societies, but later anthropological research has shown that it can well exist in apparently tightly integrated 'traditional' village societies – which are tightly integrated only for those members of society who fully master and are faithful to its basic values, not for the powerless and marginalised.

The ultimate goal of socialisation is to ensure that the actor internalises the values, norms and forms of behaviour society is founded upon. When a norm is internalised, it is literally turned into something 'inner'; it becomes a personality trait. The norm 'Thou shalt not kill' is internalised among most of us: it is a matter of course that we normally do not kill other humans. Our language is also internalised: we speak English, French, Arabic or whatever is our vernacular, without reflecting that this is actually what we do. This also goes for elementary table manners and a number of other cultural customs. As mentioned earlier, it is perhaps chiefly through comparison with other societies that we can hope to discover such traits in our own: like all members of societies, we have a general tendency to take them for granted. This means that we have internalised central aspects of the culture where we grew up, and that perhaps we need the view from afar provided by anthropology to discover them.

Life-Stages and Rites of Passage

Many people hold that they are 'the same person' throughout their existence. In this way, identity appears as something unchangeable; as a constant core in an otherwise changing world. This issue is ultimately a philosophic one, but central aspects of it can be explored anthropologically. In later chapters, it will be shown how class, gender, age and ethnicity contribute to shaping the identity of actors in a multitude of ways in different situations; for now, we simply deal briefly with one way in which a person's identity changes through time.

All societies distinguish between life-stages in the lives of their inhabitants (see also Chapter 8). Everywhere adults have rights and duties that differ from those of children, whose rights and duties are not the same as those of old people. Many societies distinguish between a greater number of stages than these; in modern European and North American societies, for example, the period known as 'youth' or 'adolescence' has eventually been recognised as a 'natural' stage in one's life, while among the Maasai of Kenya and Tanzania, a young boy passes through several phases before being accepted as a fully developed warrior.

All societies must also solve the problem of transition from one stage to the next. How can one with certainty tell that a girl has become a woman or that an adult has become an elder? The solution is usually to be found in rites of passage. These rites are strongly dramatised public events whereby an individual or an entire age cohort moves from one status to another. The most important are usually those that mark the transition from child or adolescent to adult man or woman.

Rites of passage are frequently characterised by temporary suffering, trials and deprivation among the participants. In many of the societies anthropologists have studied, circumcision of the genitals or body tattoos function as visible signs indicating that one is to be regarded as an adult person. The rite of passage can thus be seen as an endurance test forcing the candidates to show that they deserve full responsibilities and rights as adults. They also frequently acquire important knowledge relevant for adult life during the phase of transition, which transforms them into a new kind of social person. Common forms of rites of passage in modern societies are confirmation, bar mitzvah or first communion, marriage and funeral, all of which mark stages in a person's development as a social being. Such rites are dealt with in greater detail later (Chapters 8 and 13). At this stage, it will suffice to note that actors who are in a phase of transition are frequently surrounded by taboos, prohibitions and strict rules of conduct. In some societies, they are kept in isolation for weeks. One reason for this strictness may be that the rites of passage themselves, although they are necessary for society, can be seen as a threat to the social order and to the dominant power relations in society. When one is a child, one represents no threat: one has a secure and unquestionable social status as a child; as an adult, one normally has an equally well-defined place in society. When one is wedged halfway between the two stages, however, it may seem as if 'anything might happen'. During a rite of initiation, which may last for weeks, one is in a certain sense located *outside* of society; one is neither child nor adult. Anomie is a real threat, as the candidates are for the first time able to see themselves – and society – from the outside, and perhaps reflect critically on it. Perhaps, indeed, the extended adolescence typical of contemporary modern societies may fruitfully be seen as a very long rite of passage.

So far, the development of the social person has been described as an interplay between individual and society. We now move a step further and turn towards the social organisation of communities, looking at who does what with whom, and how societies are maintained (and change) through time. A central concept in this regard is the social institution. This could be defined as a custom, a system of social relationships, including power relations, or a set of rules for conduct which endures through a long period and which in a certain sense exists independently of the persons enacting it. When, say, a nuclear family is dissolved because of death, divorce or the children's departure, the institution of the nuclear family is not affected. When a king dies and his son replaces him, this usually has little effect on the institution of monarchy.

Society exists through its institutions; when they cease to function, society changes in sometimes fundamental ways. After the French Revolution, monarchy was replaced by a new institutional arrangement in the domain of politics, namely the republic. And when aboriginal

Australian societies have been subjected to genocide, displacement or the enforced introduction of wagework and a monetary economy, so that formerly important institutions have ceased to function, those societies have either been dramatically transformed or have vanished from the face of the earth. In other words, social institutions may be a highly relevant focus for the study of change as well as continuity.

The Household

The smallest building-block in social anthropology is, as already noted, not the isolated actor but a relationship between two actors. The smallest social system is thus the dyadic relationship. There are few systems of this modest compass in the world; there are relatively few social activities which take place within the framework of a system this narrow. When the field-worker arrives in a locality, therefore, he or she will usually soon find out that the smallest and most easily accessible social system where intensive and important interaction takes place is the household. In many if not most cases, the anthropologist will actually be a guest in a household during fieldwork. Therefore, and because households (although they differ in their composition) exist in every society, it seems reasonable to begin an empirical study by exploring this social system.

A household usually, but not always, consists of people who are relatives; it also frequently, but not always, consists of people who live under the same roof. The most common definition of a household is as follows: a household includes those persons who regularly eat their main meals together. The reason that a shared domicile does not form the chief criterion is simply the fact that many peoples have living arrangements whereby men, women and youths live in different huts.

The following examples, one from West Africa and one from the Caribbean, reveal important differences between household structures and may hint at the significance of such variation for other differences and similarities between humans in societies.

The Fulani (French: *peul*) are cattle nomads who live in most of the Sahel region in West Africa from Senegal to Chad (Stenning 1962). The Fulani household usually consists of a nuclear family (husband, wife and children) or a compound family (husband, wives and children). The cattle herds are owned by the man. The household is an economic unit and has collective responsibility for animal husbandry. It is also responsible for the socialisation and economic support of the children until they marry and form new households. When all the children have married, the household eventually dissolves.

There are two things to be noticed here. First, the household changes, or evolves, according to an established pattern; it goes through a developmental cycle. Second, the Fulani household is flexible and can change its composition if this is required for economic or other reasons.

Let us first look at the developmental cycle of the household. The life of the nuclear family begins, by definition, when the first child is born. If it is a son, he receives his first calf on the same day as he is named, seven days after his birth. When he is between seven and ten years old, he is circumcised. At this stage he is old enough to work as a shepherd; he is also given several animals from his father, as the foundation of his own herd. A few years later the boy is introduced to his bride-to-be, who has been selected by the two pairs of parents. She moves in with him and stays there until she becomes pregnant. She then moves back to her own family and stays there for about two years. When she finally returns with the child, the couple form their own household.

The Fulani are Muslims and the men can have up to four wives. A household may, in other words, be comparatively large at the zenith of its cycle. Then it 'peels off' as the children begin to move out with their animals, eventually shrinking to comprise just the original, old couple. The kind of physical continuity witnessed in the households of many settled agricultural peoples, where the same dwelling house and the same fields may have belonged to many consecutive generations, does not exist

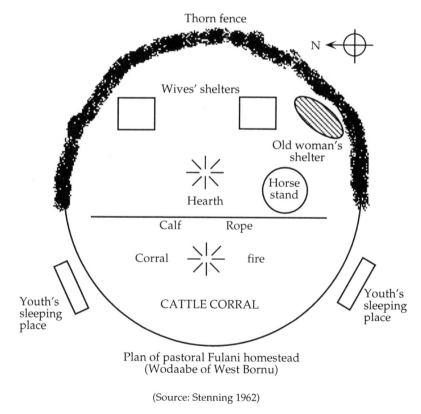

Plan of pastoral Fulani homestead
(Wodaabe of West Bornu)

(Source: Stenning 1962)

Figure 4.1: A typical Fulani household

among nomads. Yet it is obvious that the household, seen as a social system, has a constant structure and that the changes are cyclical and not irreversible. We may therefore talk of it as a social institution, which reproduces itself through several generations.

The Fulani household and the cattle herd are intimately related to each other. Ideally, the herd ought to grow at the same rate as the family; each time a son is old enough to herd, the herd itself ought to grow accordingly. However, this does not always work in practice and there are several factors which may disturb the viability of the household. Some are climatic and environmental; others are related to the organisational features of the household.

A minimum of cattle is required for survival. Stenning estimates this as 21 cows and one bull for a couple with no children, but it is extremely demanding for a couple to herd them alone, in addition to carrying out all other tasks. At the early stage of the developmental cycle of the nuclear family, the household is thus only barely viable. Frequently such a household will temporarily merge with that of the man's father, until his oldest son is able to work as a shepherd. Such an alliance with the husband's father's household can be especially important during the dry season. During this period, the Fulani are scattered over a large area; during the rainy season, they live in larger kin groups and can more easily share the work.

The situation for the new household improves as the sons grow up and can contribute their labour. In other words, the household viability depends on the relationship between two factors: labour power and other economic resources, notably cattle and available pastures. From this it follows that the size of the herd is decisive in a man's ability to have several wives (and, to some extent, vice versa). Further, a man is permitted to divorce a wife who has few or no children, since he needs labour power for his growing herd. The position of the woman in the Fulani household is thus much more uncertain than that of the man. He alone owns everything they have of value, namely the cattle herd.

The herd should not grow too large either. There are limits as to how many animals a limited number of persons can herd, and moreover the land is impoverished if there are too many animals in an area.

Marriage among the Fulani is more of an economic institution than it is in industrialised societies. The spouses have mutual obligations in that the man is obliged to ensure that the herd grows and is at good health, while the woman is obliged to give birth and socialise children. If either of them violates their duties, the other party is entitled to divorce.

The Fulani household is a self-sufficient economic unit which passes through specified, standardised stages of varying degrees of viability. The difficult art of sustaining this kind of household consists of keeping the labour–cattle relationship above the lower limit, even at difficult times of drought or disease. If food is scarce, the woman may divorce; if labour (that is, healthy children) is scarce, the man may divorce.

In modern societies as well, household viability can be a useful concept. When a European household is dissolved because the breadwinners are unable to pay the mortgage, we are actually witnessing a household which falls below the lower limit of viability.

A Contradiction-ridden Household

In all known societies, the household structure is fairly constant through a period of time, although different household forms may coexist in the same society and important structural changes may also entail changes in the household composition. When the household structure changes dramatically, this is usually an indication of other changes in the social organisation. In European societies, the shift from extended families to nuclear families in the nineteenth and twentieth centuries was generally accompanied by a shift from agrarian to industrial production. In some societies, for example among the San hunters and gatherers of southern Africa, the household structure changes periodically in response to climatic and economic changes. During dry periods they are small and flexible; during wet periods they join together in larger bands. The kind of household to be considered now is flexible in a different way. Put bluntly, it is extremely difficult to keep it together.

The Lesser Antilles of the West Indies are tropical islands largely populated by the descendants of slaves brought there from Africa to work on plantations. They are Christian (mostly Catholic), and the typical household structure is the nuclear family (see R.T. Smith 1956; P.J. Wilson 1978). In many of the villages of this area the inhabitants get their livelihood from a combination of agriculture and fishing – both for subsistence and for marketing – as well as miscellaneous forms of wagework and petty trade. The rates of migration from the West Indies to the US, Canada and Western Europe have been very high since the Second World War, and more than half of the families in many of the islands have relatives living abroad temporarily or permanently.

Although the nuclear family is considered the ideal in the Caribbean, few in Providencia, the island studied by Peter J. Wilson (1978), live in stable nuclear families. The strongest social bond is that between mother and son, and many sons are reluctant to leave their mother. Moreover, many couples live together without marrying, many married men have mistresses and women frequently have children with several men. It is far from uncommon for a woman to remain in her natal household after having children.

The problems associated with household stability can be summed up as follows. A woman has strong moral commitments towards the household she lives in, to her own children and to the men she is regularly in contact with. Usually women till the land. A man, on his part, has strong commitments to his mother, his wife, his children, his male friends, the mother(s) of his children and possibly his mistress(es). With so many obligations in different directions, it is practically impossible for a man to fulfil all of them satisfactorily. The most common domestic conflict arising in this kind of society is directly caused by the strong normative pressure on the man to spend his money outside of the household in which he lives: on his male friends, on his mother and on his mistress.

Women are also entitled to become dissatisfied with their adult sons, since they depend strongly on their economic contributions to the household, given that their menfolk are unreliable. It is quite common for close relationships between men and women, and between men and their children, to be severed. This is not due to some 'irresponsible mentality' among male West Indians, but is rather related to structural contradictions. Both men and women are faced with irreconcilable expectations.

The relationship between the household and the kin group is frequently contradiction-ridden. In the West Indian example, this contradiction is expressed as a conflict between the husband–wife and the mother–son bond, but it is nearly always the case that actors have obligations to relatives outside the household. Many live in households dominated by persons who are not their relatives (frequently they are relatives by marriage, inmarried or affines). If a woman lives with her husband's relatives, she is often entitled to move 'home' to her parents if she feels mistreated. A man can, on his part, use great resources to take care of his mother at the expense of his wife and children. We will return to this problem in Chapters 6 and 7.

The Village

Virtually no household is entirely self-sufficient. There are always a number of problems which must be solved outside of the household – concerning politics, religion, economy, children's marriage and other central aspects of existence. Even the relatively autonomous Fulani household depends on other Fulanis in matters of politics, religion and marriage, and it depends on non-Fulanis for trade. In complex modern societies, characterised by strong institutional differentiation, comparatively few needs are taken care of in the household. From Internet groups to the job market and the cafe on the corner, members of such societies are participants in many social networks of varying scale; some small and tight, some vast and dispersed. The household is nevertheless always related to other households and to social institutions existing at a higher systemic level, such as a local community or a state. At this stage, we shall focus on the village as a social system at a higher level of scale than the household.

The Dogon live on the dry savannah in south-eastern Mali, near the border with Burkina Faso (Beaudoin 1984), in an area where nomadic Fulani also live. They are sedentary farmers and cultivate millet, fruit and vegetables. They live in villages which traditionally make up independent political entitites. These villages are in many ways self-sufficient, with their own farmers, political leaders, craftsmen, fields and public rituals. The autonomy of the villages is evident through the fact that political conflicts in the area are frequently conflicts between villages, caused by disagreements over land rights or disputes at the market-place, where inhabitants from different villages meet.

The settlements in the Dogon villages are divided according to lineage membership. Each lineage has rights to cultivate specific fields and lives in a delineated part of the village. Political power is distributed among the lineages so that a member of each belongs to the council of elders, which is the highest political authority. Its leader is called the *hogon*. He is judge and chairman, and also exerts religious authority. The council of elders meets almost daily to discuss village problems ranging from land disputes, inheritance cases, crimes or conflicts with neighbouring villages, as well as planning upcoming religious festivities.

The village council and the hogon traditionally have exerted political authority over problems above the level of the individual household. (Today state institutions are gradually taking over many of their traditional tasks.) They are entitled to receive presents from the inhabitants, but are also committed to paying compensation to inhabitants who have suffered various damages. The hogon has many of the same kinds of power as the state in modern societies. He measures out punishment when the law is broken, he is 'prime minister' and 'archbishop' and he is responsible for redistribution. The presents he receives from the members of the community can be seen as taxes, and he is obliged to redistribute them for the common good. Such mechanisms for redistribution, which exist in most societies (see Chapter 11), ensure that households which are not in themselves viable may still survive.

The Dogon villages are also integrated along other lines than the purely political and judicial ones. The religious cults, in which all adult men participate, are significant. It is considered important to establish and nurture a sense of continuity with the past, and all lineages of a village can refer to a distant ancestor who allegedly founded their current settlement. The soil is spoken of as ancestral land and it cannot be sold. In this way, the Dogon villages become very stable. In- and out-migration have traditionally been uncommon. This pattern has been widespread among many African agricultural peoples, but during the twentieth century, and particularly since the Second World War, it has changed, largely due to colonialism and the growth of a state educational system and a capitalist labour market.

Flexibility and Fission

The Yanomamö, who live in the forest area near the border between Brazil and Venezuela, represent a different pattern regarding village organisation (Chagnon 1983). They are horticulturalists, which means they practise a simple form of agriculture with neither draught animals nor plough, and their most important working tool is the digging stick. Their form of production can also be labelled 'swidden agriculture', meaning that people burn off the vegetation in an area before planting it. A swidden plot of land may be used for a few years before the soil is temporarily so impoverished that people have to move on to a new area. Swidden agriculture is particularly widespread in the Amazonas region, in south-east Asia and in Melanesia.

Because of the nearly constant danger of war, the Yanomamö villages are moved relatively often, frequently quite long distances. In addition, they move short distances in order to be near the gardens currently under cultivation. Among the Yanomamö, a garden has a lifespan of four to five years. In other words, their villages are much less permanent as physical structures than those of the Dogon.

The Yanomamö villages are, materially speaking, composed of a *shabono*, a single, large communal hut which may shelter up to 200 persons. Most of the inhabitants are relatives. They practise a system of marriage that we would call bilateral cross-cousin marriage (see Chapter 7), which means that a young woman must marry a man who is recognised as her mother's brother's son and her father's sister's son. Their kin terminology is classificatory; in other words, they use kin terms to describe whole categories of persons whom they are not necessarily biologically related to (see Chapters 6 and 10).

The Yanomamö have a less complex division of labour than the Dogon; it generally follows gender and age. The youngest and the oldest are entitled not to work, while the women are mainly responsible for agricultural activities, and only the men go hunting.

The village headman and the shaman are the highest authorities in the villages. Neither of these offices is hereditary; they are achieved through outstanding personal qualities and through successfully competing for power with others.

Since the division of labour is rather simple, it might be thought an advantage for each household to run its own business independently. However, there are sound reasons for the Yanomamö to stick together in larger groups. First, there are necessary tasks which have to be done collectively, such as hunting and rituals. Second, the Yanomamö are constantly involved in feuds with their neighbours, and naturally there is both strength and security in numbers when they are regularly faced with this kind of situation.

One of the main reasons for feuding is the quest for women. Villages which are successful in military terms thus tend to grow. When the Yanomamö village has reached a certain size, however, it is split as one or several lineages moves out and builds its own shabono elsewhere. There is always a conflict prior to this kind of village fission, but as Chagnon (1983) has shown, conflicts do not lead to fission before the village has reached at least 200 inhabitants. There must therefore be another reason for the fission apart from the conflict itself. In this context,

Chagnon argues that only a limited number of people can be organised politically on kinship principles when the division of labour is as limited as in this case. His argument is strengthened by the fact that villages where the inhabitants are closely related prove to be more stable than those where the internal kin cohesion is weaker. In the stable villages people tend to be related to each other in several ways simultaneously, because the same lineages have exchanged women for generations and therefore have stronger moral obligations vis-à-vis each other than is the case in less stable villages.

Social Integration in Villages

In all of the societies discussed so far, kinship is very important. Among the Fulani, the father–son relationship forms the very spine of the social organisation, since the fathers are responsible for the sons acquiring their own herds. In Providencia, the mother–son relationship is such a strong bond that it affects life in the nuclear family adversely. The Dogon are physically organised along kinship lines; both place of settlement and land rights follow the lineage, each lineage has a political representative, and the distribution of political power follows kinship lines. Finally, among the Yanomamö kinship is the main principle of loyalty and belonging, and the powerholders in this society draw on support from their kin to maintain their position. Kinship is thus a fundamental organising principle in these (and other) societies.

The role of the village council and hogon of the Dogon, or the headman of the Yanomamö, often consists of mediating between kin groups with opposing interests. However, they are also responsible for 'foreign policy'. There is no legitimate authority outside of the village, and each village is thus an independent political unit. To the villagers, the village is the centre of the universe. Family, livelihood, childhood memories, physical protection and future all lie there. (Here we should keep in mind that the tense is the ethnographic present. Neither the Dogon nor the Yanomamö are today unaffected by the state and world capitalism.)

One may thus ask why the Fulani do not live in villages. The answer is that the pattern of settlement in any society depends on a number of factors. The Fulani live in an area where there has traditionally been little competition over land rights. The savannah between the Sahara and the more humid southern parts of Western Africa has always been thinly populated. The Fulani have had no competitors, there has been no imminent threat of war and they have depended on large grazing areas per household. They have also been flexible enough to unite in larger entities when required; the wet season has been a period for intensive ritual activities. In fact, it can be ecologically disastrous to enforce village organisation among cattle nomads, as some colonial and postcolonial regimes have tried in African countries. In Chapter 10, we shall nevertheless see how dispersed nomadic peoples may merge into larger entities when threatened by an external enemy.

Suggestions for Further Reading

Napoleon A. Chagnon: *Yanomamö. The Fierce People*, 3rd edition. New York: Holt, Rinehart & Winston 1983.
Margaret Mead: *Coming of Age in Samoa*. Harmondsworth: Penguin 1978 [1928].

5 PERSON AND SOCIETY

To say that societies function is trivial, but to say that everything in a society is functional, is absurd.

—*Claude Lévi-Strauss*

The person is a social product, and society is created by individuals. In earlier chapters, this apparent paradox has been illustrated in several ways. It has also been made clear that there will always be some aspects of society which change and some aspects which remain the same, if we regard the system through a certain period. In this chapter, we draw some theoretical lessons from these themes, and also propose a model of the relationship between person and society on the one hand, and the relationship between structure and process on the other. These two dichotomies are fundamental components of the analytical framework of this book.

Social Structure and Social Organisation

The totality of social institutions and status relationships makes up the social structure of society. It has been common to assume that this structure, in a certain sense, exists independently of the individuals who at any point in time happen to fill particular positions. Radcliffe-Brown once expressed it like this:

The actual relations of Tom, Dick and Harry or the behaviour of Jack and Jill may go down in our field note-books and may provide illustrations for a general description. But what we need for scientific purposes is an account of the form of the structure. (1952, p. 192)

Social structure may thus be perceived as the matrix of society, emptied of humans; the totality of duties, rights, division of labour, norms, social control, etc., abstracted from ongoing social life. The point of this kind of conceptualisation is to develop an abstract model of a society which brings out its essential characteristics without unnecessary details and which may be used comparatively. A principal concern of Radcliffe-Brown and his contemporaries was to point out the functions of social institutions, to show how they supported and contributed to the maintenance of society as a whole. The general function of religion, for example, was held to lie in its ability to create solidarity and a sense of community, and to legitimate power differences. The chief function of the ancestral cult of the Dogon may thus be said to be that it creates societal continuity and family solidarity, that it ties actors to the land through strong normative bonds and that it indirectly prevents revolt or revolution against the social order. The function of household organisation may be said to be, in nearly every society, to create stability and to secure the continuity of society through socialisation. When external influences, such as the introduction of capitalism, change the conditions of existence for households, one might say that the original household organisation has become dysfunctional: it is no longer practical and so eventually disappears. Within a structural-functionalist mode of thought, all social institutions thus appear as functional; if they are not functional, they vanish.

In classic structural-functionalism, from Durkheim and Radcliffe-Brown, society was often thought of as a kind of organism, as an integrated whole of functional social institutions. Alfred Kroeber (1952) described culture in a similar vein, by comparing it to a coral reef where new coral animals literally build upon their dead relatives. Seen as a whole, the coral reef (culture) is qualitatively different from the sum of its parts, and its form develops and changes gradually without the knowledge of the coral animals (actors).

The existence of certain social institutions was thus explained by reference to their function. Certain peoples believed in witchcraft, it was said, at least partly because the belief indirectly strengthened social integration and the stability of society – without the actors' knowledge of this function of witchcraft (see Chapter 14). In his theory of primitive religion, Durkheim therefore argued that when people believe that they worship supernatural powers, they really worship society.

Several problems have been pointed out in relation to this kind of argument. One obviously problematic aspect of structural-functionalism is the belief that a description of social structure might be tantamount to a good description of social life. If this were the case, we would have to expect people to act diligently and predictably according to a pre-established system of norms of sanctions. In fact this is not the case, as anyone who has done fieldwork knows. People break the rules, make exceptions, interpret norms in different and sometimes conflicting ways, and so on. An example could be the pattern of settlement among the transhumant Sami of northern Scandinavia (Pehrson 1964). According to the Sami, a woman ought to join her husband's group at marriage (the technical term for this is virilocality). However, in practice only about half of them actually do so, and there is often a good reason for making an exception. Pehrson thus draws the conclusion that the transhumant Sami actually do not have a rule about post-marriage residence. Holy and Stuchlik (1983, p. 13) do not agree in this. They argue, rather, that the rule of virilocality definitely exists, since the Sami themselves say that the woman ought to join the man's group, even if the rule is often violated. This is obviously a valid point. In many societies, sexual infidelity is quite widespread, even if most of the persons in question would agree that there is a rule to the effect that such a practice is morally objectionable.

Raymond Firth (1951) tried to resolve this problem through the distinction between social structure and social organisation. The structure is the established pattern of rules, customs, statuses and social institutions. Social organisation, on the other hand, is defined as the dynamic aspect of structure; in other words, what people actually do: their decisions and patterns of action within the framework of the structure. This distinction is analogous to the distinction between status and role.

Firth's innovation represented an attempt to conceptualise social process; that is, society and social life seen as something which happens rather than something which is. This distinction does not imply that actors continuously break the rules and norms valid in their society, but rather that systems of rules do not specify exactly how people are to act. Even perfect knowledge of the Bible is certainly not adequate if we wish to understand how Christians act. The move from structure to process expressed in Firth's model has been characteristic of much later anthropological research.

Social Systems

The term 'social system' has been used a great deal here with no further definition. It can be defined as a set of social relations which are regularly actualised and thus reproduced as a system through interaction. A social system is further characterised by a (more or less) shared normative system and a functioning set of sanctions; that is, a certain degree of agreement or enforced conformity concerning the oughts and ought-nots of interaction within the limits of the system.

Up to now, we have dealt empirically with social systems at three levels: the dyadic relationship, the household and the village or local community. Do these levels thereby represent different cultures? If an actor engages in a relationship with her husband, in another relationship with her family and in a third relationship with her village, does that make her a member of three cultures? Of course not. But different social statuses are activated in the three cases, and the kinds of relationship engaged in may vary greatly. There are aspects of life which can only be shared with one's spouse, and there are other events (such as public rituals) which would not be meaningful unless they are public. Culture may thus be understood as that which makes it possible for two or several actors to understand each other. It is not a 'thing' which one either has or does not have, and it can be relevant to talk of degrees of shared culture. Similarly, every actor is integrated, or participates, at several systemic levels in society. An adult may be a member of a nuclear family, a profession, a political grouping and a nation. One may also conceptualise one's 'levels of belonging' in more geographic, or spatial, terms: one is a member of the nuclear family, a neighbourhood, a town, a province and a nation. There are also many other possible ways of delineating systemic levels in society.

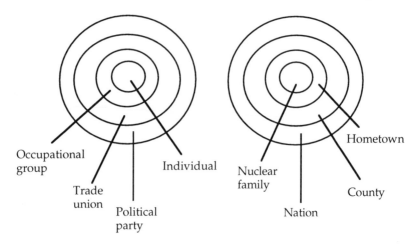

Figure 5.1: Two possible ways of conceptualising group membership in modern societies

These systems exist only to the extent that they are maintained through regular interaction.

The ethnographic examples of the last chapter reveal several systemic levels. Among the Fulani, the household, the kin group and the larger group assembling in the rainy season are relevant and important systemic levels which exist (or are activated) under particular circumstances. In the Caribbean village, the natal household remains an important systemic level for the male actor throughout his life. Among the Dogon and Yanomamö, on the contrary, the household, the lineage and the village seem to be the most important systemic levels.

Distinctions between relevant systemic levels depend on which persons are related in which ways to which others. Put simply, it concerns which groups persons belong to, and what is the purpose of these groups. In anthropological studies, the analytical interests of the anthropologist are also important. Should one concentrate one's research efforts on the household, the kin group, the village or the nation-state? An obvious answer is that one might begin by finding out how the inhabitants of a society themselves relate to their different webs of relationship; what appears as most important to them, and with whom do they carry out important tasks?

It is important to be able to distinguish between social systems and social structure. A social system is just as abstract as the social structure, but it refers to a different kind of phenomenon. Social systems are delineable sets of social relationships between actors, whereas social structure (usually) refers to the totality of standardised relationships in a society. Both of those concepts may, however, be conceptualised as socially created channels and frameworks for human action, which provide both opportunities and constraints.

The Boundaries of Social Systems

If we define a social system as a set of social relationships which are created and re-created through regular interaction, it makes sense to say that the boundaries of the system lie at the points where interaction decreases dramatically. In a relatively isolated village community, as among the Dogon in colonial and precolonial times, it would be appropriate to say that the relevant social system stops at the village boundary. The interaction engaged in by the inhabitants with outsiders is (traditionally) sporadic and relatively unimportant. Religion, family life, politics and production have all taken place within the limits of the village. However, concerning some activities, such as trade, the village appears as a sub-system; as a part of a larger system. Systemic boundaries are in this way not absolute, but relative to a kind of social context or a set of activities.

Society, if we think of it as an integrated whole, may also be divided analytically into various sub-systems. In the Dogon village, one such sub-system is the religious and ritual one, in which certain but not all members of society take part. Another sub-system, involving a different set of actors for different ends, would be the lineage organisation; a third would be the household, and so on. The relationship between such sub-systems is of great importance in anthropological research, since we aim at an understanding of the intrinsic connections between different social institutions and activities.

Social Networks

The term 'social network' has in recent years entered the everyday vocabulary of many societies. In day-to-day speech, it refers to an ego-centred set of relationships, as when people talk of 'my social network'. It may also be used to refer to a set of relationships activated for a particular end, without necessarily being organised around a single person. The analytical meaning of the term social network is thus related to the meaning of social systems; generally, we may say that a network is a person-dependent and thus not very enduring social system.

The first anthropologist to use the expression social network was John Barnes, originally an Africanist, who carried out fieldwork in Bremnes, western Norway, in the early 1950s (Barnes 1990 [1954]). Each person in the parish belonged to several groups; the household, the hamlet, the professional group and so on. For analytical purposes, Barnes identified three kinds of social fields in Bremnes. First is the territorially delineated field, which is hierarchically organised through public administration. Second is the economic field, which consists of many mutually dependent but formally independent entities, such as fishing boats, fish oil factories, groceries and so on. These two fields have a certain stability through time, to some extent independently of the actors. The third social field Barnes delineated, however, 'had no units or boundaries; it had no co-ordinating organization. It was made up of the ties of friendship and acquaintance which everyone growing up in Bremnes society partly inherited and largely built up for himself' (1990, p. 72). These ties existed between social equals, and were continuously modified as actors changed their circle of acquaintances.

A main point in Barnes's study is that this kind of society lacks the stable corporations typical of African societies. An important contributing reason for the lack of corporations in Bremnes, he argued, was the bilateral kinship system: kin reckoning which includes both the mother's and the father's side.

I have my cousins and sometimes we act together; but they have their own cousins who are not mine and so on indefinitely … Each person is, as it were, in touch with a number of other people, some of whom are directly in touch with each other and some whom are not. (Barnes 1990, p. 72)

It is this kind of system of relations that Barnes proposed calling social networks. Here it should be noted that networks often have no boundaries and no clear internal organisation, since any person may consider him- or herself the centre of the network.

Barnes further holds that one of the most important differences between small communities and large-scale societies is the fact that the networks are denser in the former than in the latter. When two people meet for the first time in a large-scale urban society, it is quite rare for them to discover that they have many common acquaintances; in small-scale societies, on the contrary, 'everybody' knows each other in many different ways – through kinship, common friends and neighbours, shared school experiences, professional life and/or intermarriage.

The network has a fleeting and impermanent character. The term is therefore most appropriate in descriptions of social fields, or sub-systems, which primarily exist by virtue of ties between concrete persons, and which therefore are transformed, or disappear, when those persons for some reason cease to maintain the ties.

Scale

We frequently say that anthropologists have traditionally studied 'small-scale societies' as opposed to 'large-scale societies'. But what is scale? It could be seen as a measure of social complexity in a society (see for instance F. Barth 1978). The scale of a society can be defined as the total number of statuses necessary for the society to reproduce itself. If we compare the Yanomamö village with the Caribbean one, it becomes evident that the latter has a larger scale than the former. The Yanomamö community is small in size and relatively simple in terms of its division of labour. In the Caribbean village the division of labour is more complex: there are ties of mutual dependency between a large number of persons because of professional specialisation, and the village is intrinsically linked to systems of much larger scale (the state, foreign countries through migration, etc.). If we move on to industrial societies, the level of scale is enormous: the mutual dependency may encompass millions of persons. If some of their statuses cease to contribute to the upholding of the system, it will change: if, say, all bus drivers in the Netherlands go on strike, this will, directly or indirectly, affect the lives of most of the Dutch.

Scale may also be regarded as a measure of relative anonymity: the larger the scale, the fewer the actors of the system one knows personally. We now turn to an example indicating the possible uses of the concept of scale.

Case Noyale is a village on the south-western coast of Mauritius, an island-state in the Indian Ocean (Eriksen 1988). About 700 people live in the village, which has approximately 170 households. The main source of livelihood is fishing, but many villagers have other work. Some work at a sugar plantation nearby, some are independent farmers, some work at a hotel 5 kilometres away and so on. The village has a grocery, a few small shops, a post office and a dispensary.

As in many other societies, the extended family is seen as an ideal among Christians in Mauritius. This portion of an extended family in Case Noyale, on their way home from Mass, may indicate that the nuclear family can be a more practical alternative in certain situations. (Photo by the author)

In a certain sense, one may say that Case Noyale is a social system of relatively small scale. The division of labour and the specialisation in the village itself are limited, and there are few local organisations with specialised aims. Virtually all of the villagers know each other.

On the other hand, it is ultimately not very helpful to regard Case Noyale as an isolated small-scale system. About 20 per cent of the adults work outside the village, and several of those who work within it (including the Catholic priest and the schoolteacher) live elsewhere. The fishermen sell their catch to an intermediary, a 'banian', who drives to and from town daily. Several of the teenagers of the village attend secondary school at Rose-Hill or Quatre-Bornes, towns which are about an hour away by bus. The inhabitants receive much of their knowledge about the outside world through radio and television; the school has state funding; the products sold in the grocery are largely imported from abroad, and so on.

From this sketch, it can be extrapolated that scale can be highly relevant in the study of agency. Scale sets limits to the scope of options for action, but simultaneously it is the product of action. In Case Noyale, the first teenager who went to secondary school became a participant in a system of larger scale than his friends were involved in. Every time someone files a court case at the District Court of Rivière Noire, he or she activates a level of scale higher than is common. To most villagers at most times, the village of Case Noyale is the relevant social system. This is where they go to primary school, work, marry and buy necessary commodities. However, Case Noyale may also be regarded as an integrated part of the nation-state of Mauritius (school, public transportation and other facilities are organised at a national level, and the fish is eventually sold at the national fish market) and even, in some respects, as a part of the global economic system, since the backbone of the Mauritian economy is the sugar industry.

In order to say anything meaningful about the scale of a society, it is necessary to investigate social relations carefully. Above all, we must identify which tasks the members of society are faced with and which options they have in carrying them out. If these tasks – subsistence, socialisation, politics, religion and so on – depend on many actors with specialised statuses, the scale is by definition larger than would be the case in a society where nearly everybody knows nearly everything. Scale is also, as we have seen, situational in the sense that all actors move from situations of small scale to those of larger scale, and back again, on a daily basis.

Group and Grid

Distinctions between small-scale and large-scale societies are still used in social anthropology, even if this kind of distinction is problematic as most actors are involved in social fields of large as well as small scale. Mauritian village life does not preclude having French penfriends or regular inter-action with Australian tourists, or consuming Burmese rice; just as the nuclear family and the personal friendship remain real possibilities for the inhabitants of Germany.

Another way of classifying societies, which concentrates on the principles of social control rather than size and complexity, has been proposed by Mary Douglas (see for example, Douglas 1970). In many of her theoreti-

cal studies in anthropology, sociology and social philosophy, she draws
on a classificatory scheme that runs along two axes (Figure 5.2), which she
labels 'group' and 'grid'. Along the 'group' dimension, persons and
societies may be classified according to their degree of social cohesion, while
the 'grid' dimension describes the degree of shared classifications or
knowledge. Purely personal notions, which are not shared with others,
belong below zero. Strong group indicates that other persons exert strong
pressure on the individual; strong grid indicates that people are rigidly
classified at the societal level, which leaves little space for individual idiosyncrasies.

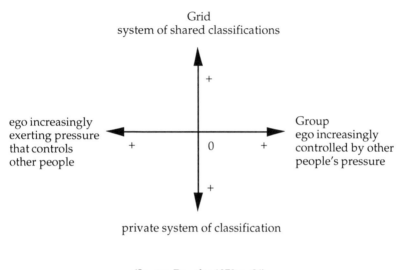

Grid
system of shared classifications

ego increasingly
exerting pressure
that controls
other people

Group
ego increasingly
controlled by other
people's pressure

private system of classification

(Source: Douglas 1970, p. 84)

Figure 5.2: Grid and group

One 'strong grid, strong group' society is, in Douglas's view, the Tallensi
of Ghana as described by Meyer Fortes during colonialism. 'Here the
public system of rights and duties equips each man with a full identity,
prescribing for him what and when he eats, how he grooms his hair, how
he is buried or born' (Douglas 1970, p. 87). Such societies, Douglas argues,
are strictly conformist, strongly integrated and create rigid boundaries vis-
à-vis outsiders.

Another kind of society is the 'weak grid, strong group' one, which
Douglas exemplifies by describing the situation in some Central African
societies during late colonialism (the 1950s; see also Chapter 15). In these
societies, contradictory demands are placed on people; they must be
obedient, but also strive for individual excellence. They are expected to
till the land of their ancestors, but also to earn money, which can only be
achieved through migration. Internal differentiation is unclear and

ambiguous, unlike the strong 'ritualisation' of social relationships in the previous type.

The third societal type exemplified in Douglas (1970) is the kind she calls 'strong grid', where group cohesion is weak. This is a sort of society, she argues, which might be better described in terms of temporary networks than in terms of corporate groups; where there are no chiefs and no rigid boundaries. Nevertheless, she notes, the meanings and classifications of society are shared.

The 'strong grid' type also has another variant, which can be described as the 'big-man system' (see Chapter 10), oscillating from the left to the right on the upper half of the diagram. The big man, a self-made leader in a small-scale society, tries to exert as much pressure as possible on his subjects, but as his power grows so does their discontent, and they pull him towards the right.

Where do industrial societies belong in Douglas's scheme? Admittedly, this is a simplification of her account. In reality, societies are spread out on the diagram, so that some groups or some social contexts belong, say, in the top left slot while others might be placed in the top right corner. In the view of some, industrial societies are 'weak group, weak grid': they are individualistic and anonymous, and thus others exert little social control over ego; and they are internally differentiated in such a way that boundaries between categories of persons, and between society and the outside world, are unclear. Another perspective might rather maintain that industrial societies are 'strong group' because of the power of the state in exerting pressure on its citizens. Douglas suggests, for her part, that there are remarkable similarities between 'some Londoners' and Mbuti pygmies. Both modern individualists and egalitarian hunter-gatherers may tentatively be placed close to zero on the vertical axis ('complete freedom' in Douglas's terms). A strongly integrated nation-state, such as Iceland, can perhaps be placed squarely in the top half of the diagram, while loosely integrated urban societies (Los Angeles for instance), would cluster around the vertical axis and – if social disintegration is strong – mostly in the bottom half. Rich eccentrics, vagrants and other 'outsiders', such as artists, belong largely below zero. On the other hand, religious cults and other strongly integrated groups in modern societies, like Jehovah's Witnesses, could be firmly placed with the Tallensi in the top right area of the diagram.

Douglas's scheme can be very instructive as a tool for thinking about humans in society. It is simple, non-evolutionary and can be fruitful for investigating the relationship between cohesion and other dimensions of social life, such as cosmologies. Its central premises are Durkheimian, and Douglas states explicitly that too little sharing and too weak social control (in other words, a condition approaching zero) is tantamount to anomie and disintegration. While role analysis and models of scale and networks take the social actor as their point of departure, Douglas's work reveals a distinctly systemic approach. A possible implication of the model could be that people who are not fully integrated are pathological and that social and symbolic integration is the 'aim' towards which every society strives. Douglas emphasises that 'societies' do the classifying, and though people relate to it individually and may even create a private classificatory system, what matters sociologically is the shared system of knowledge and norms.

Society and Actor

The founder of Social Darwinism, Herbert Spencer, proposed that social relationships ought in general to be founded on voluntary contracts between individuals. Spencer was an early proponent of a school of thought which may be called individualist, as opposed to collectivist. Individualist thought (or methodological individualism) is often associated with Max Weber, whereas collectivist thought (or methodological collectivism) is associated with Marx and Durkheim. The difference between these approaches to social life has been stated succinctly by Holy and Stuchlik (1983, p. 1), who say that anthropologists try to find out either what it is that makes people do what they do, or how societies work. Most anthropologists probably hold that they do both, but there is an important difference between the perspectives. Later chapters distinguish between actor-centred and system-centred accounts, and it will become clear that the two approaches may indeed lead to different, if complementary, kinds of insight.

Actor-centred accounts, which stress choice, goal-directed action and individual idiosyncrasies, emerged in European social anthropology in the 1950s as critiques of the then dominant structural-functionalist models. The structural-functionalists regarded society as an integrated whole where the social institutions 'worked together', more or less in the same way as body parts are complementary to each other. The individual was not granted a great deal of interest, and individual agency was seen more or less as a side-effect of society's reproduction of itself.

Can 'society' have 'needs' and 'aims'? asked the critics rhetorically, and replied in the negative. Society is no living organism, they said; it is only the arbitrary result of that myriad of single acts which take place. Further, they pointed out that it is misleading to use biological metaphors in the description of society. The sharpest critics of structural-functionalism instead emphasised that society existed largely by virtue of interaction. Norms, therefore, were to be seen as a result rather than as a cause of interaction (Barth 1966).

The structural-functionalist concept of function was also subjected to severe criticism. Already in 1936, Bateson had written that the term 'function' is an expression from mathematics which has no place in social science (Bateson 1958). Functionalist explanation, it was later remarked (Jarvie 1968), is circular in that the premises contain the conclusion. Since the observed facts by default have to be 'functional', all the social scientist has to do is to look for their functions.

It is a truism that social institutions are functional in the sense that they contribute to the survival of society, since they are themselves part of the society that survives. This does not, however, explain *why* a given society develops, say, either monotheism or a witchcraft institution, or why some societies are patrilineal whereas others are matrilineal. In other words, structural functionalism promises to *explain* cultural variation, but succeeds only in *describing* the interrelationships between institutions.

From a different perspective, Edmund Leach (1954) has pointed out that societies are by no means as stable as one would expect from a structural-functionalist viewpoint. His analysis of politics among the Kachin of upper Burma reveals a cyclical system, where the political institution continuously carries the germ of its own destruction. In this regard, it is far from functional. In contemporary anthropological research, which stresses change and process just as much as stability, structural-functionalism is not an option as a research strategy, but its influence continues to be felt, particularly in its emphasis on the interconnections between different institutions in society.

The Duality of Structure

Obviously, actors make decisions, and it is equally obvious that societies change. However, actors do not act entirely on their own whim: there are bound to be structural preconditions for their acts. There are phenomena which cannot be imagined as purely individual products, which are inherently collective phenomena. Religion is often mentioned in this context, as well as language. Neither can be thought of as aspects of individuals: on the contrary, religion, language and morality are social preconditions for the production of individuals. Anthropologists who stress the role of individuals in the making of society would answer that morality, language and religion certainly exist, but that they cannot help us in predicting action and that they cannot be taken for granted. They change: we must look into what people actually do, and why they do it, in order to understand what these phenomena mean and why they are maintained or transformed through time.

It may sometimes seem as though the contrast between individualist and collectivist accounts is a problem of the same order as the question of which came first, the chicken or the egg. The individual is in many regards a social product, but only individuals can create societies. What we must do therefore is to distinguish clearly between the two perspectives and try to see them as complementary. Neither individual nor society can be conceptualised without the other aspect.

Anthony Giddens (1979, 1984) has tried to reconcile these two main dimensions of social life, agency and structure, through his general theory of structuration. The problem Giddens sets out to resolve is the same one which has been posed in various ways in earlier sections of this chapter: on the one hand, humans choose their actions deliberately and try their best to realise their goal, which is a good life (although, an anthropologist would add, there are significant cultural variations as to what is considered a good life). On the other hand, humans definitely act under pressure, which varies between people, contexts and societies and which limits their freedom of choice and to some extent determines the course of their agency.

Giddens's very general solution to the paradox can be summarised in his concept of the duality of structure. Social structure, he writes, must simultaneously be understood as the necessary conditions for action *and* as the cumulative result of the totality of actions. Society exists only as interaction, but at the same time society is necessary for interaction to be meaningful. This model combines the individual and the societal aspects of social life, at least at a conceptual level. The art of social research, in Giddens's view, largely consists of relating the two levels to each other. His model, and related models (of which there are many), try to reconcile the idea of the free, voluntary act and the idea of systemic coercion.

Peter Berger and Thomas Luckmann (1967) deal with many of the same problems as Giddens. Their point of departure is the fact that humans are, at birth, thrown into a pre-existing social world, and they re-create this world through their actions. In addition, Berger and Luckmann emphasise the ways in which each new act modifies the conditions for action (what Giddens calls the recursive character of action). The ancient Greek philosopher Heraclitus said that a man cannot enter the same river twice, because both man and river would have changed in the meanwhile; Berger and Luckmann would hold that a man cannot undertake the same act twice, since the first act would change the system slightly.

The social system, or structure, would according to this perspective consist of the process of ongoing interaction, but it also consists of frozen action. Both social institutions and material structures such as buildings and technology are products of human action. However, they take on an objective existence and appear as givens, as taken-for-granteds which humans act upon: they determine conditions for agency. In this way, Berger and Luckmann argue, the institutionalisation of society takes place and society, although the product of subjective action, becomes an objective reality exerting power over the individual consciousness. Thereby they answer their own main question, namely that of how living human activity (a process) can produce a world consisting of 'things' (social structure and material objects).

Just as Kroeber's coral reef reproduces itself while slightly modifying itself through every new event, human action relates to earlier human action in the reproduction of and change to society. New acts are not mechanical repetitions of earlier acts, but at the same time they are dependent on earlier acts. The first act determines where the next begins, but not where it ends.

Berger and Luckmann's influential model is consistent with Marx's notion of labour and the 'freezing' of social life; he once wrote that the dead (labour) seizes the living (labour). The creative aspect of human activity is sedimented as dead material, be it a building, a tool or a convention. Social life, and the eternal becoming of society, can thereby be seen as an immanent tension between ongoing human action and the social institutions' limiting effect on the options for choice; between the solid (structure, institutions) and the fleeting (process, movement).

Social Memory and the Distribution of Knowledge

Societies can be delineated through enduring systems of interaction and through the presence of shared social and political institutions with a certain continuity through time, although neither boundaries nor continuity are ever absolute. A related feature of integration, which emphasises the cultural rather than the social, concerns knowledge and acquired skills. Whereas it was for years common to assume that the members of a society (at least a small-scale society) shared the same basic outlook and values, detailed ethnographic evidence as well as critical voices from various camps (which could for the sake of brevity be labelled Marxist, feminist, postcolonial and postmodernist) have revealed that knowledge is unevenly distributed and that members of a society do not necessarily have shared representations.

The issue concerning to what extent culture is shared within society is a complex one which has led to a lot of heated debate, some of it clearly based on misunderstandings, and let us therefore initially make it clear that sharing at one level does not necessarily imply sharing at another. Societies appear both as patterned and as chaotic, depending on the analytical perspective employed and on the empirical focus. Language, for example, is by definition shared by the members of a linguistic community, but this certainly does not mean that everybody masters it equally well. Indeed, oratorical skills are an important source of political power in many societies. The unequal distribution of linguistic skills, and its consequences for power in society, is shown in a very simple and instructive way through the work of Basil Bernstein (1972) and William Labov (1972), two sociolinguists. Briefly, Bernstein wanted to show why working-class children in Britain generally had poorer school results than middle-class children. He found that the language acquired in working-class homes was less compatible with the standard version used in schools than the language spoken in middle-class homes was. The dominant code of society, that considered 'proper English', was thus identical with the sociolect of the middle class. Meanwhile Labov showed, in a study of black children in the US, that the linguistic difference between blacks and whites did not represent a lower 'cognitive complexity' among black children, but rather that their way of expressing complex statements differed from the dominant idiom in such a way as to impair them in school. The linguistic code favoured in schools, in Labov's analysis, was not 'more sophisticated' than the black sociolect, but rather a hidden mechanism for ensuring white middle-class dominance.

Social inequality is reproduced at the symbolic level through the transmission of different kinds of knowledge through socialisation. It has been customary to believe that all members of a 'primitive' small-scale society by and large obtained the same body of knowledge and skills, but anthropological research has revealed that social differentiation and political power in such societies is just as closely related to differences in knowledge and mastery of symbolic universes as in modern complex ones. Moreover, such self-reproducing patterns of difference are difficult to eradicate even if one actively tries, as has been done in social democratic societies, to ensure that every member of society has access to roughly the same body of knowledge and skills. They are intrinsic to social organisation and the division of labour, and the differences in the transmission of knowledge are connected with other social differences to which we shall return in later chapters.

There are many ways of accounting for differences in skills and knowledge within societies. Feminists have tended to follow one or both of two lines of argument: (i) women experience the world differently from men because they are women; (ii) it is in the interest of patriarchy (male rule) to keep socially valuable skills away from women. Analyses inspired by Marxism tend to link the study of knowledge and skills to that of power and ideology (see Chapters 8, 10 and 13), while social anthropologists inspired by Durkheim may relate such differences to the division of labour, which thereby contributes to the integration of society. It should be noted that the designation of 'valuable knowledge' and, more generally, the very definition of the world, is a form of power (see Bourdieu 1982; see also Chapter 14). Nonetheless, values and rules of conduct are taken for granted as much by the powerful as by the powerless, and their taken-for-grantedness can contribute to explaining the maintenance of a social order which might otherwise appear as unjust – they make the social order appear natural and therefore inevitable – as well as accounting for some degree of cultural continuity.

Paul Connerton, in a study of social memory (1989), argues for a distinction between three kinds of memory: personal memory (which is to do with biography and personal experiences), cognitive memory (which relates to general knowledge about the world) and, importantly, habit-memory, which is embodied rather than cognitive. Connerton argues that habit-memory is in highly significant ways created and reproduced through bodily practices embedded in rules of etiquette, gestures, meaningful postures (such as sitting with one's legs crossed), handwriting and other acquired abilities which the actors do not normally perceive as cultural skills but rather as mere technical abilities or even 'social instincts'. Like Foucault (1979) before him, Connerton stresses the social and political implications of bodily discipline in reproducing values, 'inscribed' knowledge and social hierarchies.

In an original attempt to explain the transmission, spread and transformations of social representations, Dan Sperber has proposed what he

Prague, January 1990. Kneeling in front of a statue of King Václav, the patron saint of Bohemia, citizens place flowers and light candles to show their respect for the great men of the nation. Through this ritual, people give a strong symbolic expression of their sense of community. In the same place, the student Jan Palach immolated himself after the Soviet invasion of 1968. (Photo: Nora Gotaas)

calls an epidemiology of representations (1985, 1989). Using an analogy from medical science, but also obviously drawing on Lévi-Strauss, Sperber stresses that representations spread in a different way from viruses, which are simply duplicated. 'For example', he writes (1989, p. 127), 'it would have been very surprising if what you understand by my text were an exact reproduction of the ideas I try to express through this means'. Knowledge and skills therefore, in Sperber's analysis, change (are transformed) slightly each time they are transmitted through communication, although the actors may be unaware of this happening.

Although the mode of communication depends on a number of factors, including communications technology, the basic 'epidemic' character of knowledge transmission is, in Sperber's view, universal. Interestingly, he offers a method for the study of representations which does not presuppose direct access to the minds of the actors, by focusing on that which is public and communicated, yet enables the researcher to identify both variation and change, and – perhaps – properties of the mental make-up of the informants. The epidemiological model further seems to overcome shortcomings of some other approaches to knowledge in its ability to account for both sharing and variation, both continuity and change.

Agency beyond Language and Self-consciousness

Notions of choice and freedom are common in actor-centred accounts of social life. We should therefore keep in mind that far from all action is chosen in a conscious sense. Much of what we do is based on habit and convention, and in most situations it does not occur to us that we could have acted differently. In an extremely influential, but convoluted work on the organisation of society, Pierre Bourdieu (1977) discusses the relationship between reflexivity or self-consciousness, action and society. Like the other theorists discussed in this section, he wishes to move beyond entrenched positions in social science and provides a critical review of positions he deems inadequate. In a discussion of interpretive ant'·ropology (particularly the American school of ethnomethodology), he stre ses that one should not 'put forward one's contribution to the science of pre-scientific representation of the social world as if it were a science of the social world' (Bourdieu 1977, p. 23). And he continues (idem):

Only by constructing the objective curves (price curves, chances of access to higher education, laws of the matrimonial market etc.) is one able to pose the question of the mechanisms through which the relationship is established between the structures and the practices or the representations which accompany them.

In other words, for a full understanding of society, it is not enough to understand the emic categories and representations of society. Indeed, at least in this regard Bourdieu comes close to Evans-Pritchard's research programme, which consisted of studying the relationship between emic meanings and social structure.

Bourdieu's concept of culturally conditioned agency has been particularly influential. He uses the term 'habitus' to describe enduring, learnt dispositions for action. The habitus is inscribed into the bodies and minds of humans as an internalised, implicit programme for action. At one point, Bourdieu defines it as 'the durably installed generative principle of regulated improvisation' (1977, p. 78). The habitus can also be described as embodied culture, and being prior to self-conscious reflexion it sets limits to thought and chosen action. Through habitus, the socially created world appears as natural and is taken for granted. It therefore has strong ideological implications as well as cultural ones and, we should note, it refers to a layer of social reality which lies beyond the intentional. Informants cannot describe their habitus in the course of an interview, even if they want to. Drawing on his own fieldwork as well as recent research in neuroscience, Robert Borofsky (1994) confirms Bourdieu's perspective by distinguishing between *implicit* and *explicit* knowledge. Implicit memory, which is unintentional and not conscious, cannot be reproduced verbally, but is nevertheless a form of cultural competence which informs action.

In several of his books on epistemology, Bourdieu criticises social scientists for overestimating the importance of representations and reflexivity in their comparative studies of society and culture. This cognitive, and especially linguistic, bias, Bourdieu argues, is characteristic of our occupational specialisation and tends to lead us to ignore the fact that the social world is largely made up of institutionalised practices and not by informants' statements. Other anthropologists (such as Bloch 1991) have also pointed out that the social world is underdetermined by language; in other words, that there are large areas of social life and of cognition which are not only non-linguistic, but which cannot easily be 'translated' into language. The transmission of knowledge and skills, Maurice Bloch (1991) argues, frequently takes place without recourse to language. Many cultural skills can only be explained by showing them in practice. In other words, if an over-reliance on interviews is a methodological pitfall, an overestimation of the linguistic character of the social world is an epistemological error.

We have now introduced some of the most fundamental theoretical issues of social science, including anthropology. It should be noted that after the critique of structural functionalism in the 1960s, anthropology has made a distinctive move in two directions: First, there has been a shift from emphasis on structure to emphasis on process. Change is now seen as an inherent quality of social systems, not as an anomaly. Second, there has been a no less significant shift from the study of function to the interpretation of meaning. As an implication, anthropology has in the eyes of many moved away from the social sciences in the direction of the humanities. Be this as it may, it is beyond doubt that contemporary anthropologists often are cautious of positing explanatory accounts of social processes, and concentrate instead on understanding and translation.

Suggestions for Further Reading

Fredrik Barth: *Models of Social Organization*. London: Royal Anthropological Institute, Occasional Papers, no. 23 (1966).

Peter L. Berger and Thomas Luckmann: *The Social Construction of Reality*. Harmondsworth: Penguin 1967.

Mary Douglas: *How Institutions Think*. London: Routledge 1987.

Anthony Giddens: *Central Problems in Social Theory*. London: Macmillan 1979.

6 KINSHIP

No society (I believe) is bloody-minded enough to ban sex from marriage, and there is an obvious convenience in combining the two; but sex without marriage one can have and one does.

—Robin Fox

Generations of anthropologists have been flabbergasted at the intricate kinship systems existing in many 'primitive' societies. Several famous examples of such complicated systems are to be found in the Australian aboriginal population. These peoples, traditionally hunters and gatherers, have the simplest technology in the world. They lack metals, domesticated animals and writing, and in most cases they do not even have the rudiments of agriculture. Nonetheless, many of these nomadic groups have kinship systems so complex that it may take an outsider years to comprehend them fully. They can name a large number of different kinds of relatives, they have accurate rules determining who can marry whom, and the groups are subdivided into moieties, clans and sub-clans.

The study of kinship has always been a core topic in anthropology. Towards the end of the 1940s kinship was so central, especially in British social anthropology, that despairing lay people (and students) spoke ironically of the subject as 'kinshipology'. Many non-anthropologists have reacted with incomprehension at the great interest in kinship still prevalent in the profession.

What is it about kinship that makes it so important? The simple answer is that in very many societies kinship is the single most important social institution. The kin group, in many cases, takes care of one's livelihood, one's career, one's marriage, one's protection and one's social identity. Chapter 4 revealed a first glimpse of the importance of kinship, and indicated that there is a close interrelationship between the kinship system and other aspects of social organisation. In some cases, what anthropologists delineate as the kinship system may indeed be coexistent with social organisation, since the members of society, and most of their activities, may first and foremost be organised along kinship principles.

There are many social ways of organising, and thinking about, kinship. Although it is a widespread cultural notion in 'Western' societies that kinship is related to biology and blood ties (Schneider 1984), anthropological research generally analyses it as cultural classifications of people and as aspects of group formation. This chapter introduces some central features of kinship seen as social organisation, and discusses different ways of reckoning kin. In the next chapter, the focus is on marriage systems and symbolic aspects of kinship.

Incest and Exogamy

All known human societies prohibit sexual relations between persons who are classified as close blood kin, which includes at least the father–child, mother–child and sibling relationships. This does not of course mean that such relations do not occur, but rather that there is a norm prohibiting it. This universal rule is often spoken of as the incest taboo. There are significant cultural variations concerning who is included in this taboo; in many societies, persons others might regard as very distant cousins are included in the prohibition. Sanctions against violations of the incest taboo are not universally strong; however, marriage between close kin is always strictly prohibited.

Why is the incest taboo universal? Since the time of Tylor and Freud, several explanations have been put forward. Several anthropologists have pointed out the social advantages of the rule, including the expansion of the group through the inclusion of new members and the forging of alliances across kin boundaries (see Chapter 7).

A functionalist explanation of the incest taboo, common among non-specialists, is that widespread incest would lead to biological degeneration, and that functional mechanisms preventing incestuous practices are therefore called for. This kind of explanation is not satisfactory. Notably, it does not explain what it is that makes people reject incest, since they are in many cases ignorant of its possible negative effects on the genetic material.

Some anthropologists have argued that people who have grown up together will scarcely feel mutual erotic attraction, while others have invoked the term 'instinct' to explain why close kin do not feel sexually attracted to each other. Lévi-Strauss has argued that men divide the women surrounding them into two mutually exclusive categories, 'wives' and 'sisters', and that only the former are seen as potential sexual partners. He holds that the exchange of women between kin groups is, when all is said and done, an effect of reciprocity, which is a fundamental structure of the human mind, be it conscious or unconscious.

Some anthropologists have even argued against the use of the term 'incest' at all (Needham 1971), since its meaning varies cross-culturally. Most would nevertheless agree that it is a useful concept, referring to sexual intercourse between persons who are locally (emically) defined as close relatives.

There are societies which prescribe their members to marry their relatives, though never the very closest ones. This kind of practice is called endogamy; one marries inside the group. The opposite practice, whereby one marries outside of the group, is called exogamy. The two concepts are relative: the Yanomamö are endogamous at the level of the ethnic group (they scarcely marry non-Yanomamö) but exogamous at the level of the clan. They are divided into a number of exogamous clans (named groups with a common ancestor), and are required to marry persons who do not trace their genealogy to the same ancestor as they do. Since they reckon kinship along the male line (patrilineality), father's sister's children and mother's brother's sister do not belong to one's own clan (they are cross-cousins) and are thus classified as marriageable. Among many Middle Eastern peoples, on the contrary, marriage with father's brother's child (one's parallel cousin) is widely practised. In a sense, all human groups are both endogamous and exogamous to varying degrees: one is expected to marry 'one's own kind', but not someone classified as a close relative. Who is a close relative and who is not is naturally culturally specified, although the people classified as parents, children and siblings in Europe are virtually everywhere seen as close kin.

Corporate Groups

Kinship concerns much more than the reproduction of society and the transmission of cultural values and knowledge between the generations, although these aspects are certainly important. Kinship can also be important in politics and in the organising of daily affairs. In many societies, a man needs support from both consanguineal kin (blood kin) and from affines (in-laws) in order to follow a successful political career. In other societies, family members join forces in economic investments. Among the Hindus of Mauritius, for example, it is common for groups of brothers and cousins to set up a joint business. Although there may be no rule to the effect that one has to be related to run a business together, kinship can give a practical advantage. One can usually trust one's relatives, since they are tied to oneself through webs of strong normative obligations.

In many societies, and especially stateless ones, the kin group usually forms the basis for political stability and for the promotion of political interests (see Chapter 10). The group is tied through mutual bonds of loyalty and can often function as a corporation in situations of war, as well as in peaceful negotiations over, say, marriage payments or trade. In this kind of society marriage does not take place between single 'autonomous' individuals, but between groups.

Inside the kin group, norms specify roughly how one is to behave towards different categories of kin. These norms prevent the dissolution of the group and ensure that people carry out their duties. The entire division of labour may thus be organised on a kinship principle. Corporate kin groups tend to be unilineal, which means that new members are recruited on a genealogical principle, either becoming a member of the father's kin group (patrilineal system) or the mother's kin group (matrilineal system).

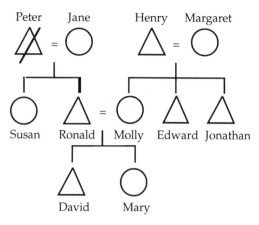

A triangle denotes a man, a circle a woman, and the equals sign that they are married (sometimes depicted by a horizontal line connecting the two from below). A horizontal line connecting two persons from above indicates that they are siblings. A diagonal line through a symbol indicates that the person in question is dead. In other words, Ronald and Molly are married, and their children are David and Mary. Ronald's sister is Susan, and Molly's brothers are Jonathan and Edward. Ronald's mother is Jane, and his father Peter is dead. Molly's parents are Henry and Margaret. The term 'ego' is used in many kinship diagrams about the person the kinship terms are related to.

Figure 6.1: Kinship symbols

Inheritance and Succession

Group membership, politics, reproduction and social stability have been mentioned as important aspects of kinship. A further important dimension of the kinship institution is the judicial one: it is no coincidence that a large part of the anthropological kinship vocabulary derives from Roman law.

Blood is thicker than water, it has been said in many parts of the world (though not everywhere), and the famous return of the Biblical lost son was celebrated with a great feast. Fratricide and patricide are considered the most serious crimes imaginable in many of the world's societies, and parents have always meddled in the marriages of their children – both before and after their consummation. These nearly perennial problems are tied to the fact that kinship is connected with inheritance and succession. Both institutions are to do with the transmission of resources from one generation to the next. Inheritance concerns the transmission of property, while succession refers to 'the transmission of office' (Rivers 1924); transmission of specified rights and duties as ascribed statuses.

All societies have rules regulating who is to inherit what when someone dies, although these rules are often contested or interpreted in varying ways. There is no universal link between the kinship system and the rules of inheritance in societies. There are patrilineal systems of descent where men and women are equals in terms of inheritance, and there are systems which give priority to one of the genders, usually the male. In some societies the eldest son receives a larger part of the inheritance than his siblings (primogeniture); others follow the opposite principle and give priority to the youngest son (ultimogeniture). Whereas the corporate principle functions in an integrating way, inheritance is a source of potential disruption, since it reveals conflicts of interest among the relatives.

Rules of succession are often closely linked with the principle of descent. In patrilineal systems, a son (or a younger brother) will frequently take over the commitments of the deceased; in matrilineal systems, a man commonly succeeds his mother's brother. However, it should be remembered that many forms of succession do not follow genealogical principles at all, for example in societies where chiefs and shamans are appointed or elected on the basis of personal merit. This is the case among the Yanomamö and in many other small-scale societies.

Ways of Reckoning Kin

Formally, there are six possible principles for the transmission of kin group membership and other resources from parents to children (Barnard and Good 1984, p. 70). As already noted, the same principle does not have to hold true for succession, inheritance and descent, although the three are frequently lumped together, particularly in patrilineal societies.

1. *Patrilineal*. Transmission of membership and/or resources takes place unilineally through the father's lineage.
2. *Matrilineal*. Transmission of membership and/or resources takes place unilineally through the mother's lineage.
3. *Double*. Some resources are transmitted through the father's lineage, others through the mother's lineage. The two lineages are kept separate.
4. *Cognatic*. Resources can be transmitted through kin on both mother's and father's side (bilaterally).
5. *Parallel*. Rare variety whereby men transmit to their sons and women to their daughters.
6. *Crossing* or *alternating*. Rare variety which represents the opposite of the previous one: men transmit to their daughters, women to their sons.

This simplistic typology should not lead anyone to believe that, for instance, persons in patrilineal societies 'are not related to' their mother's relatives. Practically all kinship systems organise kin relations on both the mother's and the father's side, although rights, names and group membership frequently give priority to one side. In a patrilineal society, one's commitment to the father's lineage is, in most situations, stronger than one's commitment to the mother's.

Cognatic or Bilateral Descent

In most of Europe and North America, kin on both sides are in principle regarded as equally important. Both mother's and father's relatives of both genders are our relatives, and we often do not distinguish systematically between the two lineages terminologically. In English, for example, we do not have separate kinship terms for father's mother and mother's mother (but such distinctions exist in the Scandinavian languages for example).

Most of these societies have traditionally given the father's side a certain priority, since the father's surname has been passed on to the children. However, in recent years many women have begun to retain their maiden name after marriage, and often the children's family name therefore becomes that of the mother.

As shown in the example of Bremnes in the previous chapter, it is difficult to organise stable, tightly incorporated groups within the framework of a bilateral kinship system. The kin group cannot be clearly delineated, since ego's relatives will always have relatives to whom ego is unrelated. Most societies which are constructed about incorporated kin groups therefore base them on a unilineal principle. However, in some parts of the world, particularly in the Pacific, cognatic corporate groups exist. They are constructed on an eclectic basis, drawing pragmatically on both matrilateral and patrilateral kinship.

A cognatic or bilateral way of kin reckoning creates problems in the construction of genealogies as well. For each generation one moves back in time, the number of kin is doubled. We have two parents, four grandparents, eight great-grandparents, sixteen great-great-grandparents and so on. Genealogies thus tend to be shallow in this kind of society – most persons are unable to name ancestors more than three or four generations back and, as mentioned, corporations based on kinship are relatively rare. Instead, it could be said that class endogamy, particularly among the upper classes, often forms the basis of group solidarity and a pooling of resources reminiscent of the logic of kinship corporations.

Patrilineal Descent

The lineage in a patrilineal system includes, at least, ego's siblings and father, father's siblings and the children of the men in the group. Father's sister's children, however, do not belong to ego's group, but rather to her husband's group.

The lineage is usually larger than this, and its size depends on the structural or genealogical memory of the group. If one includes, say, every descendant of a shared ancestor ten generations back, the group will naturally be much larger than if one starts reckoning at an ancestor five generations back. This kind of difference is not caused by mere variation in memory or forgetfulness, but is rather related to organisational features of society. In a society with a long genealogical memory it is necessary, or at least possible, to organise fairly large kinship-based networks and corporate groups – much larger ones than societies which stop their kin reckoning two or three generations back. An example of the latter kind

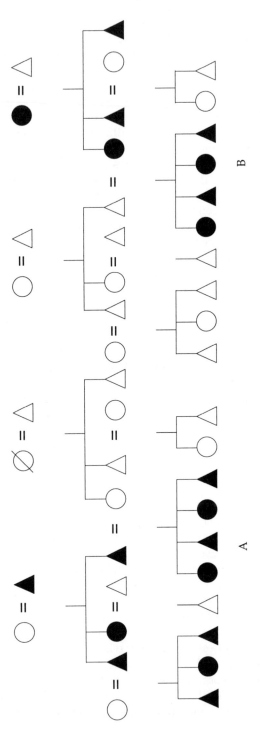

Figure 6.2: Patrilineal system (A) and matrilineal system (B). Shaded symbols stand for members who belong to the same lineage.

of society is the San hunters and gatherers of the Kalahari, where the social group is small and genealogies are shallow. Let us consider an instance showing what patrilineally based kin groups do.

When the Dogon settled where they live now, according to the myth, each village was founded by several brothers, who were the ancestors of one or several present-day clans (Beaudoin 1984). All of the descendants of an ancestor live in the same hamlet, called a *ginna*. The word ginna is used about the clan's land, about the family house where the clan chief (*ginna bana*) lives and about the smaller houses where the households are based. Most of the land is administrated, and distributed among the heads of household, by the ginna bana. The concept of ginna thus groups what anthropologists see as property, place of residence, social rights and duties, and politics, in a single kinship term.

Only men and their children are members of the lineage. The wives/mothers belong to other lineages which are centred elsewhere. Marriage is usually organised by the two fathers, who strengthen informal ties of friendship in this way. The Dogon are exogamous at the lineage level. Divorce does occur; as the patrilineal principle is all-encompassing, the father and his lineage are entitled to keep the children when this happens.

Since kinship is formally only recognised through the father, every Dogon has kinship obligations towards a limited number of relatives, notably close male agnates (patrilateral kin); that is, one's father, brothers and father's brothers.

In addition to the patrilineal principle of descent, the pattern of residence is virilocal. This means that the newly married settle in the man's household or at least in his ginna. In this way, all of the most important resources controlled by the Dogon men – land rights, politics, children and relatives – are concentrated in the same geographical place.

The system seems to be most beneficial to the men, who control the most important resources. Women in patrilineal and virilocal societies are outsiders and are often associated with danger; in some African societies they are prone to be accused of witchcraft. Their own agnates may be far away in a different village, and in a certain sense they live among strangers throughout their married lives. Married women thus represent a threat to the cohesion of the lineage, since they are strangers within the community. This reminds us of the potential conflict, mentioned in Chapter 4, between the household and the lineage. The man's loyalty becomes divided, and sometimes difficult situations may arise, where he may have to choose between loyalty to his lineage and to his nuclear family.

Patrilineal systems are capable of concentrating all valuable resources in a single principle, namely the principle of descent through the agnatic line: succession, inheritance, property rights, place of residence, marriage partner, children and political rights. We now turn to looking at matrilineal systems, which present a less tidy picture.

Matrilineal Systems

Although most peoples in the world are classified by anthropologists as either patrilineal or cognatic, many groups, particularly in Melanesia, Africa and North America, are classified as matrilineal.

It is a common misunderstanding that matrilineal kinship systems are simply inversions of patrilineal ones, where women have taken the place of men. Some may even believe that matrilineality is the same as matriarchy. This is wrong. In matrilineal societies, just as in patrilineal ones, men usually hold formal political offices and control important economic resources. This implies that matrilineal systems tend to be more complicated than patrilineal ones. In Figure 6.2 above, the difference between a simplified patrilineal and a simplified matrilineal system is illustrated. Biologically, the kin relations are identical on both sides of the diagram; in practice, however, we see that person A belongs to a kin group composed in a very different way from person B's group.

The Trobriand islanders, who were first studied by Malinowski during the First World War, are one of the most thoroughly studied matrilineal peoples in the world. The inhabitants of Kiriwina (the largest of the Trobriand Islands) are all members of matrilineages, which form four matriclans altogether. The most important task of the clan, which includes several lineages, is to arrange marriages. The lineage, which collectively owns land, magical incantations and other resources, is the most important corporate group in Trobriand society (Weiner 1988).

Both female and male relatives of mother, mother's mother and mother's mother's mother (etc.) belong to one's matrilineage. One's father, however, belongs to a different lineage, namely his own matrilineage. So far, the matrilineal system appears as a mirror-image of the patrilineal one.

However, the political power remains with men, although descent is traced through women. Each matrilineage has a male chief. Moreover, important resources are transmitted through inheritance from men to other men, usually from mother's brother to ego. The mother's brother also acts as an authority to his sister's children, while the father is expected to be kind and gentle (Malinowski 1984 [1922]) – quite the opposite of the general situation in patrilineal societies. Further, the Trobrianders are virilocal: the newly wed couple settle with the man's family, not with the woman's.

The Trobrianders are horticulturalists and the staple food is the yam (a tuber rich in carbohydrates). However, each household does not primarily cultivate yams for its own consumption. Rather, they grow yams for their matrilineal relatives. A man and his household thus grow yams for the man's sister. (Women also grow some yams for daily consumption in gardens allocated to this purpose.) The islanders also give yams to other relatives, and a man may redistribute yams given to his wife by her brothers. The purpose of this traffic in yams may be seen to be purely symbolic – as a tangible reminder of kin obligations – but it has a political aspect as well. The woman's husband controls the yams and he is obliged to repay her brother for it – either by giving him presents or through political support. A man with several wives thus has good opportunities for acquiring political power, since he receives a lot of yams not required for food, which may thus be invested.

'Matrifocality'
A well-known example of a 'very consistent matrilineal system' (Radcliffe-Brown's expression) is the Nayar people of the Malabar coast, southern India. Among the Nayars, stable nuclear families do not exist and the man has no rights in his children – only in his sisters' children (Gough 1959). According to custom, the marriage is broken off after only a few days and the woman is later allowed to take lovers. Her children belong to her matrilineage, and the men concentrate their efforts on socialising their sisters' children.

In addition to being matrilineal, this kind of arrangement can be described as 'matrifocal'. This is no kinship term, but rather a description of a household type. It means, simply and literally, that 'the mother is the focal point'. The term is used about households where the father for some reason is peripheral, where the marriage bond is unstable, as in many Caribbean societies, or – as an extreme case – among the Nayars. Matrifocality is rarely relevant for inheritance and succession, group formation and kin terminology. The phenomenon may occur in patrilineal as well as matrilineal and cognatic societies. It has been pointed out that in modern societies such as the US, matrifocality is particularly widespread among the poorest sections.

At this point we leave the Trobrianders, whose exchange system is dealt with in some detail in Chapter 11. Here we should note that matrilineal systems in general create a sharper conflict between household and lineage than patrilineal ones. The most important authority in the socialisation of children, the mother's brother, lives outside the household; and the head of household has profound obligations towards his sister, who also lives outside the household. The fact that the Trobrianders are virilocal (which is not common among matrilineal peoples) complicates matters further.

Differences between the Systems

Let us now sum up the central differences between matrilineal and patrilineal systems of descent.

Both kinds of systems are usually dominated politically by men. Inheritance, particularly land rights, often follows men. In patrilineal societies, such rights are transmitted from father to child (frequently from father to son); in matrilineal societies, they are transmitted from mother's brother to daughter's son.

Ascription of group membership varies along the same lines. In a matrilineal society, ego will be a member of the same kin group as his or her mother, mother's mother, mother's brother, mother's brother's children, etc.; in a patrilineal society, one belongs to the same group as one's father, father's father, father's brother, father's brother's children, etc.

In patrilineal systems, the wives of the men ensure the continuity of the group; in matrilineal systems, the men's sisters do it.

In certain societies, ego can take over certain rights through his or her father and others through the mother, but wherever kin-based corporations exist, one of the principles is nearly always followed in this respect. In certain rare cases, furthermore, one is a member of two lineages, one patrilineal and one matrilineal. This kind of system (dual descent) should not be confused with cognatic or bilateral kin reckoning. Among the Herero of Namibia, for example (Radcliffe-Brown 1952), everybody is a member of two separate lineages – a matrilineal one through the mother and a patrilineal one through the father. Some rights are vested in the patrilineage and others in the matrilineage. Thus the men ensure the continuity of the patrilineages (their sons and daughters become members of their patrilineage), while the women, similarly, ensure the continuity of the matrilineage.

Clans and Lineages

So far, we have used the terms clan and lineage without defining them. In much of the professional literature, they are used nearly as synonyms, although clans tend to be regarded as larger, less tightly incorporated groups than lineages. As a general rule, we may say that a lineage consists of persons who can indicate, by stating all the intermediate links, common descent from a shared ancestor or ancestress. A clan encompasses people who assume shared descent from an ancestor/ancestress without being able to enumerate all of these links. Among the Pathans of Swat valley, northern Pakistan, thousands of persons regard themselves as members of the patrilineal Yusufzai clan, assuming by general consent that they are agnatic descendants of the mythical Yusuf without being able to 'prove' it (Barth 1959).

Thus lineages are generally historically more shallow, and as a consequence smaller, groups than clans. In many societies, including the Trobriand Islands and Swat valley, several lineages considered to be related occasionally form alliances and so appear as clans – as kin groupings at a higher systemic level.

Anthropologists have developed concepts about several kinds of clan organisation, but we should keep in mind that these notions are our own and not those of the informants. One widespread form is the conical clan, which is hierarchically ordered with a centralised leadership. There is one recognised leader, usually the oldest man of the lineage, at each level, and the clan as a whole has a chief at a higher level. Conical clans are typical of relatively stable chiefdoms, which nevertheless – unlike states – are based on kin loyalty, not on loyalty to the law or to the flag.

Another model of clan organisation, which has been very influential in studies of African peoples, is the segmentary clan, which has largely been studied as a political form of organisation. The Nuer of southern Sudan, which were studied by Evans-Pritchard in the 1930s (Evans-Pritchard 1940, see Chapter 10), are probably the most famous example of a segmentary clan organisation.

Unlike the conical clan system, the segmentary clan is non-hierarchical; it is acephalous (literally 'headless'), meaning that it has no recognised leader but is composed of structurally equal lineages and sub-clans. All members of the clan regard each other as relatives, but they have clear notions about relative genealogical distance: some are close relatives, while others are more distant. In peaceful periods, and when grazing land is abundant, the household may function as an autonomous unit, more or less like the Fulani household. If a feud with another group develops, or if there is a drought, the lineages and sub-clans may unite at a higher level, temporarily, as corporate groups.

These two types of political clan organisation are the most elegant ones at the level of models, but they are not the only ones extant. In the New Guinea highlands it is quite common for the local group to be organised as an independent, patrilineal, exogamous clan with customary rights to a territory. Such a group, which may include a few hundred or a thousand persons, does not usually consider itself as related through kinship to another group. Further, such patriclans are often scattered over a large area, provided potential rules of virilocality are not strictly enforced. Besides, it seems that the principle of shared descent is less important to many Melanesian peoples than it is in segmentary African societies. For example, there are societies in New Guinea where people classify each other as relatives after having eaten the same food (Sørum 1993).

Sociobiology and Kinship

At this point, a few words need to be said about a trend in anthropology which places a great emphasis on kinship and, unlike most social and cultural anthropologists, sees it as being primarily biological. Sociobiology is that branch of biological science concerned with how human agency is affected by our biological nature. Sociobiologists assume that the single most important driving force in human action is the drive for reproduction. Men do their utmost to spread their genetic material, and women seek men who can protect them and their offspring while the children are small and defenseless. Culture and society, including kinship systems, develop as side-effects of these inborn needs. (One of the most extreme statements of this position belongs to Richard Dawkins, who has claimed that we organisms are simply survival machines for our genes; see Dawkins 1976.) Solidarity between family members can thus be explained by the fact that they have shared genes. It would therefore be rational, from a genetic point of view, for a man to die for two of his brothers or for four of his first cousins.

The leading theorist of sociobiology, Edward O. Wilson (1975, 1978), regards the social sciences as the most recent branches of biology, which have not yet been fully integrated into their 'mother science'. Obviously, this kind of argument had to be met with strong reactions among cultural and social anthropologists, who usually emphasise the non-biological aspects of human existence and who saw Wilson's 'new synthesis' as an unwelcome and irrelevant intrusion into their domain. In his *The Use and Abuse of Biology*, Sahlins (1977) argues against sociobiology. He shows, among other things, that the actual kinship systems studied by anthropologists in no way support the idea that solidarity between humans is strongest where there is shared genetic material. Indeed, many kinship systems create enduring and strong commitments between people who are not what we would call 'blood relatives'. Homosexuality, which exists in most societies, also seems difficult to explain within this framework.

This chapter has chiefly described kinship through descent, inheritance and succession, and has indicated how corporations can be formed on the basis of notions of shared descent. In the next chapter, we move a step further and consider the importance of marriage for descent and kinship in general.

Suggestions for Further Reading

Alan Barnard and Anthony Good: *Research Practices in the Study of Kinship*. London: Academic Press 1984.
Robin Fox: *Kinship and Marriage*. Harmondsworth: Penguin 1967.
Marshall D. Sahlins: *Tribesmen*. New York: Prentice-Hall 1968.
David M. Schneider: *A Critique of the Study of Kinship*. Ann Arbor: University of Michigan Press 1984.

7   MARRIAGE AND ALLIANCE

They are our enemies, we marry them.
—*Nuer proverb*

Seen from a male point of view, women are a scarce resource. No matter how male-dominated a society is, men need women to ensure its survival. In matrilineal systems, the men's sisters do this; in patrilineal societies, their wives do it; and in cognatic or bilateral societies, sisters and wives each do part of the job. A man can have a nearly unlimited number of children – in theory, he can beget several children every day – while a woman's capacity is usually limited to one child per year, and moreover in many societies many children die before they grow up. From the perspective of human reproduction, one may thus state that sperm is cheap while eggs are expensive. This fact may be a partial explanation of the widespread tendency to the effect that men try to control the sexuality of women, as well as the tendency for men to regard the women of the kin group as a resource they do not want to give away without receiving other women in return.

There may be several reasons why men in most societies want many children. They often need the labour power of the children for their fields or herds; and children can also form the basis of political support or be seen as an old age insurance policy. There are also biological explanations for the male 'drive to reproduce'.

In many societies, polygyny (where a man has several wives) is widespread. Polyandry (where a woman has several husbands) is much rarer. In fact, in the Ethnographic Atlas, a large database with relevant statistics on 863 societies, polyandry occurs only four times. Now, regarding the marriage institution as such, its rationale is evidently, at least partly, its ability to produce and socialise children. Comparatively speaking, romantic love is rarely seen as an important precondition for a good marriage. Rather, marriage is frequently arranged by kin groups, not by the individuals concerned; if the parties happen to like each other, this may be seen as a kind of bonus. Whether or not persons choose their spouses, marriage is very commonly perceived as a relationship between groups, not primarily between individuals.

The ideology prevalent in 'Western' societies to the effect that marriage should be built on pure love, which may even transcend class boundaries, is peculiar if seen in a comparative perspective. Among the Maasai, for example, the famous cattle nomads of East Africa, it is seen as a distinctive disadvantage if the romantic love between the spouses is too powerful. In this society, marriage is chiefly seen as a business relationship, the purpose being to raise children and make the herd grow. If the spouses fall in love, the result may be jealousy and passionate outbursts with adverse effects on business. Many Maasai women regard marriage as a necessary evil (Talle 1988). On the other hand, it is not true, as some believe, that high divorce rates exist only in modern societies. Divorce occurs in most societies in the world, and some 'traditional' peoples have higher divorce rates than the inhabitants of Hamburg.

Dowry and Bridewealth

In European and some Asian societies, the dowry has traditionally been an important institution (it is sometimes described as an 'Indo-European institution'). It means that the bride brings gifts from her family into the marriage, often household utensils, linen and other things for the home. The institution can be seen as a compensation to the man's family for undertaking to support the woman economically. A dowry can also be an advance on inheritance. In some societies, the payment of dowry entails a considerable economic burden. The costs associated with having daughters marry are a main cause of the high rates of female infanticide in India.

Bridewealth (sometimes spoken of as 'bride-price') is more common than dowry in many societies, particularly in Africa. Here the groom's kin is obliged to transfer resources to the bride's kin in return for his rights to her labour and reproductive powers. The payment of bridewealth establishes the rights of the man in the woman and her children. If the bridewealth is not paid, the marriage may be void, and disagreement over bridewealth payments is traditionally a common cause of feuds among many peoples.

In societies where bridewealth is common and the agnatic kin group is strong, the levirate may occur. This means that a widow marries a brother of the deceased (the *levir*), and in this way the patrilineage retains control of the woman and her children after the husband's death. The sororate, where a widower marries a sister of the deceased, is not a simple inversion of the levirate: in most cases it means that the woman's kin group commits itself to replacing the dead woman with a living one.

Payment of bridewealth creates several kinds of moral bonds between people. First, it creates a contractual tie between lineages, being a sign of mutual trust. When the bridewealth is paid over a long period, for example through bride-service whereby the groom works for a certain period for his parents-in-law, the bonds are strengthened further. Second, the system of bridewealth strengthens solidarity within the paying group. Frequently, several relatives must contribute to the payment of the price, and often the groom must borrow from his relatives. Such loans may create long-term debt and profound obligations on the part of the groom towards his lineage relatives.

The Bedamini men of New Guinea usually have to pay bridewealth to the kin groups of their future wives. Chains made of dogs' teeth, like the headband worn by this man, are a common means of payment. This man has nevertheless succeeded in obtaining two wives without paying. After having seen him dance at public feasts, they elected to elope with him. (Photo: Arve Sørum)

Moieties and Marriage

Exogamous groups must by definition obtain women from outside. It is a fact that property, inheritance and political office tend to follow men in most societies, and that men often take the formal decisions regarding who is to marry whom. So even if the pattern of residence should be uxorilocal (that is, the groom moves in with the bride's family), the woman's brothers and other male relatives tend to determine her matrimonial destiny, even if they live with their wives in a different village.

The simplest form of woman exchange would consist in the exchange of sisters: I give my sister to you, and you give me yours in return. In lineage societies, it is corporations rather than persons who exchange women. If a society consists of two kin groups who regularly exchange women between them, the society is divided into moieties. Frequently, moieties have a division of labour in addition to exchanging women.

The moiety system of exchange is widespread among Australian peoples. In studies of these marriage systems, it has been pointed out that the outcome of a moiety system is eventually a kind of classificatory cross-cousin marriage. It happens like this: in a fairly small group, like the Kariera of Central Australia, all members of society define themselves as relatives. They reckon patrilineal descent and are organised in two exogamous 'marriage classes'. They can marry anyone of the right gender who is not classified as a sibling. The Kariera, like the Yanomamö and many others, have a classificatory kinship terminology, which means that they use a single term to describe many different persons, in this case everyone belonging to the same gender, generation and clan, independently of biological kinship. The Kariera thus use the same term to describe a father, his brothers and other males of the same generation and same clan. One cannot marry persons considered as siblings, a category which includes those analytically labelled classificatory parallel cousins (father's brother's and mother's sister's children). On the other hand, father's sister's children and mother's brother's children, and everyone included in the same category, which we would call classificatory cross-cousins, are marriageable.

Seen through a certain period, this kind of system takes on the form of a moiety system based on two patriclans which exchange women between them. A man marries where his father married, which is into his mother's patriclan. Both father's sister's children and mother's brother's children belong to this clan, since father's sister also married into that clan.

A similar example, which may further illustrate the logic of exchange within a moiety system, is provided by the Yanomamö. A Yanomamö man marries a person classified as father's sister's daughter and/or mother's brother's daughter. A woman, similarly, marries a person classified as father's sister's son and/or mother's brother's son. The patrilateral parallel cousins belong to one's own group, as do the matrilateral parallel cousins, since mother's sister by definition is married to father's brother. Remember that we are talking about a classificatory kinship system and not a system which distinguishes terminologically between biological kin and others.

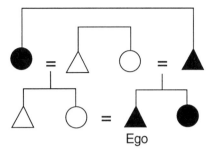

Ego

Figure 7.1: Bilateral cross-cousin marriage among the Yanomamö. The shaded persons belong to ego's patrilineage. The model is highly simplified; in reality, a much larger number of persons would be involved.

The Yanomamö use the term *suaböya* about all marriageable women, who are classificatory mother's brother's daughters and/or father's sister's daughters. However, although there are only two kinds of same-generation women in Yanomamö terminology – wives and sisters – they distinguish in practice between 'close' and 'distant' cross-cousins. Many parents therefore try to marry their children into lineages with whom they want to forge alliances.

Through a statistical analysis of several Yanomamö villages, Chagnon (1983) has shown that political stability is highest where the biological kinship bonds are strongest. Obviously, the members of groups which have exchanged women for several generations are related in more ways – both in terms of kinship and other obligations – than persons who have a purely classificatory kin relationship. Further, it is obviously in the interest of women to marry 'close' cross-cousins as they live in the same village as themselves. Thus the women can be close to their brothers, whom they may need for protection.

The ideal model of cross-cousin marriage among the Yanomamö, as depicted in Figure 7.1, would create a very stable system where the inhabitants of the *shabono* were very close relatives. However, in practice the Yanomamö are often forced to develop links beyond the confines of the village, both to reduce the danger of war (see Chapter 10) and to look for wives. As a consequence, the inhabitants of the shabono are less close relatives than they would ideally be.

Exchange and Rank Differences

Many peoples traditionally practise the cyclical exchange of women between more than two groups, so that, say, clan A gives women to clan B, which gives women to clan C, which gives women to clan D, which in turn gives women to clan A. Within this kind of system, a woman can only be 'paid for' with another woman.

A system where three or more groups are mutually linked through some kind of cyclical exchange of wives may be on a larger scale than moiety systems, since it depends on a greater number of relationships to function. Such a system, where one distinguishes categorically between wife-givers and wife-takers, is called an asymmetrical alliance system, whereas a moieties constitute a symmetrical alliance system. While the latter implies equality between the groups, an asymmetrical alliance often, but not necessarily, implies rank differences between the groups.

The Kachin of upper Burma practise exogamy at the level of the patri-lineage (Leach 1954). Their rules for wife exchange reveal a more complex and more hierarchical social organisation than that of the Yanomamö. Among the Kachin, wife-givers ('mayu') have higher rank than wife-takers ('dama').

The Kachin, who are rice cultivators, are divided into three main categories of lineages: chiefly, aristocratic and commoner. Women move downwards within this system as every lineage is mayu to those with lower rank than themselves. The dama is obliged to pay bridewealth to its mayu, but is usually unable to pay immediately. Frequently, therefore, the groom has to work for years – sometimes for the rest of his life – for his higher-ranking parents-in-law. In this way, since wives are 'expensive', the rank differences between mayu and dama are reproduced and strengthened through time.

All of the examples so far have dealt with exogamous marriage systems. Group endogamy also exists, particularly in highly stratified societies where considerable resources are transmitted through marriage. European royal families and Indian castes are thus known to be endogamous. However, we should remember that endogamy and exogamy are relative terms. All peoples are exogamous at least at the level of the nuclear family; conversely, few peoples would encourage their children to marry anybody without any discrimination. Even in societies where individual freedom of choice is stressed as a virtue, such as the United States, 'race endogamy' is common.

Descent and Alliance Theory

A principle point in the study of marriage rules and practices concerns politics, alliances and stability. Since all groups are exogamous at some level, marriage necessarily creates alliances outside the nuclear family, the lineage or the clan. These kinds of alliances have been emphasised by many anthropologists, who have implicitly or explicitly argued against those who regard descent and lineage-based solidarity as the most fundamental facts of kinship.

Some influential, classic studies of kinship, notably Evans-Pritchard's (1940) and Meyer Fortes's (1945) studies of the Nuer and the Tallensi, respectively, focused strongly on descent-based corporations. They showed how groups with shared unilinear descent – be it factual or fictitious – were cohesive and could be mobilised politically (see Chapters 6 and 10). This corporate group, united through shared ancestry, was seen as the fundamental fact of kinship in stateless societies.

New Guinea and the Anthropologists
New Guinea is the second largest island in the world, with a total area of 810,000 square km (the size of Great Britain is 244,046 square km). The population numbers about 3.5 million, and since 1975 the island has been divided between the western half, Irian Jaya, which belongs to Indonesia, and the eastern half, the independent state of Papua New Guinea.

New Guinea has a great number of endemic species of plants and animals, that is species which do not exist elsewhere. The landscape is dramatic and varied, containing barren swamps as well as jagged mountains and deep valleys which make large parts of the island relatively inaccessible. However, human settlement in both lowland and highland New Guinea dates back several thousand years. Most of the island's many hundred ethnic groups are traditionally horticulturalists, who have settled in scattered pockets ranging from the coast to valleys located up to 4,000 metres above sea level. Many of these people, especially in the highlands, keep large herds of pigs.

The linguistic variation in New Guinea is exceptional. Over 700 languages are spoken, and 500 of them – the highland languages – do not seem to be related to any other language groups. For the most part, they are also mutually unintelligible.

The coastal areas, where Melanesian languages are spoken, have been known to outsiders for centuries, first to Malayan and Indonesian seamen and, later, to Europeans. The highlands were virtually unknown outside the island until recently. In fact they were generally assumed to be uninhabited until by pure chance a group of natural scientists in the early 1930s discovered a large people there, the Enga. Crossing a hilltop just before dusk, the expedition was amazed to discover a fertile valley full of little fires and neatly cultivated gardens. Although missionary activity, the state and the monetary economy have later, especially since the 1960s, come to influence life in the highlands, many aspects of traditional culture and social organisation remain strong.

Since the discovery of the New Guinean highland peoples by Europeans, the island has been the object of intense attention from anthropologists, who immediately saw it as an enormous resource for the young comparative science of culture and society – containing as it did many relatively isolated 'Stone age' peoples displaying a great cultural variation. The inflow of anthropologists has eventually led to a certain irritation among many New Guineans, who feel that the anthropologists see them as ethnographic curiosities or even as relics from a bygone age.

Several anthropologists reacted against the elegant logical models of segmentary clans presented by the Africanists (Kuper 1988). In particular, this was the case of those who had done fieldwork in New Guinea, where it had been expected that the patrilineally based communities would be organised in segmentary lineages. However, it transpired that New Guinean societies included persons who did not belong to the patrilineage, and that they lacked the mechanisms for fusion and fission that had been described for the Nuer and the Tallensi. The Chimbu of highland New Guinea, for example, could just as well be described either as a cognatic system with a patrilineal basis, or as a patrilineal system with many exceptions. Thus the general validity of the models proposed by Evans-Pritchard, Fortes and others was questioned on empirical grounds – and it was concluded that they had probably exaggerated the importance of the unilineal descent groups at the cost of underestimating the importance of cognatic and affinal (in-law) ties. An interesting detail in this regard may be the fact that the anthropologists who focused on the structured, systemic aspect of kinship were associates of Radcliffe-Brown, while the critics who stressed the primacy of practice over abstract structure, notably Audrey Richards, were in many cases students of Malinowski.

Elementary and Complex Structures

In a famous study of kinship, *The Elementary Structures of Kinship* (1969 [1949]), Lévi-Strauss challenges descent theory in a more theoretical way. He does not regard shared descent, but rather the development of alliances between groups through the exchange of women, as the fundamental fact of kinship. Taking his cue from structural linguistics (which stressed relationship as fundamental to language) and the sociology of Marcel Mauss, who emphasised reciprocity as a basic mode for humanity (see Chapter 11), Lévi-Strauss develops a highly original view of the institution of kinship. Indeed, he argues that the very formation of society occurs when a man gives his sister away to another man, thereby creating ties of affinity.

A central element in Lévi-Strauss's perspective is the idea that all kinship systems are elaborations on four fundamental kin relationships: brother–sister, husband–wife, father–son and mother's brother–sister's son. Lévi-Strauss regarded this 'elementary structure', or 'kinship atom', inspired by similar structures from structural linguistics (see Figure 7.2), as fundamental to kinship and to human society as such. Some societies are constructed directly on the 'elementary structure', including societies based on classificatory cross-cousin marriage as well as societies based on asymmetrical alliances. 'Complex' systems, in Lévi-Strauss's terminology, add further relationships to the four fundamental ones as determining factors in marriage. He emphasises that elementary systems have positive rules; they do not only specify whom one cannot marry, but also whom one can marry (as among the Yanomamö). Complex systems, prevalent in modern societies and based on individual choice, have only negative rules and are therefore unable to create long-term alliances between kin groups.

The mother's brother is an important character in Lévi-Strauss's kinship atom. Granted the universality of the incest prohibition, and granted that men control women, the breeding of children ultimately depends on his

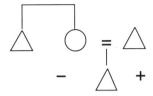

Figure 7.2: The kinship atom

willingness to give away his sister. Inspired by an earlier argument by Radcliffe-Brown, Lévi-Strauss argues, further, that the relationship between a man and his maternal uncle is crucial. If the spouses are intimate, the wife will have a distanced relationship with her brother and vice versa. If one has a close, tender relationship with one's maternal uncle, the father will be a strict and severe person and vice versa. The 'severe uncle' usually, but not always, appears in matrilineal societies.

Claude Lévi-Strauss (b. 1908) is the founder of structuralism, an ethno-graphically informed theory about the ways in which the mind works. His most fundamental tenet is the principle of binary oppositions, the view that the mind organises the world in contrasting pairs and develops coherent systems of relationship from such a starting-point. Structuralism is chiefly influenced by two bodies of thought: French sociology, especially the work of Durkheim and Mauss, and structural linguistics such as that of Ferdinand de Saussure, Roman Jakobson and others. Lévi-Strauss is a prolific writer who has synthesised and re-analysed enormous amounts of ethnography recorded by others, and his main works include *The Elementary Structures of Kinship* (1949), *The Savage Mind* (1962; see Chapter 14 of this book), the two volumes of essays entitled *Structural Anthropology* (1963, 1976), the four volumes of *Mythologiques* (1966–71) and the more personal, melancholic travelogue *Tristes tropiques* (1955).

Since he has argued that his very abstract models of thought and clas-sification are universal, Lévi-Strauss has been subjected to severe criticism from more empirically oriented anthropologists, who have often pointed out that his general schemes do not fit their ethnography. There is neverthe-less no doubt that Lévi-Strauss is the single most influential anthropologist from the period after Malinowski and Radcliffe-Brown – especially in France and other Latin countries, but also in the Anglo-Saxon world. It should finally be pointed out that his project, like Gregory Bateson's, is somewhat different from that of many anthropologists. Rather than trying to find out how societies work, or what makes people act as they do, the ultimate aim of his studies has been to reveal the principles of the functioning of the mind. He would therefore regard, say, kinship terminology not as a result of social organisation, but in the last instance as a product of the universal structures of the mind.

Lévi-Strauss's argument is complex and covers much ground, both theoretically and empirically. An important point, pertinent to the earlier discussion about descent and alliances, is nevertheless that his line of thought implies that alliances between groups are more fundamental than shared descent. Affinality is thus a universal key to the understanding of the integration of society. The nuclear family, which was earlier considered to be the smallest building-block of kinship, becomes a secondary structure within this schema, since it presupposes the brother–sister relationship and affinality.

Prescriptive and Preferential Rules?

Lévi-Strauss regarded the principle of cross-cousin marriage as a fundamental expression of reciprocity between kin groups with an elementary kinship system. These groups would also, according to him, have positive as well as negative marriage rules. Such elementary systems would also have unilineal descent systems and would exchange women at the level of the group.

Rodney Needham, a translator and critic of Lévi-Strauss, held that the latter's model was only valid in societies with prescriptive marriage rules, even if the distinction between prescriptive and preferential systems (which Needham proposed) was not elaborated in *The Elementary Structures of Kinship* (Needham 1962). Lévi-Strauss rejected this view, and stated that he regarded the kinship atom as a universal elementary structure, that his theory about the exchange of women was valid for all unilineal societies and that the distinction between prescriptive and preferential systems was irrelevant. In practice, he argued, so-called prescriptive systems are preferential, and in theory so-called preferential systems are prescriptive. Prescriptions thus only exist at the normative level, and in practice such rules are never followed perfectly.

It thus seems necessary to distinguish between categorisations of persons one can and cannot marry (such as rules of exogamy) and cultural preferences concerning whom it is particularly beneficial to marry. To individuals, marriage practices may be perceived as prescriptive rules if their parents arrange the marriage, but at a societal level it would be misleading to use this model as a description of the overall practices. What Lévi-Strauss speaks of as prescriptive rules simply amount to the categories the members of society think through; Needham's distinction makes it possible to distinguish between these categories and the strategies actors follow to achieve specific, culturally defined aims.

Even perfect knowledge of categories and rules does not enable us to predict how people actually will act, and at this point we might recall Firth's distinction between social structure and social organisation. Rules and norms are not identical with the social application of rules and norms.

Most kinship phenomena can probably be interpreted from an alliance perspective as well as a descent perspective. Both alliances and descent are aspects of every kinship system, although, as Kuper (1988) has remarked, descent theorists largely concentrated on societies where agnatic lineages were particularly important in the organisation of society, whereas alliance theorists were more concerned with the study of societies where the forging of alliances between kin groups was crucial. It is nevertheless quite possible to identify important alliances in societies usually thought of in terms of descent groups.

Claude Lévi-Strauss, the originator of structuralism, which is arguably the most original attempt at theoretical synthesis in twentieth-century anthropology. This photo was taken around the time he wrote *The Elementary Structures of Kinship*. (Photo courtesy of the Royal Anthropological Institute)

Kinship, Nature and Culture

In many modern societies, it is customary to think of kinship in terms of biology. Europeans generally see themselves as more closely related to their siblings than to their cousins and more closely related to first cousins than to second cousins. Classificatory kinship seems to be more or less absent in this kind of society. However, it transpires that even this kind of society has kin terms which derive from social organisation rather than from biological kinship. Among the Yanomamö, all of the women of one's patrilineage are regarded as 'father's sisters', and all of the men in mother's patrilineage are regarded as 'mother's brothers'. In the parental generation of ego, only two kinds of men and two kinds of women exist: fathers, mother's brothers, mothers and father's sisters. Among the Kariera and several other Australian peoples, all members of a moiety of the same generation and gender can be spoken of with the same kin term. All 'brothers' are brothers for nearly all practical purposes, even if they do not have shared biological descent.

In most European kinship terminologies, some affines are labelled 'uncles' and 'aunts', namely those who have married our parents' siblings. In many Indo-European languages, moreover, there is no terminological difference between biological and affinal uncles and aunts. The European kinship terms brother-in-law and sister-in-law may also refer to two different kinds of relatives. A brother-in-law may be the brother of ego's spouse; he may also be ego's sister's husband. Kin, in other words, do not come naturally; they must be created socially, and this is at least partly fashioned so as to facilitate tasks to be solved and to create order in an otherwise chaotic social world.

Arguing against those who have emphasised the biological foundations of kinship, Needham (1962) and David Schneider (1984) have argued that kinship is an invention with no necessary connection with biological facts, and they both stress that it is the invention of anthropologists. At least, the examples in this chapter have shown that the kinship system in a society does not follow automatically from biological kin relations. When descent is important in order to justify claims to land, it may be common to manipulate genealogies. Laura Bohannan (1952) has dealt with this in a study of the Tiv of Nigeria, an agricultural people organised in landholding segmentary patriclans. In this society, the structure and origins of the lineage are frequently consciously manipulated for the benefit of the interests of the living. Anne Knudsen (1987, 1992), writing about kinship, vendettas and mafia in Corsica, shows that of the total number of cousins (male collateral kin) a person has, only a small proportion is socially activated. Only the kinsmen one has shared interests with are in practice reckoned as kinsmen. Frequently, those cousins who are genealogically the most distant ones, become the closest ones in practice. Geertz (1988, p. 8) puts this openness of 'facts' to manipulation and interpretation in a more general way when he refers in passing to the North African mule, 'who talks always of his mother's brother, the horse, but never of his father, the donkey'.

Some Common Denominators

As we have seen, there are many different ways of resolving the problems associated with kinship, but all societies have some common denominators: all have rules regulating incest and exogamy. In all societies, alliances are forged between persons or descent groups, whether their importance is marginal or significant. All societies also seem to have developed a social organisation where mother and child live together during the first years of the child's life (a possible exception being societies with a high density of kindergartens). All societies have also developed functioning reproductive institutions, and all have rules of inheritance.

Further, many societies have also developed forms of local organisation, with political, economic and other dimensions, which are based on kinship. Both religion and daily rules for conduct may in such communities be based on respect for the ancestors and ancestral spirits (see Chapter 13). Differences in power are also often related to kinship. Kinship, indeed, is often the master idiom for society and human existence. What, then, is the role of kinship in societies which lack corporate kin groups, prescriptive marriage rules and ancestral cults?

Kinship and Bureaucracy

It is doubtless correct that kin-based forms of organisation continue to be important in many societies after having gone through processes of modernisation, that is after the inhabitants have become citizens and taxpayers, wageworkers and TV audiences. In most modern states, family dynasties exist in the realm of finance (and sometimes in politics), and genealogies remain important to individual self-identity. The nuclear family is an important institution in modern societies, and in many such communities kinship is decisive for one's career opportunities, political belonging, place of residence and more.

The capitalist labour market, however, is ostensibly based on formally voluntary contracts and individual achievement – not on kinship commitments and ascribed identity. It is therefore customary to regard the kin-based organisation as a contrast, and possible threat, to the bureaucratic organisation characteristic of both the labour market and the system of political administration in modern state societies. Kin-based organisation is based on loyalty to specific persons, while bureaucratic organisation ideally is based on loyalty to abstract principles, notably the law and contractual obligations. Kinsmen may be obliged to help each other out, whereas bureaucrats have committed themselves to following identical procedures and principles no matter who they are dealing with. According to a kinship ideology, it is appropriate to treat different people differently; according to a bureaucratic way of thinking, everybody is to be treated according to identical formal rules and regulations. When a person of high rank employs one of his kinsmen, others may call this practice nepotism (literally, particularism favouring nephews), that is 'unfair' differential treatment on the basis of kinship. According to a kinship logic, such a differential treatment is not unjust, however, but is rather an indication of loyalty and solidarity. The two logics, which coexist in virtually every society today, are thus difficult to reconcile in theory – they represent opposing moralities.

Max Weber (1978 [1919]) was the first social theorist to write systematically about the differences between kinship-based and bureaucratic organisation. His point of departure was the industrialisation of Europe, and he demonstrated a clear interrelationship between the industrial revolution, the growth of anonymous bureaucratic organisation based on formal rules and the weakening of kinship bonds. Although he was critical of some aspects of bureaucracy (he feared the inflexibility of the 'iron cage' of bureaucracy), Weber regarded this form of organisation, based on anonymous principles of equal treatment and a clear distinction between a person's professional and private statuses, as a distinctive advance over the particularistic principles that had dominated earlier. Talcott Parsons, who later developed Weber's theory further (1977), regarded modern societies as achievement-oriented and universalistic, as opposed to 'traditional' societies, which he saw as ascription-oriented and particularistic. This distinction means that a person's rank and career opportunities in a modern society depend on his or her achievements and achieved statuses, and that equal treatment for all (notably equal civil rights and equality before the law) is an important principle. In a traditional society, on the contrary, Parsons held that ascribed statuses, frequently connected with kinship, were more decisive; in other words, that it was less important what a person did than what he or she was.

Dichotomies of this kind are always simplistic. First, it is definitely not true that particularistic principles are absent in modern societies. Second, anthropological research has shown that there exist many 'traditional' societies which are highly achievement-oriented, where individual achievements are more important than lineage membership. This is the case, for example, among many hunters and gatherers, as well as in highland New Guinea. Further, the very term 'traditional societies' is extremely inaccurate since it lumps together a mass of highly diverse societies – from a Quechua village in the Andes to the Chinese empire.

On the other hand, dichotomies of this kind can be useful as conceptual tools, and provided we do not confound them with descriptions of an empirical reality they can be helpful in the process of organising facts. We should never forget, though, that they are ideal types (Weber's term); stylised, abstract models of aspects of the world, which are never encountered in their pure form 'out there'.

The relationship between kin-based and bureaucratic organisation must always be explored in an empirical context. Then we will discover that the two principles very often function simultaneously; that they are not mutually exclusive in practice. A person may support both ideals of formal justice *and* kinship solidarity in different situations.

Metaphoric Kinship

A lesson from the study of bureaucratic organisations is that the introduction of universalistic principles (formal rules, contracts, etc.) does not simply do away with particularistic principles: the two sets of rules coexist, just as individualism has not made the family superfluous, although many of its former functions have been taken over by other institutions. Let us now consider if a kinship way of thinking may have survived in other, less obvious ways in modern state societies.

Due to industrialisation and the integration of large, heterogeneous populations in nation-states, it has in many contexts become impossible to maintain clan- or lineage-based social organisation. In this kind of society, everybody is dependent on a large number of persons one is not related to, and each person is responsible for his or her life, largely without support from the kin group. The labour contract has replaced the clan land and the family trade, and social mobility is high. A marriage ideology based on individual choice has replaced the former lineage-based marriages. The monetary economy and the ideology of universal wagework has turned questions of subsistence and place of residence into individual and not collective issues.

This may lead us to believe that kinship has ceased to be important. However, it has important symbolic dimensions in addition to its social organisational potential. It is, in most known human societies, a main focus for subjective belongingness, sense of security and personal identity. In these fields, it seems clear that kinship has at least partly been replaced by metaphoric kinship ideologies such as nationalism. Nationalism presents the nation as a metaphoric kin group. Like lineage ideologies, it stresses the contrast between 'us' and 'them', and although it may be internally egalitarian and universalistic, it favours particularism in relation to other nations (see Chapter 17). The nation may also function as a lineage in certain judicial contexts. If a citizen dies with no personal inheritors, the state inherits the estate. The state may also, in certain cases, assume the parental responsibility for children.

A decisive difference between nationalism and actual kinship ideology is the fact that the nation encompasses a large number of people who will never meet personally; it promotes an anonymous community between people who do not know each other. If we wish to develop an ideal-typical distinction between societies of large and small scale, it may be useful to place the boundary at this point: if important aspects of one's existence depend on people one does not know, one belongs to a social system of large scale.

Kinship and Gender

To round off these two chapters about kinship and marriage, it may be relevant to reflect on the relationship between kinship and gender. During the heyday of 'kinshipology', up to the 1960s, anthropologists were, with a few notable exceptions, not very interested in gender. When reading the classic studies of Boas, Kroeber, Malinowski, Radcliffe-Brown, Evans-Pritchard and Fortes today, the absence of analyses of gender and the social and cultural production of gender differences is striking. In studies of kinship, a male perspective is often taken for granted. Certainly, women have a place in these studies; they sometimes appear as wives, mothers and sisters, but rarely as independently acting persons. They appear as resources which society (that is, men) controls; they are exchanged between groups, are married, accused of witchcraft and so on. Additionally, classic anthropological studies of kinship have rarely explored how particular kinship systems create particular kinds of gender relations – what sort of ideology justifies men's power over women – or even reflected on the fairly obvious fact that a kin relationship is often a gender relationship as well.

Today there exists a growing literature which tries to see social life from a gender-neutral perspective or even with an explicit female bias. Since the 1970s, many important studies on the fundamental importance of gender as an organising principle in society and culture have been published, and some of these studies are dealt with in the next chapter. However, surprisingly little of this literature links up with the study of kinship (see Collier and Yanagisako 1987; Howell and Melhuus 1993). For if Lévi-Strauss is right in that the sister–brother relationship is fundamental in the social production of kinship, it is surely not without interest that this kin relationship is also a gender relationship. The following two chapters deal with various criteria, starting with gender, that are used to classify people into mutually exclusive categories, which often entail differences in power.

Suggestions for Further Reading

Kuper, Adam: *The Invention of Primitive Society: Transformations of an Illusion*, Chapters 10–11. London: Routledge 1988.
Leach, Edmund: *Lévi-Strauss*, Chapter 6. Glasgow: Fontana 1970.
Needham, Rodney, ed.: *Rethinking Kinship and Marriage*. London: Tavistock 1971.

8   GENDER AND AGE

All animals are equal, but some are more equal than others.
—*George Orwell*

In all societies, there are differences in power between persons. There is not a single society where all adults have exactly the same influence over every decision, where everyone has exactly the same rights and duties. Social differentiation and equality are, in other words, universal phenomena. The Romantic ideas of the eighteenth and nineteenth centuries about the 'original primitive society', where all humans supposedly had the same rank and were political equals, was completely devastated when the first professional ethnographers returned from the field. Even among very small groups, and even among peoples with very simple technology, differential rank existed. Unlike what many 'armchair theorists' thought, small-scale societies do not lack internal differentiation. Marx and Engels were thus right in assuming, in the mid-nineteenth century, that there are universal criteria for social differentiation, which are the distinctions between older and younger people, between men and women and between insiders and outsiders, 'us' and 'them' (the latter is dealt with in Chapters 16–17).

Not all social differentiation entails unequal access to rank and power, and we may therefore distinguish between vertical and horizontal differentiation. The vertical dimension refers to inequalities in power or rank, while the horizontal dimension encompasses those aspects of social differentiation which do not express unequal rank – differences which may, for example, be expressed through the division of labour. Most forms of social differentiation nevertheless have a vertical or hierarchical aspect.

There are enormous and anthropologically important variations in forms of differentiation. In small-scale societies with a limited division of labour, such as hunter-and-gatherer societies, social differentiation is simple and may just be defined by age and gender. In many horticultural and agricultural societies, religious leaders and chiefs have recognised statuses setting them apart from the rest of the people, although those statuses are not necessarily hereditary. In more complex agricultural communities, there tend to be hereditary political offices, often a professional bureaucracy and a professional army, and there may be great differences between the rich and the poor; the powerful and the powerless. In some societies, ascribed statuses (such as caste in India) are decisive in formal social differentiation; in others, achieved statuses may be more important in determining a person's social rank and place in society.

There are many theoretical perspectives on such criteria for social differentiation as gender, age, class and caste. Some of the most vigorous debates in anthropology have indeed dealt with issues related to differentiation, power and rank. This and the following chapter, which discuss some of the most important criteria for differentiation, are therefore far from exhaustive.

Gender

There are two fundamentally different ways of regarding gender differences. On the one hand, there are certain biological differences between men and women; the genitals look different and function differently, women give birth to children, men usually have larger bodies, and so on. At this level, it is customary to use the term 'sex' instead of gender.

On the other hand, in practice gender differences are codified and institutionalised socially and culturally, and it is largely this kind of differences anthropologists focus on, which is distinguished from (biological) sex by the term 'gender'. All human societies conceptualise differences between men and women, and all consider such differences to be important in certain regards. However, there are important variations in the ways the relationships between men and women are worked out, and therefore it is difficult to generalise about gender. Gender can best be studied as a relationship – men are defined in relation to women and vice versa – and this relationship is conceived of differently in different societies.

Gender was for a long time relatively neglected in anthropological research, which is perhaps surprising, since gender identity may well be the most fundamental basis for personal identity. Malinowski, who has often been praised for his ethnographic detail, is now said to have neglected important women's institutions completely and exaggerated the contribution of men to the reproduction of Trobriand society (Weiner 1988). In many other classic studies too, social actors are more or less seen as equivalent to social men. This kind of perspective may be called androcentric (*andros* is Greek for man). It seems to be changing, and gender has been a central topic in anthropological research since the 1970s. Some of this research has concerned the notion of the 'original matriarchy': the idea, common in nineteenth-century scholarship, that human society was originally ruled by women. In this regard, it has been argued that such notions, which are widespread among many peoples, are probably myths created by men to justify their own power over women (Bamberger 1974).

The relative powerlessness and allegedly universal subjugation of women have also been subjected to a great deal of comparative research, forming the basis of debate both in favour of and against Western notions of 'discrimination' and 'power'. It has been argued that although women in many societies are deprived of formal political power, they may exert considerable power domestically and indirectly. It has also been suggested that the concepts of anthropologists dealing with discrimination may be ethnocentrically biased. Even if women in traditional Middle Eastern societies seem discriminated against and powerless from a European perspective, they may perceive their situation otherwise.

Some of the most recent anthropological research on women does not primarily deal with the 'position of women', but instead concentrates on different aspects of the male–female relationship in different societies. Several anthropologists have even discovered that not only women but men too are gendered (see Gilmore 1989).

Gender is omnipresent and easily visible; perhaps this is one reason why it has suffered neglect from anthropologists who have regarded it as 'natural'. However, like kinship and ethnicity, gender is not natural and God-given, but socially created. The great cultural variation regarding conceptions and conventions about gender reveals this. Probably all societies hold notions about the 'naturalness' of certain gender differences, but such ideas are themselves cultural constructs and not a part of nature. A contemporary anthropological perspective on gender would thus not try to answer the question 'what is gender really?', but would rather look into 'the social and cultural construction of gender ... [and] the relationship between constructions of maleness and femaleness' (Strathern 1988, p. 69).

Gender in the Division of Labour

Even in societies with a simple division of labour and little occupational specialisation, women's work is distinguished from men's work. We have already seen examples of this from the Yanomamö and the Fulani. The most typical cases of communities where a division of labour based on gender is the most important are nevertheless hunter-gatherer, or foraging societies, and here it may be worth noting that humanity has consisted exclusively of hunters and gatherers for the greater part of its existence.

Some readers may have noted the use of the cumbersome term 'hunters and gatherers' instead of simply 'hunters'. The reason for this is actually an increased understanding of the importance of gender. Among such peoples, men usually hunt and women usually forage. For a long time, anthropologists and other outsiders believed that hunting was the main source of livelihood among these groups. The men of these societies spoke incessantly about hunting, and visitors were given the impression that this was the single most important activity. Detailed research on nutrition among some such groups, notably in Southern Africa, has nonetheless revealed that the most important source of nutrition are tubers, insects, edible plants and small creatures gathered by the women, while the men's hunting activities are irregular, uncertain and form no reliable basis for subsistence. Among a San group studied by Richard Lee (1968), it transpired that the inhabitants received two-thirds of their nourishment from what was brought in by gathering. Nonetheless, the men saw their society as a hunting society, and the women's routine work was not given the same symbolic importance accorded to hunting.

It seems reasonable to assume, as a hypothesis, that the influence of women is most significant where their economic contribution is important. Ester Boserup (1970) has compared the division of labour in a number of agricultural societies with reference to gender. Her main conclusion, which was surprising to many at the time, was that women in many societies, especially in Africa and in communities which do not use draught animals, carry out the main bulk of the agricultural work. It also seems that their influence is generally greater in these societies than in places where they are exclusively responsible for the domestic sphere. Boserup's controversial conclusion is that the political position of women in farming societies is generally weakened when new technology is introduced, since this technology tends to be controlled by men. In addition, land is usually controlled by men. Boserup argues that the position of women is weakened when their economic contribution diminishes; this is nevertheless a thorny issue. For what is an economic contribution? As indicated, foraging may be less spectacular than hunting, and less ritualised and talked about (just like housework in industrial societies), but it is an economic contribution nonetheless. The following example may illustrate the relationship between gender relations, the economy and the realm of ideology and power.

The Mundurucú live in the south-eastern Amazon basin (Murphy and Murphy 1985) and traditionally have a way of life comparable to that of several other Amazon forest peoples. They are politically integrated at the level of the village; each village, which has between 50 and 100 inhabitants, is politically independent. They are horticulturalists and grow tubers, fruit and vegetables, apart from fishing and hunting. That is, the men go hunting.

The division of labour is based on gender. The men are responsible for clearing the ground, but planting, weeding and harvesting are women's work. The women also gather wild fruits and nuts, while men and women cooperate in fishing. The Murphys write:

The men think of themselves essentially as hunters, not as gardeners or fishermen, the religion is oriented towards hunting, and the spirit world is closely associated with the species of game. It is the skillful hunter who is honored, not the industrious tiller of the soil. (Murphy and Murphy 1985, p. 88)

In fact the horticultural activities are more important, from a nutritional point of view, than both hunting and fishing, and they also entail much more work. The issue, however, is not purely to do with nutrition: power and prestige are also at stake. If, therefore, it is considered a more valuable thing to shoot a single antelope than to grow a tonne of taro, it does not necessarily make a difference that the taro is more important to the group's survival than the antelope is.

Mundurucú society is politically dominated by men. Like men in many male-dominated societies, they tell stories of an original matriarchal social order when 'everything went wrong', before all was eventually transformed by a mythical cultural hero. Such myths must be considered an important aspect of ideology: together with the disproportionate emphasis put on hunting as a means of livelihood, they contribute to legitimating (or justifying) male supremacy. It may nevertheless be noted that if the Mundurucú regarded female subordination as 'natural', there would be no need for such ideological myths: the stories are told as warnings that the women may rise again unless the men are vigilant.

Why, one may still ask, do men have political and economic supremacy in most known societies, when it is not true that men contribute more than women to the physical survival of the group? Let us consider some attempts to account for this more or less universal power discrepancy.

The Private and the Public

Although women may carry out as much or more work than men, they are nearly universally responsible for domestic work – child-raising, cooking and cleaning. Men, on the contrary, tend to be responsible for the household's dealings with the outside world. In hunting and gathering societies, they have to protect the woman and her suckling infants from dangers; in more specialised societies, they tend to hold political and ritual offices. Some anthropologists have seen a principle cause of the subordination of women in the fact, ultimately rooted in biology, of women's lack of physical mobility during pregnancy and suckling. These impediments to free movement serve to link the woman to the home while the man is free to roam the public space. It has thus been suggested (Rosaldo 1974) that power discrepancies between the genders are related to the distinction between the public and private spheres in society: men control the former and women are confined to the latter. The Murphys' monograph on the Mundurucú suggests that such a distinction may have something to recommend it. In the Mundurucú village, only women and children live in huts; all men live in a men's house. This house has no walls; it is constructed as a large leaning roof supported by long poles. Its open side faces the village, so that the men can at any time follow events there. The woman's place is at home and in the fields, while the men's place is in the public space, where decisions of importance for the whole village are taken.

Ortner and Whitehead (1981) have added to this perspective that there is a general tendency to the effect that women are, rightly or wrongly, culturally associated with private and particularistic projects, while men are associated with the public and common good. They argue:

[This] relates to a widespread sociological distinction suggested by Rosaldo (1974): Nearly universally, men control the 'public domain', where 'universalistic' interests are expressed and managed, and, nearly universally, women are located in or confined to the 'domestic domain', charged with the welfare of their own families. (1981, p. 7)

This distinction has been criticised as ethnocentric – it is said to be meaningful in modern societies but not necessarily in others – but it is nevertheless well established and implicitly assumed in much comparative research on gender.

Dominance and Submission

Is the subordination of women universal – do women everywhere have a lower rank and less power than men? The most common answer is yes, but the question is far from unproblematic. First, there are very significant variations between gender relations in different societies, ranging from

Among the Chewong of Malaysia, gender relations are traditionally very egalitarian, and it is common for men to look after children. As this photo reveals, even small children smoke tobacco, which is economically important to the Chewong. (Photo: Signe Howell)

nearly complete equality (as among the Chewong of Malaysia; see Howell 1989), to societies where the women's influence over their own destiny seems very limited. Second, concepts such as 'rank', 'subordination' and 'discrimination against women' are themselves problematic. Perhaps, it has been suggested, the anthropologist's own cultural background creates an unhealthy analytical bias here, in that he or she assumes, as a matter of fact, that equality is desirable, while many of the people studied by anthropologists insist that the genders ought not to be equal but should rather be complementary. Finally, it is not entirely certain that men and women understand the same thing by power and power discrepancies. Perhaps women care little about what the men see as prestige objects?

One group frequently mentioned as marked by a high degree of gender equality is traditional Hopi society in what is now the south-western United States. 'When traditional Hopi women are asked "Who are more important, women or men", a common reply is "We are, because we are the mothers", with the qualification that men are important, too, as the messengers to the gods' (Schlegel 1977, p. 186).

The Hopis, a North American Indian people famous for having preserved important aspects of their traditional culture, have a matrilineal kinship system. Unlike in most matrilineal societies, a woman's brothers and mother's brother are not strong authorities impeding her freedom of movement and agency. The spouses are considered equally valuable and complementary, and the lineage as well as the household has a female head.

On the other hand, men have formal political and religious power at the level of the village, although, as Schlegel remarks, 'women do not hesitate to speak their minds' and, as 'Hopi men readily admit, women usually get their way' (1977, p. 195). At an intermediate level between the household and the village is the clan, which is led by a brother–sister pair.

The division of labour among the Hopi is unexceptional, comparatively speaking. Only the men go hunting, and only the women grind flour; however, they share the agricultural work. Schlegel thus suggests that there may be a cultural, and not an economic, cause for the high level of gender equality among the Hopi: 'Where the ideological focus of a culture is life, and both sexes are believed to be equally necessary to the promotion of life, devaluation of either sex is unlikely' (1977, p. 205). Could this be adequate as an explanation? It is true that some male-dominated societies regard the woman's role in reproduction as marginal; the male seed is seen to play the crucial part. In many patriarchal societies, it is believed that women create the soft, perishable parts of the body, while the men create the skull and bones. But could this kind of gender ideology be the *cause* of inequality between the genders, or is it rather the *effect* of such an institutional order? No general answer to this question is proposed here; suffice it to note that in actual social process, ideology and practice function together and can only be separated analytically. In other words, it is not easy to point out what it is that determines what.

What does it mean that women tend to be 'subordinated'? Even in otherwise egalitarian societies, women rarely, if ever, hold high religious office. Among the Mundurucú, only men are allowed to play and even see the sacred trumpets used in ritual; even among the Hopi, only men can be high priests. On the other hand, it is not obviously true that priesthood is the ultimate expression of power in society. In fact, women who are deprived of public office – be it political or religious – have been known to exert considerable power informally. During my own fieldwork in societies which are apparently strongly male-dominated, I have often met men who sincerely complain that their wives, who control the domestic domain, decide everything in their lives.

In an amusing and intriguing study of a Portuguese local community in the Saloio area outside Lisbon, Joyce Riegelhaupt (1967) analyses the relationship between male and female power in a society where male power is officially all-pervasive. At the time of her fieldwork, the subordination of Portuguese women was established by law, in the domestic as well as in the public sphere. Nearly all political offices were held by men. However, Riegelhaupt discovered that women in this community were in practice sometimes more powerful than men.

The explanation for the strong position of women in this community seems to lie in the division of labour, which paradoxically allows women a more public role than their husbands. The men are responsible for agricultural work, while female members of household divide their time between housework, child-raising, some agricultural work, marketing and shopping. Since the men work in the fields, only the women stay in the village during the day. They then meet in the shops, where they may exchange information and develop networks. They also travel to Lisbon to sell commodities, and are in this way able to develop networks outside the village as well. The men, on their part, have much less contact with each other, since they work in isolation on their separate plots.

As the women market the family's produce, they are central to the domestic finances. They are also important in politics, despite their formally marginal position. Most political issues in the locality concern the maintenance of and improvements to public infrastructure; mending roads, installing water pipelines and so on. It is necessary to have personal contacts with the authorities to achieve this. Thanks to their wide-ranging networks, the women frequently succeed in persuading the wives of local political leaders to talk their husbands into taking the right decisions.

There is in other words a great discrepancy between *rules* and *practices* in this case. The law and official ideology state that men ought to be in charge of politics and the domestic economy. In practice, the women seem to exert more power than their spouses in both respects. The Saloio example indicates that the subordination of women cannot be assumed *a priori*, and it also serves as a reminder that even perfect knowledge of the explicit norms of a society does not enable us to predict how people will act.

Men: Women::Culture:Nature?

This subheading is shaped like a structuralist formula. It reads like this: 'Does the relationship between men and women correspond to the relationship between culture and nature?' A simple colon refers to a relationship; a double colon refers to a relationship between sets of relationships (see also Chapter 14).

In many societies, women are seen as being closer to nature than men, who are considered more cultivated than women. Like nature, Sherry Ortner notes in an article inspired by Lévi-Strauss's structuralism (Ortner 1974), women are regarded as undomesticated, wild and difficult to control. Therefore they represent danger (to men) and must be domesticated. Ortner mentions three related, universal aspects of female existence which may lend support to this widespread cultural view. (i) The body of the woman and its biological functions (birth, menstruation, suckling) make it necessary for her to spend more time on 'species behaviour' than the man, who is freer to concentrate on 'purely cultural projects'. (ii) The body of the woman and its functions place her in social roles which are regarded as 'lower' than those of men (cooking, cleaning, etc.). (iii) These two aspects of female existence give her a mental structure which is different from that of men and which is seen as being closer to nature. This point, we should note, is reminiscent of the public/private distinction. It also suggests that women are seen as passive while men are seen as active, which is a very widespread view, whether as regards the sexual act, the transmission of culture or the respective roles of the genders in the upholding of society.

According to this line of thought, biological differences between men and women form the starting-point for gender inequality; for example, her association with small children (who are also considered imperfectly cultured) draws her towards nature. In patrilineal and virilocal societies, it may be added, women also come from 'outside'; they belong to a different kin group from the one in which they live. All of this indicates that – and may contribute to explaining why – women are often regarded as more natural, less cultural, than men.

On the other hand, women everywhere obviously have cultural roles; in many societies it is actually the role of women to maintain and transmit tradition, and it is often considered 'natural' that women are more strongly religious than men. In many Mediterranean areas, further, men are considered sexual 'forces of nature' and, for this reason, women are themselves seen as to blame if they are raped – they ought to be cultured enough to protect themselves from the male, who is allegedly unable to contain his sexual drive. Nevertheless, there is a wealth of ethnographic support for Ortner's general assumptions, namely the fact that women give birth, suckle babies and menstruate gives them an ambiguous and sometimes 'dangerous' cultural position between nature and culture.

The notion that 'man is to woman what culture is to nature' is controversial, and most scholars agree that the model is simplistic. It has also been pointed out that the cultural distinction between nature and culture may not be as universal as Ortner, drawing on Lévi-Strauss, assumes. It may still be good to think through, however, as an aid to interpreting complex ethnographic material. The general notion that one's enemies or subordinates are somehow closer to nature than oneself is far from uncommon, and it is certainly not restricted to the male–female relationship. According to the racist ideology which served to justify slavery in North America, blacks were closer to nature than whites and were therefore better suited for hard physical work; but simultaneously they were 'like children', unable to handle responsibility and freedom. In this way, the framing of social inequality in a culture–nature dichotomy can be an important ideological instrument legitimating power differences.

'Women's Worlds' and 'Men's Worlds'?

If we accept that there are systematic differences between women and men – whether we attribute the differences to biology, socialisation or ideology – we must also admit that men and women may experience the world in different ways (related to what Ortner calls different 'mental structures'). This was the point of departure for Edwin Ardener when he wrote that the 'problem of women has not been solved by social anthropologists' (1977, p. 1). The problem of women is not identical with the problem of the 'position of women', he continues, but rather concerns the methodological and theoretical problems raised by women in relation to anthropological research. Notably, Ardener claims that women in many societies are shy and quiet, and difficult to engage in conversation on topics interesting to the anthropologist. He speaks of them as 'muted' – not literally, but in the sense that women tend to communicate in ways not immediately intelligible to anthropologists (be they male or female), while men more easily talk about their society in ways familiar to anthropological reasoning: the male cultural universe, Ardener intimates, is closer to the anthropological one than the female cultural universe. In his view, it is anthropology *as such* which has a male bias, not individual anthropologists. This argument, which has been influential in later research on gender, is reminiscent of Ortner's and Whitehead's distinction between the particularistic woman and the universalistic man. If Ardener is correct, women's worlds are generally more difficult to explore than men's worlds. Whatever the case may be, it is clear that women and men may experience the world differently in many societies. In research in the Caribbean, it has indeed been argued that women and men have opposing moralities: women try to enhance their *respectability* while men strive to improve their *reputation* (P. Wilson 1978), and the two value systems entail two quite different ways of perceiving the world. However, although the two moralities are associated with gender, they are not irretrievably linked with gender. There are 'bacchanal women' – 'femmes fatales' – who look for ways to improve their reputation, and there are also stable and predictable men who rarely touch alcohol and take their children to church every Sunday (Eriksen 1990).

This kind of society, marked by strong tensions between the genders, seems paradoxical, since it appears to be based on two, partly irreconcilable value systems. The truth is probably that similar paradoxes are common, if less visible, in other societies as well, and that it may be fruitful to explore these moral contradictions by focusing on gender. This brings us far from the original preoccupations of what is 'really' male and female (the search for essences), and shows that the study of gender is an important dimension in the study of society as such.

Age

Like gender, age is a universal principle for social differentiation and classification. Ageing is an inevitable and irreversible biological process but, like gender, age is to some extent socially constructed. In many societies a person's rank rises as he or she becomes older, regardless of gender. Indeed, Ladislav Holy states, with 'the exception of a few hunting and nomadic societies in which survival depends on the physical ability to move around ..., the nonindustrial societies emerge as distinctly old-age oriented' (1990, p. 167). In modern industrial society, by contrast, old people do not have a particularly high authority by virtue of age: they are no longer achievers and are therefore relatively not valuable in societies like these, which place a high value on individual achievement. In addition, the rapid pace of cultural change in modern societies renders much of the wisdom and cultural competence of old people obsolete.

Advanced age is often associated with deep experience, wisdom and a sound sense of judgement. In many societies, old men are the political rulers and old women are perceived as less 'threatening' than younger ones, since they have grown more 'cultivated' and are further removed from nature than younger women are. They no longer menstruate, they no longer have children; they are 'drier' and do not represent a 'threatening' sexual force. Old women may in some societies be more powerful than young men. Societies where the old in the main control the political domain are called gerontocracies.

Similarly, children and adolescents are often considered imperfect in the sense that much of their immanent humanness has yet to be realised – while they may also, for the same reason, be considered 'innocent', a condition which is a form of perfection. They have yet to be socialised, and therefore know neither sin nor virtue.

In most societies, criteria other than gender and age contribute to distinguishing between categories of people, but there are also societies which only use those criteria, in addition to personal merit. It therefore seems clear that gender and age are more fundamental criteria for social differentiation than, for example, caste, class or ethnicity.

Age Grades and Age Groups

In some societies where age is an important principle of differentiation, there are several degrees, or institutionalised stages, between youth and old age. The Baktaman of New Guinea thus distinguish between seven age grades among men, and the ritual passing from one grade to the next entails a promotion in relative rank (Barth 1975). Men of the seventh grade possess virtually the entire body of knowledge extant among the Baktaman, including various forms of secret knowledge (which is transferred through consecutive rites of passage), and it therefore seems 'natural' that they should have control over the political domain.

Life-stages as an Analytical Category?
All societies distinguish between different life-stages. Van Gennep's, Turner's and others' studies of rites of passage indicate how the process of socialisation inevitably creates ruptures in life, whereby people pass from one phase to another, bringing new statuses, rights and duties. But are such life-stages universal? This view has been argued by Colin Turnbull (1985), who presents five life-stages he considers universal. If he is correct, these stages may be used as comparative concepts; that is to say, we may expect to find the same phases in all societies. Turnbull's life-stages are as follows.

Childhood is marked by dependence on others and the rapid acquisition of cultural categories.

Adolescence is described as that period between childhood and maturity when a person moves towards sexual maturity and is gradually preparing for full social responsibility.

Youth is seen as the stage between adolescence and adulthood, which is largely described as a period of higher education. Turnbull admits that this is not a universal life-stage.

Adulthood, the fourth phase (or, in many societies, the third one), seems 'more boring', Turnbull claims, than the previous ones; it is full of responsibility, work and routine.

The final life-stage is *old age*, a period when, Turnbull writes, physical and mental defects may set in, but when the 'heart and soul' are more vital than ever before, since old persons have such a great deal of experience. Do ageing and the passage between life-stages, then, mean more or less the same thing in different societies, as Turnbull intimates? Probably not. For example, there is little doubt that the European conceptualisation of childhood was only developed in the eighteenth century.

In this way, age may function as a vertical principle of differentiation. It may also function horizontally, by dividing the population (usually males only) into peer groups who belong to the same age category. In societies lacking criteria for internal differentiation other than age, gender and kinship, such as the pastoral Nuer and Maasai societies of East Africa, men (and sometimes women) are organised into age sets of people who are not defined as kin, but who were circumcised at the same time. A special kind of solidarity, reminiscent of kinship, exists within these groups, and often age sets have special collective obligations. The formation of such sets contributes to strengthening social cohesion and integration in society, since they cross kin boundaries (see also Chapter 10). In some modern state societies, schoolmates may develop comparable ties of solidarity, not least among the English upper and upper-middle classes, where, for example, old Etonians of the same cohort are expected to support each other.

Ageing into a Gendered Person

Gender and age have both biological and cultural aspects. Age is not necessarily directly correlated with gender. Among the Bakweri of Cameroon, for example, it is nearly impossible for a man to get married before he reaches the age of 40, since he must have property and political influence to find a wife. Women, on the other hand, are married shortly after sexual maturity.

Children are often considered relatively sexless, and their socialisation frequently aims at achieving a double end: to turn them into members of society, and to turn them into men and women. For this reason, rites of passage for girls and boys usually differ markedly.

Among the people who live near Mount Hagen in highland New Guinea (Strathern 1988), it is a common view that infants are born with both male and female qualities. For them to become women and men, they have to go through a long process of learning which culminates in a series of puberty rites. Among the boys, in particular, this ritual is highly demanding. According to the Hagen people themselves, this is due to the fact that the boys have to be worked more than the girls to become properly gendered persons, that is functioning social agents. The girls need to be transformed less through cultivating rites, since they are considered to carry the necessary growth potential in their bodies already. As mentioned earlier, men are often seen as active, women as passive.

After such rites of initiation, children are clearly differentiated by gender in most societies. Such rites may take place around the time of sexual maturation or earlier. In some Middle Eastern societies, both boys and girls may go to the public bath with their mothers; after initiation, however, the boys are not even allowed to see naked women. Rites of initiation often entail circumcision of the genitals, tattooing or other visible, physical alterations, making it possible at a glance to distinguish insiders from outsiders and 'complete' humans from 'incomplete' ones. In many societies, the candidates are also subjected to great trials during the period of initiation, frequently physical pain, to give them the opportunity to prove that they are worthy of the responsibility and the rights given them as grown members of society. Among the Nuer, the initiation of boys includes the cutting of six parallel stripes across the brow from ear to ear. The cuts go 'to the bone' (Evans-Pritchard 1940), and the boys are expected not to show evidence of pain during the ordeal.

The circumcision of a Betsileo boy, Madagascar. (Photo: Øyvind Dahl)

Rites of Passage

The term rite of passage (*rite de passage*) is associated with the name of
Arnold van Gennep, who published the book *Les Rites de passage* as early
as 1909. Through such rites, van Gennep wrote, society reproduces itself.
People are given new statuses without the social structure changing, and
the public character of the ceremonies gives the inhabitants an annual
reminder of the fellowship, rights and obligations provided by society.
Since then, Victor Turner (1967, 1969, 1974) has developed van Gennep's
perspective further by looking closely into the phases and levels of meaning
provided by these rites among the Ndembu of what is now Zambia. A
general point in Turner's studies is that the rites of passage simultaneously
function as permitting integration into society *and* give the participants a
mystical experience of oneness with the spiritual world and with the
'societal organism'.

Turner follows van Gennep in dividing the rites into three phases:
separation, liminality and reintegration. Separation is characterised by the
individual's or group's movement away from a fixed point in social
structure towards something unknown. When the breach is completed,

the agent enters a liminal phase, an ambiguous stage where he or she is in a certain sense placed outside society, 'betwixt and between' (Turner 1969) two stable conditions. This puts the actor in a dangerous position. Society runs the risk that the actor refuses to be reintegrated and rejects its values and power hierarchies, while the individual on his or her part risks anomie and social homelessness. Turner writes that in nearly every society, a person in a liminal phase is 'structurally if not physically invisible in terms of his culture's standard definitions and classifications' (1974, p. 232). This difficult and dangerous liminality is nevertheless necessary in order to 'clean off' the earlier statuses of the individual, to make him or her ready to be reborn as a new category of social person.

In a study of the Kaguru, a matrilineal people in Tanzania, T.O. Beidelman (1971) writes that if a boy dies immediately after circumcision he cannot be buried in the ordinary way, since he will have died neither as a child nor as an adult, but as a liminal, indeterminate kind of person, or even non-person.

The final phase in rites of passage is reintegration. During this phase, the candidates return as new persons, usually at a higher level of rank.

Beidelman provides detailed descriptions of initiation rites among the Kaguru, and it is easy to identify the three phases analysed by Turner in these. The rites entail both moral education and physical alterations for both genders, but their content differs. The boys, who are ten to twelve years old, are led away from the village into the bush (separation), undressed and shaved. Their foreskins are then removed, and the adult

---

Victor Turner (1920–83) was trained in classic structural-functionalism, but his interests gradually developed in the direction of symbolic analysis and psychological anthropology. His first major monograph, *Schism and Continuity in an African Society* (1957), deals with social integration and fission among the Ndembu in Northern Rhodesia (now Zambia). Several of his later books deal with the Ndembu as well, but his most influential texts focus on ritual and the meaning of symbols. Unlike Lévi-Strauss, Turner emphasises the multivocality or ambiguity of symbols, showing how symbols simultaneously contribute to the maintenance of society *and* respond to existential problems. In his studies of ritual, Turner is particularly known for his treatment of rites of passage. Here he has called attention to the liminal phase, which he regards as crucial (for example in *The Ritual Process*, 1969). Turner has described the transition between different states entailed by liminality as a dynamic interplay between different forms of social integration, namely the formal 'societas' and the informal 'communitas'. To Turner, rituals are condensed expressions of a social form: by studying them in great detail, he has argued, it is possible to make statements about society and individuals in general. Other anthropologists have since tried to apply Turner's insights and concepts about liminality, societas and communitas to other contexts apart from the purely ritual ones.

men who have accompanied them then begin to teach them riddles, songs and myths which encapsulate the essence of the Kaguru world view. After circumcision, the boys have to remain in the temporary camp in the bush for a certain period (liminality), and during this period the adult men arrange various trials for them: they hide in the bushes at night pretending to be lions, tell them that they may die after circumcision, and so on. This prolonged phase is, of course, the liminal one. Finally, the boys are taken back to the village and are given several new names (reintegration).

Unlike the boys, Kaguru girls are not regarded as fundamentally transformed after initiation. Whereas the boys are taken out into the bush together, girls are initiated separately and in isolation in huts in the village, but they too are circumcised and given moral education, although to some extent they learn other things than the boys do.

The liminal phase gives the boys in Kaguru society (and in many other societies) powerful common experiences; they have gone through trials together and have become adults together. Frequently, such shared experiences create life-lasting ties of solidarity; as previously mentioned, such ties are sometimes institutionalised and serve as a mitigating political factor in societies which are otherwise based on lineage organisation.

Marriage and Death

Most studies of rites of passage deal with initiation rites. Rites relating to marriage and death are nevertheless also important. They move persons from one status to another and serve as collective reminders – just like initiation rites – of the cohesion of society, its moral values and the legitimacy of authority. In kinship-based societies, marriage gives important opportunities for forging alliances between kin groups and symbolises the continuity of society.

The mortuary rite marks the last important rite of passage in the life of any earthling. Among the Kaguru, mortuary rites are associated with two problems. First of all, one must ensure that the deceased is safely transferred from the land of the living to the spiritual world. Recently deceased persons, like adolescents in the bush, are 'betwixt and between' and must therefore be approached with great caution. They cannot be controlled as one controls living people, yet at the same time they are sufficiently close to the living to influence them. They must, in other words, be established as properly dead people as quickly as possible.

A person who has died is shaved all over (like a novice during initiation); men are laid on their right side, women on their left. Both genders are buried with their heads facing left, towards the spiritual world. Dead bodies are buried in great haste since they are considered polluting and dangerous, but the mourning period lasts for at least four days. At the end of this period the second problem associated with death turns up, namely the question of inheritance. In this situation, the issue does not merely concern how to make a good deal for oneself, but also which social ties are to be strengthened and which are to be weakened. There are social obligations, property and social statuses to be redistributed at a death.

The challenges faced at a death are perhaps universal. First, death must be given a symbolic, perhaps religious, content to make it possible for the survivors to reconcile themselves with it; and second, one must ensure that life goes on, that is, that society continues to exist more or less unaltered after a death.

Rites of Passage in Modern Societies?

Some readers may have the impression that rites of passage exist 'out there' and not 'among ourselves'. This is not the case, but it is doubtless true that such rites have a diminished importance in modern societies.

In West European societies, four major rites of passage have traditionally been important, although three of them seem to have lost some of their significance since the Second World War. While the funeral is still a social event of great importance, baptism, confirmation (or first communion) and marriage have become both less widespread and, in most European societies, less important. In part, this is due to the fact that these rituals are associated with a religion whose role in the daily life of Europeans has diminished; another partial explanation is that these rituals are no longer socially important for individuals in marking the transition from one status to another. In the Protestant societies of Scandinavia, candidates for confirmation were traditionally obliged to learn by rote quite an amount of Biblical knowledge, and failing was a real possibility. At the confirmation party afterwards, young people received 'adult' presents such as a suit and a watch – in parts of Scandinavia, cigarette cases and sets of false teeth (often made of whale ivory) were also common gifts as late as the 1930s – which signified that they were now to be considered grown-ups with full responsibilities. As confirmation takes place when children are about 14, it is easy to understand why its importance has decreased: while they were formerly expected to earn their own living after confirmation, there is no longer a dramatic change in their lives following the rite. Perhaps – but this is still uncertain – a similar explanation holds for the reduced importance of the marriage rite?

An important difference between gender and age as principles for social differentiation is the fact that one more or less automatically changes membership between age groups, while few people change their gender. In gerontocratic but otherwise egalitarian societies, boys may simply await their coming of age to achieve full political rights; they may be eligible to sit on the elders' council and may eventually become powerful ancestral spirits. This is not an option available to women in many societies.

As this chapter has stressed, the division of labour in society is fundamental to social differentiation, and the relative complexity of the division of labour may indicate the complexity of social differentiation. It has also been shown that social differentiation cannot be studied independently from politics and ideology. Both gender and age tend to be associated with politics and the division of labour, but they usually function together with other factors. In the next chapter, we consider some such criteria which contribute to the kind of complexity mentioned, namely caste and class.

Suggestions for Further Reading

David Gilmore: *Manhood in the Making*. New Haven, CT: Yale University Press 1989.
Sherry Ortner and Harriet Whitehead, eds: *Sexual Meanings*. Cambridge: Cambridge University Press 1981.
Victor W. Turner: *The Ritual Process*. Chicago: Aldine 1969.

9 CASTE AND CLASS

For unto every one that hath shall be given, and he shall have abundance; but from him that hath not shall be taken away even that which he hath.
—*Holy Bible (King James version), St Matthew 25: 29*

Like gender and age, caste in the Indian subcontinent refers to ostensibly inborn, ascribed characteristics. In theory, changing one's caste membership is as difficult as changing one's gender.

The concept of social classes is different. Although many social scientists have demonstrated that most people in class societies take over their parents' class membership (if one is a working-class child, it is highly likely that one remains in the working class), there is a great deal of mobility between the social classes, both in theory and in practice. In many societies, class membership is emically considered an achieved and not an ascribed status.

The relationship between caste and class is complex, and both concepts are difficult to define accurately. Let us begin with the concept of caste.

The Caste System

The caste system encompasses aspects of both 'culture' and 'society'; that is, it is both a symbolic system associated with Hinduism, and a set of rules and practices regulating social organisation, interaction and power in Indian society.

The caste system can be defined as a system dividing all of (Hindu) society into endogamous groups with hereditary membership, which are simultaneously separated and connected with each other through three characteristics: separation regarding marriage and contact; division of labour in that each group, at least in theory, represents a particular profession; and finally hierarchy, which ranks the groups on a scale dividing them into high and low castes.

The caste system thus entails a ranking of people according to ascribed statuses, it provides rules regulating the interrelationships between members of different castes, and it creates mutual dependence of the castes through the division of labour, which implies that certain tasks can only be carried out by members of specified castes.

Hindus from all over India make pilgrimages to Varanasi (Benares) to cremate their dead and to cleanse themselves in the holy River Ganga. (Photo: Trygve Bølstad)

Regarding ideology and religion, the caste system is based on notions of ritual purity and impurity, which serve to justify the segregation and division of labour between the castes. The variations in ritual purity imply, among other things, that a member of a high caste will be polluted if he or she eats food prepared by a member of a low caste, and that only members of the Brahmin caste are entitled to lead religious rituals. Each caste has its own rules for good conduct; for example, high castes tend to be teetotallers and vegetarians.

Varna and Jāti

It is common to think of the caste system as a hierarchy dividing the entire Hindu population into four main groups, the *varnas* (a Sanskrit word meaning 'colour'). The Brahmins (priests) have the highest rank, followed by the Khsatriyas (warriors and kings), the Vaishyas (merchants) and the Shudras (artisans and workers). Outside the varna system proper, at the very bottom of the ladder, are the so-called Untouchables, labelled thus by the British because a high-caste person had to go through an elaborate purification ritual after having touched such a polluting person. Members of the three highest varnas are called 'twice-born' because they have gone through a ceremony entailing spiritual rebirth.

Such a description of the caste system, although it is not incorrect, is simplistic and ultimately misleading. First, it should be noted that there are also non-Hindus who belong to castes; India's approximately 120 million Muslims have their own castes (usually low ones), and the many ethnic groups called 'tribals' tend to be classified as, and treated as, Untouchables. Non-Hindu societies in the Indian sub-continent, from Buddhist Sri Lanka to Muslim Pakistan, also have castes.

Furthermore, and more significantly, this fivefold partition of the Indian population is highly abstract and has a relatively modest significance in daily life. The Indian social anthropologist M.N. Srinivas writes: 'The real unit of the caste system is not one of the four *varnas* but *jāti*, which is a very small endogamous group practising a traditional occupation and enjoying a certain amount of cultural, ritual and judicial autonomy' (1952, p. 24). There are thousands of jātis in India; they all represent an hereditary profession or craft (even if it is no longer practised) and have long-standing commitments to the other jātis in the area as well as a special place in the ritual hierarchy. Most jātis are relatively small, but some are large and internally differentiated groups with asymmetrical alliance patterns between the lineage segments.

At an intermediate level between the jātis and varnas, we find the all-Indian occupational castes, for example the Lohar caste of blacksmiths, which encompasses jātis all over India.

The practical function of the varna system is mainly to make it possible for members of local jātis to locate themselves in relation to jātis in other parts of the country; additionally, it represents a fixed, abstract hierarchy and value system. 'Untouchables' (now called Dalits, meaning 'the oppressed ones') do not have a place in the varna system proper, but do belong to jātis. Members of the lower jātis, comments Srinivas (1952, p. 30), have always tried to improve their rank 'by adopting vegetarianism and teetotalism, and by Sanskritizing [their] ritual and pantheon'; this process of caste-climbing, he adds, has led to the spread of a remarkably uniform value system in the sub-continent. There seems, in other words, to be widespread agreement concerning values and criteria for distinguishing a low caste from a high one.

The Jajmani System

The traditional jāti-based division of labour in Indian villages is called the jajmani system. It consists of a set of traditional rules about the exchange of products and services between the members of different castes. In other words, each caste has specific commitments towards the others. Seen from a systemic perspective, one may say that the village is upheld as a social system thanks to the interdependence between the castes; seen from an actor perspective, one may say that it creates significant structural constraints on individual opportunities. The jajmani system is ideologically connected with and justified through religion, and thus contributes to maintaining notions about purity and impurity and about relative rank within the caste system. The fact that members of the sweeper caste actually sweep is interpreted as evidence that they are actually polluting; at the same time, they have to sweep because they are perceived as polluting. In this way, the social and symbolic aspects of caste are interconnected, and contribute to reinforcing each other by creating a correspondence between ideology and practices.

Traditionally, little money circulated through the jajmani system, which largely consisted of direct exchange of goods and services. Frequently, no exact account was kept of these prestations, since each caste had specified duties toward the others. In modern India, it can be difficult to make the jajmani system function according to traditional practice. First, the monetary economy has made it possible – and this is now widespread – to buy all kinds of services and commodities from people with whom there is no jajmani relationship. Second, changes in Indian society have created a large number of new occupations which are not legitimated through the jāti system. Third, the incorporation of Indian villages into the capitalist market and state bureaucracy has weakened the ties between the jātis. Urbanisation has made the jajmani system impractical. It did integrate the social system in villages with a stable economic system and division of labour, but it does not work properly in a large city like Bombay, with a high economic rate of change, huge inmigration and a very complex division of labour. This does not imply that every connection between jāti and profession has vanished in Bombay; it rather means this connection is more tenuous, ambiguous and open to manipulation than in the traditional village.

Caste and Social Mobility

The relationship between caste and other criteria for social rank may be complex in other, more 'traditional' settings as well. F.G. Bailey's studies of 'caste-climbing' and political conflict in the village of Bisipara (Orissa, eastern India; see Bailey 1968) reveal some of this complexity. His perspective is largely an actor-centred one.

In Bisipara, the jajmani system was still more or less intact when Bailey carried out his fieldwork in the 1950s, but some disturbing elements had entered from outside. Notably, the village had been integrated into the modern Indian state in the sense that important political career opportunities were now available to members of the low castes. Bailey describes different kinds of political conflict and competition within the village, and we shall look more closely at two: caste-climbing and caste conflict.

A person has three possible ways of improving his or her situation. He or she may try to change caste membership (which is exceedingly difficult in a small village), try to improve his or her own caste's relative rank, or dismiss the entire caste system and try to make a career outside it.

The distiller caste in Bisipara had improved its economic condition steadily for decades, but this did not entail an improvement of its ritual purity. One may, in fact, be well-off and ritually polluting and vice versa, although there tends to be a correlation between wealth and ritual purity. The leaders of the caste thus tried to convert their economic capital into ritual purity. First they had to purify their own practices through what is generally known as Sanskritisation. They ceased to perform typical low-caste rituals (such as animal sacrifice) and adopted Brahmanic rules in other respects as well, becoming vegetarians and so on.

For the distillers to be recognised as a high caste, however, they also had to improve their position within the jajmani system, and this was the most difficult part. Each caste which entered into a jajmani relationship with the polluting distillers risked being surpassed by them in the local hierarchy; on the other hand, the distillers were able to pay well for services. Eventually they succeeded – after having passed through several rungs on the ladder – in having Brahmins perform ritual services for them and were thereby considered a clean caste, but at the cost of a considerable amount of money. They converted a high economic position into a high ritual position.

This kind of social mobility, we should note, does not challenge the caste hierarchy as such: rather, it openly endorses it. The type of political conflict spoken of as caste conflict is of a different kind.

The Pan caste was a lowly, ritually polluting and poor caste whose leaders were inspired by Gandhi's notions of caste equality. On several occasions they had tried to enter a temple reserved for the high castes, but had been evicted. They then built their own temple and declared themselves a clean caste. This strategy was not accepted by the other castes in Bisipara, who saw it at a blatant breach of rules, and it did not help in improving the socially defined rank of the Pan caste.

To the Pan caste, the strategy followed by the distillers was not feasible for economic reasons. Thus some of them began to follow a third course of action, trying to improve their rank through a rivalling value hierarchy, namely the public service. By exploiting the quotas for the ritually impure in local government, they succeeded in climbing socially within a hierarchical scale where criteria other than caste membership and ritual purity were relevant.

From this sketch of social mobility in an Indian village, we see that there are three scales of rank, functioning partly independently of each other: the economic system, the caste system and public administration. Different resources are at stake within the respective systems, but all of them entail power differentiation, are legitimated through different principles and are partly incommensurable. The Brahmins of Bisipara did not recognise the Pan rise to prestige through public administration; however, through climbing in local government, members of the Pan caste became able to exert some power over Brahmins.

It should also be noted that while it proved possible to convert economic power into ritual purity, it is not possible to convert political power (in the public sector) into similar prestige. This seems to be caused by the workings of the jajmani system, which combines economic and ritual factors but does not include the state sector.

Caste: a Kind of Social Stratification?

Research on caste has always been linked to the study of the Indian subcontinent. However, it has been argued that the concept of caste can fruitfully be transformed into a comparative concept with a wider scope. Let us consider two examples of this view.

In connection with his study of politics in Swat valley, north Pakistan, Fredrik Barth (1981) describes the system of stratification in the valley. Although the Pathans are Muslims, in this area they are so strongly influenced by their Hindu neighbours that they are divided into hereditary status categories associated with varying degrees of purity, which are reminiscent of castes. The division of labour in Swat valley resembles a jajmani system: there are relations of interdependence and mutual obligations including 'saints', landowners, priests, craftsmen, herdsmen, peasants and 'despised groups' (which correspond to the Untouchables or Dalits in Hindu society).

However, the 'caste system' of Swat is not related to, or justified through, a religious superstructure. On the contrary, there is a direct contradiction between the caste system and Islam, which teaches that all are equal before God. Since the Pathans are not Hindus, Barth therefore argues that their castes are chiefly an aspect of social stratification and of the division of labour.

This view of caste as an aspect of social structure, which Max Weber also endorsed, has been argued against by Louis Dumont (1980, pp. 208–12). According to Dumont, to understand caste it is necessary to view it as an integrated part of a social and cultural totality; one cannot therefore talk of castes in isolation from the particular cultural context in which they have emerged. The presence of 'castelike systems' in non-Hindu societies is accounted for by the spread of some aspects of the caste institution. To Dumont, these 'imitations' of the caste system in Swat, among Christians in Kerala (south-west India) and among Buddhists in Sri Lanka and elsewhere, are encompassed by, and influenced by, Hindu culture without fully taking part in it. In sum, Dumont argues that caste is an aspect of Indian culture and has to be understood within a Hindu sociocultural totality. The very concept of 'stratification', Dumont has elsewhere argued (1986), is further an individualistic European concept which does not make sense in the hierarchical societies of the Indian sub-continent.

Louis Dumont (b. 1911) taught at the University of Oxford for several years, but since 1955 has worked in France. Although since the 1950s he has written many books about India and about general sociological and anthropological questions, his influence in anthropology has been particularly strong since the early 1980s. His fundamental idea, which is adapted from classic sociology (notably Durkheim and Tönnies), amounts to the notion that societies are integrated wholes and therefore qualitatively different from the sum of the parts that compose them. In his famous analysis of the caste system in India (*Homo Hierarchicus*, first edition 1968), Dumont thus argues that this system has an intrinsic logic unique to Hindu culture. Whereas the individual is accorded a special value in Europe, the Indian individual is meaningful only in relation to an encompassing, holistic cultural system. In *Essays on Individualism* (1986), Dumont criticises modern social anthropology for neglecting such fundamental differences between societies, for taking it for granted that an egalitarian, individualistic ethos is universal. One of Dumont's most important contributions to anthropological theory is his presentation of value hierarchies. In this, he argues that every society is integrated according to specific values which are expressed at a variety of levels, and that some such values determine – they encompass – other values at lower levels. The highest value of European society, Dumont claims, is the individual. Such encompassing values are seen as more fundamental than, and determine, other values in society, which nevertheless may well be opposed to them.

Gerald Berreman (1979) has taken a more radical stance than Barth in trying to make the caste concept a comparative one. He argues, among other things, that there are castes in the United States, describing the

American blacks as an 'impure caste'. Notwithstanding the official ideology of meritocracy, which holds that everyone controls their own destiny, he claims that blacks belong to a hereditary low-rank category, with low-ranking professions and polluting power if they touch members of the pure castes (whites). Before Berreman, Kroeber also argued the usefulness of such a wide concept of caste, which would clearly be unacceptable to Dumont, who sees it as intrinsically related to the totality of Indian society and culture.

Dumont's perspective on caste is clearly a systemic one, while Barth and Berreman place greater emphasis on the actor's available options. In doing the latter, it becomes possible to find important similarities between blacks in the US, Swat Pathans and Hindu villagers, although their respective cultures differ greatly. Berreman has also criticised Dumont's view of caste as a 'Brahmanic view' (Berreman 1979; see also Burghart 1990) more or less uncritically reproducing the views of those in power. The former does not, in other words, see Indian society as a totality whose members necessarily are encompassed by a relatively uniform world view.

Caste in Modern India

The caste system has a religious, or spiritual, and a practical, social aspect. It has significance for the religious position of people and their ritual practices, for their marriages and alliances and for their possibilities in professional life. It is nevertheless impossible to maintain the caste system unaltered in contemporary India, and there are four main reasons for this. First, the introduction of new professions complicates the classification of people according to jāti. Second, in many contexts wageworkers are hired on the basis of qualifications (achieved statuses) rather than caste. Third, Indian authorities actively try to level out the differences between castes through quotas for 'Scheduled castes' and 'Scheduled tribes' in the public sector. Fourth, urbanisation makes it difficult to classify the people one meets, and makes it possible for many Indians to escape from a stigmatised identity by moving to a city where nobody knows them.

Within Hinduism itself, attempts have also been undertaken to eradicate the caste system. An important reformist movement, Aryanism, has worked towards this end since the nineteenth century, and Mahatma Gandhi tried to modify the caste hierarchy by, among other things, naming the Untouchables 'Harijans', which means children of God. Today, Dalit organisations (rejecting what they see as Gandhi's patronising term for them) militate for the actual abolition of caste.

Despite these and other attempts to abolish the caste system or at least mitigate its effects, it remains very much alive. The marriage ads in the *Sunday Times of India*, for example, are classified according to caste membership. Although the jajmani system may be on the wane in many parts of India, the caste system retains a number of functions in the ritual and social spheres.

Caste outside India

From 1840 to 1917, following the official abolition of slavery in the British and French colonies, several million Indians were transported to remote colonies where they settled permanently. The cause of this mass migration was the need for new labour in the plantations after the freeing of the slaves. Many have argued that these Indians, tempted by promising labour contracts, were virtually shanghaied and that their actual situation in the plantation colonies was scarcely better than that of the slaves had been. Hugh Tinker (1974) has described the system of indentureship as 'a new form of slavery' (see also Mintz 1974). Most of the Indians came from Bihar and Uttar Pradesh – some of the most impoverished parts of India – but a fair number were also Dravidians from Tamil Nadu and Andhra Pradesh. The descendants of these Indians still live in the former plantation colonies, and they are particularly numerous in Mauritius (forming 65 per cent of the total population), Guyana (c. 55 per cent), Fiji (c. 45 per cent after the coup d'état in 1987), Trinidad and Tobago (c. 40 per cent) and Suriname (c. 35 per cent).

There is a large anthropological literature on this Indian diaspora, and many scholars have raised the question of cultural continuity and change. The caste system, for example, was modified from the day of departure from the sub-continent, since dietary restrictions were impossible to maintain on board ship and since the division of labour in the colonies made the jajmani system obsolete. In some of the societies to which these people travelled, notably Mauritius, some castes are nevertheless still endogamous, but in others, such as Trinidad, the various sub-groups have for most practical purposes merged into a single category of 'Indo-Trinidadians'. Even in Trinidad, however, only Brahmins can become orthodox (Sanatanist) priests. Furthermore, in Mauritius there has in recent years been a revival of caste consciousness in political contexts, and the low castes have formed their own interest groups.

The experience of the Indian diasporas, where neither jajmani systems nor 'panchayats' (caste councils) have survived but where notions of caste continue to exist, seems to indicate that the caste system can be both flexible and adaptive, and that it is by no means certain that social and cultural change will eradicate it. On the other hand, it is certain that caste has an extremely variable significance as a criterion for rank and differentiation – both in India and among Indians overseas. For some people, caste membership may define their place in society in great detail; for others, it may be relevant only at religious festivals, and perhaps during election campaigns.

Classes and Strata

Gender and age function everywhere as principles for the social differentiation and classification of people. Systems based on caste and/or class too are more complex in this respect and tend to have a more complex division of labour.

The term social class is usually applied to capitalist societies, although classes, strictly speaking, exist in other societies as well. The most influ-

ential theory of social classes was developed by Karl Marx in the mid-
nineteenth century. In his very wide-ranging studies of historical societies,
especially capitalist ones, the term class had a privileged place, since the
relationships between the classes, according to Marx, were decisive in
historical change.

Marx defined the classes in relation to property. The ruling class in any
society is the one whose members control the means of production (land,
tools, machinery, factories and the like) and who buy other people's
labour power (that is, employ people). Below this class, one would usually
find classes of farmers and independent craftsmen, as well as wageworkers who have to sell their labour power to survive. In modern
industrial societies, we usually speak of three important social classes: the
bourgeoisie, or capitalists, who own means of production; the petty bourgeoisie, whose members own means of production but do not employ
others; and the working class, whose members sell their labour power. In
addition, there are lumpenproletariats of unemployed, criminals, vagrants
etc., as well as an aristocracy whose members live off the interest from
property.

There are doubtless great systematic rank differences between people
even in societies where equality is emphasised. In practice, class differences tend to be reproduced over the generations, so that children take
on their parents' class membership, although there is always a certain social
mobility. Whether or not such differences are necessarily connected with
ownership of means of production, they are very important from a systemic
as well as an actor-centred perspective. It should nevertheless be noted
that the majority of social scientists support a way of thinking about
inequality which, contrary to Marxism, does not give priority to economic
property as an explanatory variable. This is sometimes labelled the theory
of social stratification, and is associated with Max Weber. Weber, writing
half a century after Marx, argued that there were several, partly independent
criteria which together gave a person a specific rank and that property was
not necessarily the most important one. Political power and intellectual
prestige could, for instance, be just as important in a given society.

An important difference between perspectives on classes or strata
concerns the significance placed on conflict. Class theory is nearly always
a kind of conflict theory, seeing the conflicts between different classes as
fundamental. Marx saw class struggle as the most central factor in social
change, since successful class struggles eventually led to changes in the
relations of production (property relations) and qualitative changes in the
social order.

Both Marxist thought about social class and other theories of social strata
or classes have been criticised for being ethnocentric. Dumont's criticism
of the wide-ranging analytical uses of the term caste is representative of
this kind of argument. Whereas some would hold that all societies are
stratified and that concepts of classes or strata are therefore universally

useful, others would stress that the concepts themselves are European and relate intrinsically to modern state societies.

We return to some of the economic and political aspects of social strata and classes in later chapters. At this stage, we concentrate on class as a principle for social differentiation and classification. The following example, which shows the introduction of capitalism in a formerly feudal society, indicates that there may indeed be important interrelationships between economic change and cultural change.

During the first half of the nineteenth century, an important shift took place in San José, Puerto Rico (Wolf 1969 [1956]). Instead of largely growing food for their own consumption, the farmers increasingly began to grow one main product for the world market. The most important product was coffee, for which there was a growing demand. Several problems had to be solved, however, for the production to become profitable. The landowners had to increase their cultivated area, and thus they also had to find wageworkers. They also had to find a source of credit (a bank or similar institution) to fund the expansion.

As long as land was abundant, it was difficult to find wageworkers, since people preferred to cultivate their own plots. Gradually, however, the coffee-growers established control over most of the available land and eventually it ceased to be free: all land now had to be purchased. This new situation led to the proletarianisation of a large number of formerly independent smallholders: they became dependent on selling their labour power.

Wolf describes the confrontation between the two systems – the capitalist one, based on purchase, sale and interest, and the traditional one, based on subsistence production – as a cultural conflict, a clash of opposing value systems. The locals described the Spaniards (most of the coffee-growers and money-lenders were Spanish) as mean and individualistic: 'They rob other people's money, but then they just sit on it. They don't spend it', and they 'don't give people subsistence plots on which to grow things to eat' (Wolf 1969 [1956], p. 178). The Spaniards, for their part, described the Puerto Ricans as lazy, drunken and unable to plan their life properly.

When this new, specialised economy was fully developed, it became possible to distinguish between four social classes in San José:

1. *Peasants.* They own a little land, cultivated on a family basis, and sell the surplus on the market, but are unable to generate enough surplus to expand their production.
2. *Middle-sized farmers.* They own more land, buy labour to grow it and make a larger profit than needed to sustain their lives.
3. *Rural proletarians.* They own no land and earn their living through selling their labour.
4. *Landowners.* They are specialised coffee-growers, buy labour on a large scale and make large profits.

Here the social classes are definitely defined in relation to the means of production. The hacienda owners rank highest; the propertyless lowest. In many traditional societies, we should note, it is impossible to rank people according to ownership of means of production, since land frequently cannot be sold or bought. Among the Dogon, we should recall, the village headman (the hogon) decides who is to cultivate which plot and land rights are tied up with kinship. In hunter-and-gatherer societies, there is no systematic difference in access to means of production; for example, all men have a bow and arrow. In Chapters 11 and 12 we look more closely into these major differences in the economic organisation of societies and their connections with political power and social organisation in general; at this point, it is sufficient to note how economic differences, and the social organisation of production (division of labour), have ramifications in the cultural sphere and engender important differences in the classification of individuals.

'Cultural Classes'

In many contemporary societies, it may be difficult to argue that access to means of production is the main criterion for the class divisions, and in this respect, Weber seems to be right *contra* Marx. Notably, large population segments in industrial societies are public servants or 'white-collar workers' – they are neither capitalists nor workers. Many highly salaried directors of companies, for instance, own only a negligible number of shares in the firm they administrate. This may necessitate a less rigid concept of class than the one developed by Marx, who wrote at a time when the main twofold division of Western societies into capitalists and working class was clearer than it is today.

In Wolf's analysis of Puerto Rico, it transpires that actors rank each other according to their symbols of wealth: what makes a difference in the ways people classify each other could thus be whether someone owns a bedspread, whether the women of the household ride a horse or a mule, whether they eat their bananas plain or with milk. Such markers were, in Puerto Rico at this time, closely linked with differential access to property. However, this need not be the case. As the economist Thorstein Veblen has shown (1953 [1899]), Americans may strive to acquire status symbols, as a form of impression management, to give the impression that they are better off than they actually are. Veblen calls this kind of strategy conspicuous consumption.

More recently, Pierre Bourdieu has developed a systematic theory of 'cultural classes', taking France as his chief empirical example (Bourdieu 1979; see also Jenkins 1993). A principal idea in Bourdieu's work is that power is connected with symbols, and that the ruling class in any society is by default the class which decides the ranking of symbols and the form of dominant discourse; in other words, the class that controls the criteria for good taste. Someone who knows the codes for decent behaviour, 'proper' speech, good taste in art and music and so on has a surplus of symbolic capital. Bourdieu admits that such differences are often connected with economic inequality, but he has analysed them as power systems in their own right. In many societies there are people, such as politicians and intellectuals, who possess a great deal of symbolic capital and wield considerable power without owning means of production.

In his great study of 'taste' in French society, Bourdieu stresses its social origin. Contrary to popular notions to the effect that taste is somehow inborn, his observations show

that the cultural needs are created by education: our study demonstrates that all cultural practices (museum visits, attendance at concerts, exhibitions, talks etc.) and preferences within literature, painting or music are closely connected with the level of education (which is measured as academic title or number of years at educational institutions) and social origins. (1979, p. 1)

Pierre Bourdieu (b. 1930) was educated as a philosopher, but has mainly worked as a sociologist and anthropologist. His ethnographic regions are Algeria and his native France, and his most important work deals with the relationship between knowledge, culture and power. In *La Réproduction* (with Jean-Claude Passeron), he shows how the French educational system reproduces class differences by presenting bourgeois ideology as 'natural'. In *Outline of a Theory of Practice* (1972) and *The Logic of Practice* (1980), Bourdieu develops a general theory and method for the study of implicit, often invisible power structures immanent in culture. In *Homo Academicus* (1984), he identifies such power structures in French academic life, but his principal empirical study remains *Distinction* (1979), which is a wide-ranging treatise on taste and power in French society: how cultural concepts of good and bad taste express, and contribute to the maintenance of, particular symbolic power relations. (See also Jenkins 1993.)

Differences in taste thereby express 'objective class differences'. For example, Bourdieu shows that knowledge of classical music is strongly correlated with education and class background, and argues that the very definition of the good taste is a manifestation of power which confirms and strengthens rank differences, as well as giving a certain prestige in itself. Just as an unclean caste in India may change its way of life in a bid to improve its rank in the caste system, 'upstarts' in modern class societies may try to appropriate as many symbols as possible that indicate good taste. Bourdieu calls this kind of strategy 'conversion of capital'; it may, in other words, be possible to convert economic capital into symbolic capital (cultural prestige). In France, for instance, aristocratic titles may sometimes be purchased. The parallel with the rise of the distillers in Bisipara should be obvious.

Although there is usually a clear connection between economic and symbolic capital, the two are not congruent: some have much of the former but little of the latter, and vice versa. This is why conversion may be an interesting strategy for actors who wish to increase their prestige. Whether the chief form of conversion follows one direction or the other depends, of course, on the dominant value system in society.

Complexity in Social Differentiation

A general principle in studies of stratification, class and social differentiation, is the rule of cumulation. This 'rule' holds that if someone is economically wealthy, he or she probably also has a good education, good health and secure employment. This line of thought has been well documented, particularly in sociological studies of modern industrial societies. As anthropologists, we nevertheless need to be aware of the great variation between societies concerning criteria for rank and perceptions of rank. Although wealth nearly always provides high rank, it is not necessarily more important than, for example, ritual purity. Advanced age may give high or low rank; female gender may be completely disqualifying or nearly irrelevant, and so on.

Further – as indicated earlier in this chapter – there are often contradictions between different criteria for rank, which can be interpreted as conflicts between value systems or between principles for the legitimation of power. A classic example is the conflict, prevalent in many African societies, between age and education. Old men in the village try to retain their power, which is legitimated through tradition, while young men returning from college may insist that their educational, achieved qualifications are superior and entitle them to higher power than their elders.

Different criteria for rank, or principles for differentiation, thus do not necessarily overlap. The social hierarchy in Bisipara, for instance, may well be conceived of as a system based on no less than five pyramids which can be distinguished analytically and which influence each other and interact to varying degrees: caste, wealth, local government, gender and age.

These principles for differentiation function simultaneously, but their relative significance can rarely be predicted. Sometimes their significance is situational. This means that in some kinds of situations, such as during a religious festival, caste membership is more important than any of the other criteria. In other situations, economic power may be the most important criterion, and so on. Does, for example, a rich woman from a relatively impure caste rank higher or lower than a poor Brahmin? It is impossible to give this question an unambiguous answer, but it hints at the complexity of social classification and differentiation.

Power and the Powerless

The last two chapters have to a great extent dealt with power and influence. Social differentiation, whether it is based on gender, age, class or caste, creates and reproduces differences in power. Often such power differences may lead to revolt and protests among the powerless, and sometimes these revolts may lead to permanent changes in the power relations of society. The French Revolution is often cited as an example of such a change: after this important event in European history, the privileges of the nobility and royal family were eventually replaced by formal principles of equality and democracy.

As this chapter has suggested, there may be quite varying notions within a society about justice, good and bad and ultimately, what the world looks like. Societies are in other words internally differentiated, not only in economic and political terms but also in cultural terms. Yet certain fundamental values are usually widely agreed upon, whether they are tacit or explicit. Even people who seem profoundly oppressed frequently support the dominating ideology, even if it may be said to contribute to their oppression. Any ideology attempts to make a certain perspective on society appear 'natural'; if it succeeds, people will perceive their own place, and the dominant hierarchy, as natural. This was the basic mechanism Marx had in mind when he wrote that the ruling ideas of society are the ideas of the ruling class.

The distinction between actor perspectives and systemic perspectives is clearly relevant when we look at inequality and differentiation, and both caste and class systems can be studied profitably through a conscious switching between the two perspectives. One is born into a caste and/or a class; the caste or class structure is a systemic property, but each actor relates to his or her position of relative power or powerlessness in an independent, unpredictable way. It is therefore necessary to grasp the duality of social process – it is simultaneously the product of agency and the objective condition for agency – in the study of power. This is shown in the next chapter.

Suggestions for Further Reading

F.G. Bailey: Parapolitical Systems. In Marc J. Swartz, ed., *Local-level Politics. Social and Cultural Perspectives*. Chicago: Aldine 1968.

Louis Dumont: *Homo Hierarchicus*, 2nd edition. Chicago: University of Chicago Press 1980.

Karl Marx and Friedrich Engels: *The Communist Manifesto*. New York: The Modern Reader 1968 [1848].

10 POLITICS AND POWER

Politics is parasitical on other social relationships.
—*M.J. Swartz*

Politics is linked with power; both power that people exert over each other, and ways in which society wields power over people by imposing institutionalised constraints on their agency – constraints ranging from property taxes to torture and genocide. However, politics also has to do with the prevention of lawlessness and insecurity; that is, it concerns law and order, the implementation of the rights of persons, conflict resolution and social integration.

Politics can be identified analytically in all societies, but by no means all societies that anthropologists have studied have political institutions distinct from other societal realms. In modern state societies, it may seem fairly easy to delineate what is politics and what is not. Political science, developed to study politics in such societies, deals with the formal political institutions; with a legislative assembly, local administration, voting patterns and other aspects of society recognised as political. In non-industrial societies, it may be far more difficult to single out politics as something distinct from the ongoing flow of social life. In industrial or post-industrial society, we think of politics as something they *have*; a specialised set of institutions. In societies with no centralised state, the political system may rather be seen as something intimately woven into other aspects of existence. Very often in stateless societies, kinship and religion are in practice indistinguishable from politics. That institutional differentiation which is characteristic of modern societies is absent in many others (see for instance Godelier 1975). This implies that it would often be fruitless to look for identifiable political institutions which could be compared with, say, parliaments. Instead, political anthropologists have to look for the political decision-making mechanisms – they must find out where and how the important decisions are being made, who is affected by the decisions, which rules and norms govern political action, how hegemony is challenged, and which possible sanctions the rulers of society dispose of.

A central problem in classic political anthropology from the 1940s to the 1960s was simply the question of how stateless societies were at all integrated: why they did not just fall apart due to lack of a central authority,

144

how they managed to resolve conflicts and how peace was maintained. Today, following decolonisation and the emergence of the postcolonial state in the South, most political anthropological studies instead focus on the relationship between the state and local communities, often showing how inhabitants of such communities resist dominance from the state.

Although complex modern societies are also dealt with below, this chapter takes politics in stateless societies as its point of departure and discusses how chiefs and 'big men' acquire their positions of authority, how the inhabitants of uncentralised, 'acephalous' societies resolve conflicts with no courts or a judiciary apparatus, and how power can be seen as the prize in political games. Seen from the vantage-point of a modern state, it may seem as though the political integration of tribal peoples like the Nuer, the Pathans and the Yanomamö is extremely tenuous and fragile; the fact is that many of these groups have revealed a remarkable structural stability, which lasted longer than most European polities have existed, although they are now to varying degrees integrated into the state and capitalist economy.

Some political anthropologists emphasise how different societies are integrated (systemic perspective). Others stress how individuals lay strategies to promote their interests (actor perspective). In this chapter, we see how both kinds of perspectives can be useful. The empirical material discussed illuminates the tension between agency and social structure, as well as the differences between kinship-based politics and politics based on formal institutions.

Power and Choice

Since the study of power is essential to political anthropology, the concept of power must be discussed briefly. One of the oldest and still most influential definitions of power is that of Max Weber, who wrote that it 'is the ability to enforce one's own will on others' behaviour' (1978 [1919]); that is, the ability to make someone do something they would otherwise not have done. According to Weber, people have power over each other. Other concepts of power, including those which are inspired by Marxist scholarship, would also include structural power; that is power relations embedded in the division of labour, the legislative system and other structural features of society. It immediately seems to make sense to talk of 'systemic' or 'structural' power in many contexts: obeyance of norms and implicit rules may easily be seen as a form of structural power – it is not easy to tell *who* it is that forces me to hold the fork in my left hand and the knife in my right. However, if we include any action dictated by cultural convention in our definition, power risks becoming diluted and synonymous with conventions, norms and, ultimately, culture. It may therefore be fruitful to follow Weber in distinguishing between power, authority (*Herrschaft*) and influence, the latter being a 'milder' form of power presupposing tacit acquiesence. Authority, in Weber's view, is taken for granted and needs no justification, while power proper is continuously being challenged and must be defended.

The differences between ways of conceptualising power correspond to the differences between actor-oriented and systemic perspectives. The great challenge of all social science, one might say, consists in trying to do justice to both.

Do people, when all is said and done, act under some form of coercion, or are they free to choose their course of action? In a sense, both statements are correct. We choose our actions, but not under circumstances of our own choice. If you live in a capitalist society and are penniless, you cannot choose to invest in the Taiwanese electronic industry. Someone cannot easily choose to dethrone the chief in a society where political offices are hereditary, and a Tiv woman cannot buy herself a plot of land as long as Tiv legislation states that only men have land rights (see Chapter 11).

On the other hand, actors make choices when they can. It may be beyond my ability to buy a factory, but I can choose between depositing my salary in my bank account or spending it on beer. And although it was impossible for the Saloio women (Chapter 8) to achieve formal political positions, they were able to exert considerable influence or power through informal channels.

This implies that virtually all humans have some potential power or influence. However, this resource, like all others, is unequally distributed. We should further be aware that power is a problematic phenomenon to explore comparatively, since the peoples we study may lack concepts corresponding to our concepts of power.

Power and Powerlessness

The reverse of the coin, powerlessness, is also an important aspect of social life. It is not the same as a modest amount of power, but should rather be conceptualised as the absence of the ability to exert power. 'Muted' groups (see Chapter 8) are powerless groups in this sense. Because of lack of communication channels, lack of organisation or similar poverty in resources, they are prevented from promoting their interests in efficient ways. In Michel Foucault's terms, powerless groups are subjugated by the dominant discourses of society; the ways in which everyday language structures the world and confirms a set of values (see also Chapters 13 and 14).

Steven Lukes (1977) has suggested that power be studied at three levels. First, it can be identified in decision-making processes, that is where decisions are actually being taken. This is the simplest perspective on power, which focuses on factual, observable events. Second, power can also be studied by looking at non-decisions; that is, all of those political issues which are dealt with within the political system but which are not adopted.

The third level on which power can be studied, which Lukes argues is often ignored by social scientists, is that including 'muted' or powerless groups, whose interests never even reach the level of negotiations. Such interests lack a voice in public life; they are marginalised and made invisible. This kind of perspective on power has been common in feminist scholarship and also in research on indigenous populations. Research on muted groups has nevertheless also shown that such groups, apparently powerless and marginalised, often develop their own strategies (sometimes spoken of as resistance) to increase their control over their own existence. James Scott (1985) has thus shown that poor peasants may maintain a fairly high level of autonomy by systematically sabotaging impositions from the authorities. Studies of slavery in the Americas (see, for example, Lewis 1983) reveal that similar strategies were widespread there.

Ideology and Legitimation

Unless they rule through sheer terror and violence, as many political regimes regrettably do, the powerholders in any society must in one way or other justify or legitimate their power. Among the Mundurucú, the men justify their power vis-à-vis the women by referring to myths describing how they gained control over the sacred trumpets. In Hindu society, the Brahmins may justify their power by referring to ascribed statuses and sacred texts, while in parliamentary democracies the legislating assemblies may refer to the 'will of the people' as embedded in election results when they initiate unpopular policies.

It is quite common to assume that power discrepancies in non-industrial societies follow tradition and ascribed statuses, whereas achievement is more important in industrial societies. This point of view has been criticised from several perspectives. First, it is not true that achievement counts for everything in industrial societies: social background and family networks may be very important there, just as in non-industrial societies. Second, there are also great differences within the vast and inaccurate category of non-industrial, or 'traditional', societies in this regard.

The ascribed/achieved distinction may nevertheless be an important one in the comparative study of politics, provided we do not link it categorically to specific societal types. This dichotomy is rather an aspect of every political system. How important are personal qualities in various political systems, we may then ask, and how important are those aspects which are hereditary and follow ascription?

The idea that all individuals in modern democracies have the same opportunities to achieve power is often regarded as an ideological (mis)-conception. Similarly, notions regarding what is 'for the common good' are often seen as expressions of ideology. In a more general vein, we may state that political authority rests on ideological legitimation: it must be justified. If the justification is accepted by the population, we may, following Weber, talk of legitimate authority.

Like power, culture and other core concepts, ideology is a difficult word to define. For now, we will adopt the suggestion that ideology is that aspect of culture which concerns how society ought to be organised; in other words, it concerns politics, rules and the distinction between right and wrong. Ideology is a normative kind of knowledge; it may be implicit or explicit, and it may be challenged.

Although there seem to be groups in every society which are relatively powerless, there tends to be widespread acquiescence in the values a society is based on – even among the people who seem to be losing out because of them. Many Marxist theorists, including Marx himself, have described this phenomenon, whereby people seem not to be aware of their own good, as 'false consciousness'. Because of considerable power disparities in society, the powerful are able to promote their own world view much more efficiently than other groups and to give it an air of 'naturalness', thereby making deeply ideological notions part and parcel of the taken-for-granteds of society.

The notion of false consciousness has an immediate appeal. It seems likely that oppressed groups do not know their own good; otherwise they would have revolted, would they not? On the other hand, it is far from easy for an anthropologist, an outsider to society, to argue convincingly that a group is the victim of delusions of which its members are not themselves aware. With what right can researchers claim that they know the 'objective interests' of a group better than they themselves do?

It is rarely necessary for an anthropologist to take a stance regarding the issue of false consciousness. When we study political systems comparatively, it is usually unnecessary to decide whether the group is 'right' or 'wrong' in its world view and ideology. Above all, the comparative anthropological study of politics is concerned with showing how political systems function and how people act or are prevented from acting within them, as well as indicating the relationship between ideology and social practice. It should nevertheless be kept in mind that actors rarely see the full context and consequences of their acts, and that the anthropologist's analytical task consists in working this out.

Integration and Conflict in Kinship-based Societies

Because of Evans-Pritchard's classic, and contested, study of political organisation among the Nuer of the southern Sudan (1940), this nomadic people has virtually become a paradigm case in the study of politics in stateless societies. We shall therefore look at the political dynamics of the Nuer, writing in the ethnographic present, in some detail.

The Nuer are cattle nomads with an economic way of life as well as an ecological environment reminiscent of the Fulani. Not only do cattle form an important part of their economy, they are also central in Nuer myth and symbolism.

Although the Nuer live in small local communities, every individual has ties of solidarity tying him or her to other people scattered over an enormous territory. Each has obligations and commitments towards his or her patrilineal kin; but is also tied to other groups.

First, a Nuer is a member of an agnatic lineage. Several lineages together form a sub-clan, and several sub-clans form a clan. This principle – the division of clans into equivalent sub-clans and lineages at several levels – is called 'segmentation'. From a male Nuer's perspective, loyalties and commitments generally decrease with growing genealogical distance (see Figure 10.1).

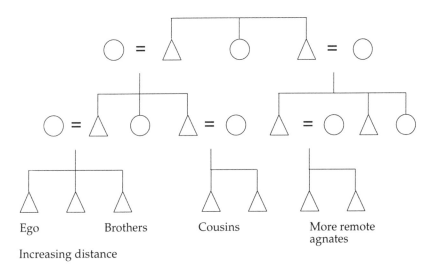

Ego   Brothers   Cousins   More remote
                                                 agnates

Increasing distance

Figure 10.1: Degrees of genealogical distance in a patrilineal system.
(Sisters and female cousins are not included in ego's generation)

A different principle for dividing up Nuer groups is the territorial one, which usually corresponds roughly to kinship; at least Nuer men tend to live near their close male relatives. Although not everyone who lives in a Nuer village belongs to the same clan, each village is associated with a clan in roughly the same way as European nation-states are associated with ethnic groups.

In addition to these overlapping principles for belongingness – agnatic kinship and place of residence – each Nuer man has obligations towards his age mates; the men he was initiated together with, as well as his affines (members of clans his siblings and himself have married into) and possible trade partners. These cross-cutting ties, which create complex systems of loyalties that cannot be reduced to mere concentric circles, reduce the danger of feuds between lineages. The local community is recruited through agnatic kinship, matrilateral kinship and affinality (Gluckman 1982 [1956]). If a man becomes entangled in a blood feud based on agnatic kinship loyalties, he thus runs the risk of having to direct his revenge towards his nearest neighbour and collaborator. Many Nuer therefore try to avoid open conflict with other lineages as far as possible.

Despite the mitigating effects of this mechanism, feuds occasionally do burst out among the Nuer. The cause may be disagreement over bridewealth, suspicion of cattle theft or murder. A feud may last for years, occasionally flaring up in violence, and one reason for its prolonged character is the existence of ties of mutual obligations between the feuding groups.

Segmentary Oppositions

Because of the political commitments entailed by kinship among the Nuer, conflicts rarely involve only two people. Usually, they would at least be helped by their closest agnatic kin. In larger conflicts, such as murder or disagreements over grazing rights, the kin group is united at a higher level. The general principle is 'myself against my brother; my brother and I against our cousins; our cousins, my brother and myself against our more distant agnates' and so on, until one reaches the level of the whole Nuer tribe, which is united against the Dinka, the traditional arch-enemy. Interestingly, since the breakout of civil war in the late 1970s the Nuer and Dinka have periodically united at a yet higher level of segmentation against the Muslim government of the Sudan.

This form of organisation is called a system of segmentary oppositions. Evans-Pritchard describes it like this:

A tribal segment is a political group in opposition to other segments of the same kind and they jointly form a tribe only in relation to other Nuer tribes and adjacent foreign tribes which form part of the same political system, and without these relations very little meaning can be attached to the concepts of tribal segment and tribe. (1940, p. 147)

The largest units – the tribes – thus only exist when they are in conflict with other tribes. It is thus through conflicts that the Nuer are integrated politically at various levels.

In a segmentary political system, the compass of the political community depends on the scope of the conflict. If the Nuer had aristocratic lineages or even a king, the situation would naturally have been different. A necessary condition for segmentation is the equality, or equivalence, of the segments at each level: lineage A corresponds to lineage B, clan X to clan Y, and so on. It is therefore impossible to state unambiguously which group a Nuer belongs to: group membership is conditional on the situation.

One answer to the question of why the Nuer are not perpetually in conflict with one another – since the potential for conflict is ample and no central government or legislative system exists – is the presence of cross-cutting ties. However, they also have an institution reminiscent of a court of justice in the 'leopard-skin chiefs' (also known as men of the earth), who are not chiefs in the ordinary sense but who are generally respected as neutral intermediaries in situations of conflict. The leopard-skin chief

---

Edward Evan Evans-Pritchard (1902–73) belonged to the first generation of Malinowski's students, but became much closer to Radcliffe-Brown's structural-functionalist school. His studies of the Azande and the Nuer rank among the most important monographs of British social anthropology. Evans-Pritchard's fieldwork in southern Sudan took place at various times during 1926–39, and his first monograph was *Witchcraft, Oracles and Magic among the Azande* (1937). The book was innovative in that it united a largely structural-functionalist analysis of social integration with an interpretive account of the Azande belief system and cosmology, showing the interrelationship between social structure and culture without reducing one to the other. His next major study, *The Nuer* (1940), was no less important and exerted a major influence on theories of political integration among stateless peoples, although criticism of his lineage model eventually grew. As a professor in Oxford from 1946, Evans-Pritchard mediated between divergent traditions in anthropology, introducing Mauss and Lévy-Bruhl to the Anglophone milieu (although he was unimpressed by Lévi-Strauss). At an important lecture in 1950 ('Anthropology and History', published in Evans-Pritchard 1962), he formally announced a break with Radcliffe-Brown's view of anthropology as a kind of natural science and argued that it should instead be viewed as one of the humanities.

---

listens to both parties and makes what he deems an appropriate settlement. However, there is no formal system of sanctions forcing people to follow his advice.

The leopard-skin chief usually comes from a small lineage and is thus considered a 'neutral' go-between in situations of conflict. However, he may often have acquired considerable wealth in cattle as payment for his services, and therefore has to be seen as a fully fledged political actor, and an important one at that, although he is officially placed outside the political conflicts. This kind of ambiguous position is not unusual for religious leaders.

Like the Yanomamö (Chapters 4 and 6), the Nuer are primarily integrated through kinship, and they reproduce political stability both through shared descent and through alliances with other kin groups. Unlike the Yanomamö, as we have seen, they are organised in a segmentary way, which means that they have potential for corporate political action on a larger scale than the former. It should nevertheless be pointed out that we have dealt with both peoples in the ethnographic present, and in fact at the time of writing the Nuer are engaged in a protracted civil war against the Sudanese government, while the Yanomamö are negotiating with state authorities over land rights. Some of their leaders have appeared on international television and have participated in global conferences for indigenous peoples. It is thus no longer entirely accurate to state that the limits of the Yanomamö polity can be drawn at the point where it is no longer possible to organise a larger number of people along kinship lines.

The notion that one's loyalty is connected to many concentric circles which are activated in different situations is not only relevant to the study of stateless societies, but can also be applied to contexts in modern complex societies. The French nationalist leader Jean-Marie Le Pen has actually presented his own loyalties as a set of segmentary oppositions, stating that he prefers his daughters to his nieces, his nieces to his neighbours, his neighbours to people from other parts of France and so on. In general, politics in complex societies may often be illuminated through models of segmentary oppositions. Every citizen belongs not only to the nation or the ethnic group – in different political situations, both larger and smaller groups may be capable of demanding one's loyalty. In the Europe of the European Union, one might add, citizens can similarly be Barcelonians, Catalans, Spaniards and Europeans in different situations. Here too the principle of conflicting loyalties applies, since European citizens are also, for example, environmentalists, jazz lovers or lesbians.

Ascription versus Achievement

Melanesia includes New Guinea and many other smaller islands to the east, including the Trobriands. The border between Melanesia and Polynesia is at Fiji; Polynesia consists of a great number of islands in the southern Pacific, covering a vast area from New Zealand to Hawaii.

Traditional Melanesian societies are generally autonomous village units integrated on the basis of kinship (Sahlins 1963). There are tendencies to segmentation, but it is rare for the groups to form alliances at a higher level than that of the village. In other words, they are politically integrated at the village level. The political leaders of Melanesian societies are characteristically 'big men', individuals who have acquired power because of their personal qualities.

Polynesian societies are different. Many of them have traditionally developed states with hereditary, royal leadership. In Hawaii and elsewhere, there were professional armies, tax collectors and bureaucrats. This kind of division of labour was unknown in Melanesia.

Leadership in Melanesia depends on personal achievement. Within every village, there is competition between men who wish to be 'big men'; who aspire to make decisions on behalf of the village and wish to be respected and powerful. Such a status is acquired through the exchange of gifts with a large number of people, thereby creating ties of mutual obligation with as many persons as possible. A 'big man' should therefore have many relatives and several wives as a starting-point for his networking. When an established 'big man' dies, a new group of younger men will start competing to build similar positions.

Traditional Polynesian societies were ruled by feudal landlords rather than by 'upstarts'. The leaders belonged to royal or aristocratic lineages (in most Melanesian societies all lineages are equal), and the authority of the king was seen as the will of the gods. The surplus produced by the farmers was sufficiently large for the aristocrats not to engage in manual work. When a chief died, his position was immediately filled by a younger kinsman. Contrary to the Melanesian system, power in this system is thus institutional and not individual.

Sahlins (1963) has compared the two systems. It appears that they reach their respective critical points in very different – some would say opposite – ways. The egalitarian, achievement-oriented Melanesian system makes it possible for enterprising individuals to obtain power by forging inter-personal ties of reciprocity with other people. When he wants to expand his area of influence, a man has to start giving presents to strangers, sometimes even in villages other than his own. During the first phase, he will get nothing in return: it takes time to build up confidence. However, this kind of enterprise is risky for the 'big man'. In many cases his own kin and co-villagers will complain that they give him valuables without receiving enough in return, since he invests the surplus 'abroad'. In some cases this kind of situation may lead to the downfall of the 'big man': he might be deposed, killed, or chased from the village.

The problem immanent in the Polynesian order is of a different kind, but this system too carries the germ of its own potential downfall. Gradually the professional state bureaucracy grows larger; thus the taxes must be increased and there is the risk of reaching a point where the burden on the taxpayers becomes so heavy that they revolt against the aristocracy.

These two contrasting examples reveal an important difference regarding the level of political integration. The Melanesian system is kinship-based, egalitarian and characterised by equality and achievement. The Polynesian system, by contrast, is hierarchical and ascription-based, founded on dif-ferences between the aristocracy and commoners. The Melanesian system collapses when the principle of equality is not taken care of sufficiently, while the Polynesian order folds when the institutionalised hierarchy is no longer legitimate.

An important difference concerns the ability of the respective societal types to accumulate surplus. The swidden agriculture practised in Melanesian societies did not make it easy to produce much more than the requirements for subsistence, while irrigation technology developed in the volcanic Polynesian islands made it possible to support a class of full-time soldiers and bureaucrats. If such a large surplus had been generated in a Melanesian society and had been channelled in the direction of a 'big man' and his family, one might well conclude that the outcome could have been a political system of the Polynesian type. Indeed, Sahlins remarks (1963; see also Keesing 1981), there are tendencies in some Melanesian societies, such as the Trobriand Islands, towards the development of hereditary, ascription-based political power and thereby a firm distinction between aristocratic and commoners' lineages. The necessary condition for such a development is the production of a surplus which is sufficient to make a division of labour possible where a segment of the population does not need to engage in agricultural work at all. These 'transitory' cases may point to some of the preconditions for the development of a state.

This comparison reveals differences in legitimation as well as limits to the number of people who can be integrated into different kinds of polities: it is clear that the centralised Polynesian system was able to integrate many more people than the egalitarian Melanesian one. It possessed powerful means of coercion in the form of soldiers supported materially by agricultural surplus; and it had a class of professional administrators similarly fed. The Polynesian system described by Sahlins was clearly a case of what Claessen and Skálnik (1978) have spoken of as 'the early state', which, as Skálnik (1992) has later remarked, serves to mitigate the simplistic dichotomy often invoked between 'state societies' (that is, 'ourselves') and 'stateless societies' (that is, 'the others').

Politics as Strategic Action

So far in this chapter, politics have been analysed from a largely systemic point of view. Although the focus has to some extent been on remarkable individuals, such as 'big men', the underlying question has been: how are societies integrated? Let us now pose a different question, namely: how do actors go about maximising political power?

It may be convenient to distinguish between two complementary definitions of politics. First, they can be defined as agency; as the establishment of authoritative decisions. Second, they may be seen as a system, in which case the word refers to the circulation of power and authority in a society.

In the discussion of the Melanesian 'big man', it became clear that motives of personal gain among 'big men' indirectly create political cohesion in Melanesian communities. If we were to apply such a perspective consistently, we would give the impression that 'societies' do not exist as anything other than the unintended consequences of a mass of strategic actions. Simultaneously, of course, actors have to lay their strategies within a system (or society) which places constraints on their course of action. This duality of social life has been discussed earlier; we will now examine its relevance in the study of political processes.

The Swat Pathans of northern Pakistan are cereal farmers (Barth 1959). A tiny minority of the population, the Pakthuns, own virtually all of the land, while the majority of the rest of the population are their tenants. The Pathans are patrilineal, and all formal political power is vested with men. Only sons can inherit from their fathers, but all sons have rights of inheritance. There is a desperate shortage of land, and the most important political issues in Swat valley concern competition over land rights. In such disputes, lineage segments may appear as political corporations. Unlike the Nuer, however, the Pathans do not usually align themselves with close agnates, but rather with distant ones. The reason is that because of the rules of inheritance, the Pathans' plots of land border those of their close agnates and so they compete to expand into each other's land. The Pathans thus align themselves with distant agnates, whose plots are far away and therefore uninteresting, against close agnates. In this way, 'politics makes strange bedfellows' in Swat valley. (Brothers, however, do not compete for land: the norm of fraternal solidarity is stronger than the drive for expansion.)

In order to expand his fields, a Pakhtun needs a large political following: he needs many clients. They can cultivate his fields and can be mobilised as soldiers if need be. Clients and land are thus the main resources competed for. Since there is no arable land not already under cultivation, the competition for clients and land can truly be seen as a zero-sum game: what one actor gains, another loses. Moreover, Barth emphasises, the game is played between individuals, not among lineage segments. Alliances and blocs are formed situationally by individual actors on a pragmatic basis.

Maximisation or Class Struggle?

Barth's classic study of politics among the Swat Pathans focuses on individual strategies for maximisation: how individuals invest their resources, how they try to outwit each other to maximise value (locally defined as land and clients). In a reinterpretation of Barth's analysis, Talal Asad (1972) argues that the power disparities of the Swat were such a fundamental characteristic of the political system that an analysis which did not take them into account had to be misleading. First and foremost, he refers to the unequal access to land, which keeps a majority of the population in poverty and powerlessness. He then points out that the patron–client

Fredrik Barth (b. 1928) was educated at the universities of Chicago, Oslo and Cambridge. He has carried out fieldwork in a variety of locations, mostly in Asia, from Iraqi Kurdistan and southern Persia to Bhutan and Bali. His first full-scale monograph, *Political Leadership among Swat Pathans* (1959), was an important contribution to the then ongoing critique of structural-functionalism. Drawing on theories of games and actor-oriented models of maximisation, Barth analyses politics not as a means of social integration but as an instrument for individuals to maximise power. *Models of Social Organization* (1966) is a theoretical essay presenting a dynamic, actor-based alternative to the stable models of culture and society then still prevalent in British social anthropology. Barth has also edited and contributed to important books in the study of ethnicity (*Ethnic Groups and Boundaries*, 1969) and research strategies in complex social systems (*Scale and Social Organization*, 1978). Since the 1970s, he has mainly worked on questions related to the distribution of knowledge and its consequences for the conceptualisation of culture and society. *Ritual and Knowledge among the Baktaman* (1975) and *Cosmologies in the Making* (1987) are based on fieldwork in New Guinea, while *Balinese Worlds* (1993) challenges a widespread view of Balinese culture as homogeneous and uniform, and develops a generative model of Balinese culture which attempts to show how variation rather than similarity is created.

system prevents the clients from developing class-consciousness which might lead them to revolt. Since they are themselves divided by loyalty to different patrons, they are unable to organise their interests as a class. Rather than fighting the oppressors, they fight each other.

Asad proposes to replace Barth's individualist theory-of-games perspective with a Marxist analysis focusing on property and power disparities. It is evident that the two approaches pose radically different questions, both of which are relevant to the study of politics but which lead to very different conceptualisations of the political field. Asad presents a systemic perspective where individual acts become relatively uninteresting since they follow from the systemic parameters; Barth's analysis zooms in on the individual actor's strategies, whereby the systemic form becomes chiefly a result of action. Both interpretations are valid, but the controversy reveals that they may lead to very different results.

The Postcolonial State

The politics and political culture of complex state societies are dealt with in greater detail later, notably in the context of cultural complexity in Chapters 15 to 18. Nevertheless a few aspects of state politics are considered here, partly to avoid the impression that most societies in the world are stateless. They certainly are not, although the role of the state varies greatly between local communities – from being nearly absent to being an important actor in most public situations. Some, like Pierre Clastres (1977), would regard the emergence of the state, and the enforced incorporation of non-state peoples into the state, as the most important watershed in cultural history. The main lesson to be learnt from the examples discussed above, apart from their ethnographic and historical value, lies in the comparative models and approaches to politics they exemplify. Today the modern state is present and is articulated in local communities nearly everywhere in the world. The general tendency, most textbooks on politics in Third World societies would argue, is for localities to be subjugated to state legislation and surveillance. In Max Weber's famous words (1978 [1919]; cf. Giddens 1985), the state has a double monopoly on taxation and the legitimate use of force where it exists. It ensures new power constellations and places new demands on its subjects or citizens, and it very often uses force or the threat of force in order to ensure loyalty and obedience among groups that question its legitimacy.

The following example may be interesting as it displays a kind of process rarely studied by social scientists concerned with the state, namely one of progressive liberation of the state from the people.

The Central African state of Congo, studied by Kajsa Ekholm Friedman (1991, 1994), became independent from France in 1962. It was thinly populated and rich in natural resources. Nevertheless, the country has experienced a nearly continuous economic decline througout its period of independence; in the early 1990s the state was disintegrating in important ways: schools, hospitals and roads were not being maintained, corruption and nepotism were serious obstacles to bureaucratic efficiency, and the state did nothing to alleviate the misery of poverty-stricken areas. In many ways, the state was absent from public affairs in the country. Yet the public service was a very large employer, and since the means of production were state-owned, the state had ample funds.

Ekholm Friedman's analysis focuses on two levels: the state organisation, government and its employees; and actors situated in local communities. The state itself, she argues, has liberated itself from the people by ensuring an independent source of income through foreign trade and aid from donor agencies. Unlike the traditional African chiefs, with whom she explicitly compares Congo's contemporary rulers, the latter do not need to ensure the support of the country's inhabitants: they can do without the citizens' taxes and do not require their services as soldiers. Borrowing a metaphor from Goran Hyden, Ekholm Friedman compares the Congolese state with a balloon floating above the country.

The state administration is based on patronage rather than meritocracy, with kinship as the most important principle. Thus a few very large extended kin groups control the entire state bureaucracy and are morally required to employ their relatives. As a result, Ekholm Friedman notes, many highly educated Congolese prefer to stay abroad after completing their studies, since they will never get a job with the state.

Tacit Acquiescence

Why do the people not revolt against such injustice? The answer, in Ekholm Friedman's analysis, lies in their cosmology and local organisation. Because of economic changes and migration, the local clan is no longer able to organise people in corporate groups. Further, Congolese tend to consult witchdoctors, clairvoyants or religious leaders rather than forming trade unions when they have a problem. Indeed, Ekholm Friedman places a great emphasis on the 'magical world view' prevalent in Congo in accounting for the citizens' tacit acquiescence in the excesses of the ruling families, showing how Congolese political movements have rapidly been transformed into religious cults.

'Whether looking at historical accounts or at the world today', David Kertzer (1988, p. 39) writes, 'one is most struck not by the rebellions of the oppressed who rise up to destroy the political system that exploits them. Rather it is the overwhelming conformity of the people living in such societies that is most impressive.' Kertzer accounts for this situation by emphasising the role of rituals and ideology in making the social order appear natural and inevitable; his term for this is 'mystification' (see also Chapter 13). It is doubtless true that dominant discourses and habit-memory (see Chapter 5), instituted through bodily practices and commemorative ceremonies in Connerton's phrase (1989), are often important legitimising instances. However, the curious feature of the

Congolese situation is that the state does not, unlike the Polynesian chiefdom, seem to exploit and oppress its citizens: it ignores them.

It should also be noted that tacit acquiescence is certainly not a universal phenomenon. Perhaps especially in South and Central American countries, social movements and peasant revolts aiming at the establishment of a more just political and economic order have been common, and have sometimes been successful in changing the social order and dominant power relations (Gledhill 1994). In Asian societies too, including China, India, the Philippines and Indochina, powerful social movements organising peasants have been, or are, politically important. Perhaps the comparative lack of success of such movements in African countries can be accounted for through Ekholm Friedman's study? Her work reveals a state which is both strong and weak; it fails to mobilise people, but is tightly organised and controls a great deal of wealth. Indeed, Ekholm Friedman concludes that the changes in Congo, both at the state level and in local communities, represent some of the least well-functioning combinations of modernity and African tradition conceivable. The inhabitants fail to organise their interests politically; the clan has ceased to function as a network channelling jobs, political organisation and social security; but the newly emancipated individuals have no abstract labour market to turn to. The state administration, for its part, legitimates and reproduces its power through kinship organisation, but it has severed the traditional ties of mutual obligations the aristocratic lineages used to have with their subjects.

Political Violence

Many contemporary societies are, as is well known, less peaceful than the disintegrating Congo studied by Ekholm Friedman (where ethnic violence has, incidentally, since broken out). One of these has for decades been Northern Ireland.

Allen Feldman (1991), writing about paramilitaries and militants in Northern Ireland, is concerned with the ways in which people are conditioned to committing violence; to using their bodies as tools for a cause, risking death in the act. Feldman scarcely discusses the large-scale political aspects of the conflict, but focuses narrowly on the experiences and narratives of those most immediately involved: the paramilitaries. His book 'is about the instrumental staging and commodification of the body by political violence' (Feldman 1991, p. 8), and shows how the political

---

Opposite. Following the decision of the Norwegian parliament to build a hydro-electric power plant at the Alta river in 1979, a group of Sami staged a large, peaceful demonstration in front of the parliament building in Oslo. The hydro-electric plant was located in an area traditionally populated by Sami, who questioned the legitimacy of the decision. The Sami tent, physically juxtaposed with the parliament building, symbolised the powerless position of the indigenous population in the face of centralised state authority. The demonstration led to an upsurge of popular sympathy with the Sami cause. (Photo: Bernt Eide) subject is created 'within a continuum of spaces consisting of the body, the confessional community, the state, and the imagined community of utopian completion: United Ireland or a British Ulster' (p. 9).

Long quotations from paramilitaries of the militant Provisional Irish Republican Army (IRA) and Irish National Liberation Army (INLA) support the author's argument about the ways in which the body is being turned into an object or an instrument; the vocabulary developed to talk about bodies, living or dead, is particularly striking. Euphemisms for killing, including 'to do [someone]', 'to knock his cunt in' and 'to fill him in', are frequently used in their narratives. Important, concerted forms of resistance developed in prison further indicate the importance of the body as political instrument, and Feldman thus analyses 'the Dirty Protest' (refusal to wash), 'the Blanket Protest' (refusal to wear the prison uniform) and the recurrent hunger strikes. These ways of circumventing the prison's control over the inmates' bodies, which is evident in frequent beatings and in intimidating forms of physical surveillance, through objectivating one's own body in illegitimate ways, are seen, following Foucault, as ritualised acts of collective resistance whereby each individual inmate – especially in the case of hunger strikes – gives his individuality to the community and relinquishes control over his own body. The dramatised contrast between Loyalist and Republican, between Protestant and Catholic, is thus brought to a climax not only through the violent acts, but also through the hardships and humiliations experienced in prison.

Feldman does not, it should be noted, purport to explain the conflict in Northern Ireland; but he gives an understanding of why some of the inhabitants have committed themselves to violent action. He analyses political violence as a result of particular bodily experiences codified through an antagonistic political ideology. In this way, violence, which has in recent years become a central focus for anthropological theorising (Riches 1986), becomes understandable. In relation to the earlier discussions about agency and structure in politics, it should also be noted that Feldman's model encompasses both dimensions in its focus on the socially conditioned body – which simultaneously expresses aspects of the person and of the social system.

Political violence takes many forms. The marginalisation and muting of large groups through paranoid terror, torture and massacres has been dealt with by Michael Taussig (1984), who writes about the many silent, powerless victims of colonialism and postcolonial state violence in South America. Political violence as civil war has been analysed in a study of Sri Lanka by Bruce Kapferer (1988), who shows how the image of the demonic Tamil is nourished and created by Sinhalese nationalists who use particular interpretations of ancient Sinhala myths and sacred texts to support the view of Tamils as devils. In a similar vein, Peter van der Veer (1994) describes how militant Hindus in India have developed a certain interpretation of the past in order to justify strong anti-Muslim sentiments. (Later, particularly in Chapters 13 and 17, the appropriation of the past for political purposes is discussed further.) Do these varied forms of political violence – from Belfast to Ayodhya in India – have anything in common?

In anthropology, the concept of war, a characteristic form of political violence, has proved difficult to define comparatively (Descola and Izard 1992) since wars differ greatly in character. A war in the New Guinea highlands, for example, does not necessarily result in many casualties; quite unlike the wars engaged in by European states in the twentieth century. What about political violence as such? Perhaps Feldman's analysis, focusing on the fusion of physical experiences and a powerful demonising ideology, can be useful in comparison. For it is a sad fact that many anthropologists will probably have to try to understand political violence, frequently expressed as 'ethnic violence', in years to come.

Anthropology is a holistic discipline in the sense that it aims at an understanding of the interrelationships between different aspects of society. Later chapters draw on these preliminary insights into political processes and develop them further. Questions to do with ideology, power and legitimation are returned to, and politics in complex state societies are also explored further. The next chapter, which deals with exchange and consumption, therefore integrates perspectives on politics with perspectives on economy.

Suggestions for Further Reading

Fredrik Barth: *Political Leadership among Swat Pathans*. London: Athlone 1959.
Pierre Clastres: *Society against the State*. Oxford: Mole 1977.
John Gledhill: *Power and its Disguises. Perspectives on Political Anthropology*. London: Pluto 1994.
John Middleton and David Tait, eds: *Tribes without Rulers*. London: Routledge & Kegan Paul 1970 [1958].

11 EXCHANGE

Money is to the West what kinship is to the Rest.
—*Marshall D. Sahlins*

Just as the anthropological study of politics is markedly different from the discipline of political science, economic anthropology distinguishes itself in important ways from the economic sciences. Anthropologists have always – at least since Malinowski – wished to call attention to the ways in which the economy is an integrated part of a social and cultural totality, and to reveal that economic systems and actions can only be fully understood if we look into their interrelationships with other aspects of culture and society. Just as politics ought to be seen as part of a wider system which includes non-political aspects as well, the economy cannot be properly studied as an isolated 'sector'. It has to be demonstrated in which way it is a cultural and social product, and this can be undertaken in modern societies as well as traditional ones, although the economic system of modern societies is widely seen as 'rational' and based on 'market principles'. A book aptly titled *The World of Goods* (Douglas and Isherwood 1978) tries to give an anthropological answer to the question of why people in modern societies want commodities. The drive for consumption witnessed in these societies is far from natural, even if it is taken for granted within academic economics and among lay people. Why is it, for example, that people want to eat food A instead of food B, if it can be shown that both are equally nutritious and even that food B is less expensive? The full answer must be sought in an analysis of the cultural categories of the society in question, not in an analysis of 'rational choice' and maximisation of value. For although it may be true that people everywhere try to maximise value, what is considered valuable varies cross-culturally and between individuals.

Apart from providing valuable insights into other peoples' economic life, anthropological studies of consumption and exchange can show that the capitalist way of arranging the economy is far from the only possible way. The capitalist economy, by now globally hegemonic, is a newcomer to the world. Seen from the perspective of cultural history, humans have been hunters and gatherers for over 90 per cent of their existence and horticulturalists or agriculturalists for most of the remaining time. If we

162

envision the history of humanity as a full day and night, modern industry appeared at five minutes to midnight. This is one main reason that this chapter takes non-capitalist economies as its initial point of departure.

Consumption in the Capitalist Market

A comparative approach to consumption clearly indicates that economy does not simply amount to methods for material survival. Let us consider food. Why is it that the steaks of the middle classes are rarer than those of the working classes? Why did no 'haute cuisine' develop in Africa when it did in Asia as well as Europe (Goody 1982)? Why did the inhabitants of Båtsfjord (northern Norway) start eating shrimps in the 1970s – creatures which had formerly been used exclusively as bait and were considered 'inedible' (Lien 1988)? Why do many North Americans refuse to eat horse meat (Sahlins 1976)?

When we ask this kind of question, it becomes evident that consumption concerns much more than the mere satisfaction of inborn needs. This is perhaps more easily observable in modern than in traditional societies, since the consumer has more choice in the former (it is not entirely without reason that these are labelled 'consumer societies'). However, traditional societies have their own 'consumer cultures' and are also increasingly integrated into a capitalist system of exchange. People across the world watch television, buy food, sweets and clothes in shops: they consume. By satisfying needs for food, clothes, etc. in culturally circumscribed ways, they communicate to others who they are – sometimes through conspicuous consumption. A theory which restricts itself to arguing that consumption amounts to the rational satisfaction of needs, not questioning how these needs are perceived locally, cannot explain why some people prefer blue trousers to red ones, or why pictures of weeping Gypsy children are regarded as vulgar by the educated middle classes in Europe (Bourdieu 1979). In order to find answers to this kind of question, an anthropological approach to the economy is necessary – it becomes necessary to study consumption as a cultural system.

In anthropology, economy may be defined in at least two markedly different ways. One is systemic, as the production, distribution and consumption of material and non-material goods in society. The other is actor-centred, as the ways in which actors use the available means to maximise value. These two perspectives, sometimes labelled substantivist and formalist views, respectively, correspond to the two perspectives on politics demonstrated in the last chapter and, indeed, to the general tension in social science between actor-oriented and system-oriented accounts. Just as Dumont argues against what he sees as an ethnocentric conceptualisation of caste (Chapter 9) and Asad argues against an actor-oriented account of politics in Swat (Chapter 10), Sahlins (1972) has argued against the model of the 'rational agent' (*homo economicus*), a premiss on which much economic science rests, as a comparative concept. Individuals who maximise value and base their economic behaviour on cost-benefit calculations, he contends, are characteristic of capitalist societies, but the very concept of the maximising individual is meaningless in societies where the unit of production is not the individual, but rather the household. Drawing on the agricultural economist Chayanov's findings among Russian peasants, Sahlins argues that peasants do not maximise profits, but instead work just enough to survive and to generate an adequate surplus; they are 'optimisers, not maximisers'. Against this, a 'formalist' would nonetheless reply that this proves only that peasants have different economic priorities from, say, stockbrokers; that the values they maximise are different from those of people in capitalist societies, not that their economy functions on qualitatively different principles. Leisure time, it could thus be claimed, may be a 'value' which can be 'maximised'.

This controversy concerns differences and similarities between people in societies ('are the others basically like "ourselves" or are they qualitatively different?'), as well as posing the perennial problem of fashioning context-free, comparatively useful concepts. We shall keep the problem in mind while considering some empirical material as well as some central issues in the anthropology of exchange.

The Economy as part of a Social Totality

The Trobriand Islanders are, it should be recalled, matrilineal, but virilocal horticulturalists. The most famous of Malinowski's monographs about this people, *Argonauts of the Western Pacific* (1984 [1922]) is chiefly a study of one of the most famous and striking social institutions in the region, namely the kula trade, which is a large-scale trade network in shell bracelets and necklaces. Not only the kula trade, but also other aspects of the Trobrianders' economy were subjected to great interest and wonder when Malinowski returned with his material from the islands after the First World War. He showed, contrary to widespread expectations, that 'savages' were by no means driven by lowly material needs in everything they did, that they had a sophisticated religion and that a complex kinship system and a multitude of regulated practices upheld society and contributed to the fulfilment of far more needs than the purely biological ones. In *Argonauts*, Malinowski also argues against those who supposed that 'savages' were extremely 'rational' individualists who acted on pure self-interest. The Trobriander, he writes,

works prompted by motives of a highly complex, social and traditional nature, and towards aims which are certainly not directed towards the satisfaction of present wants, or to the direct achievement of utilitarian purpose ... [A]ll, or almost all of the fruits of his work, and certainly any surplus which he can achieve by extra effort, goes not to the man himself, but to his relatives-in-law. (Malinowski 1984 [1922], p. 61)

Someone walking about in a Trobriand village just after harvesting will notice large heaps of yams displayed in front of many of the huts. This, as noted in an earlier chapter, will not be the household's own produce, but rather gifts received from kin and (possibly) political clients. The size of these heaps of yams thereby gives an indication of who is particularly powerful in the community. Malinowski tells of an especially important chief in the village of Omarakana, who had 40 wives and received 30–50 per cent of the total production of yams in Kiriwina. Exchange of yams, in other words, does not just contribute to reproducing social bonds and ties of kinship; it also has a highly visible political aspect.

In a capitalist economy, money is the common denominator for what is commonly thought of as economic activity, and it serves to single out an economic institution in those societies as something apparently separate from the rest of society. This kind of boundary may nevertheless be contested from an anthropological viewpoint, since it fails to include unpaid domestic work, for example, in the economy. In many societies, including the Trobriand Islands, there is no word for 'economy' as an institution separated from social life in general. When a man performs garden magic to make his yams grow, when he works hard for months just to give away his crop and when he exchanges shells with distant partners through the kula trade, he does not speak of this as an 'economic' activity: all of it is is seen as a general part of his existence. With the Trobrianders, as with many other peoples, rights in women and children have an aspect which Westerners might call economic, since wives provide both labour and yams from one's affines. But nobody would claim that women and children, seen from the viewpoint of the Trobriand man, are solely an 'object of investment' to be regarded purely as an economic asset. When we single out the 'economic' aspect of the social life of the Trobrianders, therefore, this is in a sense an artificial abstraction, since it does not exist in Trobriand society itself. We nevertheless depend on this kind of abstraction for comparison to be possible in anthropology, even if it does not form part of native cultural categories.

In principle, a capitalist economy recognises only one form of commodity exchange, namely market exchange based on the laws of supply and demand. Among the Trobrianders, a multitude of forms of exchange (about 80, according to Davis 1992b) are included in what we would translate as 'trade', and some of the most famous varieties are the following.

Gimwali is market exchange, reminiscent of capitalistic commodity exchange. Pigs, vegetables and other foodstuffs are traded and bargaining is accepted. *Laga* is payment for magical incantations bought from non-relatives. *Pokala* is usually a kind of tithe; yams or similar paid to one's social superiors. It can also refer to payment for magical incantations bought from relatives. *Sagal* is food which is distributed free of charge at public events such as funerals. *Urigubu* are yams given to one's sister's or mother's husband. *Wasi* is the exchange of fish for vegetables which takes place between coastal and inland villages.

Kula, finally, refers to the cyclical exchange of two kinds of valuables: shell necklaces and shell bracelets. The trade takes place over a large area of the south-western Pacific. The necklaces circulate clockwise, the bracelets anti-clockwise. The kula trade takes place both locally, within each island, and between the islands. The most valuable objects travel furthest. The people who travel with the shells are agents or partners of powerful men, usually aristocrats, in the various islands. Kula valuables are always named after their former owners.

It is difficult to argue that the kula trade is 'profitable'. The rule is actually that one exchanges two objects of exactly the same value. When a deal is completed, one may keep the bracelet or necklace for a while – perhaps several years – before putting it into circulation again. What is the purpose of this trade? Malinowski writes somewhere that the Trobrianders seem to exchange kula valuables 'for the sake of it', but elsewhere he argues that they have to be understood as token prestations, as a kind of symbolic valuable. He is not clear, however, as to what they symbolise. Pursuing the analysis of the kula trade further, Weiner (1988) argues that its main source of motivation is the quest for fame. The names of earlier owners are connected to kula shells, and the most valuable shells remain in circulation for a long time. In accordance with this reasoning, Jerry Leach (1983) has pointed out that the Trobrianders are generally proud of the existence of a book like *Argonauts of the Western Pacific*: like their own kula trade, this book contributes to increasing their fame. The kula trade, as with other forms of trade among the Trobrianders, may be classified as an economic activity, but its significance has ramifications far beyond what is usually thought of as the economy.

Marshall D. Sahlins (b. 1930) was originally a student of the cultural ecologist Leslie White, and his early work was characterised by an evolutionistic mode of thought. In *Social Stratification in Polynesia* (1958) and *Moala* (1962), Sahlins analyses the relationship between state formation and kinship organisation in Polynesia, and shows which mechanisms create social integration and conflict at various levels, thereby developing the model of the segmentary lineage in new directions.

Sahlins's later work has been informed by a strong cultural relativism, and much of it is inspired by Marxist and structuralist thought. In *Stone Age Economics* (1972), he attacks individualistic and universalistic perspectives on economic systems (including dominant trends in economic science), showing how the economy is always culturally constituted. In *Culture and Practical Reason* (1976), he argues against the notion of the 'rational actor' and shows how all human life-worlds – including the presumedly 'rationalised' bourgeois society – presuppose a level of symbolic meaning. In later books, including *Islands of History* (1985), Sahlins proposes a non-ethnocentric historiography, which is nevertheless strongly marked by structuralist influence.

Gifts as Total Social Phenomena

When a Trobriand islander gives yams to his affines, he does not require an immediate counter-prestation. The yams could thus be classified as a gift. The same could be said of the pocket money given by a European father to his daughter. She is not expected to pay it back. However, in both cases, the givers do anticipate some kind of counter-prestation. The Trobriander expects his affines to help him when necessary, and the European father may expect some kind of gratitude or even that the daughter will feel responsibility for him when he grows old.

Many of the world's economies have traditionally been described as 'gift economies' (Strathern 1988); that is to say that the distribution of goods takes place with no fixed price. Within the household and the lineage, goods are distributed according to individual needs and rights, and gifts are also an important means of making contact with outsiders: a means of creating peace, friendship or, as in the case of the Melanesian 'big man', political loyalty. If it is the case that friends make gifts, Sahlins writes (1972, p. 186), gifts make friends as well. In societies where the exchange of gifts is very widespread, this contributes significantly to systemic integration. In a shrewd analysis of some of the categories of Norwegian culture, Eduardo Archetti (1991 [1984]) notes that whenever one buys a cup of coffee for someone in a university canteen, the recipient will hold out a few coins in payment the moment one returns with the drink. Archetti interprets this as an unwillingness to enter into a morally committing relationship with others. To accept the coffee as a gift would imply a vague debt of gratitude which Norwegians are reluctant to incur.

Some criteria are necessary if a transaction is to be defined as gift-giving. Apart from the absence of a fixed price, the return gift or prestation should not be given at once. Only when these conditions are met is gift exchange socially integrating by its creation of webs of vague obligations on the part of large numbers of people. In some societies, such as the Polynesian ones Mauss deals with in his famous essay on the gift (1954 [1924]), virtually everyone in a local community has vague long-term obligations towards each other connected with gift exchange.

The gift is a characteristic expression of reciprocity. The obligation to give implies the obligation to receive; the recipient again commits him- or herself to making a counter-prestation to the giver. The analytical interest of a gift thus lies chiefly in its social and cultural aspects, not in the purely economic aspect. Mauss describes a particularly important category of such gifts as 'prestations totales' or total social phenomena: they involve the entire person and embody, by symbolic association, the totality of social relations and cultural values in society. Through such *prestations totales*, 'all kinds of institutions are simultaneously expressed: the religious, judicial, moral and economic' (Mauss 1954 [1924], p. 1). In modern societies, the exchange of wedding rings is, perhaps, the ultimate *prestation totale*.

Potlatch, Reciprocity and Power

A famous social institution which was once widespread on the north-western coast of North America is known in the literature as *potlatch* (Boas

1897; Mauss 1954 [1924]; Benedict 1970 [1934]). The potlatch was practised
by Kwakiutl groups and their neighbours. These peoples were prosperous
hunters and fisherfolk, and lived in more hierarchical societies than is
common among groups with this kind of livelihood. The aristocrats within
the system continuously had to defend, and to try to improve, their relative
rank by giving spectacular gifts to each other. This phenomenon, which
could be described as competitive gift exchange, contains a mechanism
for acceleration. When chief B received a gift from chief A, he would have
to surpass the latter in his return gift. This competition could, in some cases,
culminate in the destruction of considerable material wealth. Each winter
the chiefs invited each other to large parties, where abundant food and
drink were served and lavish presents were given to the guests. In addition,
they destroyed valuables, throwing salt fish away and setting fire to tents
and carpets; in the old days, Boas wrote around the turn of the century,
they even threw slaves into the sea to show off their wealth.

At the return party, the hosting chief would have to surpass the previous
host in destructive capabilities. The chief who could afford to destroy most,
achieved the highest rank in the regional hierarchy.

Institutions similar to the potlatch exist among many other peoples. The
purpose of the waste is to establish a political hierarchy with oneself on
top. Mauss (1954 [1924]) has identified a milder form of potlatch in the
French custom of trying to surpass others by giving lavish wedding
presents. Mauss describes the potlatch institution as a 'perverted' form
of the more widespread phenomenon of reciprocity, which is an important
social institution in many societies.

Mauss's essay on the gift has been extremely influential in later anthropological theorising on reciprocity and exchange. In Lévi-Strauss's theory
of kinship (1949; see also Chapter 7), a principal axiom is the universality of exchange, a notion indebted to Mauss, as a fundamental human mode
of existence. Marriage systems, politics and everyday social interaction alike
have been analysed in terms of exchange, both in Mauss's wide sociological
sense and in a more restricted 'economic' sense, and this shows clearly
the inadequacy of a division of the social world into political, economic,
religious and other 'sectors'.

In his wide-ranging studies of symbolic power, Pierre Bourdieu has also
drawn on Mauss and the social logic of reciprocity. In one of his Kabyle
ethnographies (the Kabyles are Berbers in Algeria), he describes a situation
where 'the generalization of monetary exchange' enters into a relationship formerly defined through reciprocity:

[A] well-known mason, who had learnt his trade in France, caused a scandal, around
1955, by going home when his work was finished without eating the meal traditionally given in the mason's honour when a house is built, and then demanding,
in addition to the price of his day's work (one thousand old francs), an allowance
of two hundred francs in lieu of the meal. (Bourdieu 1977, p. 173)

Here the mason was trying to convert a personal ritual gift to a decon-
textualised and quantifiable economic sum. Bourdieu explains that the

mason thereby exposed 'the device most commonly employed to keep up appearances by means of a collectively concerted make-believe', the pretence that the economic transaction really amounted to a generous exchange of gifts. In pursuing this line of analysis, Bourdieu in a sense turns Mauss on his head, by focusing on the ways in which gifts and 'total social phenomena' conceal power relations and exploitative practices. The kind of social integration and mutual obligations created through reciprocity is not necessarily beneficial to everyone involved. Indeed, feudal lords in medieval Europe frequently sustained their power by offering gifts to their subjects. It could also be argued that development aid from North to South is a subtle technique of domination intended to ensure the continued submission of Southern governments to global policies pursued by the rich countries. The former dictator of Uganda, Idi Amin, clearly understood this aspect of reciprocity when, some time in the 1970s, he sent a shipload of bananas as emergency aid to crisis-stricken Britain.

Forms of Distribution

Gifts are socially integrating at the same time as they define and reconfirm specified relationships between individuals. Commodity exchange in a capitalist system works in a different way. When buying food at the supermarket, it is exceedingly likely that one will not remember the face of the cashier later.

In an important study aiming at explaining the historical transition to capitalism, Karl Polanyi (1957 [1944]; see also Godelier 1991) distinguishes between three different principles in the circulation of material goods, or forms of distribution: reciprocity, redistribution and market exchange. Reciprocity is the dominant principle of distribution in gift economies such as those found in the egalitarian societies of Melanesia. Such communities are to a great extent integrated through the principle of reciprocity; through those mutual obligations created by gift-giving.

Redistribution means that a central actor (such as a chief or a state administration) receives goods from the members of society, which he commits himself to redistribute to them. This kind of system confirms and strengthens the legitimacy of the ruler, as well as creating a social safety net for the needy. Redistribution is thus centralised and can be described as a hierarchical principle of distribution, whereas reciprocity is a decentralised, egalitarian principle of distribution.

The third form of distribution is the market principle, which is based on a contractual relationship between the exchangers. The market is anonymous and involves abstract rules about contractual liberty (that is, one can choose one's trading partners). It normally creates an impersonal form of interaction.

Although the market principle dominates in modern capitalist societies, redistribution in feudal societies and reciprocity in egalitarian small-scale societies, in Polanyi's scheme one form of distribution does not exclude the others. In most societies, all three principles are at work in different situations and different social fields, as witnessed in the Trobriand example, although their relative significance varies. Polanyi's point is that the principles of distribution are adapted to fit very different kinds of society.

In Polanyi's and Sahlins's view (Sahlins 1972), the redistribution principle supports a centralised and hierarchical political structure, while the market principle is capable of integrating an enormous number of people in a single web of exchange as it is anonymous and based on abstract rules, and reciprocity proper creates solidarity on the basis of horizontal interpersonal obligations. As Bourdieu's Algerian example shows, however, this kind of typology makes sense only at an idealised model level since all societies embody a variety of exchange forms.

Money

Reciprocity, or gift exchange, is more important as an economic institution in kinship-based societies than in modern state societies, and can be a key to an understanding of fundamental differences. However, what we may think of as market exchange is certainly not uniform either, and it functions in different ways in different societies.

In most places, there are rules regulating what can be sold and purchased and what cannot. Even in modern capitalist societies, there is general agreement that there are values which cannot be bought – love, friendship and loyalty, for example. Still, it is easy to see that the scope of a capitalist market economy is much greater than that of a village market; not only with respect to its scale and the selection of goods, but also in the sense that all commodities are comparable: they are measured on a shared scale, namely that of money. A collection of short stories becomes 'equivalent' to three packs of cigarettes because they have the same price (or exchange value, in the Marxist terminology). Money renders different goods and services comparable by measuring their value on a shared scale.

As the example of the Trobriand Islands shows, the exchange of goods and services may be much more complicated than this and may thus involve a wider repertoire of social relationships. How can three hours of work be compared with a suckling pig or a bag of rice if one cannot measure them on a common scale? In many traditional societies, barter has been a common form of exchange. 'Primitive money', or special purpose money, has also been widespread, the functions of which are reminiscent of money in modern societies. In large parts of West Africa cowrie shells functioned as a kind of money, insofar as one could buy food and other subsistence items for them. The sale and purchase of labour and land, however, are frequently unthinkable in traditional societies, where land is tied to the kin group and labour cannot be measured (not least because time cannot be measured on a shared, objectified scale; see Chapter 14). Special purpose money has functioned as a means of payment in a restricted way: some, but not all material goods and services could be mediated by them. Thus special purpose money has not, unlike the general purpose money characteristic of the contemporary world, functioned as a value standard: it has not been capable of measuring and comparing all kinds of material goods and services on a common scale.

In traditional societies, there are often different categories of goods that are incommensurable in value, that circulate in different, relatively closed spheres. We now turn to considering an example of such an economy and its transformation, which also gives an indication of general changes taking place in traditional subsistence economies being integrated into the capitalist system of production and exchange.

Economic Spheres among the Tiv

The Tiv are traditionally farmers who live in the savannah belt of central-eastern Nigeria (Bohannan and Bohannan 1953; P. Bohannan 1959). They are patrilineal and also transfer land rights along the patrilineage. As in many other kinship-based societies, it was traditionally not possible for Tiv to buy and sell land, since the land ultimately belonged to the ancestors. Personal identity was, as one might expect, intimately tied to the lineage land.

The Tiv grew cereals, fruit and vegetables and kept livestock. They produced food for subsistence in addition to a surplus which was either redistributed or sold in the market. Their system of distribution was multicentric, which is to say that economic resources were distributed according to different principles and did not form a uniform 'single market'. (The opposite of a multicentric economy is a unicentric system, where one institution, usually the market, dominates completely.)

Until about the Second World War, the Tiv had three economic spheres, or centres, in their economy. These were ranked morally. The lowest was the subsistence sphere, where cereals and other foodstuffs, kitchen utensils, spices and tools circulated. These commodities were exchanged in the market and were thus commensurable: they were the same kind of products.

The second sphere was the prestige sphere. Here cattle, brass rods, magical paraphernalia and a highly valued, imported cloth circulated. In this sphere, brass rods functioned as a means of payment.

The third and highest sphere was where women and children were exchanged. Generally, a person could only be paid for with another person. If my lineage received a woman from yours, you could only be repaid with another woman from my lineage. Payment, obviously, did not have to take place immediately.

Within each sphere, exchange was considered morally neutral, which was to say that someone did not become subject to condemnation for exchanging fowls for pots, or brass rods for magical aids. Problems arose only with exchange *between* the spheres, when values were converted. Since there was no common denominator encompassing all three spheres, there were no rules as to the amount of subsistence goods required to pay for prestige goods. It was considered foolish and irresponsible to convert downwards, selling off brass rods for grain, for example – this was possible, but not a well-advised thing to do. Prestige objects were an indication of symbolic capital and were comparable to, say, aristocratic titles in Britain or France, or ritual purity in Hindu society. To rid oneself of brass rods therefore entailed a qualitatively different loss than selling off one's agricultural surplus did. Similarly, only a desperate lineage would sell off its women for brass rods, since the ultimate aim of Tiv men was to have as many wives and children as possible.

With the effective colonialisation of the interior of Nigeria, great changes, observed by the Bohannans during their fieldwork, took place in Tiv society. The colonial government created a peaceful situation (*pax Britannica*) enabling villagers to extend trade networks over much larger areas than had been possible earlier. The Tiv now had access to hitherto unknown imported goods, and trade became on the whole much more important than it had formerly been. Many Tiv left the subsistence economy entirely and became small capitalist farmers producing specialised crops, notably sesame seeds, for the international market. Those crops were sold for money (general purpose money, that is pounds and shillings), which was now spent on food and other necessities.

The introduction of general purpose money had important consequences for Tiv society, and the monetary economy proved to be irreconcilable with the former, rigid distinction between spheres of circulation. Money entered the system at all levels, and in a matter of a few years, brass rods, white cloth, fowls and grain alike could be measured on a common scale. As early as the 1950s, Paul Bohannan reports (1959), the Tiv used money as a value standard even when engaged in direct barter: even when they exchanged ten pounds of tomatoes directly for a chicken, they agreed that the price for both was five shillings and that they were therefore equivalent. Money, in other words, became a common denominator for all goods. Eventually bridewealth began to be paid in cash. Many felt this was a devaluation of women, since the new practice indicated that they were a commodity of the same kind as pots and chickens.

In accordance with the distinction between actor perspectives and systemic perspectives employed elsewhere, it should be noted that Bohannan's analysis of change in Tiv society represents a typical systemic perspective. Change, in his analysis, is caused by exogenous factors (outside factors) modifying the system as a whole. In an actor-oriented analysis of the breakdown of economic spheres in another African society, the Fur in western Sudan, Barth (1967) instead emphasises endogenous factors of change. He shows how an enterprising individual (an entrepreneur) discovers new, profitable ways of exchanging goods through conversion between spheres, and the result is roughly the same as in Tiv society; a breakdown of the moral economy, and the universalisation of the market principles of monetary exchange based on supply and demand.

As usual, both the actor-centred and the systemic perspective can be illuminating in understanding social process.

It would be too facile to draw the conclusion, on the basis of Bohannan's rendering of changes in the Tiv system of exchange, that the monetary principle (or 'general-purpose money') is inevitably 'morally bad'. Its spread has different consequences in different societies and to different persons, and an implication of Bourdieu's argument is that monetary exchange liberates the exchangers from the web of moral obligations, including hierarchy, entailed in reciprocity. Instead, monetary exchange creates new hierarchies. Social disruption is not necessarily undesirable and it may entail a liberation from feudal bonds. In several European societies, a change in domestic reciprocity relations has led to changes in the marriage institution since the 1960s. It is evident that the sharp increase in divorces is connected with the increased economic independence of women: they now earn their own money and are no longer forced into webs of reciprocity with male breadwinners. Many of the women concerned perceive this as an improvement. The same could be said of the challenges posed to the institution of arranged marriages in countries such as Pakistan and India and among immigrants in Europe. In some segments of these populations, particularly in the middle classes, young men and women are no longer willing to be exchanged by their kin groups. Insofar as they are economically independent of their families because of participation in the capitalist labour market, they may actually marry on the basis of individual choice rather than being part of a family-based system of exchange. Although it may certainly be relevant to evaluate the moral and political aspects of a transition from a subsistence economy to capitalism – and the change has certainly been disastrous to many, not least Africans – the initial anthropological task lies in mapping out the social and cultural consequences of the changes.

Money as Information Technology

The collapse of the economic spheres, or the moral economy, of the Tiv entailed a wider comparability of values formerly regarded as incommensurable, as different in kind. The economy thereby lost its moral character and was gradually disengaged from the cultural values which had originally constituted it. Pure market principles of supply and demand replaced rules of right and wrong as well as distinctions between 'high' and 'low' values. Because of the introduction of general purpose universal money, however, the Tiv were also enabled to communicate economically through trade on a much larger scale than before. The brass rods, the former special purpose money of the Tiv, had no value outside their tribal area, whereas pounds sterling (and later Nigerian nairas) had the same value over an enormous area. The sesame seeds grown by a Tiv after the introduction of general purpose money could be sold to a wholesale retailer in the nearest city and might eventually end up on a breakfast table in

Birmingham. For their own part, the Tiv could from now on buy, say, printed T-shirts and radios for money; goods which could not be bought for brass rods. With the introduction of general purpose money, the Tiv thereby became integrated into a global system of production, distribution and consumption.

The economy of any society is always part of a wider social and cultural context, and the introduction of general purpose money in any society, including Tiv society, has profound consequences. As noted, money challenged the traditional value hierarchy, altered the pattern of agricultural production and led to changes in marketing strategies and in

The capitalist system of market exchange is today virtually omnipresent, but it does not lead to total homogenisation: local cultural contexts remain different from each other. (Photo by the author)

consumption. Money was the medium enabling (or forcing) the Tiv to become economically integrated on a larger scale. In this way, money may be regarded as a form of information technology. The brass rods also had this function, but on a much more local scale. Money is impersonal and anonymous. It can be accumulated and invested. It makes communication and exchange on a vast scale possible: I can draw money from my bank account from a bank or ATM in any country in the world, and the money is a common denominator making it possible to compare a vast number of goods and services of the most diverse origins. Perhaps it could be said that the relationship between money and brass rods is comparable to the relationship between television and personal conversation? It is certainly no coincidence that the spread of the monetary economy has usually been concomitant with the spread of state institutions, literacy and quantified, linear time, all of which can be seen as standardising devices accompanying the transition from small-scale to large-scale integration.

The Meaning of Artefacts

Clearly, as Appadurai (1986, p. 5) observes, 'things have no meaning apart from those that human transactions, attributions and motivations endow them with'. Their meaning thus varies cross-culturally, and moreover 'abstract objects' such as words or services may take on the character of goods or commodities. In the Trobriand Islands, for example, magical incantations are inherited and sometimes purchased. There is no easy answer to the question of what turns an object (or non-material resource) into a commodity, but as the earlier discussions on exchange, gifts and trade have shown, a study of the circulation of goods (in the wide sense, encompassing non-material valuables) can be highly illuminating. Since commodities are by definition scarce (Georg Simmel, quoted in Appadurai 1986, p. 3, says that 'we call those objects valuable that resist our desire to possess them'), the circulation of goods tells us about the cultural values dominant in a society. In the famous introductory chapters to *Capital*, Marx (1906 [1867]) describes how commodification entails the exchangeability and comparability of highly different objects, and several writers inspired by him, including György Lukács (1971 [1923]) and Jürgen Habermas (1967), have written about the spread of the commodity logic in modern society; how the market principle enters into a variety of social relationships formerly organised according to a different, more 'human' logic, and thereby contributes to social alienation and 'commodity fetishism'.

Contemporary anthropological perspectives on commodity circulation and consumption tend to differ from this line of thought, focusing not on alienation but rather on the ways in which commodities mediate and define social relationships and self-identity – in other words, their cultural meaning and social significance. Referring *inter alia* to Bohannan's study of economic spheres among the Tiv, Appadurai (1986) introduces the concept of regimes of value, which he defines as systems within which there are more or less consistently shared notions of value and exchange-ability. Several such regimes may coexist within any society. Economic spheres clearly constitute such discrete regimes of value, but it is also obvious that many other distinct regimes exist in modern capitalist societies as well. Bourdieu (1988) has thus analysed academia as an arena for the exchange of prestige and power, which thereby makes up a field in which only a minority of the population participate. Studying regimes of value can thus be a strategy for exploring diversity in a society, since the concept presupposes that there is no uniformity in the evaluation of commodities.

Although there is a calculative dimension present in all exchange, as both Appadurai (1986) and Daniel Miller (1987, 1994) acknowledge, it cannot be divorced from its cultural content and social implications. On the one hand, objects and artefacts form part of the taken-for-granted part of our environment and thereby contribute to shaping our habitus – they 'order people' (Miller 1994, p. 404); on the other hand, they are consciously selected through consumption to create meaning and a particular self-identity. In a study of an English working-class housing estate, Daniel Miller (1988) shows how interior decorating conveys very specific messages about the people who live in each flat. The kitchens, which were initially identical, have been shaped self-consciously by their inhabitants, who, using standardised products available in shops, combine them in personal ways to express their individuality. Rather than seeing them as the alienated victims of 'commodity fetishism' (the orthodox Marxist view), Miller analyses the consumers as conscious actors who appropriate the material culture of their environment to strengthen their own sense of personhood and identity. Viewed in this way, things become important elements in cultural projects; they objectify social relationships and hierarchies, are used in the articulation of self-identity, are variously interpreted by different persons, and contribute to defining social relationships. Social and personal memory can also be embedded in artefacts; not just in tombstones and cathedrals, but also in mundane objects like 'old beer cans, matchbooks and comic books' (Kopytoff 1986, p. 80). In Miller's words (1994), 'com-modities as well as gifts have the capacity to construct cultural projects wherein there is no simple dichotomy between things and persons'.

A Reconsideration of Exchange

In the anthropological literature, it has been common to contrast 'the West' and 'the Rest' with regard to the logic of exchange (for a classic study, see Sahlins 1972). It should therefore be emphasised that the picture is less clear-cut than the previous discussion may suggest. Reciprocity and market exchange are not mutually exclusive, nor is it easy to draw a clear distinction between them. As Sahlins himself has noted in a recent essay on economic and cultural change in the Pacific (1994), tribal peoples in highland New Guinea have by now become wageworkers, and money has bridged the boundaries between formerly discrete spheres. However, he adds, the highlanders do not invest the money chiefly in radios, cassette recorders and other paraphernalia of modernity, but in traditional institutions. The money may, for instance, enable them to sacrifice more pigs to the ancestors than they were formerly able to. We should not, therefore, believe that the introduction of a new economic system necessarily kills the old one, or that societies are either 'traditional' or 'modern'.

A different, more fundamental critique of the classic dichotomy between reciprocity and market exchange is represented in a fascinating essay by John Davis (1992b), who argues forcefully and elegantly against what he sees as an arbitrary distinction between gift-giving and market exchange. He is sympathetic to the project initiated by Mauss and developed further by Sahlins (1972), where the wider social and cultural contexts of exchange are revealed and where it is shown that non-industrial economies must be understood in cultural terms. However, Davis sees a shortcoming in that anthropologists, while showing the limitations of economic science when applied to non-industrial societies, have not developed similar cultural accounts of exchange in modern industrial ones. After discussing some of the forms of exchange made famous in Malinowski's studies of the Trobriands, he thus goes on to show that there are indeed at least as many distinct cultural categories of exchange in British culture (Figure 11.1), each of them associated with a particular, culturally based evaluation. Quite contrary to those who complain of the 'commercialisation of Christmas', Davis is 'rather pleased since it seems to me that it could be put the other way around: it could be an instance of the gifting of the market, and could be a demonstration of the instability of markets relative to the continuing strength of gift-giving' (1992b, p. 53). Reciprocity is also an important part of everyday social interaction in any society, perhaps especially significant in the household. Davis's essay is a contribution to the current anthropological project of deconstructing simplistic boundaries between

alms-giving	expropriation	reciprocity
altruism	extortion	renting
arbitrage	futures trading	retailing
banking	giving	robbery
barter	huckstering	scrounging
bribery	insider dealing	shoplifting
burglary	insurance	shopping
buying/selling	marketing	simony
charity	money-lending	social wage
commodity-dealing	mortgaging	swapping
corruption	mugging	theft
donation	pawning	tipping
employment	profiteering	trading
exploitation	prostitution	wholesaling

Figure 11.1: Part of the British repertoire of exchange types. (Source: Davis 1992b, p. 29)

'us' and 'them', 'moderns' and 'traditionals', 'Gemeinschaft' and 'Gesellschaft'; in Appadurai's words, 'to restore the cultural dimension to societies that are too often represented simply as economies writ large, and to restore the calculative dimension to societies that are too often simply portrayed as solidarity writ small' (1986, p. 12).

This does not mean that all systems of exchange are 'the same'. The breakdown of the 'economic spheres' among the Tiv and other peoples was an irreversible change with profound social implications. The generalisation of monetary exchange certainly does alter social relations and social scale, but its local importance needs to be studied empirically. In the next chapter, we consider social and cultural implications of changes in a different aspect of what we call economy, namely production.

Suggestions for Further Reading

Arjun Appadurai, ed.: *The Social Life of Things. Commodities in Cultural Perspective*. Cambridge: Cambridge University Press 1986.

John Davis: *Exchange*. Buckingham: Open University Press 1992.

Bronislaw Malinowski: *Argonauts of the Western Pacific*, Chapter III. Prospect Heights, IL: Waveland Press 1984 [1922].

Daniel Miller: *Material Culture and Mass Consumption*. Oxford: Blackwell 1987.

Marshall D. Sahlins: *Stone Age Economics*. Chicago: Aldine 1972.

12   PRODUCTION AND TECHNOLOGY

We live in a consumer society. I am quite sure that we will dispose of the 'natural peoples' when it becomes clear that they do not fulfil the intellectuals' demands for purity, that they do not incarnate Nature, but rather in many respects are more 'artificial' and 'civilised' than ourselves.

—*Hans Peter Duerr*

Humanity's Exchange with Nature

The idea that there is an interrelationship between ecological conditions and ways of life is old; it appears in the Enlightenment philosophy of the mid- to late eighteenth century (for instance in Montesquieu and in Marquis de Sade's non-pornographic writings). Montesquieu, among many others, held that the main cause of Europe's technological and scientific advances was the harsh climate, which required the inhabitants to be inventive and sharp-witted to survive. Somewhat more recently, the human geographer Ellsworth Huntington (1945) argued for climatic determinism in a study where he shows, among other things, the statistical correlation between rainy days and booklending at libraries in Boston. On sunny days, the inhabitants of Boston tend not to borrow books. (In other words: too much sun seems to make people uninterested in intellectual pursuits.) Even today, many lay people assume that Africans never invented the combustion engine and the microchip because their material survival was so easy that they never 'had to use their brains'.

From a comparativist perspective, it is easy to argue against this kind of mechanical determinism, the idea that one single causal factor (in this case climate) can account for the principal cultural variations in the world. For one thing, there are other regions in the world with climatic conditions comparable to those prevalent in Europe, in pre-conquest North America and southern Australia, for example, which have not developed along the same lines. In Indonesia, under roughly the same ecological conditions, there are rice cultivators, horticulturalists and hunters and gatherers.

There is no simple causal link between ecological conditions and social organisation. However, there is no doubt that nature – in both senses of the word (see Chapter 3) – sets limits to the options available to humanity. If it is true that our inner nature is identical everywhere (this is the dogma

of the mental unity of humanity), that is certainly not the case with respect
to external nature. If the climate is too cold, one cannot grow bananas; if
it is even colder, one cannot even grow wheat. But there is no one-to-one
relationship between ecological conditions and society: any ecosystem offers
several different possibilities, although it also inevitably excludes some.

System Theory and Ecology

Ecological analyses were originally developed as a part of biological
science, as a method for the description and analysis of processes and
interrelationships in nature. However, ecological ways of thinking are also
applied in fields other than that of biological nature. The Chicago sociologist Robert Park thus developed an 'urban ecology' in the 1920s, using
ecological models to describe ethnic dynamics in Chicago. A couple of
decades later, cybernetics and systems theory were developed as general,
abstract theories about how systems work in general. A central idea in
Gregory Bateson's work (1972, 1979) is the notion that very different kinds
of systems function according to the same general principles. Writing on
communication among dolphins, on schizophrenia, on biological evolution
and initiation in New Guinea, Bateson consistently argues that very different
phenomena are connected by an underlying pattern – which could be a
metaphor, a kind of process, formal commonalities or something similar.
He and other system theorists have struggled to depict culture and society
as a continuous process.

Many anthropologists see systems theory as an alternative to models
focusing on form and classification, regarding it as a method for the conceptualisation of social life as something dynamic and continuously
changing. Others criticise systems theory for dealing inadequately with power
and intentionality.

It is necessary to distinguish sharply between ecological analyses
dealing with biological processes and those applying ecological thinking
to other domains. In the latter case, ecological models are used metaphorically as models, in roughly the same way as some structural-functionalists
used biological models of the integration of organisms as metaphors for
the integration of societies.

Cultural Ecology

Cultural ecology is largely an American speciality in anthropology; it is
associated with Julian Steward and Leslie White, who were particularly
influential in the 1950s. British anthropology has tended to stress the
primacy of social organisation, while continental European anthropology,
notably in France, has generally been more concerned with questions of
cognition and symbolisation than with ecological determinants. As Kuper
(1994) has pointed out, cultural ecology can be traced back to Darwin and
(to a lesser extent) to Marx, and is an entirely different research programme
from both Boasian relativism (where culture is more or less self-explana-
tory) and British social anthropology, which harks back to the sociological

schools of Durkheim and Weber. In its original form, as in Steward's writings (see Steward 1955), cultural ecology is a doctrine about cultural evolution seen as a result of the interaction between different kinds of material factors: demography, ecology and technology. Unlike Marxists, Steward did not regard relations of production as decisive. In his general model of cultural evolution, he distinguishes between different levels of sociocultural integration, by which he means roughly the same thing as in the discussion earlier in this book on small and large scale, namely the varying size and complexity of societies. In Steward's scheme, however, material factors determine a society's level of sociocultural integration. The lowest level of integration, exemplified by the Shoshonean Indians in his own work, was that of the family. The highest level was that of the state.

Cultural Ecology and Marxism

In one of his most deterministic – and most famous – statements, Marx wrote that whereas the hand mill creates a society led by feudal landlords, the steam mill creates a society led by industrial capitalists. A cultural ecologist might, perhaps, retort that whereas a tropical savannah creates societies of pastoralists and millet-growers, a tropical rainforest creates societies of hunter-gatherers and horticulturalists.

There are several interesting parallels between cultural ecology and Marxism. Both schools of thought emphasise the importance of material factors in social and cultural change, and both turn against sociobiology and would argue that 'human nature' can be moulded in an almost infinite number of different ways. Both emphasise the importance of factors located outside human consciousness ('objective' factors).

The key difference between the two schools of thought concerns the role of human agency and social contradiction. In Marxism, the main contradictions in society are seen to lie in the social organisation of the relationship between technology and property, between labour and capital (in capitalist societies); and the chief driving force in history is class struggle. Cultural ecologists would rather focus on the interaction between demographic factors, ecological adaptation and technology in their accounts of historical change.

The Marxian criticism of Malthus may illustrate this important difference. In an early demographic study, Thomas Malthus (1982 [1798]) wished to show that population growth necessarily led to impoverishment. His fundamental idea was that whereas food production grew arithmetically (1, 2, 3, 4, etc.), the population grew geometrically or exponentially (1, 2, 4, 8, etc.). Marx and Engels accused Malthus of treating human beings as mere 'objects' and societies as static. Instead of the Malthusian concept of overpopulation, Marx proposed the notion of relative overpopulation, which occurs when the productive forces (technology plus raw materials) are unable to satisfy human needs. The densely populated Japanese archipelago is poor in natural resources, but is nevertheless able to give its 130 million

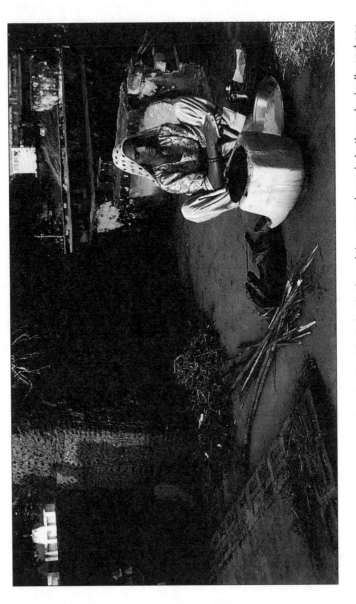

In the view of some cultural ecologists, the Hindu institution of the sacred cow is both ecologically and economically functional. This woman in Bombay is exploiting cow dung in at least two ways: as a building material and as fuel. In addition, cows provide milk and manure, and give birth to bullocks. (Photo: Trygve Bølstad)

inhabitants one of the highest material standards of living in the world, thanks to the advanced forces of production there. Malthus's formula is misleading because, unlike Marxist and sociocultural analyses, it does not take technological innovations into account. The 'green revolution' of the 1970s, for example, where new cereal breeds were introduced, led to a spectacular growth in Indian food production, although it has been criticised for increasing the gulf between well-off and poor farmers.

In this sense, the Marxists, who stress the primacy of the social over the environmental, have won over the cultural ecologists. On the other hand, the ecological crisis of our time suggests that there is an absolute upper limit to the population the world is capable of supporting – that an ecological concept of absolute overpopulation might be helpful in addition to the sociological concept of relative overpopulation. Marx did not predict such a development; to him, natural resources were free, and there is a conspicuous lack of environmental perspectives in his writings.

Both Marxism and cultural ecology raise ambitious and fascinating questions about the relationship between the factors that shape people's lives: they provide very powerful explanatory schemes. It should therefore be stated why this book has not been written in the spirit of either Marxism or cultural ecology. First, both give marginal attention to factors associated with human consciousness. Partly for this reason, they become highly functionalistic as modes of explanation and tend to leave out much of what is the very stuff of anthropology, namely cultural projects. Second, there is a tendency to the effect that grand theories of this kind reduce a multitude of cultural and social processes to dependent variables – to products of 'objective' factors. In this way, we run the risk of losing the highly complex interplay between a variety of factors, which takes on specific and sometimes unique forms in different societies. It is obvious that if we see them as general theories of society and culture, neither of the two is capable of accounting for all aspects of culture, society and cultural variation – including phenomena that anthropologists wish to explore. By embracing such powerful, all-encompassing theories wholesale, one does run the risk of using a bulldozer where a teaspoon might have been the appropriate tool.

A commonly invoked criticism of cultural ecology is, moreover, its tendency to apply a vocabulary borrowed from natural science to human societies. Peoples thereby become 'populations', human agency becomes 'behaviour' and the technical terms, while they look scientific, do not give a clear understanding of phenomena to do with consciousness, interaction and intentionality (Ardener 1989; Ingold 1994a). Of course, humans are, like other organisms, subjected to natural laws. But they also place themselves outside these laws; they reflect, classify and theorise on them, and this complicates matters seriously for someone who enters the study of human relations armed with a vocabulary developed for the study of insects and other non-verbal creatures. Perhaps, indeed, cultural ecology teaches us little about ecology but rather more about culture? Consider this example.

The Wet and the Dry

'Whatever Morocco and Indonesia might have in common' writes Geertz (1971), '– Islam, poverty, nationalism, authoritarian rule, overpopulation, clean air, spectacular scenery, and a colonial past – the one thing they do not have in common is climate'.

Indonesia is wet, and Morocco is dry. With this contrast as a starting-point, Geertz discusses differences of social organisation in a Moroccan and an Indonesian (Balinese) locality. First, it is obvious that farmers in the two societies must grow different crops. The Moroccans studied by Geertz cultivate wheat and olives; the Balinese grow rice in irrigated paddies. Water is a scarce and costly resource in Morocco, while it is free and abundant in Bali. Southern Bali is criss-crossed with systems of irrigation canals, while such systems are scattered and clearly delineated in Morocco. What are the consequences of these simple differences for social organisation?

The Balinese irrigation systems are organised through *subaks*, irrigation cooperatives led by elected foremen. All owners of land automatically become members of the local subak, and are joint owners of the canal network. Although farmers each grow their rice independently, irrigation and maintenance of the canals has to be organised centrally. This is the role of the subak, which calls for coordination and cooperation. Geertz also argues that religion and ritual life are intimately linked with rice cultivation and the growth cycle of the plant. In an earlier study (Geertz 1963), he further showed how similar patterns appeared at a variety of levels in Javanese society (organised along similar lines as the Balinese), namely what he called 'involution' or the tendency to intensify and elaborate inwards instead of expanding outwards. This was necessary in the economy due to the lack of available land combined with population growth; however, Geertz found the same kind of process in Javanese religion, poetry and music.

The Moroccans relate to water in a very different way from the Balinese. Not unexpectedly, the situation is one of stark competition over water rights between families. The wells are few and scattered, and the population is also much more scattered than in Bali.

In principle, water is individually owned, but since several families have to share the same well, ownership of water in practice means time-shares in the well; farmers each have a fixed time when they are allowed to use the well. The competition over water thus becomes an individual zero-sum game: what one family gains, the others lose. Unlike the Balinese system, where everyone has to cooperate, this system is based on competition.

Continuing his comparison of Morocco and Bali, Geertz finds a similar opposition between individualism and collectivism in many other contexts too. However, although he acknowledges his debt to Steward, he is careful to stress that he does not intimate that there are simple ecological or climatic causes for cultural phenomena:

This is not geographic determinism. It is an argument that the kind of socio-cultural analysis that applies to kinship, village politics, child raising, or ritual drama applies equally, and not just in these two societies, to human transactions with the environment. (Geertz 1971)

Clifford Geertz (b. 1926) is a leading proponent of hermeneutic (interpretive) method in anthropological research. He has been strongly influential – both as an inspirator and as a target for criticism – on the 'postmodernist' trends of anthropology in the 1980s and 1990s, which has subjected dominant concepts and forms of explanation to severe criticism. His early books on Indonesia range from cultural ecology (*Agricultural Involution*, 1963) to religion (*The Religion of Java*, 1960) and nation-building (*Old Nations, New States*, ed., 1965). Since the mid-1960s, Geertz has concentrated on the study of symbolic systems. He has compared the study of culture with the study of texts, and argues that a cultural system can be 'read' in a manner analogous with the reading of a novel. Geertz's view, powerfully expressed in *The Interpretation of Cultures* (1973) and *Local Knowledge* (1983), has been criticised for exaggerating the importance of culture and symbols at the expense of interaction and social structure, and for exaggerating the degree to which cultures are integrated and coherent. Nevertheless, Geertz continues to exert considerable influence, and his position has been seen as an alternative to 'objectivist' modes of explanation such as structural-functionalism, structuralism and Marxism.

Human Modifications of Ecosystems

Geertz, like many others writing on the nature–society relationship, does not propose a strong hypothesis regarding causal links. This kind of equation includes sociocultural factors as well as environmental ones – in other words, culture and society are not mere effects, but also part of the cause. Humans do not act mechanically on environmental factors, even if such factors affect their actions directly and indirectly.

Some anthropologists writing on pastoralists have worked out accurate formulas which describe the exact interrelationship between the number of animals in a given area, viability limits for households and ecological sustainability. Among the Fulani (see Chapter 4), the lower limit for viability was set at 21 cows and a bull for a young household. There was also an upper limit to the size of herds; both due to social limitations (a household can only herd so many animals) and because too large a herd would lead to the degradation of the grazing land and ultimately lead to desertification.

This way of reasoning makes it tempting to assume that societies are self-regulating in that they do not undermine the ecological conditions for their survival. The global environmental crisis of our time indicates that this is certainly not always the case. Moreover, environmental crises on a smaller scale have occurred earlier too; many pre-industrial societies altered their environment in irreversible ways. Large parts of the Middle

East have been desertified during past millennia, chiefly due to over-grazing and deforestation, and similar processes seem to be taking place in parts of sub-Saharan Africa and elsewhere today.

The very fact that it is possible for human societies to undermine the ecological conditions for their own survival ought to prove that we are far from determined by, and perfectly adapted to, our ecosystem. However, this fact also serves as a reminder that there is a continuous, and necessary, mutual exchange between society and environment. Some societies have proven remarkably stable in that they have reproduced a technology which did not alter their environment irreversibly in ways requiring technical innovation or dramatic social change. The Mbuti pygmies have been discussed in an earlier chapter; another example might be the horticultural societies of highland New Guinea. Recent archaeological findings seem to indicate that roughly the same kind of technology which is dominant today was present there thousands of years ago.

Provided the climate remains constant, it seems as though two inter-related factors may dramatically speed up processes of change in the ecological environment: population growth and technological change. Technological changes tend to imply an intensified exploitation of natural resources and an increased use of energy. Population growth is often, but not always, a result of technological change. An area which is capable of sustaining perhaps 1,000 hunters and gatherers, or 2,000 horticulturalists, may perhaps be able to support 20,000 farmers with tractors and chemical fertiliser, but they will not be able to revert to horticulture and have in this sense lost flexibility (Bateson 1972).

Technology

Technology, in a very general meaning of the word, consists of the systematised acquired skills and manmade material implements humans reproduce and apply in their dealings with nature. However, it is a notoriously difficult term to define; in a review of recent studies on technology, Bryan Pfaffenberger (1988) notes that few of the anthropologists dealing with the topic have bothered to do so. One of those who have done is Tim Ingold, who describes technology as 'a corpus of culturally transmitted knowledge, expressed in manufacture and use' (1979). He stresses, it should be noted, its sociocultural character, and links it to the superstructure in a Marxist sense – along with other kinds of culturally transmitted knowledge. It should also be remarked that technology literally means 'knowledge about technics', and therefore 'technology is to technics what ... linguistics is to language, for instance, or ethology to behaviour' (Sigaut 1994, p. 422). Technology is thus a theory about technics, or as we might say, techniques.

Referring to the political scientist Langdon Winner, Pfaffenberger discerns two main pitfalls common among anthropologists in their dealings with technology. The first is technological somnambulism, which sees techniques as either trivial or irrelevant to social organisation and culture. Technical implements are according to this view simply made and put to use, and exert little influence on the way people think and act.

The second pitfall is technological determinism, which claims, often without substantial argument, that technology is of paramount importance for culture and social organisation, as 'a powerful and autonomous agent that dictates the patterns of human social and cultural life' (Pfaffenberger 1988, p. 239). Karl Wittfogel's famous thesis of 'Oriental despotism' (1959) falls into this category. Wittfogel held that the structure of irrigation systems in rice-growing areas in Asia, which he called 'hydraulic societies', inevitably led to political centralisation and despotism.

In his critical article, Pfaffenberger outlines a view of technology which does not, unlike the positions mentioned, 'gravely understate or disguise the social relations of technology' (1988, p. 241). Like artefacts, discussed in Chapter 11, technologies and techniques are cultural products which form part of ongoing processes in society and can therefore not be studied separately from those relationships. Techniques shape our relationships, but our relationships also shape techniques. The tractor makes sense as a means of production in very different kinds of society, even if it alters the concrete productive process in similar ways everywhere. It is nonetheless obvious that technology frequently does affect society and culture in profound ways. The introduction of the microcomputer in the rich countries from the late 1970s onwards has not, as anticipated, led to a decrease in the use of paper; but it has transformed parts of the labour market by creating new kinds of jobs and skills. Through the introduction of modems, CD-ROM discs and Internet facilities such as electronic mail and electronic bulletin boards, the microcomputer has enabled and encouraged millions of people to change the structure of their stream of social interaction in significant ways. What is interesting to anthropology is not the techniques in themselves, but which skills people employ and for what purposes, how they are transmitted and objectified, and how the distribution of skills is related to the production of cultural meanings and social organisation. Furthermore, as Pfaffenberger (1988) suggests, technology, seen as often implicit doctrines about relevant techniques, can be studied as a form of ideology – he calls it 'a mystifying force of the first order' (p. 250). This is not least because technology tends to be regarded as 'natural'.

Techniques are embedded in the habitus and in knowledge systems, and technologies may be studied as ideology. However, the techniques result in the creation of material objects, which, unlike words and actions, 'have an enduring physical presence as components of the environment within which communicative events are framed' (Ingold 1994b; cf. D. Miller 1994). It was in this regard that Sartre (1960) introduced the concept of 'le champ pratico-inert' – the practical-inert (field of action), the material field of building and artefacts which directs human action. Sartre argues that the sheer materiality of architecture and other 'inert material structures' inevitably shapes and freezes social relationships, restricting freedom

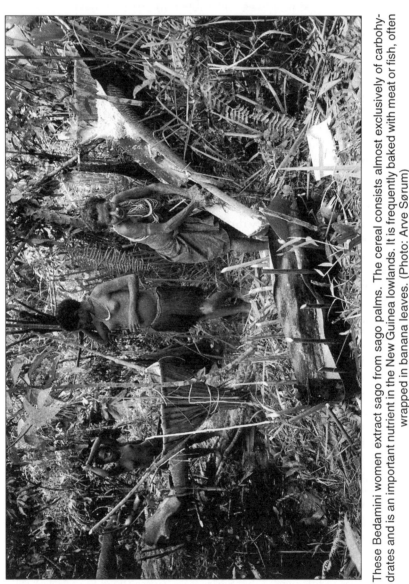

These Bedamini women extract sago from sago palms. The cereal consists almost exclusively of carbohy-drates and is an important nutrient in the New Guinea lowlands. It is frequently baked with meat or fish, often wrapped in banana leaves. (Photo: Arve Sørum)

and confirming hierarchies. At this point, he comes close to material determinism, and to argue against his view it would be sufficient to demonstrate how identical material structures can be used in significantly different ways. On the other hand, this also means that the relationship of humans to technologies embedded in durable artefacts – whether or not they are means of production – needs to be studied empirically.

Systems of Production

The world's systems of production may be classified according to various criteria. During the Cold War, a major distinction in everyday language was between capitalist and socialist systems; those characterised by private ownership of means of production and those where the state owned the means of production, respectively. In Marxist scholarship, an important distinction is drawn between the capitalist mode of production and the various 'pre-capitalist' modes. Within this body of thought, the relations of production (property and the ability to control other people's labour power) and forces of production (raw materials, technology) make up a mode of production, and this is considered decisive for the organisation of society.

A different way of conceptualising the differences between economic systems classifies societies according to the dominant mode of subsistence. This, we should note, is not the same as a mode of production, but is related to dominant production techniques. A society of hunters and gatherers may well be capitalistic, provided its members sell their surplus individually in the market-place and buy the bulk of their subsistence goods. Hunters and gatherers may thus, technically, have the same mode of production as industrial societies. Similarly, agricultural societies may well be based on collective as well as individual ownership. The same form of subsistence may in other words be dominant under different modes of production.

The following typology aims at suggesting some interrelationships between modes of subsistence and other aspects of culture and society, including technology and the human relationship with the wider ecosystem.

Hunters and gatherers, or foraging peoples, generally have a division of labour based on gender and age, and a simple technology. Usually they are organised in small, family-based groups (or 'bands'); they are small-scale societies with (generally) an egalitarian political organisation. They tend to produce small surpluses and generally have limited opportunities for storage. Most such groups therefore have an economy based on immediate return, which does not encourage long-term planning. Some 20,000 years ago all humans were hunters and gatherers; today they exist in scattered pockets in Australia, Southern Africa, the forests of Central Africa, South-East Asia, the Amazon basin and the circumpolar areas. Everywhere they are gradually being integrated into states, and because of loss of territory their traditional mode of subsistence is becoming increasingly difficult to maintain.

Horticulturalists generally have a more complex social organisation than hunters and gatherers, but they too tend to have a division of labour based on gender and age. Their productive technology includes simple cultivating tools (the most common one is the digging stick), while a widespread technique for manuring consists of burning off fields before planting them (swidden or slash-and-burn agriculture). The main source of nourishment is usually a tuber (yams, manioc, taro, sweet potato), but it may be dry rice or maize. Usually land rights are linked with lineages. Their economy, obviously, implies delayed return. Most horticultural peoples have limited possibilities for storage and produce a limited surplus. Today most horticulturalists are found in the Amazon, in Melanesia, scattered throughout Africa, in South-East Asia and in Madagascar. They are confronted with some of the same problems and challenges as hunters and gatherers, and many are becoming proletarised (see below).

Agriculturalists are, by conventional definition, distinguished from horticulturalists through the use of ploughs and draught animals. They are often organised at a higher level of scale than horticultural people, and produce enough surplus to have a differentiated division of labour which may include professional specialists such as priests, soldiers, scribes, blacksmiths and chiefs. Many cultural historians hold that the most important watershed in human history lay in the transition to agriculture, which made a hitherto unknown social complexity possible. Agriculturists' social organisation is frequently hierarchical, and land rights in such societies are usually based on kinship.

Does Protein Deficiency lead to War?

A long-lasting controversy has concerned the causes of war among Amazonian peoples. According to Marvin Harris, the main cause was the scarcity of protein; he argued that the groups were forced to expand their territory in order to get more food. Napoleon Chagnon, by contrast, held that the quest for women was more important. On the eve of Chagnon's departure for fieldwork among the Yanomamö, Harris and he discussed the topic at a public meeting at Harvard. Harris argued that the Yanomamö probably ate less protein than a Big Mac equivalent per day (that is, 30 grams), and dared Chagnon to find out. If he was wrong, he said, he would eat his hat.

In the event, it transpired that there was no correlation between protein deficiency and war. The Yanomamö were well nourished, and in fact, the frequency of war was highest in areas that were particularly rich in protein. Confronted with Harris's view, the Yanomamö themselves admitted that they were fond of meat, but added that they were even more fond of women (Chagnon 1983, pp. 85–6). Chagnon does not relate, however, whether or not Harris actually ate his hat.

Pastoralists emerged after the agricultural revolution and not before it, as is often assumed. They always, or nearly always, live in some kind of symbiotic relationship with settled agriculturalists with whom they exchange products. The division of labour is usually based on gender and age, and the social organisation may be as simple as that of hunters and gatherers, a fact connected with the need for mobility and flexibility required by their economic system. The technology of production is flexible and mobile, and the main economic resource comprises animals (in contrast to agriculturalists, who see their chief resource as land, and to hunters and gatherers, as well as many horticulturalists, who see labour as their most important economic resource). Ownership of animals is frequently individual.

Peasants are a special case of agriculturalists. Perhaps the majority of the world's population today are peasants. The most commonly acknowledged definition (Wolf 1966) describes them as agriculturalists partly integrated into the world economy. Many of them have to pay rent for the land they cultivate: in peasant societies, land has become a commodity (it can be purchased), unlike the case in traditional agricultural societies. They produce food for subsistence, but also depend on selling and buying in a general purpose money market.

Industrial societies are characterised by a very complex division of labour, specialisation of knowledge, separate political and economic institutions, a complex mechanical technology and social integration at a very high level of scale. Production is organised on the basis of individual labour contracts. Nobody produces food first and foremost for subsistence (even farmers tend to be specialised and buy food in shops), and the anonymous commodity market is a central institution in the economic life of any actor. Industrial societies have centralised states, anonymous labour markets, written legislations and systems of social control integrating an enormous number of people on the basis of principles other than kinship.

Do typologies of this kind make sense? They are certainly simplistic, and today there are scarcely any 'pure' forms left. However, such a breakdown may nonetheless be useful in providing a list of ideal types which reveals the interrelationship between production technology, mode of subsistence and other aspects of culture and society. Later chapters discuss the relationship between oral and written religions, between mechanical and 'concrete' time and between different modes of thought. If it can be agreed that it was not a complete coincidence that anthropology emerged in industrial society and not in a pastoralist society, for example, we need to make clear distinctions between kinds of societies to understand how the diversity of humanity expresses itself in different, but not unconnected ways. When we do so, it is equally important to remember that these distinctions only exist at the level of the model to facilitate comparison, and that the world outside is always more complex than our models of it.

Capitalism as a System of Production

Throughout the twentieth century, and at an expanding rate since the Second World War, peoples all over the world have become participants in a global world economy. Although global systems certainly did exist earlier (Friedman 1994), the contemporary world system has a formal uniformity, represented chiefly in capitalism and the modern state, which lacks precedents. The shirt I am wearing as I write this was made in India and my trousers were produced in Portugal; the computer I work on was assembled in California; the coffee I am drinking is Colombian and the rolling tobacco I relish is French. The system of production, consumption and exchange is truly global, and few of the world's peoples are totally unaffected by it.

According to an influential theory about the capitalist world system (Wallerstein 1974–9), capitalism is not only the dominant mode of production today, but it also sets the limits for – and constrains – other modes of production, whether they are 'pre-capitalist' or 'socialist'. The capitalist mode of production is ever expanding, according to Immanuel Wallerstein, who sees it as completely hegemonic in our time.

Wallerstein subdivides the capitalist world system into three distinct fields: the core, the semi-periphery and the periphery. In the periphery, economic development depends on the investments and needs of the core areas, and the economy in these areas is subjected to unpredictable fluctuations in market prices, low wages and low rates of investment. It has also been pointed out that the peripheral areas – notably Africa, Latin America and most of Asia – largely produce raw materials for the world market, at prices determined by the demand in the rich countries.

This kind of theory, much of it influenced by Marxist thought, is called dependency theory since it stresses the fundamental dependence of the peripheral, poor countries on the rich ones and the exploitation of the former by the latter. Although it can be very revealing, it is general and abstract and does not always fit the territory (Worsley 1984, 1990). Frequently, poverty and class differences in the countries sometimes spoken of collectively and simplistically as 'the Third World' can be explained by looking at local power disparities, as in the case of Congo (Chapter 11), and there are also today several examples of former producers of raw materials which have become industrial countries. On the other hand, there are doubtless very important power disparities between 'North' and 'South'. If wagework was uniformly remunerated on a global basis, Colombian plantation workers would earn about as much as apple pickers in the United States, while in fact most of them will never be able to afford a TV set. The underground railway recently opened in Calcutta had been largely dug out by hand. This tells us something about the price of labour in peripheral countries, and such disparities are a fundamental feature of the contemporary world economy.

The kind of theory represented in Wallerstein's and others' grand models of the world is nevertheless too sweeping in its generalisations to be immediately applicable to anthropological research. To anthropologists, it is necessary to study processes of change as they are expressed locally, taking as our point of departure aspects of local life. This implies an emphasis on local peculiarities that are generally neglected in world-system theory, which deals with social facts at a different level. General theory may supplement and inform anthropological research, but it cannot replace it. Let us therefore turn to a couple of empirical cases revealing local contexts of integration into the capitalist system of production.

From Peasants to Proletarians

In many parts of the world, two modes of production coexist side by side. Marx and others have assumed that one mode would always be dominant and that it ultimately would replace the 'earlier' (usually 'pre-capitalist') one. But in many societies this has not happened. The most important reason is perhaps that it is profitable for capitalists to keep non-capitalistic modes of production going. If a labour migrant moving from Luoland, western Kenya, to Nairobi is to earn enough money for his own survival, his salary may have to be at least, say, 500 shillings a week. However, if he has a 'shamba' (farm) and a wife and children to work it in his tribal area, it may be sufficient to pay him 400 shillings, as he will then be able to go home at the weekends, bringing food back to town with him. This is actually what a great number of wageworkers in the South do.

It may be said that capitalism, in this kind of context, is parasitic on other modes of production. In large parts of the world, capitalism and subsistence agriculture are combined in the way suggested above. Although many people have become involved in wagework, they may still depend on producing food for subsistence. In other cases, the change may be more fundamental, more or less eradicating the subsistence sector. The following example indicates some of the changes induced by the transition from a peasant mode of production to capitalist wagework.

Ganadabamba was traditionally a typical local community in Peru (S. Miller 1965). Most of the 1,000 inhabitants were Indian peasants and contract workers; the few inhabitants of European and mixed descent worked as administrators at the local *hacienda* (estate). The peasants generally controlled the land they rented from the hacienda; that is, the male head of household controlled it. His control of land was the basis for his local prestige, and although they had to pay rent for the land, land rights were inherited from father to son.

In the lower areas (under 2,500 metres above sea level) maize was grown; in the higher areas, the potato was the main crop. There was wide-reaching exchange between the regions, and this functioned as a form of reciprocity in creating friendship and mutual obligations between the groups.

In connection with rites of passage, religious festivals and harvesting, large public feasts (*fiestas*) were organised. The entire village took part, and the feasts functioned as public rituals in the sense that they gave a visual, dramatised expression of both solidarity and local hierarchies.

From the beginning of the twentieth century, population pressure and scarcity of land forced a number of villagers to travel to the coast as plantation workers. In the early years, they regularly returned to Ganadabamba in the harvest season. They regarded the wagework at the coast as a temporary solution. Unlike the situation in the highlands, where the amount of work was regulated by the seasons, plantation work was constantly hard. Social life on the plantation was, moreover, unstable and unsatisfactory. There were no clubs or gathering places for the contract workers and there was no strong moral community. Individuals were left isolated; it was impossible to bring one's family along to the coast.

Eventually the Indian settlements on the coast became more permanent and the family structure was re-stabilised, largely through female co-migration. The social situation for the proletarised Indians was nevertheless quite different from how it had been when they were peasants. They now had greater opportunities for social mobility; they could change their jobs, go on strike for wage increases and organise themselves in trade unions. Their children were offered schooling. Simultaneously, they became much more vulnerable than they had been earlier. When people were dismissed by the management, they now had no economic safety net. Other consequences were perhaps even more profound, and are related to the fundamental differences between the respective logics of peasant production and capitalist production.

Capitalism and Peasantry Compared

Capitalist production is split up: the individual worker carries out only a small part of the process of production. It is based on formal hierarchies and individual labour contracts, where the incumbents of the various statuses are replaceable. The production is mediated by money, and the value of the work is calculated as a function of money and measured labour time. The purpose of production is the accumulation of profits, and because of competition technical innovations are necessary.

Peasant production is holistic: the individual takes part in all phases of the process. The organisation of work is based on kinship, local conventions and local hierarchies. The purpose of the production is first and foremost to satisfy the needs of the household. Peasants compete with others only to the extent that they sell products in the market, which is not a main activity. Labour time is not a scarce resource in a peasant economy and it is not measured.

Wageworkers take part in a global system of production, distribution and consumption; peasants are largely integrated locally. Wageworkers further become citizens in ways which peasants do not; as the Peruvian example shows, they may be organised in country-wide unions with an elected leadership and thousands of members who are unrelated and do not know each other except in an abstract way. The unions make demands of the state and the employers, usually in a written form. Peasants (and other 'traditional peoples') have no similar means of making demands towards others apart from their relatives and local powerholders; they usually master no information technology other than the spoken word. Wagework, further, has an individualising effect: the economic unit is the individual instead of the household. Wageworkers can be replaced, and can change their jobs, while peasants are tied to their plot of land.

Wageworkers are integrated into several anonymous structures which contribute to shaping their lives. They can spend their salaries anywhere, buying anything from anybody. The literacy they (usually) acquire enables them to communicate on a very large scale, at least in principle. They pay taxes to the government, are committed to following the written laws of the country and may make certain demands of the state. Abstract time, which measures the value of their labour power, is another anonymous structure; it is not only valid for you and me but for everybody who follows it, and it serves to synchronise a very large number of persons in an anonymous way. A brief comparison with the mechanisms of social integration prevalent among, say, the Dogon, the Yanomamö or the Trobriand Islanders would indicate that capitalism and wagework entail not merely 'economic' changes, but also profound social and cultural changes. There is no simple determinism or a one-to-one relationship, but the capitalist system of production and exchange, once it has become an integral part of local society, inevitably creates new kinds of social relations as it contributes to defining premisses for social relations far beyond the domain of production.

Suggestions for Further Reading

Philip Burnham and Roy Ellen, eds: *Social and Ecological Systems*. London: Academic Press 1979.
Tim Ingold: *Evolution and Social Life*. Cambridge: Cambridge University Press 1986.
Kay Milton, ed.: *Environmentalism*. London: Routledge 1993.
Eric Wolf: *Peasants*. Englewood Cliffs, NJ: Prentice-Hall 1966.

13 RELIGION AND RITUALS

Rituals always have a desperate and manic aspect.
                              —*Claude Lévi-Strauss*

In a study of the Basseri pastoralists of southern Iran, Fredrik Barth (1961) expresses some surprise regarding their lack of religious interest. His surprise is caused by the fact that religion seems to loom large in the lives of most of the peoples described in classic anthropological studies. This may be a major reason why religion has always been a central field of inquiry in anthropology, even if, as Evans-Pritchard (1962) has pointed out, social scientists have themselves often been indifferent or hostile to religion.

In attempting to give non-ethnocentric, comparatively useful definitions of politics, economy, nature, gender and other core concepts, it has repeatedly been shown that we run into problems usually related to the fact that these notions are in use, and have a specific meaning, in our own society and in the anthropological vocabulary, but not necessarily in other societies. This makes them problematic as 'etic' concepts.

This problem is certainly valid where religion is concerned, and few concepts of social science have been defined, revised and criticised more often than this one.

Only a little more than a century ago, it was commonplace in the professional literature to distinguish between religion and paganism on the one hand, and religion and superstition on the other. The concept of paganism was associated with non-Christian religions and, in particular, their practices of public rituals which expressed aspects of the content of the religion. The concept of superstition was largely reserved for descriptions of invisible interrelationships in the world which neither science, authorised religion nor 'common sense' could account for. From this kind of perspective, Islam and African ancestral cults would be located in the domain of paganism, while, say, the Trobriand Islanders' belief that they die because of witchcraft and the common notion, in the Mediterranean region and elsewhere, that some persons are possessed by the evil eye, would be expressions of superstition. In contemporary anthropology, this corresponds to a frequently invoked distinction between religion and knowledge. Religion may thereby be said to include forms of social belief in supernatural powers which are public and which are given public expression through rituals. Knowledge can be defined so as to include 'facts' which people are reasonably certain of and act upon, and which also have a social origin.

Of course, knowledge can have a religious character, and the distinction is not absolute. In this chapter, we nevertheless concentrate on the social notions associated with contact with the sacred and the hereafter, and its expressions through ritual; leaving other forms of knowledge to the next chapter.

Have I still not defined religion properly? If so, I join a large group of anthropologists in struggling with this concept. Ever since anthropologists began to study forms of belief in alien communities seriously, there has been disagreement as to what religion is. One of the oldest definitions, supported by Tylor, defines religion simply as beliefs in supernatural beings. The question of what is supernatural immediately poses itself here, for does that not vary just like every other form of knowledge – is it not the case that what is natural for us is supernatural to others and vice versa? Is the garden magic of the Trobrianders, which is as necessary to them as manure is to us, part of their religion or part of their production technology? Are ancestral spirits supernatural? If so, who says so?

Is Understanding Religion Compatible with Believing?
This provocative question is the title of an article by the philosopher Alasdair MacIntyre (1970). His answer is, simply, no. According to MacIntyre, religion must be understood in sociological and logical terms, as stabilising and legitimising ideologies and as systems of signification and action which provide a certain shape and meaning to the world and to human existence, which explain why we are here and what happens when we die. If one is to believe in religion, he continues, one has to move to a completely different mode of thought, which easily accepts contradiction and lack of coherence, appealing to concepts such as 'the absurd' (Kierkegaard), 'paradox' (Karl Barth) or 'mystery' (Marcel). The sceptic and the believer, he claims, have no shared conceptual world – the sceptic, who 'understands' religion, cannot conceptualise the reality of the believer. MacIntyre further seems to hold that the social context of modernity, which has created modern social science, is incompatible with religious faith since it is based on a wholly secular form of thought.

Many anthropologists would be inclined to disagree with MacIntyre (see Evans-Pritchard 1962). Few would contest, for example, that Catholics such as Victor Turner, Mary Douglas and E.E. Evans-Pritchard have contributed substantially to our understanding of religion.

Another possibility in the struggle for a definition lies in following Durkheim, who assumed that a distinction is made between the profane and the sacred in every society, and who confined religion to the sacred domain. Durkheim also wanted to show how the function of religion in 'primitive societies' consisted of creating solidarity and integration through rituals and 'collective representations'. In a famous statement, he claimed that religion at its most profound level means society's worship of itself. This view has its problems (notably the problems of functionalist explanation), for example in not explaining why the inhabitants of one society believe in ancestral spirits whereas their neighbours believe in forest spirits, granted that both would be socially integrating beliefs.

A rather different approach to religion is represented in an influential essay by Geertz, 'Religion as a Cultural System'. He defines religion like this:

(1) a system of symbols which acts to (2) establish powerful, pervasive, and long-lasting moods and motivations in men by (3) formulating conceptions of a general order of existence and (4) clothing these conceptions with such an aura of factuality that (5) the moods and motivations seem uniquely realistic. (Geertz 1973, p. 90)

In other words, he argues that instead of looking at the social functions of religion, we ought to explore what religion means to people, how it helps to make sense of the world and how it gives a meaning and direction to human existence. We should study religion itself, not its social causes, and the ultimate aim of such an investigation ought to be how the world and human existence appear meaningful to the believer. This hermeneutical, or interpretive, procedure is evident in Evans-Pritchard's earlier work on Nuer religion (1956), which is a detailed ethnographic exposition aimed at translating Nuer beliefs into European (and Christian theological) concepts, thereby rendering them comparable to other religious phenomena, as well as relating religion to social organisation.

The approach advocated by Geertz and foreshadowed by Evans-Pritchard has been very influential in anthropological research on religion in recent decades. This shift in perspective is a part of the general change in anthropological thinking mentioned earlier, whereby the main trends have swung from an interest in functions, structure and social integration, which was dominant until the 1960s, to a concern with the interpretation of meaning, symbols and social process. Several examples of this change have been noted in earlier chapters; in the study of religion, it has brought, among other things, a growing interest in relating meaning to experience and in understanding cosmologies. This chapter shares such a concern, but in the sections dealing with rituals – religion as practice – we return to some of the problems first articulated by Durkheim, as well as presenting approaches to understanding the ideological aspects of religion and ritual.

Oral and Written Religions

The distinction between oral and written religions is important and has a bearing on other aspects of culture and society too. Written religions are based on a sacred text, or 'religions of the book' as Goody (1986) calls them, are linked to a sacred text (like the Koran) or a collection of sacred texts (like the Bible), and the believers are expected to have at least a minimal knowledge of the contents of the works. Such religions, including Judaism, Islam and Christianity, regard their content as tied to the text and not to a particular cultural context. Since they are text-bound, these religions can be disseminated throughout the world to peoples who in other regards live very different kinds of lives. Islam, for example, is the main religion in countries as different as Java, Niger, Egypt and Iran; whereas Christianity dominates in countries like the Philippines, El Salvador and Germany. The written religions, and particularly the monotheistic ones with their origins in the Middle East, can also be described as religions of conversion – systems of belief to which one can be converted and in which one has to affirm one's faith. Unlike other religions, they tend to be exclusive and not to accept 'syncretism'. Christian missionaries in Africa have therefore despaired at the sight of Africans cheerfully worshipping their God as well as water spirits and ancestral spirits.

Some written religions fulfil this pattern only partly; notably the Asian ones (Hinduism and Buddhism are the largest) which have a less fixed doctrine, are more flexible and insist less on obedience to texts than the monotheistic script religions do.

However, the kinds of religion characteristically studied by anthropologists are markedly different from religions based on scriptures. First of all, they are locally confined. No Nuer or Kaguru in his right mind would expect the whole world's population to become 'disciples' of their revered spirits or even of their highest god, *thoth* (Nuer) or *mulungu* (Kaguru). The gods are frequently physically associated with revered places in the tribal area. For this reason, missionaries and others misguidedly held tribal peoples to be 'animists': holding the belief that trees, springs and rocks are imbued with divine powers ('anima' is Latin for spirit). Second, oral religions tend to be embedded in the social practices of society, whereas written ones are often more detached from other social institutions. This distinction, which is not absolute, corresponds to the previously discussed institutional differentiation in modern societies, which is largely lacking in small-scale traditional societies. However, we should note that one of the first specialised (non-food producing) occupations that develops as societies become more differentiated is the priestly one. Shamans, that is people who through the medium of the trance enter into communion with the spiritual realm, exist as a specialised profession even in acephalous and otherwise undifferentiated communities, such as traditional Inuit society.

A somewhat related distinction, which was introduced by Robert Redfield (1955), concerns little and great traditions. Redfield argues that different strains and logics of religion and knowledge exist side by side in many societies; they may be radically different, but are often interrelated. The Mediterranean belief in the evil eye, for example, clearly belongs to a 'little' tradition (neither Christianity nor Islam – the 'great' traditions of the region – supports the notion), as does the worship of saints in Muslim societies. In some coastal Portuguese communities, villagers believe in a wide range of healing rituals, sorcery, magic supposed to secure fishing luck and 'supernatural' explanations of misfortune (Brøgger 1990). These beliefs exist alongside the official doctrines of the Catholic church, although they contradict the teachings of Christianity and seem to have done so for centuries. The same individuals believe simultaneously in the 'great' and 'little' traditions. In other societies, such as Indian ones, there may be a more clear-cut social distinction between the religious traditions. Brahmanic Hinduism is the official 'great' tradition, its beliefs and rituals sanctioned in the ancient Veda texts and centuries of monitored ritual practices. Low-caste Hindus nevertheless have their own rituals and beliefs, often more reminiscent of oral than written religions, which coexist with the 'high' or 'great' tradition but are socially segregated from it.

Oral religions are characterised by their local relevance, relative lack of dogma and tight integration with the 'non-religious' domains. An ethnographic example may illustrate these points.

An Oral Religion in Africa

According to the Kaguru, God (*mulungu*) created the world, but they are uncertain as to when it happened (Beidelman 1971, p. 32). This God appears quite rarely in the lives of the Kaguru, however; usually they consult ancestral spirits instead of bothering the great mulungu when they are in trouble.

The ancestors (and perhaps particularly ancestresses – the Kaguru are matrilineal) arrived from the north and the east in a mythical past, founded the present-day clans and divided the land between them. Each clan is assumed to have a 'mystical' connection (Beidelman's term) with its land. For the harvest to be good, the clan members must carry out annual rites so that the ancestral spirits will bless the land and secure its fertility. Notions and practices of this kind clearly go a long way to explain why land cannot be sold or bought in many traditional African societies.

When the Kaguru wish to consult an ancestor or a different spirit, they leave the village and enter a hillside or go into the bush. Usually, the consultations concern practical issues such as rites of passage and festivals intended to ensure the fertility of soil and women. The ancestral spirits are believed to wield real power over the living. A Kaguru woman who had lost several children thus blamed her deceased father, claiming that he was feeling lonely and had called her children to come and keep him company. Since the spirits are this powerful, it is important to pay them respect continuously and sacrifice to them regularly. They enter into every realm of life: birth, rites of passage, fertility and politics.

The Afterlife

The Kaguru, like virtually every people in the world, are concerned with the afterlife. All existent religions deal with death and try to reconcile life and death. Most peoples have notions about an afterlife which in a sense represents an idealised version of life here and now, devoid of the trivialities, problems and frustrations of this life. The Kaguru envision the afterlife as a mirror-image of life in Kaguruland, but marked by abundance and lack of conflict. The Norse Vikings, for their part, assumed that people (or at least men), after an honourable death, came to Valhall, where the fire burned day and night, there was plenty of fighting and an abundance of roasted meat. During fieldwork in Trinidad, moreover, I once found a pamphlet from a North American missionary organisation in my mailbox. It painted, in vivid colours, the Christian paradise as a kind of amusement park, where people could fly, where there were video shows presenting highlights from Biblical times and so on. The more intellectually oriented, and orthodox, versions of Christianity, like other written religions, rather depict the afterlife in more abstract terms. Oral religions tend to be more concrete on this point too. According to the traditional religion of the mountain Sami of northern Scandinavia, people are allowed to keep everything, including their reindeer herds, in the afterlife, the main difference being that pastures are abundant there. This kind of notion explains why the Sami (and many other peoples) were buried with their favourite clothes on, with their tools and, in the case of some hierarchical societies, their favourite slaves. Notions of the afterlife, be they abstract or concrete, obviously give an impression of continuity and serve to demystify death.

It should be added, though, that there are also peoples who do not believe in an afterlife; this unusual view seems to be particularly widespread in two of the most individualistic types of society we know of, namely hunters and gatherers (Woodburn 1982) and modern industrial and post-industrial societies.

The Logic of Ancestral Cults

The great attention given to ancestors and ancestral spirits, which is found in most non-literate societies, also clearly deals with the problem of continuity – both in society and in the individual lifespan – when a life is suddenly stopped. In an article on ancestral cults in Africa, Kopytoff (1971) has observed that there is not necessarily a sharp distinction between living humans and ancestral spirits. Living people become wiser, 'drier' and less mobile the older they become; the ancestors are thus perceived, he argues, merely as *extremely* wise, dry and immobile persons. There is no rigid boundary between life and death in this scheme, rather a gradual transition to another phase, which begins long before death.

The respect paid to ancestors also has a politically legitimating and socially stabilising effect. When age is a criterion of wisdom and a qualification for political office, which is nearly inevitable in kinship-based societies, politics becomes conservative. The ancestors showed the way, the elders are their intermediaries and their younger descendants have to listen and obey. As Robin Horton (1970) and others have pointed out, a great many rituals in African tribal societies are dramatic re-creations of the past intended to please the ancestral spirits by showing that the living are faithful to the values and practices taught by their elders.

The political aspects of ancestral cults are significant in practice, even if they cannot explain why people hold beliefs in ancestral spirits. In a general sense, one may perhaps state that any religion, like other kinds of ideology, must simultaneously legitimate a political order and provide a meaningful world view for its adherents, such as a reconciliation with one's own inevitable death. The death of a ruler, which signifies discon-

Religious cults drawing on a variety of sources, which are sometimes described as 'syncretic', are common in large parts of South and Central America. The saint depicted in this photo from highland Guatemala, San Simón, is a cigar-smoking conquistador dressed as an Indian. (Photo by the author)

tinuity, is always associated with crisis, and the belief in ancestral spirits may mitigate the effects of the rupture.

It should be remarked at this point that we have added a political dimension to Geertz's cultural definition of religion, which may lend some support to Marx's famous statement to the effect that religion is the opiate of the people. By this he meant that it functioned as a drug and diverted interest from the real political issues to silly fantasies about a happy afterlife for the pious and obedient. (Of course, a religious non-Marxist might retort that Marxism is the opiate of Marxists.) We now turn to a closer look at the interrelationship between the cultural (ideational) aspects of religion and its social and political dimensions.

Ritual: Religion in Practice

Most people in the world are faced with various practical problems of an economic and social character. Some of them can only be resolved with the help of specialists, and in many societies such specialists are people with a priviliged access to higher powers. Other kinds of problems are existential ones; they may deal with the mystery of birth or the fear of death, or simply the ultimate meaning of life. Rituals are largely directed towards problems of the latter kind, dramatising them and giving them articulation – if not necessarily resolving them.

Ritual has been defined as the social aspect of religion. If we may define religion as systems of notions about the supernatural and the sacred, about life after death and so on (with its obvious political implications), then rituals are the social processes which give a concrete expression to these notions. Very generally speaking, we may suggest that rituals are rule-bound public events which in some way or other thematise the relationship between the earthly and the spiritual realms.

The issue is somewhat more complex than this suggests, although it may be a fruitful beginning towards a useful definition. In fact, several of the greatest anthropologists of the twentieth century have devoted many years to trying to understand ritual. Since the early structural-functionalist accounts of rituals as manifestations of society's worship of itself, where the integrating functions of ritual were stressed, anthropology has eventually developed quite complex theories about what ritual is and how it works. One principal perspective emphasises that rituals simultaneously legitimate power, and are thus important vehicles of ideology, *and* give the participants strong emotional experiences; another perspective focuses on the ability of rituals to give people an opportunity to reflect on their society and their own role in it. Victor Turner stresses the multivocality or ambiguity of ritual symbols (1969). One of the most famous analyses of rituals does not even deal with a religious ritual but a cockfight (Geertz 1973), while in the mid-1990s a team of Norwegian anthropologists carried out research on the 1994 Winter Olympics, which they see as an enormous ritual celebrating and legitimating modernity.

This is, in other words, a very complex field, and it is important because the ritual can be seen as a synthesis of several important levels of social reality: the symbolic and the social, the individual and the collective; and it usually brings out, and tries to resolve – at a symbolic level – contradictions in society.

Rituals and Integration

Max Gluckman (1982 [1956]) has described a number of curious rituals from Southern Africa, whereby customary rules, conventions and hierarchies are turned upside down. One of them took place among the Swazi at the coronation of a new king. When this was about to happen, every citizen was expected to mock and criticise the king in public, making a grand spectacle of his inadequacy. Similarly, open social criticism was allowed at the medieval carnivals in parts of Europe, but not during the rest of the year. Actual social conflicts are allowed to play themselves out as theatrical performances. Gluckman describes several other 'rituals of rebellion' and concludes that 'by allowing people to behave in normally prohibited ways, [they] gave expression, in a reversed form, to the normal rightness of a particular kind of social order' (1982 [1956], p. 116).

Gluckman thus sees these rituals as functional in that they transform conflicts in a harmless direction, but he is also aware that strong experiences on the part of the participants are necessary for the rituals to be possible at all. In other words, he sees an interaction between individual motivations and societal 'functions'. In a famous study of ritual among the Tsembaga Maring in highland New Guinea, Roy Rappaport (1968) looked almost exclusively at the functional aspect.

The Tsembaga Maring are horticulturalists and pig-raisers organised in local groups of 200 to 300 persons. Their political system is egalitarian, with the 'big man' and shaman the only formally recognised authorities. They are considered warlike and are frequently at feud with neighbouring groups. Rappaport argues that there is an intrinsic functional link between war activities and the ritual cycle of the Tsembaga.

Every twelfth to fifteenth year, the Tsembaga organise the *kaiko* festival, which lasts for a full year and culminates in a declaration of war on the enemies of the local group. At the kaiko parties prior to this, large numbers of pigs are sacrificed to the ancestors and lavish ceremonial gift exchange takes place within the group. This year-long religious ritual begins when there are 'enough pigs', say the Tsembaga. Rappaport, however, holds that the kaiko festival begins when there are so many pigs in the village that they destroy more values (crops) than they produce (meat). The kaiko can thus be seen as a regulating response to the competition from and parasitism of the pigs. Moreover, when there are many pigs the population is less concentrated – the women, who are swineherds, have to move further and further away from the village during the day – and more vulnerable to military attacks.

The violent activity following the large-scale pig slaughter also serves to disperse the population, since the losers of the war have to move and raise new settlements, thus decreasing the pressure on the ecosystem.

The ecosystem, including the people in it, is analysed as a self-regulating system. Rappaport shows that the kaiko begins, and violence breaks out, when the number of pigs and humans in a given area has reached a critical level; then the ecosystem is near the limits of its sustainability. After the completion of the ritual cycle, the critical values decrease and the system is stabilised.

Rappaport's monograph was debated for years after its publication. The critics pointed out that a system cannot be 'rational' in this way – that an ecosystem cannot conceivably know the limits of its sustainability and trigger rituals and war when the critical values appear. It was also stressed that humans are themselves the causes of their actions, that they take decisions within a cultural universe and that it is highly unlikely ecological fluctuations can 'create' rituals. What Rappaport succeeds in showing is, in the end, a statistical correlation between ecological pressure and ritual activity.

The problems inherent in Rappaport's analysis, which he has himself addressed (1984), are the classic problems of functionalist explanation. Although the rituals are 'functional' in the sense that they contribute to the long-term survival of Tsembaga society, this does not explain why they exist. Other institutions would also have taken care of that; besides, other societies change too. Functionalist accounts of rituals were challenged in Edmund Leach's monograph on the Kachin (1954). Contrary to what his teachers had told him, Leach discovered that the religious–ritual complex among the Kachin in no way functioned in an integrating way; that it rather spurred dissension and imbalance.

Ideological and Social Ambiguities

Unlike their neighbours the Shan, who are Buddhists, the Kachin worship their own gods and spirits (*nats*). The world of nats is conceived of as an extension of the earthly hierarchy, since the nats are ancestral spirits. They belong to lineages, and in a manner analogous to the distinctions of society, the Kachin distinguish between aristocratic nats and commoner nats.

Kachin society, Leach argues, is not stable socially or ideologically, and there are two rival views of how society should be run, called 'gumlao' and 'gumsa'. Gumlao refers to an egalitarian ideology with no ranking of lineages and conscious attempts to avoid the tendency towards hierarchy inherent in the mayu–dama relationships (see Chapter 7), while gumsa refers to a more hierarchical form. To some extent, Leach shows that Kachin societies oscillate between gumlao and gumsa. Now each local community has a patron saint, a *mung nat*, who is worshipped and sacrificed to during a ritual lasting for several days at a public place in the village. During hierarchical gumsa periods, the mung nat is regarded as a spiritual member of the chief's lineage; within the egalitarian gumlao system, he is considered the ancestor of all the lineages. The sky nat Madai, the ruler of the spiritual realm, is only recognised within the gumsa system.

Edmund R. Leach (1910–89) was initially educated as an engineer but was, according to himself, converted to social anthropology at the age of 25. His stationing in Burma during the Second World War gave him the ethnographic raw material for a book which has become one of the most important monographs of the subject, *Political Systems of Highland Burma* (1954). This was an explicit attack on the then hegemonic view that societies were generally well integrated and stable, and that myths and ideology first and foremost strengthened such a stability. Leach described a society which continuously carried the germ of its own transformation, whose political system changed in a cyclical manner. His next monograph, *Pul Eliya* (1960), from Sri Lanka, was much more ethnographic in character, but at around the same time he launched his attack on what he saw as the exaggerated interest in ethnographic 'butterfly collecting' at the expense of theoretical development (*Rethinking Anthropology*, 1961). Leach was a sharp polemicist and had a lifelong dialogue with Lévi-Strauss and structuralism, which he regarded with a mixture of admiration and scepticism.

Leach's argument is as follows. The spiritual world is construed as a mirror-image of society. Rituals – which largely consist of private and public sacrifices – are chiefly indirect and oblique ways of talking about society. Therefore it is understandable that one does not sacrifice to the 'king' of the spirits during the egalitarian gumlao phases.

Further, there is an intrinsic relationship between the myths (religion, or the cognitive aspect of religion) and the rituals, since the rituals dramatise the myths. However, Kachin myths are ambiguous and can be told in different ways. Some of these confirm the gumsa system; other, only slightly modified versions, confirm gumlao ideals. The different slants can be presented at the same time by different persons wishing to make different points. Leach shows that this ambiguity in myth and ritual practice in no way creates social stability. The inconsistencies in the Kachin ritual system are, in his view, fundamental and are therefore an eternal source of tension in society. Quite unlike what Durkheim, Malinowski and others had argued, Leach shows that the myths and rituals positively encourage a lack of stability, since they offer themselves to conflicting interpretations. Kachin beliefs and rituals nevertheless always function ideologically in the sense of legitimating a particular power structure, but the ideology, reflecting instability in Kachin social organisation, is ambiguous.

Much later research on ritual has concentrated on one of the dimensions Leach deals with, namely what he calls 'symbolic statements about the social order'. One interesting study in this vein is Bruce Kapferer's analysis of demon exorcism among the Sinhalese in Sri Lanka (1984). I shall not go into the details of the ritual; suffice it to say that these exorcisms are large, well-attended and heavily dramatised events which usually take place in the front yard of the home of the patient (the possessed person). In his analysis, Kapferer stresses that the rituals enable the participants to see the world more clearly than usual, and to reflect on their own position in it. For this to be possible, however, they must be able to move to and fro between the ritual, spiritual context and the everyday context: otherwise the two realms would remain separate. Paradoxically therefore, Kapferer writes, the part of the audience which is furthest away from the central stage is best able to carry out this kind of reflection. The patient, the relatives and the first rows of spectators are too immersed in the event to reflect on it, while the people at the back, sipping their tea and chatting together in low voices, are able to see the ritual at a distance and thereby use it consciously in their self-reflection. Here Kapferer finds a quite different pattern from Geertz (1973) in his famous analysis of the Balinese cockfight, where he argues that the only participants who fully understand all the symbolic nuances of the fight (which is laden with cultural symbolism) are those who are central betters – who are placed at the inner circle near the fight itself. Only they engage in what Geertz calls 'deep play', which may be an euphemism for religious communion. In Kapferer's example, the opposite proved to be the case: the people of the inner circle understood little, because they were too deeply immersed in the drama.

It is very likely that this difference is caused by differences between the respective empirical findings. Such dissimilarities, of course, seem to complicate even further the matter of building a general theory of ritual. Nevertheless, we should be aware that from the system ecology of Rappaport, to the complex multi-level analysis of Leach, to the hermeneutic approach represented by Kapferer and Geertz, there is a clear continuity in that they all agree that ritual is an oblique, indirect way of making complex statements with a strong ideological dimension about society. Through a number of studies of the Ndembu of present-day Zambia, Victor Turner (1967, 1969, 1974) has developed a sophisticated model of ritual symbolism, which sums up many of the concerns taken up by others.

The Multivocality of Symbols

The use of symbols is central to rituals, and this does not just involve which symbols are used, but also their mutual relationship and their meaning (what they symbolise). In Christianity, white symbolises virtue and purity while black signifies evil and darkness; the number seven has a sacred air, and the wafer consumed at communion has the paradoxical quality of being simultaneously an ordinary wafer and a part of Christ's body. The wafer can thus be seen as a liminal object forming a bridge between this world and the spiritual realm. In this way, it can truly be said that rituals both say something and do something. Moreover, many of the symbols of

Christianity are ambiguous, or multivocal to use Turner's preferred term;
several meanings can be read into the number seven, and it is not universally
agreed what the holy communion really means.

Among the Ndembu, the milk tree (*Diplorrhyncus mossambicensis*) is a
central symbol at initiation rituals (Turner 1967). The tree is notable in that
it secretes a thick, white, milkish fluid when its bark is cut. The Ndembu
explain that it is important in the initiation of girls because the milk tree
stands for human breast milk and for the breasts themselves. They also
say that the tree 'belongs to mother and child'; that it symbolises the
mother–child tie. In other words, it seems to have two main meanings: a
biological and a social one. The Ndembu also emphasise that the milk tree
expresses the continuity of the matrilineage and the cohesion of the tribe.
'The milk tree is our flag,' said an educated Ndembu, invoking an apt
analogy to an important multivocal symbol in nation-states.

Turner also notes that the milk tree can symbolise contradiction and
fission. Especially at the girls' initiation rites, the tree forms the focus for
the female spirit of community and their opposition to male dominance;
the women dance around it, sing libellous songs against the men and so
on. Further, says Turner, the tree represents the individual novice, as a
young milk tree is being blessed at the same time that she enters the
liminal phase. Thus, the tree represents the tension between individual
and society. It can also represent a conflict between the mother of the novice
and the other women: she loses her child who is becoming an adult, and
is not allowed to join in the dance around the tree. Finally, the milk tree
may represent the matrilineage of the novice and so serve as a reminder
of the contradiction between the unity of the tribe and the separation of
the lineages.

The milk tree is a dominant symbol, and Turner argues that all rituals
are focused on similar symbols. Dominant symbols have the following characteristics. First, they are condensed, that is to say many different
phenomena are given a common expression. Second, a dominant symbol
amounts to a fusion of divergent meanings. In this way, otherwise different
people can sense likeness and express solidarity through these symbols
– such as flags in nation-states, which mean different things to different
people and so are able to give different people the impression that they
are the same. Third, dominant ritual symbols entail a polarisation of
meaning. At one pole (the ideological), there is a set of meanings to do
with the social and political order of society. At the other pole (the sensory),
physiological and biological meanings are expressed. (To this, we would
probably add emotional meanings today.) The milk tree thus represents,
at one pole, matrilineality and the unity of Ndembu society (among other
meanings); at the other pole it expresses breast milk and the mother–child
relationship.

A major insight in Turner's work is that symbols have to be multivocal,
or ambiguous, to create solidarity: since people are different, they must
be capable of meaning different things to different people. This could be

said of rituals in general too, and Leach's Kachin study is a clear case in point. Another important insight from Turner, who belonged to a generation of British anthropologists concerned with bridging the gap between interpretation of meaning and accounting for social structure, is the idea that ritual symbols must speak both about politics (social structure, legitimation) and about existential or emotional cravings: they must be capable of fusing personal experiences with political legitimation if they are to be effective.

The Inherent Complexity of Ritual

In an important study of the changing significance of circumcision rituals in Madagascar, Maurice Bloch (1986) has developed further the points made here concerning ritual, social integration, ideology and power.

The Merina (formerly known as Hovas), who live in the Malagasy highlands, are the most powerful ethnic group in the island, having ruled most of its area for centuries, subjecting neighbouring peoples to Merina rule. Strongly hierarchically organised, the Merina succeeded in retaining some of their traditional power during French colonialism, even after surrendering to France in 1895. The Merina have a bilateral kinship organisation, and the fundamental unit of local organisation is the *deme* (Bloch 1971), consisting of a largely endogamous local group associated with a particular territory. The Merina are famous for their imposing tombs and their elaborate ancestral worship. In his principal study of Merina ritual, Bloch concentrates on male circumcision, which is the single most important public ritual.

Merina boys are circumcised very young (between the ages of one and two years old), and this ritual involves practically the whole local group, as well as deme members living elsewhere. They give contributions to the child's family which are proportional to their closeness of kin. During the ritual they sing and dance throughout the night, thereby dramatising the unity of the kin group. The circumcision usually takes place in the child's parents' house, but other deme members are appointed as the child's 'father' and 'mothers'. The child's 'father' is the circumciser, while the 'mothers' are young women who have a special responsibility for the child during the ritual, which can last for days. Other people also have special assignments; adolescent boys are expected to act mischievously and make practical jokes, while the men cook the food, which is usually a female task.

In a largely structuralist analysis of the symbolism of the ritual, Bloch describes how symbolic meanings are contrasted and inverted, and how both the social and the cosmic order are dramatised in suggestive, non-verbal ways. The unity represented in the ancestors' tombs and the division represented in the houses (inhabited by people from different lineages) are juxtaposed, while the male–female opposition is also expressed at a variety of levels. For example, the ritual always takes place during the cold season; in Bloch's view, this establishes a continuity between the life-giving ceremony of circumcision and the stone tombs of death and deme unity. The fact that the circumciser and 'mothers' are not close kin to the child, which negates biological kinship, also lends support to this view. During the very complex proceedings, objects and acts represent different forces and social relationships which interact in ambiguous ways; these include strong vital elements (which are 'wild' and include the *vazimba*, the mythical enemies of the Merina), intermediaries (which mediate and domesticate those vital forces, making them useful to the Merina), the tomb (unity and undifferentiated descent) and devalued entities (such as 'women on their own' and division; Bloch 1986, p. 99).

The central contradiction in the ritual is, in Bloch's multi-layered analysis, the symbolic association between blessing and its opposite, namely violence. Violence is enacted both symbolically and literally; the latter does not just occur in the act of removing the child's foreskin, but also in the killing of a bull to be consumed during the ritual. Each act of violence, however, is associated with a *tsodrano* or blessing ritual, where important men and women call on God and ancestors to give them their blessings. These elders then 'blow water' onto the child and the spectators, thereby mediating the blessings given by God and the ancestors. This contrast – between blessing and violence, life and death – is in Bloch's view a central contradiction in Merina ideology.

Drawing on sources enabling him to trace descriptions of the ritual back to the eighteenth century, Bloch shows how its central symbolic features have remained remarkably uniform despite important social and political upheavals – the growth of the centralised Merina state, colonialism and independence – and despite great variations in its size and social importance. During the period of the centralised state, the royal circumcision was the main state ritual, and was used to legitimate royalty, tax collection and centralised hierarchy at the expense of weakening the demes. For this purpose, the symbolic content of the ritual was altered slightly, although its key elements remained unchanged. During French colonialism the ritual was a small-scale family undertaking, whereas since independence in 1960 it has increased in importance and taken on anti-elite connotations. Bloch's detailed analysis of both the symbolic and social elements of the ritual process and its changing historical significance shows that ritual is not determined by an easily intelligible set of factors.

Bloch expresses dissatisfaction with conventional anthropological approaches to ritual. On the one hand, various functionalist explanations (Marxist as well as non-Marxist variants) are inadequate for reasons discussed earlier in this chapter. On the other, what he calls intellectualist and symbolist views, including those of Geertz and Evans-Pritchard (1956), which 'see religion as a speculation on nature and an intellectual accommodation of the beyond' (Bloch 1986, p. 8), fail to place the beliefs and rituals in a proper social context. In concluding his own historical analysis of the Merina circumcision ritual, Bloch concludes: 'Rituals are events that *combine the properties of statements and actions*. It is because of this combination that their analysis has proved endlessly elusive' (1986, p. 181).

A fact which cannot be elaborated here, but which should be kept in mind, is that it is not always easy to distinguish clearly between theatrical and ritual performances. Schechner (1994, p. 622) proposes a continuum where the theatre represents entertainment and the ritual efficacy; the theatre stands for fun and appreciation, the ritual for results and beliefs. However, not least in contemporary Western dramatism, the object of a theatre performance may well be to make the audience reflect on the conditions of existence (consider, for example, the relationship between the Sinhalese exorcism ritual and Beckett's plays) or to act politically (as with Brecht).

An Actor-centred Perspective on Ritual

Actor-based definitions of politics and economy are presented in Chapters 10 and 11. Rather than stating that politics, for example, is the social distribution of power, authority and rights, or that economy is society's routine for production, distribution and consumption, one may thus define politics and economy as aspects of action.

Edmund Leach (1968) has proposed a definition of the same kind regarding ritual. Common anthropological definitions would locate it in ritual institutions – churches, mosques, sacrificial grounds, etc. – and focus on the systemic level. This would ultimately be misleading, Leach argues, and instead he calls attention to the ritual act, seeing rituals as an aspect of culturally standardised actions. The expressive, symbolic aspect of a conventional act – everything which is not obviously goal-directed – is ritual, says Leach, and he points out that ritual acts do not necessarily take place in what we think of as 'ritual contexts'. This kind of definition, we should note, does not exclude the more 'substantivist' definition focusing on the ritual institutions, but complements it by focusing on the acts themselves and not merely the social framework.

Political Ritual in State Societies

Careful to avoid a simplistic reductionist explanation, Bloch analyses the ideological dimension of ritual perhaps more carefully than any earlier anthropologist. One of his main points, which he shares with many other anthropologists, is that rituals and ritual symbolism have to be ambiguous because they are representations of a social world that is contradiction-ridden. So 'the message of ideology cannot be maintained simply as a statement ... because it is by its very nature in contradiction with human experience in the world' (Bloch 1986, p. 195). This is important. Ideology always simplifies and imposes hierarchy and a particular social order. In the case of the Merina, ideology as mediated by the circumcision ritual also served to justify state violence.

In modern state societies, the oblique ideological dimension of ritual is no less evident than in non-modern societies (see Handelman 1990). National flags, for example, are sufficiently ambiguous (or multivocal) to be able to create a symbolic bond and a sense of community between persons who are very different and who represent contradicting interests. Insofar as they are able to interpret the flag in different ways, and thus identify with it on different grounds by relating it to different kinds of personal experiences, citizens can actualise themselves as a nation through such simple national symbols. In this way, state rituals may indeed function as charters for collective action.

In situations of social transformation, rituals belonging to the former social order may be reproduced, although their meaning may change, in order to give an impression of legitimacy. As Kertzer notes (1988, p. 46), New Year celebrations have been a constant feature of Russian society since pagan times. When the Russians became Christian, the church merged these festivities with Christmas, and after the 1917 Bolshevik revolution the new Soviet leaders actively sponsored the festival after a brief interlude of attempting to abolish it, but tried to remove as much of its Christian content as possible (see also Mach 1993, pp. 130 ff.). During periods perceived as turbulent, where, say, a new political power structure tries to replace the old one, the new leaders may try to appropriate ritual symbols associated with the old, familiar order in order to create an impression of continuity and legitimacy. Such a use of familiar symbols in order to render an unfamiliar situation familiar, whether or not this is intentional, is characteristic of the legitimation of contemporary ethnic movements (Abner Cohen 1974) and nationalism; this is dealt with in Chapter 17.

It is perhaps nowhere more evident than in the study of religion, rituals and practical/cognitive systems of knowledge that anthropological research generates insights which would not have been available without fieldwork. For instance, contrary to much theoretical philosophy, anthropological research has shown how it is fully possible, in practice, to hold notions which are contradictory in theory. Different kinds of knowledge are used in different kinds of situations, and as long as they are not confronted in the same situation they may easily coexist in the mind of one person. In a study of medical systems in polyethnic Mauritius, Linda Sussman (1983) shows that Mauritians may well consult three or four different kinds of doctors – who in a sense work within totally different realities and have irreconcilable views on illness and healing – to be on the safe side. If they have a backache, they may see a Chinese herbal doctor, an Indian ayurvedic doctor, a European physiotherapist and an African traditional healer.

The general point here is that meaning is use: that religious as well as other knowledge becomes important to people only when it can be used for something, only when it is connected to their experience. Rituals, in this regard, dramatise the rather abstract tenets of religion, render the content of religion concrete and recognisable, link it to experience and legitimate the social and political order. Moreover, different kinds of knowledge are made relevant in different situations. Therefore it does not necessarily lead to a practical contradiction to believe in both the Bible and the scientific theory of evolution, as long as the two bodies of thought are kept in separate realms. Similarly, a Kachin may be favourable to both gumlao and gumsa values, but not simultaneously; and a West Indian may be (indeed, most are) favourable to values of both respectability and reputation.

Suggestions for Further Reading

E.E. Evans-Pritchard: *Theories of Primitive Religion*. Oxford: Clarendon 1965.

Clifford Geertz: Religion as a Cultural System, in Clifford Geertz, *The Interpretation of Cultures*. New York: Basic Books 1973.

Max Gluckman: *Custom and Conflict in Africa*, Chapters 4–5. Oxford: Blackwell 1982 [1956].

Victor W. Turner: *The Forest of Symbols. Aspects of Ndembu Ritual*. Ithaca, NY: Cornell University Press 1967.

14 MODES OF THOUGHT

Animals are divided into (a) belonging to the Emperor, (b) embalmed, (c) tame, (d) sucking pigs, (e) sirens, (f) fabulous, (g) stray dogs, (h) included in the present classification, (i) frenzied, (j) innumerable, (k) drawn with a very fine camelhair brush, (l) *et cetera*, (m) having just broken the water pitcher, (n) that from a long way off look like flies.
> —*Jorge Luis Borges (quoting from 'a certain Chinese encyclopedia')*

Whorf's Hypothesis and the Problem of Translation

Benjamin Lee Whorf was an insurance salesman in the US in the 1920s. A recurrent problem in his job concerned the interpretation of words; their precise meaning was often extremely significant with regard to indemnity payments. What did it mean, for example, that a fire was 'self-inflicted'? And what did it mean that a drum of petrol was 'empty'? In some cases, it could be empty of petrol, but full of petrol gas and highly explosive. A fire which was caused by an empty petrol drum exploding could, however, not be defined as self-inflicted. Whorf's company lost some money on such cases.

Some years later, Whorf developed an hypothesis on the relationship between language and the non-linguistic world which has enjoyed great influence in anthropology. Whorf's teacher in linguistic anthropology, Edward Sapir, played a part in the development of the idea, and the hypothesis is sometimes named the Sapir–Whorf hypothesis, but I shall speak of it as Whorf's hypothesis (Whorf 1956). It postulates that there is an intimate connection between the categories and structure of a language and the ways in which humans are able to experience the world. Whorf paid special attention to the language of the Hopis, which was almost without nouns as we know them and which also lacked the standard verb conjugations common to Indo-European languages. Since the language of the Hopis had these peculiar characteristics, Whorf argued, they would experience the world in a fundamentally different way from the descendants of European settlers in North America, who had brought their languages and grammars to the continent. The language of the Hopis was process-oriented and focused on movement, whereas English and other European languages were oriented towards things and nouns in general.

Whorf argued that there was an intrinsic connection between the life-world of a people and its language; that every people will develop the linguistic tools it needs to solve tasks perceived as necessary, and that the language of a people will therefore be a significant source of knowledge about their mode of thought, their cosmology and their everyday life.

An immediate implication of Whorf's hypothesis is the problem of cross-cultural translation, one of the perennial problems of anthropology. Is it necessarily possible to translate, say, the life-world and culture of the Azande into English? Or could it rather be that their form of life is so closely connected with the Zande language that such a project is doomed to fail – because we will always be forced to interpret them in our own terms, and not in theirs, when we try to describe them in a language other than their own? Whorf himself did not hesitate to describe the differences between the Hopi language and English in comparative, or 'etic', terms, and in practice he thus carried out cultural translation. Such translations are necessary for anthropology to be possible, but they are not unproblematic.

The Notion of the Pre-logical Mind

Such issues are fundamental to anthropology as a comparative social science. They do not concern research methodology only; they also deal with the question of whether all humans think in roughly the same way, or if there are culturally specific modes of thought which follow different logics and cannot be faithfully reproduced in a foreign language. When the German explorer von den Steinen reported, in the late nineteenth century, that the Bororo of Amazonas described themselves as red macaws, many – among them Lévy-Bruhl – drew the conclusion that the Bororo were clearly unable to think logically. For how can it be possible to think that one is a parrot and a human being at the same time? The Bororo mode of thought thus had to be pre-logical; this people violated Aristotle's principle of contradiction, which states that an object cannot both have and not have one and the same property at the same time and in the same respect. One cannot, in other words, both believe and not believe that one is a parrot. (Later it became evident that the Bororo by no means contradicted themselves, but rather spoke metaphorically in a way incomprehensible to von den Steinen. He interpreted them in too literary a sense.)

The general problem of translation is still with us, although it has been reformulated many times since the early 1930s. The problem has three main aspects. First, do 'primitive', non-literate peoples think in a fundamentally different way from ourselves? Second, if so, is it possible to understand their life-world and to translate it into a comparative anthropological terminology? Third, is the anthropological terminology inherently culturally embedded, or does it represent a kind of context-free, and therefore comparatively useful, kind of language? There are many ways to approach these issues, and the only answer on which nearly all anthropologists agree, is that any differences in modes of thought are not innate – they are not caused by 'racial' differences. We must, therefore, study and compare culture and social organisation, even when the topic is the relationship between abstract modes of thought among different peoples.

The Mental Unity of Humanity

One of the central dogmas of anthropology is the principle of the mental unity of humanity. This indicates that the innate characteristics of humanity are roughly the same everywhere – not in the sense that humans are identical, but rather in that inborn differences do not account for cultural variation. If, for example, one had believed that the 'races' had varying degrees of intelligence, one might have accepted that there were inherent genetic causes for the fact that Africans in colonial times were illiterate and engaged in ancestor worship whereas British gentlemen drank port and quoted Shelley. If this had been correct, the entire modern anthropological endeavour would have been superfluous, since it would have been futile to search in culture and social organisation for causes of human variation.

The scientific grounds for claiming that different human groups have systematically varying mental faculties has never been convincing. The variation *within* each group has frequently been shown to be greater than the variation *between* the groups. Within any random sample of individuals, there will be some 'smart' and some 'stupid' people, some enterprising and some lazy individuals, and so on; but it cannot be shown that, say, the Sami are intelligent whereas the Mbuti are stupid. This is to say that human groups worldwide are endowed with roughly the same innate faculties and potentials, and that cultural variation must be accounted for by referring to events taking place after birth.

Many kinds of cultural variation have been accounted for in this way in previous chapters. Neither the kula exchange of the Trobrianders, the ancestor cults of the Kaguru nor the agricultural technology of the Dogon have been explained through reference to inborn characteristics of the 'races'. This chapter focuses on variations between different cultural modes of thought, which are some of the most difficult cultural differences both to understand and to account for in comparative terms. We begin by discussing whether it may be reasonable to believe in witches, and then move on to classification, cultural knowledge and the relationship between thought, power and social organisation.

Witchcraft and Knowledge among the Azande

The Azande are a patrilineal people of agriculturalists who live largely in southern Sudan, a few hundred kilometres south-west of Nuerland (Evans-Pritchard 1983 [1937]). Their cosmology presumes (in the ethnographic present tense) the existence of a number of spirits of different kinds, including ancestral spirits. In addition, the institution of witchcraft is central to their daily life and world view. It is seen as the individual ability to create misfortune for others in spiritual ways. Only some Azande possess this ability. Unlike magic, which involves medicines and magical formulas, witchcraft is a purely spiritual, generally involuntary activity: the witchcraft power frequently commits its acts while the carrier (the witch) is asleep.

Edward Evans-Pritchard surrounded by Azande informants.
(Photo courtesy of the Royal Anthropological Institute)

Death and other unfortunate circumstances are usually seen as caused by witchcraft. Traditionally, witches were executed ritually, but by the time of Evans-Pritchard's fieldwork in the late 1920s this practice had been abandoned, although the belief in witchcraft continued; even decades later, when many Azande had been proletarised, witchcraft beliefs were common (Reining 1966).

The witchcraft institution provides answers to important questions and explains why people suffer misfortunes. It cannot explain in general why one develops a fever after a snakebite, but it does offer an explanation for why a certain person was bitten by a certain snake on a certain day. The scientific doctrine about cause and effect cannot provide explanations of this kind: it cannot tell why the granary had to collapse just when several Azande were resting in its shade. Although the poles supporting the granary were destroyed by termites, the victims held that the accident was ultimately caused by witchcraft.

The notion of witchcraft is not incompatible with a belief in causality. A Zande might agree that certain diseases are caused by bacteria in the drinking water, but he would also want to know why he became ill when his neighbour did not. He would look for the cause in his enemies, whom he would suspect of witchcraft.

Evans-Pritchard suggests that witchcraft is invoked as an explanatory principle 'whenever plain reason fails'. When somebody is accused of witchcraft, a prince or a witchdoctor consults an oracle to decide the matter. The most important is the poison oracle, which consists of a portion of poison and two fowls. The first fowl is served poison; if it survives, the accused is innocent, but if it dies, he or she is guilty. Then the validity of the verdict is double-checked by administrating the poison to a second bird.

Evans-Pritchard took witches more seriously than anybody had done earlier, and was concerned to show how the belief in witches made sense and was perfectly rational within the Zande world. He was among the earliest to criticise and discard the idea that there existed a specifically primitive, 'pre-logical' mentality. His aim was to explore the interrelationships between thought and social structure, but not to reduce the former to the latter.

However, at two important points Evans-Pritchard indicates that when all is said and done the Azande are wrong in assuming that witches exist. First, he introduces a sharp distinction between the witchcraft logic and the scientific logic, and frequently makes statements to the effect that 'obviously, witches do not exist'. He also distinguishes clearly between mystical notions, notions based on common sense and scientific notions. Since witchcraft is invisible and (in 'our' view) supernatural, a cosmology based on such beliefs falls squarely into the first category and must be less valid, on objective grounds, than scientific notions.

Second, Evans-Pritchard's monograph ends with a primarily structural-functionalist explanation of the witchcraft institution: the belief in witches and similar institutions exists, ultimately, because they contribute to social integration and check deviant behaviour – not because they produce valid insight and understanding.

Winch's Criticism

The philosopher Peter Winch, reacting against Evans-Pritchard's distinction between mystical and scientific notions, started a lengthy and heated debate on comparison, rationality and cultural translation when he wrote a paper in 1964 entitled 'Understanding a Primitive Society' (Winch 1970). Winch rejects the idea that there are universal standards available to compare witchcraft beliefs and science. To him, science just as much as witchcraft is based on unverifiable axioms. Winch also claims that Oxford professors are scarcely less superstitious than Azande; they too trust blindly in forces they do not fully understand. One of his examples is drawn from meteorology. How many of us really understand its principles? Yet we watch the weather forecasts.

Winch agrees that ideas and notions must be tested in order for their validity to be justified. This, he argues, is done both in scientific experiments and in the Zande consultation of poison oracles, and there is no difference in principle between the two procedures.

Further, Winch claims that scientific experiments are meaningless to someone who is ignorant about the principles of science. For this reason, science – like witchcraft – is not inherently meaningful, but makes sense only within a particular, culturally created frame of reference. He compares the helplessness of an engineer deprived of his mathematics with the predicament of a Zande without access to his oracles.

To Winch, it is also important to note that the lives of the Azande seem to function well; that their relationship to witchcraft makes their existence meaningful, and that the system by and large is consistent.

The disagreement between Evans-Pritchard and Winch ultimately amounts to divergent views of science. Whereas Evans-Pritchard holds that the Azande are wrong, Winch argues that all knowledge is culturally constructed and that it can therefore only be deemed right or wrong within its own cultural context. Winch questions anthropology's assumption that its comparative concepts are culturally 'neutral' – when all is said and done, he suggests, even anthropology is a cultural practice.

He draws extensively on Ludwig Wittgenstein's theory of language games (1983 [1958]), where the latter argues that knowledge is socially created and that different systems of knowledge (language games, or in Winch's sense, cultures) are incommensurable and can therefore not be ranked hierarchically or, strictly speaking, compared. This line of reasoning, which Winch applies not only to anthropological analysis but also to the anthropologists themselves, can be glossed as a strong version of Whorf's hypothesis, and it seems to render different cultural universes incommensurable for want of a neutral language of comparison.

Let us pose the question differently. Why is it that anthropology as an academic discipline developed in Western Europe and the US, and not, say, in the Trobriand Islands or Zandeland? As an experiment in thinking, we may imagine a Zande anthropologist who arrives in Britain to look into the local cosmology and cultural perception of death. She would quickly discover that the witchcraft institution is absent in that country, something which clearly must be accounted for. If she is a faithful structural-functionalist, she might search for functional causes for the strange denial, among the British, of the existence of witches. Perhaps she would eventually draw the conclusion that the denial of witchcraft, the blind faith in 'natural causes of death', strengthened social integration in British society, since it prevented open conflict between families and lineages.

This kind of argument seems to lend support to Winch's relativist position. However, it is a matter of fact that social anthropology did not develop in Zandeland but in Britain and other northern countries, and this must also be taken into account. Perhaps the hypothetical example of the Zande anthropologist is best seen as a warning against simplistic func-tionalist explanations, but not as an argument against anthropology as a generalising, comparative discipline. Later in this chapter, some reasons are suggested as to why the Zande did not develop their own compara-tive science of society and culture.

Classification

Durkheim and Mauss were among the earliest to explore the interrela-tionship between social organisation and patterns of thought. The basic idea in their book *Primitive Classification* (1963 [1903]) was that thought is a social product and that different societies thereby produce different kinds of thought. (Unlike Winch, they did not question the privileged position of scientific thought.) A great portion of the book discusses primitive systems of classification; and since its publication, the study of classification has been a central concern in anthropology.

Classification, in the anthropological sense, entails dividing objects, people, animals and other phenomena according to socially pre-established categories or types. This is an important part of the knowledge system of any society, and knowledge is always related to social organisation and power. Arguments have just been presented against the notion that some kinds of knowledge are 'objectively and universally true', and in exploring systems of knowledge it is necessary to be aware of the interrelationship between knowledge and other parts of the social world; this includes one's own knowledge.

Just as witchcraft beliefs may seem 'irrational' to the ethnocentric observer, alien systems of classification may seem unsystematic to someone who takes the Western system for granted. Ethnographic studies have revealed great variations in the ways other people classify. One famous example is the Karam of highland New Guinea, who do not regard the cassowary as a bird (Bulmer 1967), although Linnaeus (the founder of the scientific system of plant and animal classification) would definitely have done so. The cassowary resembles an ostrich: it has feathers and lays eggs, but does not fly. Therefore the Karam do not consider it a bird. On the other hand, they classify bats together with birds (as flying creatures), even though we 'know' that they are 'really' mammals.

For a long time, anthropologists tried to show that the logic of any system of classification was intrinsically connected to the usefulness of plants and animals; that it was simply a functional device for the material reproduction of society. This idea eventually had to be abandoned, and we now turn to showing why.

Cannibalism

In which sub-field of anthropology does research on cannibalism properly belong? In the study of economic systems, politics, religion, cultural ecology, symbolism and modes of thought, classification – or in the autocritique of anthropology? Let us outline some highlights in research on cannibalism.

Some scholars, including Marvin Harris, held that the assumed widespread cannibalism among the Aztecs was caused by protein scarcity. Others, notably Sahlins, argued that there was enough protein available, and that the ritual consumption of human hearts was instead a deeply religious act.

According to Lévi-Strauss's theory of symbolic relationships between different kinds of food, boiled and roasted food constitute a binary pair of oppositions. In accordance with this model, Lévi-Strauss held that it was likely that endocannibals (who eat parts of deceased relatives) would boil such food, while exocannibals (who eat enemies) would roast it. In a bid to test this 'hypothesis', the Harvard anthropologist Paul Shankman processed data from 60 societies assumed to practise cannibalism. He found that 17 boiled while 20 roasted; six did both. The rest used other techniques for preparation, including baking. Shankman found, further, that there was no correlation between the categorisation of the eaten and the mode of preparation (Harris 1979).

It must be said, in defence of Lévi-Strauss, that anthropological reports of cannibalism are uncertain and tend to be second-hand. Indeed, they are so uncertain that William Arens, in *The Man-eating Myth* (1978), argues that cannibalism has probably *never* existed as a cultural custom. All the sources he has consulted suffer from weaknesses and inconsistencies. For the Spanish conquistadors, for example, it was useful to depict the Aztecs as bloodthirsty cannibals to justify their destruction of that highly advanced civilisation. Arens, referring to a mass of anthropological research, could not find a single reliable eye-witness account of cannibalism. He points out that many peoples tell stories to the effect that the neighbouring tribe is cannibalistic, which may explain why the belief in cannibalism is so widespread. In fact, he intimates that a rule against cannibalism may be as universal as the incest taboo.

If Arens is at least partly right, cannibalism has to do with classification, but not classification of food. Instead, it concerns the classification of people, and both anthropologists and other people have been involved in this kind of classification.

Classificatory Anomalies

The Lele of Kasai (in present-day Zaïre) distinguish meticulously between different classes of animals (Douglas 1975). For instance, birds are characterised by feathers, their ability to fly and the laying of eggs, and are thereby distinguished from other animals. However, there are certain animals that do not fit neatly into this logic. The monitor lizard and the tortoise are examples of such exceptions: they lay eggs, but walk on all fours and lack feathers. Douglas describes such 'deviant' creatures as anomalies; they fail to fit in. The anomaly, like the liminal phase in Turner's model of the ritual process (Chapter 8), is both outside and inside; it threatens the established order. Anomalous animals are subjected to certain rules; one can only eat them under specific circumstances, women are not allowed to touch them, and so on.

Natural Symbols

An original view on the relationship between nature and society is expressed in Mary Douglas's writings on cultural conceptions of nature, purity and pollution (1966, 1970; see also Chapter 5 here). Her thoughts on this issue are inspired by Lévi-Strauss's position on the universality of the culture–nature distinction, by Durkheim's and Mauss's work on classification and by British structural-functionalism. Her general argument is as follows.

Humans are classifying beings who distinguish between order and disorder, inside and outside, pure and impure. The reason why the pig is considered unclean in the Middle East, for example, is that it is a non-ruminating cloven-footed animal and therefore does not fit into the classificatory system for animals. Cultural ecologists, among them Marvin Harris, would rather argue that the pig is considered impure because it is a potential carrier of trichinas.

Douglas deals with the social classification of the body from the same perspective. The socialised body is ambiguous: it is simultaneously cultural and natural, both orderly and chaotic. Its natural aspects, including ageing and bodily functions, are threatening and potentially dangerous, since they are symbolic reminders of the continuous threat of chaos and dissolution to the fragile social organism (society). The cultural body thereby becomes a metaphor for society, and the boundaries of the body are metaphors for the boundaries of society. For this reason, Douglas argues, it is socially important to circumscribe bodily functions with strict cultural (and cultivating) rules. Menstruating women, for example, are seen as polluting in many societies and are sometimes secluded.

The most important anomalous creature among the Lele is the pangolin (*Manis tricuspis*). It has, the Lele explain, the tail and body of a fish and it is covered with scales, but it gives birth like a mammal. It has four small legs and climbs trees (Douglas 1975, p. 33). This animal, it turns out, has an important place in the mythology and ritual life of the Lele. There is a cult of fertility centred on it. The reason, argues Douglas, is that the pangolin is anomalous in a crucial way: in addition to everything else, it gives birth to only one offspring at a time. In this regard it resembles a human more than an animal. Just as the parents of twins and triplets (who are also anomalies on this score) are seen as mediators between the human and the spiritual worlds, the pangolin is seen as a mediator between humanity and the animal world.

Anomalies are usually associated with danger and pollution. One example, described by Douglas elsewhere (1966), is the pig in Middle Eastern religions: as a cloven-hoofed but not ruminant mammal, it was not classified as edible since edible animals ought to be both cloven-hoofed and ruminant – it was an anomaly. The rather more positive status of the pangolin is caused by the fact, Douglas argues, that the Lele have succeeded in turning a potential curse into a blessing, exploiting the ambiguous status of the animal to their advantage. The pangolin is not economically important, and yet it occupies a central place in Lele cosmology: it is a mediator.

Totemic Classification

When the Bororo spoke of themselves as red macaws, to the bewilderment of von den Steinen, they referred to a system of classification known in the professional literature as 'totemism'. Totemism – the term is of Ojibwa origin – is a knowledge system whereby each sub-group in a society, usually a clan, has a special, ritual relationship to a class of natural phenomena, usually plants or animals. Totemism has traditionally been particularly widespread in Australia and the Pacific, the Americas and Africa. For example, the totems of the Algonquin in Quebec include the bear, the fish and thunder in a symbolic system whereby natural phenomena are seen to correspond to aspects of society. The question posed by many anthropologists, from Frazer onwards, was the exact nature of this correspondence.

Malinowski, writing on totemism in the Trobriand Islands, held that totemic plants and animals were chosen because they were inherently useful to the maintenance of society (1974 [1948]). Radcliffe-Brown, who developed a more complex view of totemism, drew on Durkheim's notion that the attitude towards a totem was caused by a special relationship between it and the social order, and that the ultimate function of totemism was to maintain social integration (1952 [1929]). The totem is thus a tangible identity marker for a group; Durkheim himself mentions flags as a kind of totem.

Radcliffe-Brown then poses the question of why certain animals and plants are chosen as totems. Like Malinowski and others before him, he assumes that there must be a practical reason, so that, for example, experts in bear hunting take the bear as their totem. In this way, totemism could be seen as a symbolic expression of the division of labour in society.

In a later article, Radcliffe-Brown (1951) raises doubt about his earlier assumption that totemic animals are economically useful to society. At this

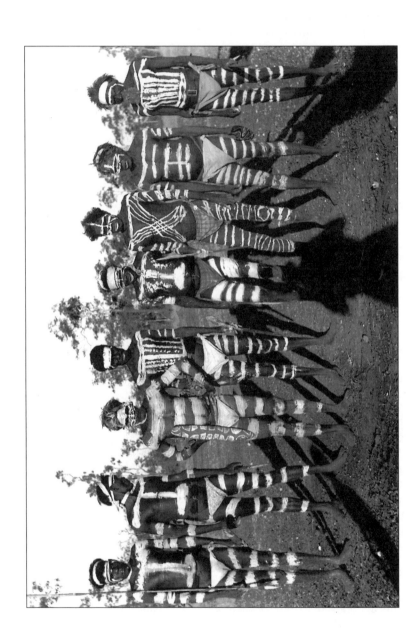

point, he rather focuses on their symbolic meaning. However, he fails to draw a clear conclusion, and Lévi-Strauss is generally credited with resolving the enigma of totemism in anthropology (1963, 1966 [1962]). Drawing on an enormous mass of recorded ethnography, largely from North America and Australia, Lévi-Strauss shows that there is no inherent connection between the utilitarian value of a creature and its significance in the totemic system. Instead, he argues, certain animals are chosen because of their mutual relationship – that is, not because of their direct relationship to groups in a segmentary society. The differences between totemic animals (the way they are perceived by the people) correspond to the differences between groups in society (see Figure 14.1).

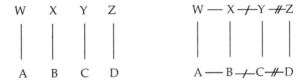

Figure 14.1: Radcliffe-Brown's early view of the relationship between totemic animals and clans (left) and Lévi-Strauss's view (right)

Totemic animals contribute to the creation of order; up to this point, Lévi-Strauss agrees with earlier theorists. However, as he puts it, they are not chosen because they are good to eat, but because they are 'good to think' (*bons à penser*).

The system of totems and the clans in society are further connected symbolically in two complementary ways, through metaphor and metonymy. A metaphor is a symbol which stands for something else, in the way the milk tree among the Ndembu stands for fertility among women (Chapter 13). A metonym is rather a part which symbolically expresses a whole. Metaphorically, the king may be represented by a lion, metonymically by the crown he wears on his head. The relationship between metaphor and metonymy can be said to correspond to the relationship between melody and harmony (see E. Leach 1976; Lakoff and Johnson 1980). A metaphor acquires its meaning through its association with the object it represents, while metonymy consists of using a part to represent the whole.

In a totemic system therefore, each totemic animal stands metonymically for the whole chain of totems, just as each clan stands for the whole society (as a single word may represent the whole sentence). Simultaneously, of

---

Opposite Among Australian peoples, body painting has several layers of meaning: it is decorative, it is socially differentiating and it depicts symbolic links between humans and natural phenomena. The patterns seen on these men from Northern Australia indicate with great precision which totemic group they belong to – their moiety as well as their clan and sub-section. In this way, body painting can function as a kind of social map. (Photo: Johannes Falkenberg) course, the totems are metaphors for each clan. The relationship between the bear and the eagle corresponds to the relationship between the bear clan and the eagle clan. Now, the totems themselves – say, the bear and the eagle – are arbitrary; what counts is the relationship between them.

Undomesticated Thinking

A major concern in Lévi-Strauss's work on totemism was to invalidate notions to the effect that there existed a 'pre-logical, primitive mode of thought' – although he follows a different path from Evans-Pritchard. The structuralism of Lévi-Strauss seeks to reveal not similarities in actual reasoning, but universal underlying principles for thought and symbolisation.

In *La Pensée sauvage*, 'Undomesticated thinking' (misleadingly rendered in English as *The Savage Mind*, Lévi-Strauss 1966 [1962]), the fundamental cognitive processes among modern and non-modern peoples are seen as identical. People everywhere think in terms of metaphor and metonymy, and above all they think in contrasting pairs, so-called binary oppositions. This general model depicting organising principles of thought resembles Bateson's theory of information (1972, 1979), where he argues that only differences that make a difference can create knowledge. Both Lévi-Strauss and Bateson are concerned to show that what is essential are relationships rather than the objects themselves.

Lévi-Strauss argues that fundamental thought processes are identical everywhere, but he also indicates that people with different kinds of technology at their disposal will express their thought in very different ways. Those who depend on script and numbers clearly think along different lines than non-literates, he says. Lévi-Strauss compares the literate and non-literate styles of thinking, and describes the latter as the science of the concrete (*la science du concret*). When a non-literate person, living in a society with no script, is to think abstractly, he or she is forced to align his or her concepts with concrete, visible objects. Spirits, for example, are abstractions described in terms of their visible manifestations; this explains why many early explorers and missionaries erroneously thought that tribal peoples 'worshipped trees and rocks'. Originality, in this kind of society, is possible through novel juxtapositions of concepts referring to familiar objects. Lévi-Strauss describes this thought operation as *bricolage* (a 'bricoleur' can be translated as a handyman, a jack-of-all-trades). This creative, associational and 'playful' mode of thought is contrasted with that of the 'engineer'; the abstract science dominant in Western societies, imprisoned and disciplined by writing and numbers.

However, bricoleurs have a limited repertory of symbols at their disposal. Engineers, who creates abstractions from abstractions, may rather try to transcend the familiar. They are tied up – their thought is tamed or domesticated – by writing and numbers, but at the same time they are liberated from the direct communication with natural objects enforced on the 'untamed thought' of the bricoleurs.

The distinction between bricoleurs and engineers should not be seen as absolute. Today most societies in the world are 'semi-literate', and even Lévi-Strauss himself admits that some modes of thought reminiscent of bricolage, notably in music and poetry, exist even in throughly literate societies. Still, the distinction can be a useful starting-point for an exploration of the interrelationship between knowledge, technology and social organisation.

The Social Construction of Emotions

Knowledge, belief systems and classification are social products, and a great deal of research has been carried out regarding their variations and relationship to power structures and other elements of social organisation. Other aspects of culture have been studied less thoroughly until recent decades; one such is emotions. Many anthropologists still take them more or less for granted and presume that they are inborn. The capacity for love, hatred, empathy, aggression and so on is thus seen as more or less uniformly distributed in the world, and it has also been tacitly assumed that emotions function in roughly the same way in different societies. This view has been challenged, especially since the late 1970s, by scholars who argue that emotions are socially constructed. For example, it has been shown that the European distinction between 'reason' and 'emotion' does not exist in societies such as those of the Ilongot of the Philippines (Rosaldo 1980), the Ifaluk in the Pacific (Lutz 1988) and in Bali (Wikan 1992). It has also been argued that aggression, believed by many to be inborn, is a cultural product (Howell and Willis 1989), and that there exist societies where no concept comparable to our notion of aggression occurs (Howell 1989).

Writing as Technology

In *La Pensée sauvage* Lévi-Strauss distinguishes between what he calls 'cold' and 'hot' societies. Cold societies see themselves as essentially unchanging, while hot societies are based on an ideology perceiving change as inevitable and potentially beneficial. This distinction corresponds not only to the bricoleur–engineer dichotomy, but also to the distinction between 'traditional' and 'modern' societies. For the sake of the argument, the contrast between these societal 'types' is overstated here, but the reader should keep in mind that 'modern' and 'traditional' are ideal types, and that real societies on the ground are much more complex than this simple dichotomy implies.

The role of script as a form of technology has been discussed by generations of anthropologists (see for instance Goody 1968; Ong 1982; Finnegan 1988; Street and Besnier 1994). In a number of books, Jack Goody has argued that the introduction of writing may have fundamental effects on thought as well as social organisation, and his idea of the 'Great Divide' between non-literate and literate societies is close kin to Lévi-Strauss's studies of totemic versus historical thinking and the bricoleur–engineer contrast – characteristically, one of Goody's books on literacy is called *The Domestication of the Savage Mind* (1977). It could be said that just as Marx turned Hegel on his head (or on his feet!), Goody tries to operationalise and sociologise Lévi-Strauss. Controversial among anthropologists who hold that this kind of distinction is simplistic (for example, Halverson 1992), Goody's main arguments nevertheless merit an outline here.

The introduction of writing, Goody argues, enables people to distinguish between concepts and their referents. Writing allows us to turn words into things, to freeze them in time and space. Speech, by contrast, is fleeting and transient and cannot be fixed for posterity. In this sense, writing entails a reduction of speech: the two are not 'the same', and the written version of a statement lacks its extra-linguistic context – facial expression, social situation, tone of voice, etc. Writing can indeed be seen as a kind of material culture; like artefacts, it is solid and enduring, and it can be analysed as objectified subjectivity (T. Barth 1991).

Writing arguably liberates thought from the necessity of mnemotechnics; we do not have to remember everything, but can look it up instead. By implication, writing makes the accumulation of vast amounts of knowledge possible in ways orality is unable to. Writing also narrows the meanings of thoughts in the sense that it lends itself, Goody argues, to accurate critical examination in ways which oral statements do not. We may isolate a small bit of human discourse and subject it to thorough examination in ways that cannot be achieved in societies which lack writing. However – and this is a criticism that has repeatedly been levelled against this kind of theory – there are many examples of literate societies where criticism (in the scientific sense) is not encouraged. On the other hand, it may be retorted that writing is a necessary but not sufficient condition for science as we know it. This argument, one may agree, goes a long way towards explaining why the Azande did not develop their own comparative science of culture and society – but it does not alone explain why many literate peoples have not done so.

Writing also has great potential importance for social organisation. It has been noted that it was used at a very early stage (ancient Mesopotamia) for lists, inventories of the amount of grain in the granary, the number of slaves and animals in the city and so on. As the Christian evangelists witness, censuses were also used very early in the history of writing. Writing thus facilitates not only analytical thought, but also the surveillance of vast numbers of people. It can therefore be regarded as an important kind of technology in the political administration of complex societies.

Finally, a chief use of writing in most literate societies has lain in the building of archives, some of which eventually become history. Lévi-Strauss, commenting on the 'totemic void' in Europe and Asia (1966 [1962]), concludes that these societies have chosen history instead of totemic myths. He does not see history as inherently 'truer' than myth, but rather as a special kind of myth.

The difference between literacy and orality should not be overemphasised: there is by no means a clear-cut distinction. It is nevertheless obvious that the uses of script form an important part of the technology of a society. An abstract ideology such as nationalism, for example (see Chapter 17), is scarcely imaginable without the information technology of writing, which enables members of society to disseminate ideas over a vast area, thus creating bonds of solidarity between millions of individuals who will never know each other personally.

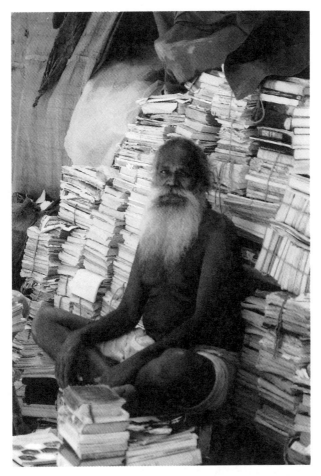

A bookseller in Madras, south India. (Photo by the author)

Time and Scale

Abstract time, that is the kind of time represented in clocks and calendars, may have effects analogous to those of writing. In the kind of society where most of the readers of this book were raised, it is generally believed that time is something one may have much or little of; something which can be saved, something which 'is money', something which can be measured independently of concrete events. Concepts like 'one hour' or 'one week' are meaningful even if we do not say what they contain by way of events. Time, in this kind of society, is conventionally conceptualised as a line with an arrow at the end, where a moving point called 'the present' separates past and future. This kind of abstraction is a cultural invention, neither more nor less. In a certain sense, clocks do not measure time but create it.

Societies lacking clocks do not 'lack time', but rather tend to be organised according to what we may call concrete time (although, as usual, there are very important variations). In this kind of society – historically speaking, the vast majority of human societies – time exists only as embedded in action and process, not as something abstract and autonomous existing outside the events taking place. Rituals do not take place 'at 5 o'clock', but when all is ready – when the preparations are completed and the guests have arrived. In clockless societies, time is not a scarce resource, since it exists only as events. One cannot 'lose' or 'kill' time there.

Past and future take on a different meaning in societies with and without an abstract concept of time, respectively. Obviously, peoples without dates and calendars do not date previous events in the same way that we do. Bourdieu, further, has written of the Kabyles that they were shocked to learn of the way the French related to the future (Bourdieu 1963). 'The French see themselves as greater than God,' they said, 'for they believe that they can control the future. But the future belongs to God.' Many peoples, moreover, do not conjugate verbs in the future tense. One philosophically sound way of explaining this may be that events in the world create time, and since no events have yet taken place in the future, the future cannot constitute a time (Tempels 1959).

Linear, quantified, abstract time is not detached from social organisation, but it did not arise mechanically in response to 'societal needs'. Just as writing, a tool for political control and the advancement of science, was first developed for ritual purposes, the first Europeans to use clocks were monks who needed them to coordinate their prayers. However, abstract time has taken on an important place in the social organisation of contemporary societies. Lewis Mumford has written that the most tyrannical and authoritarian device developed in modern societies was neither the car nor the steam engine, but the clock. The philosopher Henri Bergson, writing in the early decades of the twentieth century, was concerned to save the subjective experience of time, *la durée*, which was threatened by quantified, mechanical time.

Why is it that people living in modern societies have become slaves of the clock, as it were, while others seem to manage perfectly well without it? The answer must be sought in the social organisation of society. If I wish to travel, say, from Oslo to Prague, it would be extremely inconvenient to have to go to the airport and wait for a day or two until a sufficient number of passengers to Prague have found their way to the airport. It seems more reasonable that the airline states that the departure will be at 11 a.m., that all of the passengers agree on the meaning of 11 a.m. and thus appear at the airport more or less simultaneously. In other words, the concept of abstract time and the omnipresence of clocks make it possible to coordinate the actions of a much larger number of people than is possible in a society with no shared, quantified notion of time. Thus, both script and abstract time make social integration at a very high level of scale possible.

Knowledge and Power

Evans-Pritchard once wrote that he believed his studies of Azande witchcraft might contribute to the understanding of communist Russia (1951). What he meant was that an understanding of the ideological under-pinnings of the knowledge system of one society may give clues as to similar structures elsewhere. Undoubtedly, knowledge systems create a particular order in the world, and this does not only concern ideologies of gender, caste, class or ethnicity as dealt with in other chapters here, but also the very structuring of experience. In his celebrated novel *1984*, George Orwell (1984 [1949]) describes a society where the language has consciously been changed by the power elite, in order to prevent the citizens from critical thought. In 'Newspeak', the word 'freedom' has thus lost its meaning of 'individual freedom' and can only be used in sentences like 'the dog is free from lice'. Although such conscious manipulation of language may be rare, there can be no doubt that the kind of insight introduced by Whorf may profitably be used to study ideology and power structures. In our kind of society, the shift from 'chairman' to 'chairperson' (or simply 'chair') and similar changes in language use indicate a growing con-sciousness about the ideological character of language and concepts.

A different approach to the relationship between knowledge and power is exemplified in the study of so-called secret societies. Initiation into such societies, common in several parts of the world, is accompanied by the acquisition of esoteric, highly valued knowledge. In some societies, such as dynastic China, literacy was seen as esoteric knowledge and kept away from the masses. In *Homo Academicus*, Bourdieu (1988) describes academic knowledge as a political resource of a similar kind. He describes the inaccessible language spoken by academics, the pompous rituals and conventions surrounding academic life in France – allegedly necessary for the 'advance of science' – as expressions of symbolic power.

The relationship between knowledge and social organisation can be illu-minated in many ways. For example, it is common to assume that culinary differentiation, particularly the development of 'haute cuisine', is connected with social differentiation and hierarchy. Everything which is taken for granted has a social origin, be it totemic classification, dogmatic belief in the blessings of liberal democracy, belief in God or the idea that one should eat with a knife and a fork. Karl Marx was profoundly aware of this kind of relationship when he wrote, in the mid-nineteenth century, that even the functioning of our five senses is a product of the whole of history up to this day.

This chapter has discussed a number of simple contrasts frequently invoked by anthropologists (especially in the past), between witchcraft accounts and scientific accounts, between the bricoleur and the engineer, between literacy and orality, between abstract linear time and concrete time, and ultimately between large-scale, 'modern' and small-scale, 'traditional' societies. This kind of dichotomy, which has never provided a satisfactory empirical description of the world, has been maintained for generations, at least partly because it facilitates the classification of social and cultural phenomena – if not entire societies. In the remaining chapters, this kind of dichotomous modelling is subjected to critical scrutiny, and both its strengths and limitations are made clear.

Suggestions for Further Reading

E.E. Evans-Pritchard: *Witchcraft, Oracles and Magic among the Azande*, abridged edition. Oxford: Oxford University Press 1983 (1937).
Alfred Gell: *The Anthropology of Time*. Oxford: Berg 1992.
Jack Goody: *The Domestication of the Savage Mind*. Cambridge: Cambridge University Press 1977.
Edmund Leach: *Lévi-Strauss*. Glasgow: Fontana 1970.
Gisli Pálsson, ed.: *Beyond Boundaries. Understanding, Translation and Anthropological Discourse*. Oxford: Berg 1993.

15 THE CHALLENGE OF MULTIPLE TRADITIONS

Now that the Polynesian islands have been clad in concrete and transformed into hangar ships anchored in the Pacific Ocean, when all of Asia is beginning to look like a polluted suburb, when cities of cardboard and sheet metal spread all over Africa, when civilian and military airplanes violate the untouched innocence of American and Melanesian forests even before they take away their virginity – what can the so-called flight from reality entailed by travelling then result in, other than confronting us with the most unfortunate aspects of our own history?

—*Claude Lévi-Strauss*

In earlier chapters, we looked at different forms of political organisation, world views and systems of economic production and distribution. It has repeatedly been noted that the ethnographic present, the tense conventionally used when anthropologists talk about different societies, is increasingly becoming a past tense (Davis 1992a). In Australia, 250 languages were spoken in the late eighteenth century. At the end of the twentieth century, there are about 30 left and, apart from English, few of them seem likely to survive for another generation. Virtually all inhabitants of the world live in states which define them as citizens (see Chapter 17), and a growing majority of the world's population depends on general purpose money in their daily life. At least nominally, more than half of the world's adult population is literate.

Urban Anthropology: Change and Continuity

One of the most visible aspects of social and cultural change in the period since the Second World War has been urbanisation. While less than 5 per cent of Africa's population lived in cities in 1900, about 50 per cent did in 1990, and the numbers for Asia and Latin America are of a similar order. There are several related causes of urbanisation. Population growth in the countryside and transitions from subsistence agriculture to the production of cash crops lead to a general land shortage and greater vulnerability; simultaneously, new opportunities for wagework arise in and near the cities. Most urban dwellers in non-industrial countries, however, are usually classified as poor, although their lot might not have been much better if they had stayed in the countryside.

A series of early studies of urbanisation in Africa has been very influential both theoretically and methodologically. The group of researchers collectively known as the Manchester School undertook an ambitious exploration of urbanisation in Southern Africa under the leadership of Godfrey Wilson and later Max Gluckman from the late 1930s to the 1960s.

Max Gluckman (1911–75) studied with Evans-Pritchard, but left for Rhodesia after the Second World War, where he was to play an important role in the so-called Rhodes-Livingstone school (later the Manchester school). Gluckman's early research was faithful to his teacher's analyses of segmentary lineages and political integration in acephalous societies, and he analysed politics among the Zulu, the Lozi and other peoples of Southern Africa. Through indicating how conflict and 'rituals of rebellion' could have an integrative effect, he added a dynamic dimension to classical structural-functionalism without abandoning its central tenets (*Custom and Conflict in Africa*, 1956; *Order and Rebellion in Tribal Africa*, 1963). Gluckman was also concerned with traditional law and judicial processes, and wrote the influential *Politics, Law and Ritual in Tribal Society* (1965). His influence on what was later to be known as the study of ethnicity was also considerable. Although Gluckman himself published little on the topic, he was an important source of inspiration for scholars who developed urban anthropology in Southern Africa and network analysis, including John Barnes, J. Clyde Mitchell and A.L. Epstein.

The development of the copper industry in North Rhodesia (today's Zambia) led to a great need for labour from the early decades of the twentieth century. The industry was concentrated in a 'belt' in the north-eastern region, known as the Copperbelt, and the miners often had to travel far to get to work. In the mining towns, they lived in barracks not intended for family life. Unlike many West African cities, such as Ibadan or Timbuktu, as well as coastal East African cities like Mombasa and Zanzibar Town, the towns in this part of the continent were founded and populated very quickly; they had no 'traditional sector' and no historical predecessors. There was thus a sharp social and cultural discontinuity between the towns and the outlying countryside. The mine-owners assumed that they could send the workers back to their villages in periods when their labour was not needed; this did not eventually come about, however. The labour migration, intended to be seasonal, led to a partial depopulation of the rural areas, and eventually entire families lived more or less permanently in the mining towns. A permanent proletarisation of a former farmer population had taken place.

In the first anthropological study of urbanisation in the Copperbelt, Godfrey Wilson (1941–2) introduces the term de-tribalisation; in other words, he emphasises the qualitative change in social integration entailed by urbanisation. From being kinship-based subsistence producers, the workers become individual participants in the world economy, he writes, describing this society as

a community in which impersonal relations are all-important; where business, law and religion make men dependent on millions of other men whom they have never met; a community articulated into races, nations and classes; in which the tribes, no longer almost worlds in themselves, now take their place as small administrative units; a world of writing, of specialized knowledge and of elaborate technical skill. (G. Wilson 1941, p. 13; quoted in Hannerz 1980, p. 124)

Wilson also notes a change in the value-orientation of the proletarianised Africans, remarking that the Africans of Broken Hill are neither a cattle people nor a fishing people, but a 'dressed' people. In town, clothes became an object of investment, a kind of special purpose money, an expression of individualism through conspicuous consumption and an expression of an emulation of a European lifestyle.

While Wilson in this early study concentrated on describing change, J. Clyde Mitchell later focused on the relationship between change and continuity in the small monograph *The Kalela Dance* (1956). The Kalela dance was performed every Sunday afternoon by labour migrants belonging to the Bisa people in the town of Luanshya. They were dressed in modern clothes and the dance did not form part of their traditional cultural repertoire. However, the dance and songs were definitely markers of 'tribal' group identity. Although the kin groups and tribal forms of organisation did not have a significant practical role in the towns, group identity was frequently overcommunicated; that is, it was given special emphasis in contexts of interaction. Moreover, the contrast with other groups became more visible here than it had been in the countryside. In towns, people categorised each other according to their place of origin (a criterion which had only rarely been relevant earlier), and many of the new forms of association made possible by the town – peer groups, clubs, etc. – were based on ethnic membership. Mitchell notes, significantly, that the notion of 'tribe' and group membership continues to be important after urbanisation, but that its significance changes in response to shifts in the overall social organisation.

Many later studies of urbanisation and change have taken their cue from the studies carried out by the Manchester school. In a study of political organisation among Hausa in the Yoruba city of Ibadan, Abner Cohen (1969) shows how cultural symbols and traditional principles of social organisation change in meaning, but remain important, when they are moved from a traditional to a modern context. To mention a couple of further examples, David Lan (1985) has shown how traditional spirit mediums and old myths gained a new significance during the civil war in Zimbabwe (in the late 1970s) and provided legitimacy to entirely new political institutions, notably the guerrilla movement; whereas Richard Wilson (1991) has provided a similar kind of analysis of political mobilisation in marginal, Indian-populated highland Guatemala, where he shows that local political entrepreneurs may innovatively draw on both local and foreign symbols and sources of legitimacy in their bid to mobilise the local population in the initially alien modern political sphere.

In situations of change, there are certain aspects of culture and social organisation which alter, and certain aspects which do not. What changes and what does not is an empirical question: there is no general answer to it.

Conceptualising Complexity

Urban anthropology in Southern Africa raised methodological issues which became increasingly relevant from the late 1950s onwards, as fewer anthropologists now studied relatively isolated villages or local communities. In a city it is practically impossible for a researcher to develop an overview of the entire social universe. Many encounters with informants are brief, and there are many members of society one has no chance of ever meeting. Obviously, it is something quite different to study social relations in Luanshya or, for that matter, New York, than it is to spend a year in a village in Kiriwina. In order to solve some of the methodological problems raised, the Manchester school developed a rigorous methodology to study social networks (see Chapter 5). They also proposed the extended case study as an alternative to the traditional, holistic style of inquiry. A case study would characteristically focus on an important public event, drawing conclusions about the wider social and cultural context on the basis of intensive exploration and interpretation of that event and its wider ramifications. *The Kalela Dance* was a typical case study along such lines.

In urban anthropology and, more generally, anthropology in modern societies, it is impossible to find out everything about everybody, due to the complexity and size of the societies concerned; in a word, their scale. Modern societies are large and highly differentiated.

There are several ways of approaching this problem. One possible solution is the case study. Another, related approach consists of focusing on a strictly delineated topic, such as the downward mobility of parts of the North American middle class in the 1980s (Newman 1988). One may also choose to concentrate on a restricted topic *and* a delineated physical field, as in Marianne Gullestad's monograph on gender and everyday life in a suburb of Bergen (1984). A third strategy could be to single out a small group in a complex society, for example an ethnic minority (such as Okely 1983). Usually such studies have to give a great deal of attention to the relationship between the group and the outside world, and may thereby shed light on a wider context in roughly the same way as a case study does.

A study combining several of these approaches is David William Cohen's and E.S. Atieno Odhiambo's monograph on Siaya (1989). Siaya is an area in western Kenya, largely populated by Luo speakers, that is a classic labour power reservoire in the capitalist sector of the Kenyan economy. About 475,000 people live in the region; another 134,000 were born there but live elsewhere, usually as wageworkers. Many households in Siaya are dependent on economic contributions from family members who work in Nairobi and elsewhere; the latter are, in return, dependent on food supplies from home. Daily life in Siaya is thus inextricably inter-twined with the lives of migrants and the workings of large-scale Kenyan society and, at a further remove, the global economy. The example of Siaya thus shows how local life is interconnected with large-scale social and cultural processes.

First, labour migration has led to significant social and cultural changes locally. Second, the national educational system, the growing social scale and the new occupational opportunities have created a Luo middle class and new forms of internal social differentiation.

Third, urban Luos have developed their own political organisations in Nairobi (Parkin 1969), and there are indeed parts of Nairobi which may be analytically included in Luoland. Fourth, Kenyan authorities have reserved an area in the highlands, far from the traditional tribal area of the Luo, for their use. This has led to a further dispersal of the population and, doubtless, a stronger social integration into the Kenyan nation-state.

Fifth, the location of Siaya close to the Ugandan border has provided ample opportunities for local entrepreneurs. From the 1940s onwards, many people from Siaya took well-paid seasonal work in Uganda. During the 1970s, this changed. Under the rule of Idi Amin (1970–9), the Ugandan economy fared poorly and labour migration was no longer an option for Kenyans. Still, the flow of values across the border did continue, this time through smuggling. The Ugandan shilling was unstable, and Kenyan currency was highly valuable in Uganda. Tea, coffee, outboard motors, stereo equipment and other commodities were sold across the border in large quantities, and people in Siaya made large profits.

This border trade, much of it illegal, also had consequences for the larger system it was placed in. Among other things, it was said that the smuggling of petrol from Uganda in the late 1970s was an important con-tributing factor to the downfall of Idi Amin.

Siaya is in many ways typical of the world in the late twentieth century. Geographical and social mobility have increased, as has social differentia-tion. Ethnic self-consciousness has been strengthened due to the increased contact with the outside world (see Chapters 16–17), and the pattern of consumption has changed. The boundaries between Siaya and the external world are no longer unambiguous. In a certain sense, Cohen and Odhiambo write, Siaya exists in Nairobi too; while aspects of Kenya, and of the wider world, exist in Siaya.

Colonialism and Local Responses

The encounter with global forces of modernity is worldwide, irreversible and ongoing. Some have argued that processes of modernisation leave few opportunities for local communities to choose their own direction of change. Doubtless, contact between 'Stone Age' peoples and industrial

society always has some dramatic and frequently painful aspects. Historically, the encounter between traditional and modern societies has
often taken place in the context of colonialism, and large-scale massacres
of militarily weaker groups form part of this history. On the other hand,
it would seriously underestimate the abilities of 'traditional peoples' if they
were to be regarded merely as helpless victims of the avalanche of
modernity. The encounter may take various forms and may be conceptualised in several ways.

The Trobriand Islanders are often mentioned as a 'traditional' people
who have succeeded in incorporating elements of modernity such as
general purpose money without losing aspects of traditional culture and
social organisation which they see as important. Back in the 1920s
Malinowski wrote in *Argonauts* that it would probably only be a question
of a few years before the kula trade and the ritual exchange of yams
vanished, as missionaries and traders had already begun to arrive at
Kiriwina in his time. Seventy years later, it seems that important parts of
Trobriand culture – including the kula trade and yam exchange – have
survived, although the changes have been formidable. A famous expression
of the Trobriander ability to incorporate new phenomena into pre-existing
meaning structures can be seen in the ethnographic film *Trobriand Cricket*
(J.W. Leach and Kildea 1974), which shows that Trobrianders use cricket
as a ritual way of communicating enmity and competition between
matriclans, and that they have modified the rules to adapt it to local circumstances. Cricket is thereby used to strengthen traditional clan identity.
On the other hand, it is clear that Trobriand culture is far from unchanged
after its colonial encounter.

A different kind of reaction to modernisation is represented in the so-
called cargo cults of Melanesia and Polynesia (Worsley 1968). These
millenary political or religious cults first emerged as a result of increased
contact with the outside world after the First World War, and some are
much more recent. They have a double aim: to re-establish traditional
authority and to achieve control of the immense wealth of the foreigners
(mostly Americans). In this, such movements represent, at the ideological level, a happy marriage, as it were, between the old and the new. For
as Roosens (1989) has remarked, indigenous peoples may wish to retain
important aspects of their tradition, but they also tend to want modern
commodities. Often, it must be added, neither aim is achieved.

One famous cargo cult is the John Frum movement in the New Hebrides
(Worsley 1968, pp. 152–60). At the cultural level, it can be described as a
mixture of Christianity, indigenous religion and consumerism. Many of
the members of the movement were nominal Christians but were disappointed by the modest returns of Christianity, which chiefly offered
prayers and songs with no tangible consequences. Early in the 1940s
therefore, Tanna men began organising meetings where they awaited
messages from the prophet John Frum. He was expected to liberate them
from the colonial domination of the British, re-establish the outlawed traditional customs, introduce a new currency 'with a coconut stamp' and

ensure abundance of material goods (cargo). Among the magical paraphernalia used by the members of the cult was the Bible, which was
assumed to have magical properties since it always seemed to accompany
the cargo which arrived by ship and plane at the island. The movement
was banned and a man suspected of being John Frum was arrested.
However, it continued to flourish and it is still active in the 1990s.

This man, a 'big man' in Tanna (New Hebrides), leads a cargo cult
in the island. He is holding a picture of Prince Philip, who is revered
as a high spiritual being by the cult. (Photo: Øyvind Vigestad)

How should such millenarian movements be understood? Are they
merely functional techniques for re-establishing mental balance in periods
marked by uncertainty and turbulence? Worsley (1968) does not think so.
He rather sees the cults as rational attempts to reform and adapt tradi-

tional society to new circumstances. It may of course be said that they do not provide the results called for, but on the other hand the reasoning of the John Frum movement is as logical as the Zande witchcraft institution, seen within the context of local knowledge and experience.

The widespread frustration which is a necessary condition for millenarian movements to arise is generally based on a discrepancy between culturally defined aims and available means: people want, for example, prosperity and political self-determination, but have no established methods for achieving these goals. There is a locally perceived gap between cultural lifestyle ideals and social reality, which is clearly a result of colonialism and increased contacts between 'the West' and indigenous peoples. In this context, it is often retorted that many peoples actually had shorter life expectations and suffered greater material hardships before colonialism. On the other hand, the *perception* of scarcity is greater today, since people are taught – through school, advertising, mass media and direct encounters – to compare themselves with a European or North American middle-class way of life. Although many Melanesians are better off in absolute terms today than they were 100 years ago, they may be worse off in relative terms. They have been relatively deprived. Poverty becomes a greater problem the moment wealth is perceived as a definite possibility.

Ways of Conceptualising Encounters

In the social sciences, it has been common to regard encounters between rich, Northern and poor, Southern peoples either in terms of modernisation or in terms of imperialism (see also Chapter 12). The former perspective, exemplified in the work of the development economist Walt Rostow (1965), presupposes a unilineal evolutionary view according to which the poor countries would eventually 'catch up with' the 'developed world'. Economic and political contact between North and South would then be beneficial, since it would lead to the 'development' of the Southern countries.

The other main view, which is influenced by Lenin's and Trotsky's analyses of imperialism, instead emphasises the ways in which the rich countries exploit the poor ones and that economic and political contact does not lead to the 'development' of the latter, but instead to their active underdevelopment. Large state debts, low prices put on the goods the poor countries sell (mostly raw materials) and the extraction of profits by multinational companies are symptoms of this situation of structural inequality (see for instance Frank 1979). Thus the decolonisation of the postwar decades did not lead to the true independence and emancipation of poor countries, since they were tied up with a global capitalist system where they were bound to lose. At the level of culture, moreover, writers influenced by the theory of neo-imperialism have argued that formerly colonised peoples become dependent on the models and knowledge systems of the former colonisers.

Anthropological perspectives on these processes differ, as we have seen, from the models of global systems. Although anthropologists may draw insights from the grand theories of development or underdevelopment, their main concern has been to show local variations in the encounters between different systems of knowledge and cultural practices. Detailed ethnographies describing colonial and postcolonial situations have indicated a need for a more nuanced understanding than that provided by the general models of global relationships. Olivia Harris (in press), writing on cultural complexity in Latin America and particularly the Andean area, has proposed a typology depicting variations in the ways in which social encounters between knowledge systems can be conceptualised.

First, she describes the model of mixing or creolisation, sometimes described as syncretism, hybridity or, in Latin America, *mestizaje*. This model, which is still used (see Chapter 18), shows how new meanings are generated from the mixing of diverse influences. What Harris sees as problematic about this is that it 'presupposes fixed points of origin for the cultures which then mix' rather than regarding the creation of meaning, in her view more accurately, as an ongoing process with no fixed starting-point or end-point.

The second model is the one of colonisation, which in the South American and Andean context implies European dominance, exploitation and violence towards Indians, including the enforced introduction of Christianity and the Spanish language. This model is strongly dualist and somewhat mechanical in its notion of power and, in Harris's view, draws a rather too strict line between European and Indian culture, reifying ('freezing') both in the act.

Third, an alternative to the rigid model of colonisation implies the attribution of 'more agency to the colonised' and a phrasing of 'the relationship in terms of borrowing'. The traditions remain discrete, but Indian elites (Harris refers particularly to Incas and Mayas) borrow knowledge from the Christians.

The fourth model is 'that of juxtaposition or alternation, where two radically different knowledge systems are both accepted without a direct attempt at integration'. Since, for example, Maya and Christian cosmologies entailed fundamentally different conceptualisations of time and of the past, they could not be mixed, but actors could draw situationally on either.

The fifth way of conceptualising the meeting is 'that of imitation, assimilation or direct identification', whereby persons self-consciously reject their own past and adopt a self-identity and knowledge system they perceive as better or more beneficial to themselves. A conversion from Indian to mestizo identity in the Andes, Harris notes, 'usually involves wholesale rejection of Indian identity, in favour of and identification with what is seen as white or Hispanic'.

The sixth and final mode discussed by Harris is that of 'innovation and creativity', where 'attention is firmly removed from contrasted knowledge systems and priority is given to autonomy and independent agency'. Unlike the five other models sketched, this kind of conceptualisation does not focus on origins.

If we look at Pacific cargo cults in relation to this typology, it becomes clear that several of the models may generate some understanding of them, and they are not mutually exclusive. In his classic study, Worsley (1968) emphasised the unequal power entailed by colonialism (the second model), the creativity of the Melanesians in coping with the new circumstances and their self-conscious borrowing of cultural traits (such as the Bible) from the Europeans.

Medical Systems

Medical anthropology is a growing sub-discipline dealing with cultural knowledge and practices about the body, health and illness. Commonly, medical anthropologists distinguish between three 'bodies', the personal, the social and the political (Scheper-Hughes and Lock 1987), all of which are socially constructed. Although the body, of course, does in an important sense exist biologically, it is imbued with cultural meanings.

Many medical anthropologists have concentrated their attention on the empirical relationship between 'Western medicine' and 'indigenous medical systems'. Although several practitioners tend to polemicise against Western medicine rather than studying it as a cultural system, the most common perspective among medical anthropologists is probably expressed in Harris's fourth model, which indicates the presence of two (or several) mutually exclusive knowledge systems which remain discrete. As mentioned in the last chapter, Mauritians who suffer from some ailment draw pragmatically on the services of medical personnel who relate to radically different, and frequently contradictory, notions about health, illness and treatment. The 'Western' medical system recognises a distinction between body and mind, for example, which is not deemed relevant within the Indian ayurvedic school. In European societies, it is also clear that many inhabitants – immigrants as well as natives – relate to distinct knowledge systems pragmatically when faced with a practical problem such as a disease, without trying to mix them cognitively or in practice.

A different model, which could perhaps be classified as a creolisation model in Harris's scheme, is represented in Robert Welsh's (1983) work among the Ningerum of New Guinea. The Ningerum are described as a 'very traditional people' who nevertheless have accepted 'Western medicine' without much ado and integrated it into their pre-existing system of knowledge. Traditionally, the Ningerum had a wide repertoire of treatments for different ailments; some complaints could be cured by anyone, while others had to be treated by specialists. Since 1963, the Ningerum have had access to a dispensary staffed by nurses drawing on a Western medical system for diagnosis and treatment. The introduction of new knowledge and new skills was easily accepted, and actively appropriated, by the Ningerum, and moreover it did not seem to alter their traditional practices, which coexisted happily with the Western medical system. Two main factors account for this painless appropriation of new knowledge. First, Ningerum nurses were trained to staff the dispensary, so it was not run by outsiders for very long. Second, the new medical practices did not interfere with the indigenous knowledge system, which – contrary to Western medicine – held that the causes of disease were always external to the body (spirits and ghosts, bad food, etc.). Treatment, in their view, would either stop the external agent or strengthen the body. To the extent that the injections and pills offered by the dispensary had positive effects on the disease, they were easily accepted along with the other kinds of treatment the Ningerum had at their disposal.

The lesson from this example may be that 'meaning is use'. To the Ningerum, it made little difference that Western medicine presupposed a cosmology and knowledge system quite distinct from their own, as long as the treatment functioned satisfactorily. On the other hand, it could be argued that the assimilation of the alien knowledge might be more difficult if Ningerum were to become medical doctors. If so, the cosmologies and not merely the practices would be confronted directly.

Medical anthropology, and the anthropology of the body in a wider sense, has a considerable potential for dealing with several classic anthropological problems in novel ways. It can shed important light on cultural dynamics in polyethnic societies, not least among immigrants in rich countries (Lock 1990); as the New Guinean example showed, it can give fresh perspectives on questions of relativism, including those in relation to development issues; and, moreover, medical anthropological research is at the forefront of cross-cultural research on concepts of personhood (see also Chapter 3).

We now turn to considering an encounter between cultural logics in the context of a development project. The following case adds to the complexity of cultural encounters, and additionally shows the importance of understanding culture and society when attempts are made to implement change through 'aid' or development programmes.

An Anthropological Perspective on 'Development'

Because of the methodological cultural relativism of the subject, it is difficult for anthropologists to see any intellectual value in a concept of 'development' which defines it, for example, as GNP (Gross National Product) per capita. Analytically, this kind of model is unacceptably evolutionist and reductionist, since it ranks societies on an ethnocentrically defined ladder as well as disregarding local, culturally specific value judgements. Among cattle nomads in East Africa, it may thus not be rational to produce as many animals as possible, slaughter them and make as big a profit as one can. For several of these groups, it is more highly valued to have a large herd than to have much money. Cattle with unusually large horns may have a special ritual value, and cattle are indispensable as bridewealth.

The cultural relativism inherent in anthropological methodology does not necessarily mean that anthropologists by default will be critical of development projects. It does imply, however, that an awareness of social and cultural variation is necessary for such projects to be meaningful. We have to take into account the fact that notions of 'quality of life', 'progress' and 'development' are locally constructed. The role of anthropologists in development projects has therefore tended to consist of providing a local context for the projects; explaining to the other professions involved (engineers, economists and others) what is unique about the locality in question.

A project in Ecuador, supported by the World Bank and led by the Ecuadorian Ministry of Agriculture, attempted to modernise and 'rationalise' the production of guinea-pigs in the rural highlands (Archetti 1992a). Guinea-pigs had been bred for centuries, and it was held that an improvement of the techniques for production might improve the standard of living of the producers. The programme nevertheless failed at an early stage, and an anthropologist, Eduardo Archetti, was hired to explore what had gone wrong.

Traditionally, guinea-pigs were kept inside the local people's huts, more specifically in the kitchen. The feeding of the animals was unsystematic, there was widespread inbreeding and it was difficult to avoid the spread of disease. The development agents suggested that cages should be built, so that the guinea-pigs could be separated by gender, fed regularly and mated in such ways that degeneration could be avoided. In the beginning, the breeders were to receive the technical equipment free of charge. Nonetheless, very few villagers accepted the offer. The Ecuadorian Ministry of Agriculture was disappointed.

Archetti quickly discovered that guinea-pigs were not just defined as any kind of food: they were a *special* kind of food, simultaneously pets and edible animals. They had an important symbolic place in the lives of the villagers. Guinea-pigs were not eaten daily, but only at special occasions such as rites of passage, religious feasts and in connection with healing. The guinea-pig had special qualities (and may in this regard be compared to the pangolin among the Lele). It was also seen as an oracle which could divine the weather and interpret social events. For this reason, it was important to have one's guinea-pigs nearby. Animals which were mildly disfigured, for example because they had an extra toe (possibly as a result of inbreeding), were considered unusually wise creatures.

In addition, it is a fact that the new method of production entailed a considerable extra burden for the already overworked Quechua women. To the women, it was thus not rational to change their techniques of production, since the proposed changes ran contrary to established local values.

Are Europeans and North Americans more rational than the Quechua women? Hardly. As Sahlins (1976) has pointed out, North Americans consider themselves rational, but they very rarely eat cats, dogs and horses, which would be a sensible thing to do from a nutritional perspective. The point is not, therefore, whether a group is 'rational' or not, but rather that there are different, culturally determined ways of defining rationality or common sense.

Is Anthropology Inherently Conservative?

After having completed his study of humans and guinea-pigs, Archetti did not draw the simple conclusion that 'cultures must be left alone' or that any attempt at tampering with long-established cultural values is either doomed to fail or is an expression of evil cultural imperialism. However, and this is his point, if such attempts are to be successful it is essential that the actors themselves must agree that the proposed changes serve their interests. Those interests, or aims, may of course change, but at this stage, he concludes, it is necessary to 'try to understand the guinea-pig in its social and symbolic totality' (Archetti 1992a, p. 153).

In relation to questions of development and cultural change, anthropology may be regarded as an inherently conservative discipline. The reason is that both social and cultural anthropology have always (i) emphasised the study of interrelationships and sociocultural wholes, and (ii) insisted on an attitude of cultural relativism, according to which any society or culture can, when all is said and done, only be understood in its own terms. From such a vantage-point, it seems only natural that changes instigated from the outside are potentially destructive.

This attitude is altering within the anthropological community. For what, really, are the 'own terms' of a society if women and men, young and old, urbanites and farmers in the same community disagree about the direction of change? In the study of guinea-pig breeding, Archetti points out that there is not just one Ecuadorian ideology about guinea-pigs, but several, and that the conflict between the Ministry of Agriculture and the rural women might well be understood as a conflict within Ecuadorian society. As a consequence, it becomes absolutely necessary to admit that societies or cultures are neither tightly integrated, unchanging nor closed systems. They change and interact with the outside world. Nevertheless, no matter how 'global' the influences from the outside may be, the responses are always local, and we have seen several examples of local ways of handling imposed changes from the outside world (see also Chapter 18).

Change and sociocultural complexity also present peculiar methodological challenges to anthropology. Some of these problems are today part and parcel of many, if not most, anthropological research projects. This added complexity does not mean that earlier work has become obsolete, but rather that it must be supplemented by new perspectives in both theory and methodology.

Decolonising the Anthropological Mind

With anthropological studies of minorities, labour migration, urbanisation, development issues and sociocultural processes in the context of nation-states and sub-cultures in industrial societies, it may seem as though anthropology is on its way home. The discipline began as the study of 'the Other'; it now increasingly includes the study of 'ourselves', or to put it more accurately: the boundaries between 'us' and 'them' are becoming blurred.

Today anthropological research is increasingly becoming available to its 'objects' as they acquire literacy and as an educated middle class capable of reading anthropological studies develops. This forces researchers to take their 'objects of study' seriously in ways which were formerly unnecessary. This development has also led to a growing understanding of the peculiar historical and ideological circumstances which led to the growth of anthropology, perhaps particularly in Europe. There the discipline entered into new domains along with French and British colonial expansion. The anthropologist, in the view of many, was an accomplice of colonialism, and the professional interest developed in the subject – on both sides of the Atlantic – may be seen to reflect domestic concerns at least as much as it reflects the concerns of 'the Other' (Marcus and Fischer 1986; Kuper 1988). Anthropologists also contribute to the making of history: their perspectives and interpretations contribute to defining the world in a particular way. There are therefore quite a few states in the 'Third World' which tend to deny access to anthropological fieldworkers because the anthropological emphasis on cultural variation is at odds with their development strategies, but also because they see it as their own right to write their own contemporary history. By no means every government in 'the developing world' is content with depictions of their country stressing the existence of headhunters, gift economies, traditional oral religions or unique initiation rituals among their citizens.

The historian and literary theorist Edward Said (1978) has criticised classic European philological and historical scholarship about Asia for propagating an image of 'the Orient' as mystical and tantalising, but profoundly irrational. If the history of the Orient were to be written by Orientals themselves, the result would be quite different – not least because we speak of an area stretching at least from Turkey to Japan. Said argues that the Western researchers have reproduced stereotypes of 'the Oriental' in their production of myths about themselves, about the 'Western world' as the cradle of progress, rationality and science. Tzvetan Todorov (1989) shows, in a similar vein, how descriptions of 'primitives' in France have closely followed domestic discourse about politics and social philosophy, and he intimates that they indeed tell us more about France than about 'the Other'. This kind of criticism is taken very seriously by many anthropologists, yet as Jean-Claude Galey (1992) argues, Orientalism and anthropology may have shared origins, but they have developed quite distinct methods and ways of conceptualising society and culture. Generally speaking,

speaking, Orientalism may nevertheless be seen as a fundamental mode of misrepresenting others, to which anthropologists are no less prone than other commentators.

As regards India in particular, Ronald Inden (1990), writing from within 'Orientalism', has documented in great detail how conceptualisations of Indian society and culture have owed more to European preoccupations than to Indian society itself. Veena Das (1994), a member of India's Subaltern Studies Group, (which is concerned with the development of postcolonial social science in the country) (see Guha 1989), argues that India cannot be represented as if the country itself were silent. Unlike their predecessors, she says, contemporary social scientists cannot lay claims to absolute truths, but 'can only insert their voices within a plurality of voices in which all kinds of statements – prescriptive, normative, descriptive, indicative – are waging a virtual battle about the nature of Indian society and the legitimate space for social sciences in this society' (Das 1994, p. 143).

To be fair, it should be added that many 'metropolitan' anthropologists have in recent years begun to study native history. In *Europe and the People without History*, Eric Wolf (1982) writes the history of the great 'discoveries' from the perspective of the 'discovered' peoples, and in *Islands of History* Sahlins (1985) compares Polynesian oral versions of history with written versions drawn up by foreigners, showing how they are all cultural interpretations of the same events and that the foreign histories are not necessarily more 'correct' than the native ones. Lévi-Strauss has, in line with this mode of reasoning, argued that history writing is the myth of our time because it, like oral myths, is based on an ideological interpretation of a very limited set of facts from the past (Lévi-Strauss 1966 [1962], Chapters 8–9). History writing, he argued in what was originally a polemic against Jean-Paul Sartre, is not a product of the past, but is rather created by the needs perceived by those who write history.

An analogous statement could be made about anthropology: it is not created by 'the Other', but by the interaction between anthropologists and 'the Other'. A consequence of processes of modernisation and decolonisation in the core areas of anthropology is the fact that our informants not only increasingly demand to be consulted on the content of our studies of them, but some of them also begin writing their own theoretical texts about their culture, history and society (Archetti 1994). This decentralisation (and some would say decolonialisation) of the discipline, although admittedly still modest, has led to new challenges for anthropologists in bringing us closer to our objects of study and, in some cases, engaging in a theoretical dialogue with them.

There exists an enormous anthropological, sociological and philosophical literature about modernity and modern society. Because of fieldwork, and because of its orientation towards non-European societies, anthropology has contributed important insights to the effect that 'modernity' and 'tradition' are not mutually exclusive, contrary to what Max Weber and other early theorists of modernity held. Modern politics, wagework and a modern state may well exist side by side with ancestral cults and lineage organisation, although there are bound to be tensions and contradictions within such complex societies. It has also been shown that people who live in 'modern' societies can retain important 'traditional' characteristics, such as, for example, nepotism and moral particularism, social cohesion at the community level and a wide range of religious beliefs ranging from virgin birth to sorcery. At the same time, there is no doubt that modernisation entails irreversible social and cultural change.

One seemingly paradoxical result of modernisation in many parts of the world is the emergence of 'traditionalist' movements praising the virtue of 'the ancestral culture'. Like cargo cults, such movements may be interpreted as strategies to come to terms with new social and cultural circumstances; adapting to the new without letting go of the old entirely and thereby creating a sense of continuity with the past in a rapidly changing world. In the following two chapters, we look into some such movements and processes in some detail.

Suggestions for Further Reading

David Lan: *Guns and Rain. Guerrillas and Spirit Mediums in Zimbabwe*. London: James Currey 1985.

Eric Wolf: *Europe and the People without History*. Berkeley: University of California Press 1982.

Peter Worsley: *The Three Worlds*. London: Weidenfeld & Nicolson 1984.

16   ETHNICITY

People become aware of their culture when they stand at its boundaries: when they encounter other cultures, or when they become aware of other ways of doing things, or merely of contradictions to their own culture.

—*Anthony P. Cohen*

A well-known musician from Finnmark, the Sami-dominated county in northern Norway, was once asked the following question by a journalist: 'Are you mostly a Sami or mostly a musician?' She tried to be accommodating and gave an answer to the question; if she had been an anthropologist, she would probably have regarded the question as absurd. This chapter, which outlines basic dimensions of ethnicity, explains why.

The Contemporary Ubiquity of Ethnicity

A cursory glance at major anthropological journals and monographs from, say, 1950 to 1994, will quickly reveal a change in the language of the subject. The terminology has generally become more influenced by hermeneutics and literary theory than by natural science during this period. Words such as 'function' and 'social structure' have become less common. Those like 'class', 'infrastructure' and 'contradiction' had a brief spell of popularity in the 1970s, while terms such as 'discourse', 'resistance' and 'symbolic capital' have steadily grown more popular since the early 1980s. Such terminological changes reflect shifts in the dominant perspectives of the subject, but they may also reflect changes in the outside world. The enormous interest in ethnicity which has developed since the late 1960s, and the growing interest in nationalism since the early 1980s, indicate some such changes. For one thing, a term like 'ethnic group', which has largely replaced that of 'tribe', simultaneously expresses that tribal organisation is no longer common and that anthropology no longer works from a rigid boundary between 'us' and 'them'. For ethnic groups (and nations) are omnipresent and exist in the anthropologist's own society as well as elsewhere.

Looking at the political situation in the world at the end of the twentieth century, the immediate impression is that most of the serious armed conflicts today have an important ethnic dimension. From Punjab to

Northern Ireland, from Tibet to Bosnia, from Sri Lanka to the former Soviet Union, there is conflict and competition between different ethnic groups regarding political sovereignty and control over territories. There are also other kinds of conflicts where ethnic groups emerge as corporate groups. Indigenous peoples and immigrant groups may, for example, demand the right to cultural survival and the right to equality with the majority, usually without demanding their own state.

Other ethnic conflicts are not expressed through institutional politics. Clashes between natives and immigrants in Germany, or between blacks and whites in the US, are usually enacted in day-to-day situations. In other words, ethnicity may be articulated at many levels of scale in complex societies.

Ethnicity does not necessarily entail conflict: it may be expressed in quite undramatic ways through everyday definitions of situations, through impression management, in religious cults and other peaceful phenomena. It can be identified at different levels of scale – from dyadic interaction to civil war.

The phenomenon of ethnicity is, in other words, a complex one. In everyday language, the concept 'ethnic group' is normally used to describe a minority group which is culturally distinguishable from the majority, and as such the term encompasses groups in very different situations – ranging from New York Jews to the Yanomamö in Brazil. In anthropology, the expression 'ethnic group' may also be used to describe majority groups, and ethnicity concerns the relationship between groups whose members consider each other culturally distinctive.

This is still rather vague. Let us therefore be more specific.

Communicating Cultural Difference

It is commonly held, not least among members of ethnic groups with a strong collective identity, that ethnicity has to do with 'objective cultural differences'. This would suggest that ethnicity becomes more important the greater the cultural differences are, and that the phenomenon is caused by the fact that different groups have lived in relative isolation from each other and have developed socioculturally in very different directions.

Anthropological research on ethnicity has shown this assumption to be false. In fact, ethnicity is frequently most important in contexts where groups are culturally close and enter into contact with each other regularly. Anthropology may therefore give an answer to a seeming paradox of our time, namely that whereas cultural differences in many regards become less apparent because of increased contact and the general processes of modernisation, ethnic identity and self-consciousness become increasingly important. The more similar people become, it seems, the more they are concerned with remaining distinctive.

Bateson (1979) has written that there must always be two of something to create a difference and thereby information. In line with this idea, we might say that the idea of an isolated ethnic group is absurd. It is through contact with others that we discover who we are, and an 'isolated ethnic group' may therefore be compared with the sound of one hand clapping – an absurdity. The fact that two groups are culturally distinctive does not create ethnicity. There must be at least a minimum of contact between their respective members. We therefore have to draw the conclusion that the members of different ethnic groups must have something in common – some basis for interaction – in addition to being different.

Ethnicity occurs when cultural differences are made relevant through interaction. It thus concerns what is socially relevant, not which cultural differences are 'actually there'. In an article on ethnic relations in Thailand, Michael Moerman (1965) has shown that many of his informants mention cultural particulars which they presume are characteristic of themselves but which they in fact share with neighbouring peoples. Indeed, a variety of criteria can be used as markers of cultural difference in interethnic situations – phenotype (appearance or 'race'), language, religion or even clothes. If any such marker is socially recognised as an indicator of an ethnic contrast, it matters little if the 'objective cultural differences' are negligible.

In an influential essay on the social nature of ethnicity, Fredrik Barth (1969) criticised a then influential view for being overly concerned with cultural content, or substance, instead of focusing on social processes in the study of ethnicity. Like Moerman (and Leach, Mitchell and others) before him, Barth emphasises that 'cultural traits' do not entail ethnicity, and suggests that the focus of research ought to be the social boundaries between groups rather than the 'cultural stuff' they contain. In fact, he says, there may be a continuous flow of people and information across ethnic boundaries even though they are maintained as boundaries. If such divisions are maintained, this must be because they have some social relevance. In the relationship between the sedentary Fur and the nomadic Baggara in the Sudan, for example, there is an economic complementarity. They are mutually dependent on commodity exchange and occupy complementary ecological niches. As Gunnar Haaland (1969) has shown, Fur may become Baggara by changing their way of life, just as Leach (1954) showed that Kachin could become Shan; but the ethnic boundary separating the groups remains untouched in the process.

Barth stresses the social process in his model of ethnicity, which provides an image of interethnic relationships as dynamic and negotiable. Ethnicity must therefore be seen as an aspect of a relationship, not as a property of a person or a group. The existence of the ethnic group thus has to be affirmed socially and ideologically through the general recognition, among its members and outsiders, that it is culturally distinctive. In addition, this cultural distinctiveness has to be related to social practices, such as religion, marriage (a rule of endogamy), language or work: for an ethnic identity to survive, it must be embedded in at least some of the social situations the actor goes through.

A further dimension of ethnicity, which was not dealt with in the volume edited by Barth but which has become politically important in many contemporary societies, is the appropriation of a shared history (Tonkin et al. 1989), that simultaneously functions as an origin myth, justifies claims to a common culture and serves to depict the ethnic group as an extended kin group.

Social Classification and Stereotypes

The studies of urbanisation in the Copperbelt (Chapter 15) are related to the line of reasoning presented systematically by Barth. In *The Kalela Dance* Mitchell clearly shows how ethnicity or 'tribalism' is expressed through a practical, everyday classification of persons. In the polyethnic situation of the mining towns of North Rhodesia, ethnicity did not have to be related to rank differences or an ethnically based division of labour. Rather, it expressed an internal cultural differentiation and emic concepts of relevant cultural differences, but it was ultimately based on social organisation in that the urbanites were still tied through kinship to their home village and traditional marriage rules. Ethnic classification, nonetheless, has something to do with the creation of order in the social environment by providing a division into 'kinds' of people. Such a classification may or may not be related to power disparities.

For a system of social classification to be effective, the actors have to believe in it. They must be convinced that there are relevant differences which distinguish their group from members of the other groups. A classification of persons into kinds of persons which stresses the commonalities of each kind and neglects their differences, depends on stereotypes to be efficient. Stereotypes are simplistic descriptions of cultural traits in other groups which are conventionally believed to exist. One may have stereotypes about workers, women and royal families; for instance, a common stereotypical idea about male homosexuals amounts to their being 'effeminate'. Phrases like 'Jews are greedy' or 'The French are passionate' express stereotypes: they refuse to take individual variations into account. Ethnic stereotypes are often morally condemning (as in 'Hindus are selfish', 'Never trust an Arab'), and such images of others may strengthen group cohesion, boundaries and one's self-perception. In polyethnic societies, people also commonly hold stereotypes about themselves; an example could be the Creoles of Mauritius (Eriksen 1988), who tend to describe themselves collectively as honest, generous folk in implicit contrast to other ethnic groups.

It is impossible to make a general statement about the relationship of stereotypes to 'facts'. They can be exaggerated, overly generalising and ideologically charged descriptions of social facts. When the Creoles of Mauritius describe the Hindus as miserly, this stereotype corresponds to one that Hindus hold of themselves as hard-working and responsible people. Stereotypes may also function as self-fulfilling prophecies. A dominating group may, for example, turn a dominated group into school dunces by systematically bombarding them with statements to the effect that they are born stupid.

There are also many stereotypes with no clear relationship to social facts. Accusations about cannibalism in many societies are typical examples: they are nearly always false (Arens 1978).

Stereotypes provide ideological legitimation of ethnic boundaries ('Don't marry one of those!') and strengthen group cohesion ('It's a good thing we're not like them'). When they are coupled with a rank system, stereotypes tend to support and strengthen it.

Ethnic Anomalies

In the study of classification and cosmology, the term 'anomaly' is used to describe animals, plants or other phenomena which do not fit into the social system of classification. The pangolin is an anomaly among the Lele (Douglas 1975), and the duck-billed platypus was seen as an anomaly within the Linnaean system of classification when it was discovered in the nineteenth century; as it is an egg-laying mammal with a duck's beak.

Anomalies occur in social classification as well. An anomaly in an ethnic system of classification may, for example, be a poor Syrian in Trinidad, where wealth is seen as a defining characteristic of Syrians. A highly educated Gypsy would appear as an anomaly in many European societies, where Gypsy identity is symbolically tied to low education. In many societies, moreover, children of ethnically mixed marriages are considered anomalies.

In certain polyethnic societies, entire categories of people may be seen as anomalous. In Trinidad, the chief contrasting pair of the ethnic system of classification is the Afro-Trinidadian/Indian contrast. The children of mixed African/Indian unions are locally known as 'douglas' (which is Bhojpuri for 'bastard') and tend to be placed in an uncomfortable position oscillating between 'both–and' and 'neither–nor' in the system of classification. In Mauritius, a similar dilemma characterises the situation of the 'gens de couleur' or 'mulattoes': people of mixed African/European origin. They are not allowed to join the ethnic community of Mauritian whites, nor are they generally perceived as good Creoles by the black Creoles (of African descent). Frequently, they are described by black working-class Creoles as 'kreol fer blan' – Creoles who try to be white.

Seen from a systemic perspectives, ethnic anomalies are helpless 'victims' of an hegemonic system of classification. Viewed from an actor perspective, however, they may sometimes be regarded as ethnic entrepreneurs who succeed in being both, say, Indian and African and switching strategically between these identifications (Eriksen 1993).

Situational Ethnicity

An important insight from the studies of the Copperbelt is the fact that ethnicity is relative and to some extent situational. As Mitchell expresses it (1966), a man may behave as a tribal in some situations and as a wageworker in others. For a North Indian Brahmin in an English city, it would be deeply insulting if a native English person were to classify him in the same category as persons he perceived as 'pitch-black' immigrants from Jamaica (in the broad category of 'non-white immigrants'). He might see himself as a white, 'clean' person, and would perhaps try to convince the native English person that he rightly belonged to a different category from the Jamaican. Such a negotiation over identity may be regarded as a struggle between different views of what the world looks like in ethnic terms, as competition between ideological descriptions of the world, or even as competition between world views. Some groups, who may be the victims of damaging ethnic stereotypes, may try to argue the irrelevance of ethnic distinctions or to challenge the prevailing stereotypes, much in the manner of the Pan caste of Bisipara (Chapter 10), switching strategically from trying to exploit the system to their own advantage to rejecting the entire caste system.

The situational aspect of ethnicity has been explored by many anthropologists. In a study of ethnic relations on the sub-Arctic north Norwegian coast, Harald Eidheim (1971) has shown how ethnicity is made relevant in various ways, in various kinds of situations, between Norwegians and Sami. Here he introduces the concepts of dichotomisation and complementarisation to describe fundamental ethnic processes. Dichotomisation refers to the articulation of ethnic relationships through mutual negations: the Sami define themselves in direct contrast to the non-Sami (usually the Norwegian). Complementarisation, rather, gives an expression of ethnic relationships within a shared language where both groups appear as culturally distinctive and as structurally equivalent. Dichotomisation is expressed through stereotypes where the other group is seen as inferior ('the Sami are dirty', etc.), while complementarisation is expressed through the school system, where both Norwegian and Sami history is taught. In complementarisation, the members of one group will compare themselves directly with the other group, stating, for example, that *we* have our history, religion, folk music and arts; while they, too, have *their* history, religion, folk music and arts. In this way, ethnicity contributes to making cultural differences comparable. Eidheim also showed the essential falseness of widespread stereotypes about the Sami. Contrary to what many Norwegians held, they were neither 'dirty', 'drunken' nor 'pagan'.

In the early 1960s the coastal Sami were a culturally stigmatised group, meaning that they were looked down upon by the dominant Norwegians. For this reason, they undercommunicated their ethnic identity in public contexts, in the shop, on the local steamer and so on. They then presented themselves as Norwegians, and overcommunicated what they saw as Norwegian culture to escape from the stigma. In private 'backstage' situations, however, they always spoke Sami and expressed their common identity.

A theoretical point from this kind of ethnicity studies is the fact that ethnicity is relational and processual: it is not a 'thing', but an aspect of a social process.

Ethnic Identity and Organisation

An important element in ethnic ideologies is the notion of the historical continuity of the group. By appealing to notions of shared tradition and history, such ideologies give the impression that the ethnic group is 'natural' and enjoys cultural continuity over a long period of time. In this way, every ethnic ideology offers a feeling of cultural belongingness and security. Such ideologies also, naturally, have a political dimension. Both ethnic identity (group identification) and ethnic organisation (politics) are important, complementary expressions of ethnicity. How strong the we-feeling is, and what a possible ethnic organisation or corporation has to offer its members, varies greatly, however. The fact that ethnicity occurs in a society gives us no indication of its relative importance in the everyday life or politics of that society. Ethnic identity may vary both situationally and in absolute terms, in the sense that one's ethnic membership may be socially relevant in a negligible number of contexts, and that one's self-perception is made up by many other elements as well as the ethnic one. For example, all North Americans except the indigenous populations are descendants of people who arrived from other continents quite recently, but in most cases this origin has little social relevance. To the Swedish-Americans of Minnesota, it may be the case two or three times a year that their ethnic identity is made visible through public rituals; for the rest of the year, they are ordinary and not hyphenated Americans. By contrast, in everyday life in a highland village in Guatemala the dichotomisation between Ladinos (of mixed origin and Spanish-speaking) and Maya Indians is very powerful, and nearly everything an individual does – from dress to food to language to work to body language – can easily be read by the other villagers as an expression of his or her ethnic membership (Nash 1988). The local community is, as it were, saturated with ethnicity.

There is no agreement among specialists as to which is more fundamental, ethnic identity or organisation. Some assume that identity, as 'we-feeling', is the most basic aspect of ethnicity and that ethnically based politics consists of transferring this collective emotional attachment to a new field. Abner Cohen, who has studied ethnicity in Nigeria, Sierra Leone and London (1969, 1981, 1993), represents the opposite position. In his view, ethnic organisation – the pursuit of group interests – is the very raison d'être of ethnic identity; he holds that the identity would vanish if it had no organisational focus, and that the ethnic cohesion as well as the we-feeling are actually created through social and political processes, especially in contexts of competition for scarce resources.

Research on ethnicity indicates that there are many variations here, although Cohen's view of ethnicity as an essentially political phenomenon is certainly valuable in the study of ethnicity in modern societies. Ethnicity, as it is enacted, is clearly a combination of both dimensions – the symbolic and the social or political. Clearly, ethnic ideologies depend on a cultural 'raw material' as a point of departure, although this 'raw material' may be manipulated. Some aspects of the identity base of ethnicity cannot, however, be manipulated. Obviously, Mauritian Hindu politicians who decide to exploit ethnicity in the quest for office will be unable to persuade a single voter that they are Hindus if they define themselves as Muslims. On the other hand, they may be able to persuade Hindus to vote along ethnic lines and may thus contribute to the formation of a corporate Hindu ideology.

It has also been argued that ethnic identities may continue to be important to their carriers even if they do not 'pay off'. The Creoles of Mauritius may provide an example: they are poorly organised politically, and define themselves in relation to ostensible cultural traits which make it difficult for them to compete with other groups in the labour market and in politics (Eriksen 1988). An important insight from Cohen and others who have studied ethnicity as a kind of political organisation is nevertheless that ethnicity attains its overall greatest importance when it is expressed as economic and political competition over scarce resources which both or all groups deem valuable.

There are thus degrees of ethnicity. Don Handelman (1977) has developed a typology of degrees of ethnic incorporation where he distinguishes between four levels; put in other terms, he classifies interethnic contexts as four distinctive degrees of social and cultural importance. His degrees of incorporation are as follows.

In the *ethnic category*, ethnicity as identity is reproduced over several generations through myths of origin and endogamy. Its social relevance outside the household and kinship levels of organisation is negligible.

The *ethnic network* is an interpersonal system of interaction, accompanied by a flow of value, which follows ethnic lines. For example, ethnic networks beyond the kinship level may be helpful in the search for a job, a house and a spouse.

The third level is the *ethnic association*, whose members are organised corporatively in certain respects. It consists of a goal-directed collective organisation which pursues shared goals defined on behalf of the ethnic group as a whole.

Finally, Handelman speaks of the *ethnic community*. Here we have an ethnic group with a clear territorial base. At this, highest level of ethnic incorporation, group members have shared interests in their ethnic identity, their ethnic networks, their ethnic associations and their shared territorial estate. It is obvious that a society where virtually all scarce resources are held by ethnic groups in this way becomes much more 'ethnified' – ethnicity becomes a more pervasive dimension in politics and everyday life – than societies where neither politics nor the division of labour are strongly correlated with ethnic distinctions. There are thus important differences in degree as to the relative importance of ethnicity.

Ethnicity and Rank

In polyethnic societies, as in others, a variety of criteria is available for the classification of people, and ethnic status never gives sufficient information to describe a person's position in a system of social classification. Ethnic categories or groups are internally differentiated according to gender, age and (often) class, and there are also other independent criteria for differentiation which have no direct relationship to ethnicity. We can illustrate this with an example from Mauritius, that polyethnic island-state in the south-western Indian Ocean (Eriksen 1988, 1992).

Both Rajiv and Kumar are Hindus around 30 years of age. Their respective positions in Mauritian society are nevertheless very different, and one may almost say that all they have in common, apart from gender and age, is their ethnic identity.

Rajiv belongs to the Babojee caste, which makes him a Brahmin; in other words, he is a member of one of the highest castes. He is the son of a wealthy merchant in Vacoas and is eventually expected to take over his father's business, where he now works. Rajiv is also expected to travel to India to find a wife from his own caste within a couple of years. He has a BA degree from the University of Lucknow. He speaks English and French in addition to Creole (his vernacular) and takes evening classes in Hindu. He owns a car. Many of Rajiv's friends and acquaintances belong to other castes; some even belong to other ethnic groups.

Kumar belongs to the Ravi Ved caste, which is one of the lowest castes in Mauritius. Like his father, he is an agricultural worker on a sugar estate in Flacq, and the family lives in a small rented house on the estate. Kumar is hardly literate and can make himself understood only in Bhojpuri (a rural Hindi dialect) and Creole, the low-status languages of Mauritius. He is married to a woman from the village and they have two children. Kumar's personal network largely consists of kinsmen, neighbours and colleagues from work, all of them low-caste Hindus like himself.

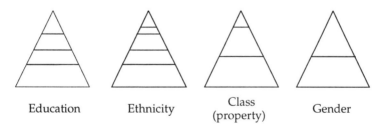

| Education | Ethnicity | Class (property) | Gender |

Figure 16.1: Four perspectives on rank in Mauritian society

According to a class analysis, Kumar belongs to the working class, while Rajiv belongs to the bourgeoisie. Their life-worlds are in many ways very different, and in this sense Kumar may have more in common with the Creoles who work in the sugar factory than with Rajiv. Nevertheless, they vote for the same party, the Hindu-dominated Labour Party.

There are political organisations and parties in Mauritius which hold that class differences and the rural–urban contrast are more fundamental than ethnic differences. Some of them have enjoyed some success in certain periods; for example, in the 1970s there were two general strikes where Creoles, Hindus and Muslims went on strike together against the state and the local capitalists, regardless of their ethnic membership. This illustrates the fact that the social relevance of ethnicity cannot be taken for granted, but is negotiable.

The example from Mauritius shows that ethnicity cuts across class. However, in many societies there is a strong correlation between ethnicity and class, so that some ethnic groups rank higher than others. Many Caribbean societies reveal such a pattern, where skin colour may frequently be read as an indication of class membership. In some places, moreover, it is possible to change one's ethnic membership as one changes one's class membership. In Peru, it may be de facto possible for Indians to become Ladinos if they acquire the way of life and external markers (dress, language) characteristic of the Ladinos (van den Berghe 1975). In Mauritius, Creoles may regard themselves as, and be regarded by others as, *gens de couleur* ('Coloured') if they acquire certain aspects of what is locally seen as a European way of life.

Both class and ethnicity are criteria for social differentiation and rank. As with the caste–class relationship discussed in Chapter 9, neither can be reduced to the other, but they do influence each other. For example, the Chinese of Trinidad, formerly a poor and somewhat despised group, have gradually become one of the richest ethnic groups in the island. As a result, people of mixed origin now tend to overcommunicate the 'Chinee' aspect of their identity. Although it is commonly assumed that ethnicity is ascribed while class is achieved, it may thus be possible to change one's ethnic membership in certain cases.

Gender is also a dimension of social differentiation which may influence the significance of ethnicity. Several anthropologists have pointed out how gender may create cross-cutting ties of loyalty, especially among women, who may develop female networks that cut across ethnic boundaries and thereby make them less rigid (Little 1978).

If the relationship between class and ethnicity is difficult to grasp analytically, it is no easier to understand fully the relationship between class and ethnicity on the one hand and gender on the other. It is obvious that a Mauritian woman who belongs to the Franco-Mauritian upper class in many ways ranks higher than a man who is a low-caste Hindu and plantation worker. At the same time, there are conceivable situations where his rank – or power – may be higher than hers, by virtue of his gender. If the public spheres of society – politics, notably – are male dominated, the Hindu worker may be able to participate and compete there, while she will be more or less strictly confined to 'Kinder, Küche und Kirche' (children, kitchen and church), namely the private sphere.

Ethnicity and class are to some extent comparable, since both phenomena are related to power discrepancies and competition in public space. Gender, on the contrary, cuts across both ethnicity and class and is not related to either of them in a simple way, yet it is important in a multitude of social situations. This is not the place, therefore, to decide which status is the most 'fundamental' out of class, gender and ethnicity. It is nevertheless a fact that the actors themselves in many societies regard ethnicity and gender as ascribed, and class as achieved. The ethnic status thereby appears as an imperative status, more compelling than other statuses. One can change one's class membership through social mobility; for most people, it is far more difficult (and sometimes impossible) to change one's ethnic membership.

Segmentary Identities

Ethnic organisation can only be including if it is also excluding, and ethnic identity is largely defined by contrasts with others. It has been suggested above that ethnicity cannot by itself define the social identity of a person. This is caused, among other things, by the fact that every person is a member of several groups, and only some of them are formed on the basis of ethnicity. For example, Cris Shore (1993) draws extensively on the theory of ethnic identification when he writes about communist identity construction in central Italy, a non-ethnic kind of identification which was nonetheless very important to the people involved and which resembled ethnicity in its functioning.

First, we may imagine the social identities of an actor as a series of Chinese boxes or concentric circles, which includes an increasing number of people as we move from the small to the large scale. As in the segmentary organisation of the Nuer (Chapter 10), the concrete situation decides which group one participates in; which community, rather, that is made relevant. To many of the inhabitants of Mauritius, their social identity as Mauritians became relevant only when the island began to attract large numbers of tourists, as well as becoming industrialised and starting to compete for markets on a global scale. Simultaneously, kinship and ethnic membership continue to play a part in many situations, such as marriage and politics, but in other regards they have been replaced by the more encompassing phenomenon of Mauritian citizenship. In kinship-based societies, a social level like the region or the state may be irrelevant to many of the inhabitants in most social situations, if their needs are by and large satisfied at lower levels of integration, such as those of the household, lineage or village.

Any person thus has many complementary social identities, and the context decides which of them is activated at any time. The model of segmentary identities serves as a reminder that identity is not fixed, is not 'innate', but is fashioned in the encounter between an individual and a social situation. The segmentary model may enable us to describe the social identities of a person as, say, citizen of the world, African, Kenyan, Kikuyu, someone from the Murang'a area, member of clan X, member of lineage A. However, as the discussion of segmentary identities in Chapter 10 indicated, individuals also have other identities which cut across a system of concentric circles. For example, a person may be 50 years old, a man, a spouse, a lawyer, a socialist, a stamp-collector and so on. He or she is a member of many groups with only partially overlapping membership. Which identity is assumed in a situation of conflict, when an individual must choose, say, between loyalty to the party and loyalty to the nation or ethnic group, is an empirical question.

The analytical perspectives on ethnicity outlined here have focused on the social construction and maintenance of ethnic boundaries, the use of history as myth to justify boundaries, the communication of cultural differences (which may be 'real' or 'fictitious') and the situational character of social identification. Several readers may feel that these views on ethnicity, while no doubt analytically useful, are overly dispassionate tools for dealing with a world torn by brutal conflicts often described as ethnic. It is true that anthropological models of ethnic relationships have rarely presupposed power asymmetry, although they do not preclude it. It is also true that the conceptualisation of ethnicity in this chapter has largely stressed the formal properties of ethnic relationships, rather than discussing, say, the civil war in Bosnia, racism in Western Europe or genocide in Guatemala. However, the standard anthropological perspectives on ethnic relationships *can* help us in understanding such conflicts, provided the analysis also takes the power relationships and the violent dimension into account.

It is characteristic of late-twentieth-century politics that ethnic identities are used in political legitimation. In Bolivia, rural non-governmental organisations (NGOs) put forward their claims to be the representatives of an oppressed class in the 1970s; the same groups now emphasise that they represent Aymara or Quechua Indians. The shift from class and gender analysis to the analysis of ethnic relationships mentioned at the outset of this chapter is clearly symptomatic of an ongoing ethnification of politics and identification in many parts of the world, which is a major topic in the remaining two chapters.

Suggestions for Further Reading

Fredrik Barth: Introduction, in Fredrik Barth, ed., *Ethnic Groups and Boundaries*. Oslo: Scandinavian University Press 1969.
Abner Cohen: *Two-dimensional Man*. London: Tavistock 1974.
Anthony P. Cohen: *The Symbolic Construction of Community*. London: Routledge 1985.
Hans Vermeulen and Cora Govers, eds: *The Anthropology of Ethnicity. Beyond 'Ethnic Groups and Boundaries'*. Amsterdam: Het Spinhuis 1994.

17 NATIONALISM AND MINORITIES

People in different parts of the world still utter different sounds, but nowadays they say more or less the same things everywhere.

—Ernest Gellner

Scarcely anyone who has travelled into the core areas of classic anthropological research since the 1960s can have avoided encountering expressions of nationalist ideology. The growth of nationalism and nation-building is an important, spectacular and highly consequential dimension of the global processes of change connected with colonialism and decolonisation. Nationalism is a kind of ideology which exists almost everywhere in the world, although it assumes very different forms. This does not mean that all the citizens of any state know about, or for that matter support, nationalist ideology – but it implies that nationalism is a cultural phenomenon of such importance that both anthropology and other social sciences have since about 1980 seen it as a main priority to try to come to grips with it analytically.

Nationalism and Modernity

In anthropology, nationalism is usually defined as an ideology which holds that cultural boundaries should correspond to political boundaries; that is to say, that the state ought to contain only people 'of the same kind' (Gellner 1983). All nationalism champions, in one way or the other, the congruence between state and the culture of citizens. While many social theorists formerly regarded nationalism as an 'archaic survival' from a remote age, which would probably be superseded through modernisation and bureaucratisation (for instance, Weber 1978 [1919]), it has gradually become clear that it is actually a product of modernity. In fact, nationalism as we know it was developed in both France and Germany around the time of the French Revolution: it has a dual origin in the French Enlightenment and German Romanticism.

The parallel between the study of nationalism and that of ethnicity is obvious; most nationalisms – some would say all – are special cases of ethnic ideologies. Since most nationalist ideologies argue the ancient nature of their nation, many have thought that this was also the case with the

261

ideology itself. This is not the case, and at this point it may be useful to distinguish between tradition and traditionalism. Nationalism tends to appear as a traditionalist ideology, glorifying a presumedly ancient cultural tradition. This does not mean that it is 'traditional' or 'ancient' itself.

The example of Norwegian nationalism since the 1850s demonstrates this point. At that time, Norway was in an enforced union with Sweden and a growing number of urban, educated Norwegians felt, inspired by similar movements elsewhere in Europe, that they ought to have their own state. They then travelled to remote valleys where they found popular traditions which seemed peculiarly Norwegian; they brought them back to the cities, exhibited them and made them appear as an expression of the Norwegian people and its 'spirit'. Thus a national symbolism was gradually developed, stressing dimensions of Norwegian rural life that were seen as unique (not found in neighbouring Sweden and Denmark, which Norwegian nationhood was defined in contrast with), and this was used to establish the idea of the ethnic Norwegian nation. A national historiography was founded during the same period, stressing the continuity with the Norse empire of the Viking age (around AD 1000), while a national literature, national art, national music and a new national language based on certain rural dialects – thereby markedly distinctive from Danish – were created. All of this effort was intended to give the impression that Norway was really an old country with a unique culture, and therefore deserved political independence.

The rural culture of Norway, in a reinterpreted form, provided an efficient political weapon, not because it was statistically 'typical' or because it was more 'authentic' than urban culture, but because it could be used to express ethnic distinctiveness vis-à-vis Danes and Swedes and because it embodied the rural–urban solidarity characteristic of nationalism. According to nationalist ideology, the important distinguishing lines between groups follow national boundaries, and internal differentiation is therefore undercommunicated. Nationalism postulates that all members of society have a shared culture, which was a radical point of view in societies which had formerly been based on ascribed rank and feudal hierarchies.

The traditionalism which is expressed through nationalism is thus deeply modern in character. The fact that the nationalists claim the Vikings were Norwegians does not mean that the nationalists are Vikings. We now need to examine more closely the relationship between nationalism and modernity, which has a strong bearing on earlier discussions of social scale, technology and forms of social integration.

Nationalism and Industrial Society

In Ernest Gellner's important book about nationalism (1983), the author stresses that nationalism emerged as a response to industrialisation and people's disengagement from 'primordial ties' to kin, religion and local communities. Industrialisation entailed a greater geographical mobility, and made people participate in social systems of a much larger scale than they had known earlier. Kin ideology, feudalism and religion were no longer capable of organising people efficiently. There was, in other words, a need for a cohesive ideology in the large-scale societies evolving in Europe in the nineteenth century, which both created social systems of enormous scale and inspired demands for individual equality and civil rights. Nationalism was able to meet such demands, and Gellner largely sees it as a functional replacement of older ideologies and principles of social organisation.

Ernest Gellner (1925–95), was initially educated as a philosopher, and an important part of his published work deals with the philosophy of science. He has contributed to anthropological debates on translation and rationality, as well as debates on the relationship between language and the world. His essays on the philosophy of social science include the collections *Thought and Change* (1964), *Spectacles and Predicaments* (1974) and *Relativism and the Social Sciences* (1985). Gellner has described himself both as a positivist and as a functionalist, and he emerges as a strong defender of anthropology as science, criticising hermeneutics as well as the Wittgensteinian philosophy of language (as represented in Peter Winch) and, more recently, 'postmodernism'. He has carried out fieldwork in Mahgreb, and in this context has published *Muslim Society* (1981).

Among Gellner's later books, *Nations and Nationalism* (1983) stands out: it has been a decisive source of inspiration in the burgeoning interdisciplinary field of nationalist studies. In this work he emphasises the modern character of nationalism, linking it to the industrial revolution. *The Psychoanalytical Movement* (1985) is a strong criticism of psychoanalysis, which Gellner dismisses on epistemological and logical grounds, as well as providing a sociological explanation of its great importance. *Reason and Culture* (1991) develops perspectives on modern society further, but from a more philosophical point of view, as the focus is on the tension between Enlightenment and Romanticism in European thought – between 'reason' and 'culture', or – as an extrapolation – between civil rights and nationalism. *Postmodernism, Reason and Religion* (1992) attacks epistemological relativism in anthropology, evaluates the merits and shortcomings of religious fundamentalism, and ends with a very outspoken defence of science as a source of understanding.

A fundamental difference between kinship ideology and nationalism is the fact that the latter postulates the existence of an abstract community; that is, as a nationalist or patriot, one is loyal to a legislative system and a state which ostensibly represents one's 'people', not to individuals one knows personally. The nation thus only exists if one is capable of imagining its existence – it cannot be observed directly – and it is in this sense that Benedict Anderson (1991) has spoken of the nation as an imagined community. In his account of nationalism, he stresses the development of mass media, particularly the printed book. With print-capitalism, he argues, an immense number of people are able to appropriate the same knowledge, and this may take place without direct contact with the author. A standardisation of language and world view on a huge scale thus becomes possible. The role of the state educational system in nation-states is immensely important here. All English schoolchildren have heard of Guy Fawkes, but few know why Pieter Stuyvesant is an important person in Dutch history. In the Netherlands, naturally, the situation is reversed.

At a cultural level, print media and standardised education imply a certain homogenisation of representations. At the level of social organisation, it facilitates geographical mobility over a large area, since it gives people in different areas roughly the same qualifications and thus makes them replaceable in the labour market. Large-scale communication and cultural standardisation or homogenisation are thus important features of nation-building, which contribute to explaining how it can be that people identify with such an abstract entity as a nation.

Both Gellner and Anderson emphasise the modern and abstract character of the nation. The nation and nationalism here appear as tools of state power in societies which would otherwise be threatened by dissolution and anomie. Nationalism is a functional ideology for the state in that it creates loyalty and facilitates large-scale operations, and it is functional for the individual in that it replaces obsolete foci for identification and socialisation, notably the family. It is thus no mere cliché that the nation-state has taken over many of the former functions of the family in modern societies, as an institution representing, among other things, social control, socialisation and group belongingness. The nation may further be seen as a metaphoric kin group. Kinship is fundamental to human organisation, and nationalism tends to emerge in situations where kinship organisation has been weakened. From having been members of lineages or villages, people also, and perhaps more importantly, become citizens through processes of modernisation. The nation-state offers both a feeling of security and a cultural identity, as well as socialisation (through schooling) and career opportunities. It demands our loyalty in roughly the same way as the family: people are willing to kill and die for their relatives and their nation (if nationalism is a successful ideology), but for few other groups. The nation-state is, in other words, able to mobilise very strong passions among its members, and Anderson (1991) has remarked that nationalism has more in common with phenomena such as religion and kinship than with ideologies like socialism and liberalism.

Some authors have argued that although nationalism is a modern phenomenon, it is rooted in earlier ethnic communities or 'ethnies' (A. Smith 1986, 1991), but it would surely be misleading to claim that there is an unbroken continuity from pre-modern communities to national ones. As the Norwegian example shows, national dress and other symbols take on a very different meaning in the modern context from that which they had originally.

The Nation-state

For a nation-state to exist, its leaders must simultaneously be able to legitimate a particular power structure and create a popular belief in the ability of the nation to satisfy certain profound needs in the population. A successful nationalism implies, in most cases, an intrinsic connection between an ethnic ideology stressing shared descent, and a state apparatus. Let us briefly consider some of the characteristics of the nation-state, seen as a mode of social organisation. It may be relevant to compare it with other forms of social organisation described earlier in this book: there are both similarities and differences between, say, the nation of France and the Dogon village.

Multiculturalism and Human Rights

The growing importance of self-conscious constructions of cultural identities, which is a global phenomenon, is evident in consumption patterns, politics and the arts. In many countries, perhaps particularly the rich ones with substantial immigrant populations, debates about 'multiculturalism' have highlighted several of these dimensions. Is it, for example, meaningful to talk of 'ethnic art', and should it be evaluated according to culturally specific criteria? To the Nigerian-English editor and critic Adewale Maja-Pierce, this kind of argument can be used to defend mediocre literature and thereby functions in a discriminating and often patronising way (Maja-Pierce, personal communication). On the other hand, as Charles Taylor (1992, p. 67) remarks, to 'approach, say, a raga with the presumptions of value implicit in the well-tempered clavier would be forever to miss the point'.

In the political field, issues of multiculturalism have focused on human rights and minority rights. Multiculturalism could be defined as a doctrine which holds that discrete ethnic groups are entitled to the right to be culturally different from the majority, just as the majority is entitled to its culture. However, as many critics have pointed out, this kind of doctrine may serve to justify systematic differential treatment of ethnic groups (as in apartheid), and may indeed, even in its more benevolent forms, be at odds with individual rights. On the one hand, then, every citizen is in theory entitled to equal treatment from the state and society at large; on the other, people with different cultural backgrounds may also claim the right to retain their cultural identity. When this cultural identity involves, for instance, arranged marriages and this institution is unlawful, the conflict between the right to equality and the right to difference becomes clear. Should groups have rights rather than just individuals; if so, how can one prevent oppression and abuse due to internal power discrepancies in the group? Needless to say, anthropologists play an important part in these modern discourses, both as participants and as analysts. After all, the very notion of multiculturalism draws on a concept of culture developed in anthropology.

Above all, the nation-state is based on nationalist ideology; that is the doctrine stating that state boundaries should correspond with cultural boundaries. Further, the nation-state has a monopoly on the legitimate use of violence, the enforcement of law and order, and the collection of taxes. It has a bureaucratic administration and written legislation which covers all citizens, and it has – at least ideally – a uniform educational system and a shared labour market for its people. Most nation-states have an official national language; some have even banned the use of other languages in public.

In other societies too, the political authorities have monopolies on violence and taxation. What is peculiar to the nation-state in this regard is the enormous concentration of power it represents. If we compare a modern war with a feud among the Yanomamö, we see the difference clearly. In the same way as the abstract community of nationalism encompasses an incredible number of people (usually many millions) compared to societies integrated on the basis of kinship (among the Yanomamö, there is an upper limit of a few hundred people), the modern state may in many cases be seen as an enormous enlargement of other forms of social organisation. This does not mean that the nation-state is 'just like other kinds of society', only bigger, but we ought to be aware of the similarities between state and non-state forms of organisation, not merely the differences.

Nationalism and Ethnicity

The difference between nationalism and ethnicity is simple if we stick to the level of definitions. A nationalist ideology may be defined as an ethnic ideology which demands the right to its own state on behalf of the ethnic group. In practice, the distinction can be much more complicated.

First, groups or categories of persons may analytically be located in a grey zone between nationhood and ethnic identity. It is simply not true that ethnic groups 'have a shared will'. If some of their members wish for independence, while others are content to have linguistic and other rights within an existing state, the category in question may appear both as a nation and as an ethnic group, depending on who is speaking. A person may also switch situationally between being a member of an ethnic minority and a member of a nation. An Argentinian migrant to France belongs to an ethnic minority while in France, but belongs to a nation the moment she returns to her country of birth.

Second, nationalism may sometimes express an ideology which represents, and is supported by, a majority of ethnic groups. This is clearly the case in Mauritius, where no ethnic group openly wishes to make nation-building an ethnic project on its own behalf. Nationalist ideology in such countries may be seen as polyethnic or supra-ethnic in that it tries to reconcile ethnic differences, but not abolish them, within a shared framework of a nation.

Third, we should keep in mind that everyday language and mass media continuously mix up the concepts of nation and ethnic group; when, for example, people speak of the '104 nations' of the former Soviet Union, they clearly refer to ethnic groups, a few of which are nations in the sense that their leaders want to have states where they are dominant.

Nationalism and ethnicity are related phenomena, but there are many ethnic groups which are not nations, and there may also be nations which are not ethnic groups – that is, polyethnic nations or countries which are not founded on an ethnic principle. Naturally, most of the world's countries are as a matter of fact polyethnic, but many of them are dominated by one ethnic group; the French in France, the English in Great Britain and so on. The model of nationalism presented above, as well as models endorsed by nationalists, rarely fits the territory. Notably, there is rarely, if ever, a perfect correspondence between the state and the 'cultural group'. This simple fact is the cause of what, in the contemporary world, is spoken of as minority issues.

Minority and Majority

Two kinds of ethnicity studies which have placed a great emphasis on power and power discrepancies are studies of labour migrants from poor to rich countries, and studies of indigenous peoples. Both types are concerned with the relationship between minorities and majorities, where the majority – usually a nation represented in a nation-state – is in several ways more powerful than the minority.

An ethnic minority may be defined as a group which is politically non-dominant, and which exists as an ethnic category. Although the term minority usually refers to inferior numbers, in the professional literature it denotes political submission. A great number of peoples in the world may therefore be seen as minorities. Their relationship to the nation-state nevertheless varies, as do the strategies of the nation-state towards these minorities.

The term minority is relative to both the scale and the form of organisation in the total social system. As has been shown earlier, any delineation of a social system is relative. This means that (i) minorities are created when the compass of the social system increases, as when formerly tribal peoples become integrated into nation-states (the Yanomamö were no minority before they entered into a relationship with the state), (ii) minorities may often become majorities if they are able to delimit the system in new ways (for example, by setting up a new state), and (iii) ethnic groups which are minorities in one place may become majorities in another.

The Sikhs make up less than 2 per cent of the total population of India; in Indian Punjab, however, they comprise 65 per cent of the population. In accordance with (ii) above, some of their leaders are struggling to set up an independent Sikh state, thereby transforming the group collectively from minority to majority status. On the other hand, Hungarians in Transylvania (Romania) and Pakistanis in Britain exemplify (iii): they are a minority, but their group is a majority elsewhere.

Power Asymmetries

So far in the discussion of ethnicity and nationalism, we have not emphasised the very important and very widespread fact of uneven or asymmetrical power relations between ethnic groups. Many studies of ethnicity concentrate on the maintenance of ethnic boundaries and negotiations over identity, without looking more closely at the ways in which power disparities may be decisive for interethnic relationships. The famous studies of ethnicity (or 'tribalism') in the Copperbelt, to mention one example, scarcely mentioned the wider context of colonial mining society, which defined Africans as second-class citizens in relation to Europeans.

Stanley Tambiah (1989) has proposed a typology of contemporary societies that differentiates them according to their ethnic composition (see Eriksen 1992 and Horowitz 1985 for different typologies of minority–majority relationships):

1. Countries which are almost ethnically homogeneous (where the dominant group has more than 90 per cent of the total population), such as Japan, Iceland and Bangladesh.
2. Countries with a large ethnic majority (75–89 per cent of the population), including Bhutan, Vietnam and Turkey.
3. Countries where the largest ethnic group makes up 50–75 per cent of the population and where there are several minorities, for instance Sri Lanka, Iran, Pakistan and Singapore.
4. Countries with two groups of roughly the same size, such as Guyana, Trinidad & Tobago and Malaysia.
5. Truly plural countries composed of many ethnic groups where no one of them is dominant; for example India, Mauritius, Nigeria and the Philippines.

One striking fact about such a typology is that it lumps together countries which are politically extremely different. Within each category there are stable and unstable countries, parliamentary democracies and military dictatorships, countries with good as well as bad records regarding human rights and so on. Ethnically homogeneous Somalia experienced civil war in the early 1990s, while there is no threat to the territorial integrity of neighbouring multi-ethnic Kenya. Eritrea's secession from Ethiopia in the early 1990s, moreover, was not an ethnic issue, as Eritrea's population is composed of about twelve ethnic groups. Mauritius, a truly ethnically plural society, is one of the most stable parliamentary democracies in the tropical part of the world. Ethnic plurality, in other words, cannot alone account for violence and political instability.

However, if we add a distinction between ranked and unranked polyethnic systems (Horowitz 1985; Tambiah 1989), it may be easier to understand why some such societies are unstable and others are not. Typically, ethnic groups which are systematically deprived of civil rights and career opportunities will tend to perceive the political order as unjust. This applies only in societies where rights are in practice unevenly distributed on the basis of ethnic membership, but this kind of situation is not uncommon. For now, we will restrict ourselves to considering asymmetrical relationships between dominant ethnic groups which control the state, and minorities.

Non-ethnic Nations?
Theories of nationalism have often been Eurocentric (Handler and Segal 1993) and, unsurprisingly, non-European countries have often failed to fit the model. If by nationalism we mean the doctrine of congruence between state and ethnic group, even the US does not seem to be a nation. In Central and South America, few people see their own country as essentially ethnically homogeneous; in Mexico, for example, the fact of 'mestizage' (cultural and racial mixing) has become a symbol of the nation. Africa presents a no less complex picture, with hardly a single ethnically homogeneous country; while large parts of Asia are also ethnically very complex – not only in fact, but also at the level of ideology (unlike in Europe, where the facts are often multi-ethnic but the ideology of nationalism is mono-ethnic). If the nation of Kenya is to be imagined by its citizens, therefore, it cannot be viewed as Luo, Kikuyu or Maasai, but as a symbolic community which exists at a higher segmentary level than the ethnic groups that make it up. In many of these countries, national ideology is therefore associated with equal rights and civil society rather than with any particular ethnic group. It may still have the ability to stir patriotic emotions and create loyalty to the state.

Would these polyethnic imagined communities still be nations in an analytical sense? That is a matter of definition. It is certain, however, that if the concept of nationalism is to be cross-culturally valid, it cannot be restricted to mono-ethnic nations: it will have to be further refined to fit the global territory.

Segregation, Assimilation and Integration

Short of physical extermination (which has actually been quite common), states may use one or several of three principal strategies in their dealings with minorities. First, the state or the majority may opt for segregation. This means that the minority group becomes physically separated from the majority, often accompanied by the notion that the members of the minority are inferior. The former South African ideology of apartheid promoted segregation, and many North American cities are segregated along ethnic lines.

Assimilation is also a possible outcome of contact between majority and minority. If it happens on a large scale, it eventually leads to the disappearance of the minority, which melts into the majority. In England, this happened to the Norman upper class which ruled the country after the invasion in 1066. The descendants of this group became, after a few generations, English.

Assimilation may be enforced or chosen. In some cases, it is practically impossible, if ethnicity is based on physical appearance. In the US, most immigrant groups have historically become assimilated; usually they lost their mother-tongue after two generations and retained only a vague memory of their country of origin. But this did not happen with the descendants of the black slaves, since skin colour is an important criterion for social classification. A black American cannot become a 'typical', that is white, American in the same way as the grandchild of a German immigrant may do. In these situations, where assimilation becomes impossible for cultural reasons, it may be useful to speak of entropy-resistant traits (Gellner 1983): the distinguishing marks of the minority cannot be removed, whether or not its members wish.

Integration is the third 'type' of relationship between majority and minority. It usually refers to participation in the shared institutions of society, combined with the maintenance of group identity and some degree of cultural distinctiveness. It represents a compromise between the two other main options.

An ethnically based division of labour is compatible with segregation as well as integration, but only assimilation and certain forms of integration are compatible with full political participation in greater society. Chosen segregation may form the rationale for a nationalist movement, or it may be an elite option chosen to keep valuable resources within the ethnic group, but most segregated minorities are 'second-class citizens', whether they are indigenous peoples or recent arrivals.

Most empirical cases of majority–minority relationships display a combination of segregation, assimilation and integration. Assimilation may well take place at an individual level, even if the chief tendency might be segregation or ethnic incorporation. Despite the fact that the Sami of northern Scandinavia have in recent decades moved towards a stronger ethnic incorporation and chosen segregation, there are still individuals who are assimilated to a majority ethnic identity (Norwegian, Finnish or Swedish, as the case may be).

In studies of majority–minority relationships, it is difficult to escape from an analysis of power and power discrepancies. The majority does not only possess the political power; it usually controls important parts of the economy and, perhaps most importantly, defines the terms of discourse in society. Language, codes of conduct and relevant skills are defined, and mastered, by the majority. The majority defines the cultural framework relevant for life careers, and thus has a surplus of symbolic capital over the minorities. For this reason, many minority members may be disqualified in the labour market and other contexts where their skills are not valued. A Somalian refugee in Germany is highly skilled if he speaks four languages, but he has no chance in the German labour market if those languages happen to be Somali, Swahili, Amharic and Arabic.

Migration

Migrants are a special kind of minority. They often lack citizenship in the host country, and they often have their origin in a country where they belong to a majority. In many cases, migrants are only temporarily settled in the host country. Sociological and anthropological research on migration from poor to rich countries has mainly concentrated on three topics: aspects of discrimination and disqualification on the part of the host population; strategies for the maintenance of group identity; and the relationship between immigrant culture and majority culture. Some researchers have also studied the relationship between the community of origin and the sociocultural environment in the host country, since most migrants maintain important ties to their place of origin (Georges 1990; Olwig 1993).

In a comparative study of two polyethnic neighbourhoods in London, Sandra Wallman (1986) discovered important differences in the relationships between majority and minorities. Bow in East London was characterised by a strong polarisation and dichotomisation between people born in Britain and immigrants, whereas ethnic relationships in Battersea, South London, were much more relaxed and less socially important. Both areas were largely populated by manual and lower white-collar workers, and they included roughly the same proportions of immigrants from roughly the same places of origin (Africa, Pakistan, India, the West Indies).

Wallman shows that the social networks of the two areas were constituted in significantly different ways. In Bow, the same people interacted in many different types of situation, and the different groups of which each individual was a member overlapped a good deal. In Battersea, on the contrary, each individual was a member of many different groups with different criteria for membership. In Bow people worked and lived in the same area; in Battersea, people tended to work in other parts of London. The British-born population in Bow was extremely stable, while Battersea was characterised by a greater flux.

These and related factors, Wallman argues, have contributed to creating fundamentally different types of ethnic relationships in the two areas. She describes Bow as a closed homogeneous system and Battersea as an open heterogeneous system (see Figure 17.1). In Battersea, unlike in Bow, there were a great number of 'gates' and 'gatekeepers': there are, in other words, many ways in which one may cross group boundaries as an immigrant. One becomes a member of the local community the moment one moves in. But in the closed environment of Bow, people have to have lived their entire lives there in order to be accepted. In Bow, the ethnic boundaries are sharper than in Battersea because the different social networks are so strongly overlapping that an immigrant will have to cross several 'gates' or fences *simultaneously* in order to become an accepted member of the locality. In practice, this is impossible.

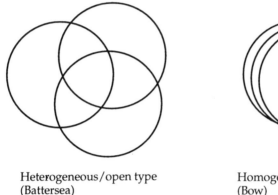

Heterogeneous/open type   Homogeneous/closed type
(Battersea)   (Bow)

Figure 17.1: Degrees of overlap between social sub-systems or fields in Battersea and Bow. (Source: Wallman 1986, p. 241)

Wallman's study strengthens the idea, discussed elsewhere in this book, that cross-cutting ties have a mitigating effect on conflict. Other researchers have, rather than choosing a sociological approach, focused on the personal identity of migrants. Here, a common perspective amounts to the view that migrants often 'live in two worlds', that they switch between different cultural codes when they move between contexts. Whereas ethnic identity may be undercommunicated in relationships with the host population, it may be overcommunicated internally.

A different, more dynamic perspective would rather focus on social and cultural change, indicating that a Pakistani identity in England necessarily means something different from a Pakistani identity in Pakistan. In some respects, such migrants are 'Anglified'; in other respects, they may self-consciously work to strengthen their cultural identity; in yet other respects, there may be strong cultural values in the midst of the community which are difficult to change even if some members of the group may want to – regarding, for example, the tradition of arranged marriages. The field of migration may in this way prove to be an interesting area for the study of cultural dynamics and change (see also Chapter 18).

'The Fourth World'

The term 'indigenous peoples' refers, in everyday language, to a non-dominant population associated with a non-industrial mode of production. This does not mean that members of indigenous peoples never take part in national politics or work in factories, but merely that they are seen to represent a way of life that renders them particularly vulnerable when faced with the trappings of modernity and the nation-state. It can therefore be instructive to distinguish them from migrants, who are fully integrated into the capitalist system of production and consumption, but who make no territorial claims.

One cannot speak of 'indigenous peoples' in a value-free way. Technically speaking, all inhabitants of the world are indigenous peoples of the planet. The term is always used in a political context in order to make specific political claims.

Indigenous peoples all over the world are placed in a potentially conflictual relationship to the nation-state – not just to one particular nation-state, but to the state as an institution. Their political project frequently consists of securing their survival as a culture-bearing group, but they rarely if ever wish to found their own state. Many indigenous peoples have too few members, and are insufficiently differentiated, for such an option to seem realistic.

The most common conflict between indigenous peoples and nation-states concerns land rights. For this reason, issues regarding these groups and their rights have become increasingly relevant – both in politics and in anthropological research – as nation-states have progressively expanded their territories and spheres of influence. As a reaction against this development, the indigenous peoples of Greenland, Australia, New Zealand, Amazonas, northern Scandinavia, North America and elsewhere have organised through global networks to protect their rights to their ancestral land and cultural traditions. In other parts of the world, including Borneo, New Guinea and large parts of Africa, such forms of organisation are still embryonic, not least perhaps because the coming of the modern nation-state has taken place at a later stage.

Perhaps paradoxically, the cultural survival of indigenous peoples necessitates important changes in their culture and social organisation. The Sami of northern Norway provide a good example of this. Only after having acquired literacy and a certain mastery of modern mass media and the national political system was it possible for them to present their political case in effective – and ultimately successful – ways. Generally, the global 'Fourth World' movement is 'Western' and modern in every respect insofar as it is based on human rights ideology, draws on modern mass media and is oriented towards political bodies such as the United Nations. Peoples who retain their traditions unaltered to a greater extent than, for instance, the pragmatic and resourceful Sami stand a much smaller chance of survival in the long run, since they have no effective strategy for handling their encounter with the hegemonic, modern state. This odd paradox of indigenous politics relates to a more general paradox of ethnicity and nationalism, namely that there is no one-to-one relationship between culture and cultural identity, although the two are connected. The distinction between tradition and traditionalism may help us to understand the difference.

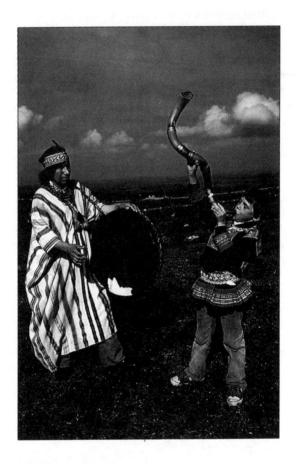

Although many of them are still deeply oppressed, indigenous peoples from all over the world have formed networks and organisations such as the WCIP (World Council of Indigenous Peoples), enabling them to exert a certain pressure on governments and on international society. This photo shows a Peruvian Indian and a Sami. (Photo: Aslak Aarhus)

Ethnic Revitalisation

That 'reawakening' of traditional culture in a modern context, which seems necessary for indigenous peoples to survive, is often spoken of in more general terms as ethnic revitalisation. The discovery, or invention, of the Norwegian past described earlier is a classic example. The concept of revitalisation literally means that cultural symbols and practices which have lain dormant for a while regain their lost relevance. However, we have to be aware that a revitalised culture is always very different from the original. Revitalisation movements are traditionalist in that they seek to make tradition relevant in a context which is not itself traditional, but modern. An instance of this kind of process is the ongoing Hindu revitalisation in Trinidad (Klass 1991; Vertovec 1992).

Several hundred thousand Indians arrived in Trinidad and other plantation colonies following the abolition of slavery in 1839. Most of them never returned to India, and in Trinidad people of Indian origin make up about 40 per cent of the total population of 1.2 million. For generations, the Indians (or 'East Indians', as they are locally called) were the poorest and in many ways most marginal part of the population: they were illiterate, rural and strongly culturally stigmatised by the dominant European and Afro-Trinidadian groups. Since the Second World War, they have increasingly taken part in the institutions of the Trinidadian state: they now have adequate schooling, trade unions and political representations; they have become occupationally differentiated and have experienced a general rise in their standard of living. Since the 1970s, Hindu symbolism and the Indian cultural heritage have played an increasingly important part in the community. In the 1980s a Hindu weekly paper was founded, and during the same period it became common for Indo-Trinidadians to go to India on vacation. Religious attendance is increasing, and political organisations aiming at strengthening the Indian identity have been formed.

This revitalisation may seem paradoxical. In many ways, the Indians have been assimilated into Trinidadian society. Virtually all Indo-Trinidadians now speak Trinidad English as their vernacular; the caste system has lost most of its functions and categories, and research indicates that the 'East Indians' have the same dreams and aspirations as the rest of the population. Nevertheless, many of them are determined to retain and strengthen their ethnic identity and Indian heritage.

This process is actually very common in ethnopolitical movements. Before 1960 the Indo-Trinidadians were socially and politically fragmented, many were illiterate, and they lacked a strong group identity. Only when they were integrated into the modern institutions were they able to mobilise political resources enabling them to function as a corporate group (or an 'imagined community'). Moreover, the concerted presentation of ethnic symbols – itself dependent on a modern infrastructure – gives a meaningful focus to the movement, in creating cohesion at the same time as responding to the individual quest for dignity.

Cultural homogenisation within the modern nation-state may contribute to explaining ethnic revitalisation in other ways as well. Since the Second World War, Indo-Trinidadians have entered into more intensive relationships with the rest of the Trinidadian population, which has led to the erasure or challenging of ethnic boundaries in a number of fields. Many Indians have therefore felt that their identity is threatened, and speak of 'creolisation' as a danger to the integrity of the Indian 'way of life'. A response to perceived creolisation has been conscious dichotomisation and overcommunication of distinctiveness. In general, we might say that an ethnic identity becomes important the moment its carriers feel that it is threatened. Evidently, this is connected to the fact that ethnicity is created by contact, not by isolation.

It would not be correct to state that ethnicity occurs exclusively within the framework of a modern state, but the ethnic dimension can be expressed in unusually powerful ways there. Although ethnicity does not necessarily relate to processes of modernisation, most ethnic studies deal with social and cultural change. In Norway, there were scarcely fewer Sami in 1940 than in 1990, but they were much less visible, less culturally self-conscious and lacked both a corporate organisation and an 'imagined' collective identity. They did not deal directly with the state and had no minority status; Sami–Norwegian ethnicity was still at the interpersonal level.

As for labour migrants and refugees, their very migration is a tangible expression of modernisation, of links mediated by the state and capitalist modes of production and consumption. Villages in Jamaica and Ghana are becoming economically tied to cities in Britain, and in the 1970s the labour market in Oslo was better known to villagers in parts of Pakistani Punjab than the labour market in Lahore.

Indigenous populations find themselves in a precarious position. In a certain sense, they are wedged between the reservation and cultural genocide. On the one hand, they may try to opt for isolation and build solid boundaries about their customs and traditions. Such strategies have nearly always been unsuccessful. On the other hand, they may try to promote their political interests through established channels, and for this to be possible they – or some of them – must go through a process of modernisation in order to learn the rules of the relevant political game. This strategy may, however, be successful, and in the final chapter it will be clear in what way.

Identity through Contrasts

In this chapter, nationalism and minority issues have been discussed as modern phenomena. It has nevertheless been pointed out that there are certain parallels with other ideologies and forms of organisation, which are more typical of the societies traditionally studied by anthropologists. One parallel with non-modern societies which deserves to be mentioned concerns the production of identification through contrasting. The Iatmul of coastal New Guinea, studied by Bateson (1958 [1936]), recounted a myth of origin which expresses a line of reasoning reminiscent of the white North American stigmatisation of black and Amerindian citizens, and which suggests that ethnicity is not a mere tool of dominance but expresses a need for order, classification and boundaries. In the earliest of times, according to the myth, there was on the shore an enormous crocodile, Kavwokmali, which flapped its huge tail, front legs and hind legs so that soil and water were continuously muddled together in an unpalatable mixture. Everything was mud: there existed neither land nor water. The great culture hero Kevembuangga then came along, killing the crocodile with his spear. The mud sank, and the distinction between land and water was a reality. Boundaries, outlines, clear distinctions appeared for the first time.

This myth, not dissimilar to the myth of origin told in the Bible (Genesis), exemplifies the social production of distinctions and classification – differences that make a difference. The production of ethnic distinctions may be regarded as a special case of this general phenomenon, which has been discussed in Chapter 14. Perhaps the fact of ethnic conflict and ethnic discrimination is better analysed not as a result of ethnicity, but rather of unjust social arrangements. Perhaps when we speak of the tragedy of nationalist war, the problem is war and not nationalism.

Finally, we should keep in mind that neither ethnic groups nor nations are eternal. They appear, flourish and vanish. Since history is always written by the victors, it is easy to forget that for every successful nationalism there are perhaps ten or more unsuccessful ones. The members of such potential nations, or their descendants, were either exterminated or assimilated in the long run.

Suggestions for Further Reading

Benedict Anderson: *Imagined Communities. An Inquiry into the Origins and Spread of Nationalism*, 2nd edition. London: Verso 1991.

Thomas Hylland Eriksen: *Ethnicity and Nationalism: Anthropological Perspectives*. London: Pluto 1993.

Ernest Gellner: *Nations and Nationalism*. Oxford: Blackwell 1983.

Anthony D. Smith: *National Identity*. Harmondsworth: Penguin 1991.

18 THE LOCAL AND THE GLOBAL

Every culture must liberate its creative potential by finding the correct equilibrium between isolation and contact with others.

—*Claude Lévi-Strauss*

An anecdote is told about a tribe of transhumant camel nomads in North Africa, whose annual migration had taken place in March since the dawn of time. Recently their migration was several months delayed. The reason was that they did not want to miss the final episodes of *Dallas* (D. Miller 1993a, p. 163).

It does not matter whether or not this tale is true. What it may tell us is that the world is no longer what it used to be – or rather, perhaps, what we used to imagine it to be. For it is easy to find evidence that changes in the world have been dramatic in earlier times too, that there has been extensive and regular communication and contact between societies, and that even in medieval times there existed truly cosmopolitan cities like Byzantium and Timbuktu. The opening words of the first classic of British social anthropology, Malinowski's *Argonauts of the Western Pacific*, read as follows:

Ethnology is in the sadly ludicrous, not to say tragic, position, that at the very moment when it begins to put its workshop in order, to forge its proper tools, to start ready for work on its appointed task, the material of its study melts away with hopeless rapidity. Just now, when the methods and aims of scientific field ethnology have taken shape, when men fully trained for the work have begun to travel into savage countries and study their inhabitants – these die away under our very eyes. (Malinowski 1984 [1922], p. xv)

Malinowski's worries concern phenomena which are today sometimes described as imperialism, or cultural imperialism, and sometimes as the globalisation of culture; that is, the worldwide dissemination of certain cultural forms and social institutions because of colonialism, trade, missionary activity, technological change and the incorporation of tribal peoples into states and large-scale systems of exchange. When the first American anthropologists started to return from Bali in the 1920s, they described, in a concerned tone of voice, how Balinese culture was about to be completely destroyed by mass tourism (which still, in the 1990s, does not seem to have come about; see Wikan 1992; Barth 1993) – and similar grim predictions have been made on behalf of many of the peoples who have been explored anthropologically. Ever since the feeble beginnings of modern comparative anthropology, practitioners have been worried about the disappearance of that cultural variation which it is our aim to explore. In the 1960s and 1970s many spoke of the importance of 'urgent anthropology', which entailed recording the culture and social organisation of the peoples still living in a traditional way before they disappeared from the face of the earth. In recent years, new concerns have to some extent replaced these, and many anthropologists now investigate, in different ways, the new complexities engendered by the increased contact between societies.

Where Are They Now?

What has become of the peoples first explored by anthropologists during colonialism? Nearly all of them are, to varying degrees, integrated into larger – in the final instance global – economic, cultural and political systems. To some, such as the Tsembaga Maring, this integration is still of relatively minor importance in their everyday life. Although wagework and a monetary economy have entered their society, they still get their livelihood from pig-raising and horticulture. Because of the increasingly efficient state monopoly of violence, it has nevertheless become difficult to go to war in the highlands.

For many of the other peoples dealt with in earlier chapters of this book, the changes have been more fundamental. The Azande have become pro-letarised – many of them found wagework in cotton and peanut plantations – and yet, it was reported in the 1960s, the witchcraft institution remains strong. The Yanomamö have been drawn into wagework too – among other things, gold has been found in their territory – and, simultaneously, they now have professional spokespeople travelling around the world to promote their interests as an indigenous population. Nevertheless, in the mid-1990s most of them chiefly live off subsistence horticulture, although the monetary sector is becoming more important. As for the Mundurucú, as early as the 1950s they were about to be drawn into a capitalist economic system. Several of the villages depended on wagework on rubber planta-tions, and in this setting their pattern of settlement was changed: the men's house was gone, and men lived with their wives and children in nuclear families. In general, the Murphys report (1985), the women were happy with the changes, which meant that men contributed more to the household; whereas the men spoke in nostalgic terms about a largely mythical past, when they fought heroic battles and game was abundant.

One of the most important changes among the Dogon since the period of French colonisation has been the fact of peace. Their old enemies, the Fulani, have efficiently been prevented from attacking them, and thus the Dogon have been able to expand their territory. Like the Fur, the Fulani, the Hausa and many other peoples, however, the Dogon have been

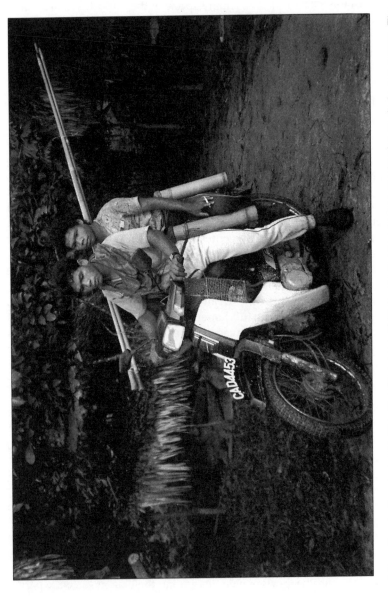

Like other indigenous peoples, the Chewong of Malaysia try to adapt to modernity on their own terms. The motorbike can be a helpful addition to a traditional activity such as hunting with blowpipes. (Photo: Signe Howell)

severely hit by the combination of recurrent droughts in the Sahel region and population growth. The Dogon are today in many ways integrated into the nation-state of Mali; the children go to school, are vaccinated and learn French as a foreign language. The monetary economy has become more widespread and certain industrial products, such as factory-made clothes, transistor radios and bicycles, have become common. As with many other African peoples, Islam has been an important factor in cultural change among the Dogon. In this respect, the increased peaceful contact with the Fulani, who are Muslims and active missionaries, has been particularly important.

Turning to the Nuer and Fur, their greatest problem apart from devastating droughts has been the long-lasting civil war in the Sudan, which has made trade difficult, apart from draining off both economic and human resources from their societies. Many Nuer fight on the south Sudanese side in the war against the Islamic north; in accordance with Evans-Pritchard's model of segmentary oppositions, one may say that they are now integrated at a higher level of segmentation than they used to be – fighting side by side with Dinka. In Darfur, as in many other local communities in the Sudan, large numbers of refugees from politically unstable Ethiopia have, particularly in the 1980s, led to a further strain on already very scarce resources.

As mentioned in an earlier chapter, the Trobriand Islanders largely seem to have adapted to processes of modernisation on their own terms. Modernisation has led to changes in political organisation, in the economy and in the politics of identity, but both the kinship system and the system of ceremonial exchange still function, even if they do not have the same meaning as before.

The kind of diachronic perspective implied in these snapshots of change provides a starting-point for anthropological studies of local life which alters and which is connected with systems of enormous scale. The main task of anthropology can no longer be to explore and describe alien ways of life for the first time, but rather to account for processes taking place at various points and various levels in the global system.

A Global Culture?

As the quotation above from Malinowski indicates, anthropologists have, since the very beginnings of the subject, been aware of tendencies towards what we may call cultural entropy – that historical process which is today sometimes described as 'the global cultural melting-pot', as 'cultural creolisation' or, rather inaccurately, as 'Westernisation'. However, one may wonder if we are not presently at the threshold of a new era in the history of humanity, the global era. The previous three chapters have exclusively dealt with phenomena belonging to modern contexts; in some cases, as with nationalism and minority issues, these topics have only been relevant for 20 to 30 years in large parts of the world. In these final pages, we investigate in what sense it may be reasonable to consider our time a 'global age' and, above all, look into the relationships between the global and the local. First of all, we need to look more closely at the term 'globalisation'. For this word does not mean that we are all becoming identical, but rather that we become different in ways that are not as they were in earlier times.

If by the word modernity we refer to everything that capitalism, the modern state and individualism mean to human existence, modernity has been hegemonic in the world at least since the First World War; that is to say, it has dominated. The dissemination of modernity has nevertheless accelerated since the Second World War. During the last few decades, there has been an intensified flow of people, commodities, ideas and images on a global scale. Since the appearance of the jet plane, and since satellite TV became common in many parts of the world, the limitations on cultural flow represented in space and time have been significantly reduced.

Modern communications technology contributes in two ways to the disengaging of certain cultural phenomena from space. First, a multitude of phenomena – including aspects of 'youth culture', prestige commodities from Coca-Cola cans to pop CDs and jeans, popular films, and political problems such as the environmental crisis – exist both globally (everywhere) and locally (in particular places) simultaneously. Second, the jet plane has made it possible for a growing number of people to move rapidly and comfortably all over the world, while telephones, fax machines, the Internet and computerised video systems make it feasible, in principle, to communicate with people anywhere in the world at any time. Space can no longer be said to create a clear buffer between 'cultures'.

To anthropology, which has generally concentrated on the study of local communities, or at least more or less clearly delineated sociocultural systems, these changes imply new and complex challenges, both at the level of theory and at the level of methodology.

Dimensions of Globalisation

Although modern societies differ in marked ways, modernity has certain shared dimensions everywhere. These commonalities, or parallels, can be observed both at the level of institutions and at the level of cultural representations.

The state and citizenship are today nearly universal principles of social organisation, although they exist in many variants. Their meaning should not be exaggerated – it is still possible, at least in some parts of the world, to live a whole life without regular contact with the state. This is nevertheless becoming increasingly difficult. Virtually nobody in today's world can entirely escape citizenship, and the state's power over its citizens is reflected in its double monopoly on taxation and legitimate violence. If agents other than the state collect taxes or commit violent acts, they are now guilty of crimes.

Wagework and capitalism are also important dimensions of globalised modernity. Capital is increasingly disembedded from territory, which means that companies and capitalists may invest virtually anywhere. If it is cheaper to produce computer chips in Malaysia than in Scotland, the microchip producer may easily move the assembly plant there. This also means that there is a globally available workforce prepared to enter into labour contracts.

Within modernity, consumption is by and large mediated by money. This simply means that people buy the goods they need in a market where general purpose money is the dominant medium of exchange. Subsistence production and barter are becoming less important.

From this, it follows that both politics and economies are integrated in an abstract, anonymous and, spatially speaking, enormous level of scale. No single person can affect this system in decisive ways, and events taking place at one point in the system can have ramifications – frequently unforeseen – in other parts of it. If the Taiwanese exports of personal computers increase one year, a fashion shop in a middle-class area in California may go bankrupt. The reason is that many of the shop's former customers have lost their jobs in the Silicon valley computer industry. These processes cannot be described satisfactorily in simple causal or intentional accounts. They take place at the abstract level of the system and can be likened to what is sometimes spoken of as 'butterfly effects': a butterfly flaps its wings in Rio de Janeiro and creates a small wind, triggering a long chain of events of growing magnitude, which eventually creates a storm in New York.

One consequence of increasing systemic integration at a global level is the fact that certain political issues affect the entire planet. The environmental crisis is an obvious example. If the rainforests of Amazonia, Indonesia and Central Africa disappear, there is likely to be a climatic change perceptible everywhere. And when the Chernobyl nuclear reactor suffered a meltdown in 1986, newspapers in Venezuela, Japan and Mauritius carried daily, worried reports about the catastrophe.

The creation of agencies and NGOs with a worldwide scope also indicates the importance of globalisation. The UN and organisations such as the Red Cross and Amnesty International, as well as Fourth World networks, have contributed to the development of a global discourse about morality and politics, although the system of sanctions is still weak. In Chapter 13 it was argued that it is difficult to find universal criteria for human rights; because of the globalisation of culture, politics and economic and military power, it seems that such criteria are about to be developed – at least in theory.

The worldwide dissemination of AIDS is another instructive – if grotesque – example indicating that globalisation is not limited to contact mediated by abstract structures such as the mass media; contact across national and regional boundaries can be physical and direct. In 1992 Thailand's president asked the authorities in Bonn to stop German tourism

World Music

Creolisation or hybridisation refers to the intermingling and mutual influencing of two or several distinct bodies of cultural flow (or 'traditions'). This kind of process does not imply that 'everything is becoming the same' or that all kinds of cultural flow are equally susceptible to mixing. Many forms of knowledge and practice remain local, and many are more influenced than influential.

One area of signification which is often mentioned as a happy breeding-ground for the exchange of diverse influences is contemporary rhythmic music. Blues, jazz and rock are thus often described as 'creolised' forms developed by the descendants of African slaves in North America. More recently, and particularly since the mid-1980s, a new trend in rhythmic music has been showcased as an expression of the creative intermingling of discrete traditions; known as 'world music' or 'world beat', this features non-European musicians in a European environment, using modern studio equipment and electrical instruments to convey, for example, 'the spirit of Africa'.

There are conflicting views on the nature of world music. Some argue that it represents a commodification and commercialisation of authentic tribal music; that the Western record companies have merely adapted African and Asian music to cater to the jaded palates of Western consumers and have destroyed it in the process. On the other hand, it could be argued that 'Westernised' artists such as Youssou N'Dour are also immensely popular in Africa itself – so how could their recordings be regarded as adulterated and 'inauthentic'? Steven Feld (1994) sees the trend of world beat as a reinvigorating force for rhythmic music in general, where Fela Anikulapo Kuti may just as well borrow from James Brown as Peter Gabriel may hire a group of African drummers. The 'Africanization of world pop music and the Americanization of African pop', Feld writes (1994, p. 245), 'are complexly intertwined', although he also discusses issues of copyright and power inequalities between the metropolitan artists and record companies, and the non-European artists.

Musical discourses are fields where identities are shaped, and for this reason the global flow of popular music can be a fruitful field for studying contemporary cultural dynamics as well as the political economy of meaning. The debate on authenticity is in itself interesting, as it reveals conflicting views of culture: as unbroken tradition, or as flux and process. These issues, we should keep in mind, are not merely aesthetic ones but are frequently politicised.

to Bangkok, the reason being that many German men who travel to Thailand buy sex from local women and thereby contribute to the spread of the AIDS epidemic in both countries.

Local Experiences of Globality

At the level of interaction, global process is expressed in a variety of different ways. The Gulf war of 1991 was discussed in Chinese villages whose inhabitants listened to daily news bulletins about the war on the radio. There are, in other words, situations where a large proportion of the world's population takes on an identity as 'citizens of the world' in the sense that they are concerned with problems relevant for all the world's inhabitants.

The fact that a cultural phenomenon is 'global' does not, however, imply that it is known to everybody or concerns every individual on the face of the earth. Even the Coca-Cola bottle, possibly the single most familiar object in the world, is not familiar to everybody. The point, however, is that such phenomena are disembedded from particular places. An event like the Winter Olympics has a truly global dimension (Archetti 1992b), even if the majority of the world's population is ignorant of it. Whether one happens to be in Montreal, Milan or Birmingham, one can follow such a sports event simultaneously, thanks to newspapers and television. This does not, we should note, imply that everyone who relates to these cultural forms perceives them in identical ways: global symbols and globalised information are interpreted from a local vantage-point (and contribute to shaping that vantage-point). In this way, a fashion magazine like *Vogue* is read differently in a tropical island such as Mauritius compared with Paris; and a soap opera like *The Young and the Restless* takes on a different meaning in Trinidad compared with the US (D. Miller 1993a). These and many other cultural phenomena are global in the sense that they are not located in a particular place; at the same time, they are local in that they are always perceived and interpreted locally.

In an analysis of British-Pakistani codifications of the Gulf war, Pnina Werbner (1994) shows how support for Saddam Hussein from this community was chiefly related not to the conflict itself, but to the local British context. Their support for Saddam was perhaps surprising, since Pakistan backed the UN forces and because it created problems for them in wider British society, which was unequivocally opposed to Saddam. However, the Gulf war was framed, particularly by some religious leaders, in a discourse about minority rights, (including the Salman Rushdie issue), where they demanded to be granted special concessions as a religious minority. The Muslim leaders were thus concerned to depict Muslims as radically different from mainstream British society, and this explains their 'confrontational posture' (Werbner 1994, p. 234). In Pakistan itself, the discourse about the Gulf war was quite different since it related to other local contexts.

Tourism and Migration

One perspective on globalisation thus consists of investigating how people, wherever they are, can participate in a shared production of meaning, appropriate the same information and yet interpret it in widely different life-worlds. A complementary perspective may be an exploration of the ways in which people move physically from place to place. Tourism and business travel are widespread forms of movement, which so far have not received significant attention from anthropologists (but see Hannerz 1992). Is it, for example, the case that place, in the meaning of locality, is entirely irrelevant to tourists and business travellers; that international business hotels are 'the same' everywhere, that a shared 'business culture' exists and that there is a shared, global 'leisure' culture – identical in Cancun (Mexico) and the Canary Islands? Further; could these cultural forms, evident in hotels, airports, boardrooms and beach clubs, profitably be seen as 'third cultures' mediating between different local cultures? These questions merit further exploration.

A related field of interest, which has been researched much more thoroughly, is migration – immigration or emigration, depending on which country one sees it from.

Labour migrants move within the parameters of modernity. They carry passports and are citizens; a precondition for their movement is their willingness to take part in wagework. For labour migration to be possible, the migrants must already be, at least partially, integrated into the cultural logic of capitalism.

Several possible analytical perspectives may shed light on their situation. One approach is to focus on the relationship between majority and minority in the host country; another is to compare the situation, culture and social organisation of migrants in the home country and in the country of destination. A third approach might be to compare different perspectives on migration. For example, Kuwait and other Gulf states attract many thousands of immigrants or 'guest workers'. From the dominant perspective of the Kuwaiti, these migrants are a 'necessary evil'; they are necessary because they carry out manual work, and they are an evil because they are seen to constitute a potentially threatening foreign element. From a humanist European perspective, frequently invoked in sociological studies of migration, the situation of the migrants can be described as a case of severe exploitation; they are underpaid, overworked and lack certain rights which – thanks to the globalisation of culture – are regarded as universal. From a third perspective, namely that of the migrants themselves, the position generally looks different. Thousands of Malaylees from Kerala, south India, eagerly await their chance to work in the Gulf. When they return to their hometown they bring money and gifts, and they frequently return to the Gulf if given the chance. The Indian minister of finance praises them publicly for bringing hard currency to the country.

Where you stand depends on where you sit. Every social and cultural phenomenon can be interpreted in a multitude of different ways, according to the perspective from which one sees it. Where interaction within the global system is concerned, ambiguities of this kind are typical, and they may remind us that people do not become 'the same' just because they engage in increased contact with each other.

Additionally, it becomes increasingly clear that the term 'Western culture' is notoriously inaccurate. Depending on definition and delineation, 'the West' contains between 700 million and 1 billion inhabitants. It is not, in other words, 'a culture', but a very large number of societies and a large number of different cultural environments. Besides, the emerging patterns of cultural variation due to migration and cultural globalisation mean that 'the West' exists just as much in a middle-class suburb of Nairobi as in Melbourne, and that Buenos Aires may be seen as a more typical 'Western' city than Bradford, where a large proportion of the population are Muslims of Asian origin. 'The West' cannot meaningfully be conceptualised as a kind of society: it must rather be regarded as an aspect of culture and social organisation not localised in a particular 'cultural area', namely what has here been called 'modernity'.

Migration and Cultural Identity

A salient feature of the world around the beginning of the third Christian millennium is mobility, displacement and exile. According to UN statistics, more than 100 million people lived outside their country of birth in 1992, and the number is growing. In addition, many descendants of migrants (who are born in their present country of residence) form, whether voluntarily or not, minorities (Chapter 17). An area which has a turbulent past and present in this respect is the Caribbean, and some of the most important anthropological studies of migration have been carried out here.

Karen Fog Olwig's studies of Caribbean culture and history (1985, 1993) reveal clearly why so much contemporary anthropological research can neither have a community focus nor be synchronous 'snapshots'. In her analyses of Nevisian society (Olwig 1993; Nevis forms part of St Kitt's and Nevis, and has about 10,000 inhabitants), she shows that this society has never been self-sufficient politically, culturally or economically – or indeed demographically. The ancestors of the present inhabitants arrived there as slaves and planters, and the Afro-Caribbean culture and social organisation in the island have developed in the interface between local factors and global processes. As part of a worldwide capitalist system, Nevisians are dependent on external forces; but Olwig also shows how they have actively shaped their own way of life. The high level of outmigration in the decades after the Second World war – few Nevisians do not have relatives living in metropolitan cities such as London, New York or Toronto – could similarly be seen as an expression of extreme dependence; but it can equally well be studied as a result of entrepreneurship and remarkable cultural adaptability.

Studying Nevisian migrants in Britain, Olwig shows that the codification and indeed creation of a distinct Nevisian identity takes place there, in intense contact with alien culture, as a counterforce to the local British identity. Further, perhaps more surprisingly, she argues that the annual Caribbean carnival in Notting Hill, West London (see also Abner Cohen 1993) can be seen not just as a construction of a Caribbean cultural identity, but also as a revitalisation of a lost English carnival tradition. Migration, far from severing ties with their island of birth, strengthens the local identifications of Nevisians, who talk of Nevis with compassion and nostalgia. They send remittances to their families, and many even invest in real estate in Nevis. The migrants and their children thus become important actors in both cultural and economic projects in Nevis, even if they live on the other side of the Atlantic.

Exile and De-territorialisation

The Satanic Verses (Rushdie 1988), the novel which has earned its author a *fatwa*, or death penalty, from Shi'ite priests in Teheran, is not primarily a book about Islam. Rather, it is about the condition of exile; about being on Air India's Flight 420 halfway between Bombay and London – permanently. In the book, Salman Rushdie shows how the shift in perspective entailed by exile creates doubt and uncertainty, because the person in exile discovers that the world, the past and (ultimately) even the truth appear differently when viewed from different positions. Ethnic revitalisation among migrant groups may be understood within this perspective. Drawing on nostalgia and a sense of alienation, such movements contrive to reinstil a sense of continuity with the past, ontological security (Giddens 1990) and personal security.

Although it has received intense attention from anthropologists and sociologists, revitalisation represents only one side of the coin. Clearly, the processes which in some cases inspire revitalisation also merit attention. These are the processes of globalisation, whereby people become embedded in shifting social and cultural networks of sometimes staggering scale, where society, in Zygmunt Bauman's view, 'proclaims all restrictions on freedom illegal, at the same time doing away with social certainty and legalizing ethical uncertainty' (1992, p. xxiv).

From an anthropological point of view, this needs to be studied empirically. Appadurai (1990) has thus proposed a framework for exploring cultural flow in the contemporary world. He distinguishes between five dimensions in global cultural flow, which have different ways of functioning.

The *ethnoscape* refers to 'the landscape of persons who constitute the shifting world in which we live'; in other words, the demographic attributes of the world – tourism, migration, exile, business travel, but also stable communities.

The *technoscape* means the 'global configuration ... of technology', which in important ways shapes the flow of cultural meaning, and also includes the uneven global distribution of technology.

The *finanscape* is the flow of capital, which has increasingly become disembedded from territories. Together, these three dimensions form a global infrastructure of sorts, but it is by no means predictable, since each 'is subject to its own constraints and incentives'.

The final two dimensions, which are ideational, are the *ideoscape* and the *mediascape*; referring, respectively, to ideological messages and mass media constructions.

A major point in Appadurai's article, and one that other writers on globalisation have also made, is that de-territorialisation – which does not merely
amount to large scale, but to the reduced importance of the spatial
dimension as such – necessitates new conceptualisations of the social and
cultural world. Ideas, technologies, people and money can be, and are,
moved about more frequently, quickly and easily across the globe in the
late twentieth century than ever before. One result, often described in terms
of displacement, is the growth of populations on the move or living in exile.
Another consequence is the self-conscious construction of place, since
place, as a space imbued with cultural meaning, can for many people no
longer be taken for granted. One's place of residence may change dramatically, or one may move somewhere else; and places are also multivocal
like symbols in the sense that they mean different things to different
people or in different situations (Rodman 1992). We should now move on
to a few further consequences of globalisation for anthropological research.

Challenging Dichotomies

A great part of anthropological theory rests on contrasting pairs, or
dichotomies, used analytically to distinguish between ideal types (Weber's
term) of societies and cultures. Some of the most widely invoked such
dichotomies are: small-scale/large-scale; oral/written; bricoleur/engineer;
traditional/modern; status/contract; Gemeinschaft (community)/Gesellschaft
(society).

An underlying assumption of this kind of dichotomy is the view that modern
industrial society is unique and stands out in relation to all other societies,
which, by comparison, are depicted as 'more or less the same'. Obviously,
these dichotomies are inadequate. First, traditional societies are not 'all
the same' – the ancient kingdoms of India and the pastoral societies of
North Africa have little in common. Second, this holds true for modern
societies as well. There are important differences between, say, Japan,
the United States and France. Third, the highly divisive distinction between
'types' of societies is untenable. In most if not all societies of the world, it
should be possible to identify 'modern' as well as 'traditional' aspects –
not least in the age of globalisation.

The world as it is studied by anthropologists is not characterised by clear,
'digital' or binary boundaries, but rather by grey zones and differences in
degree – analogic differences. It is not an archipelago of isolated cultures,
but an unbounded system of multiple interrelationships. Why then should
we bother with dichotomies at all? Strangely, perhaps, it seems difficult to
do without them. Anthropologists have for a long time been aware of the
inadequacies of rigid classificatory schemes; they have often been discarded,
but frequently only to re-emerge in a new guise. Perhaps dichotomies are
indeed necessary for the anthropological enterprise. If so, we should keep
two critical points in mind. First, the models are not identical with the social
world but a mere aid in organising facts from the social world; and second,
dichotomies may be envisaged as scales marked by differences in degree
rather than as absolute contrasts.

Some Consequences for Anthropology

Globalisation of culture does not mean that groups and individuals become culturally identical, but rather it engenders the growth of new kinds of cultural difference in the interface between the global and the local. Before moving on to some empirical examples, there follows a list of some general points concerning the consequences of globalisation for anthropological thought.

- It is becoming increasingly clear that the concepts 'tradition' and 'modernity' refer to a purely analytical distinction; that is to say, it is untenable to speak of traditional and modern societies in an empirical sense.
- The concepts of society and culture have become more problematic than ever before. The networks of communication, migration, trade, capital investments and politics cross virtually every boundary; with a few exceptions, neither states nor local communities are really clearly delineable in every regard. 'Cultures' are neither closed nor internally uniform.
- Since it has become impossible, in many cases, to delineate clearly the system being investigated, it has become more and more relevant to explore specified groups or specified cultural phenomena (such as the Olympic Games, tourism, migration) which do not make up autonomous systems in a social or cultural sense, but which can nevertheless be isolated for analytical purposes.
- Classic fieldwork has become quite insufficient as the sole method of collecting the data and insights required to understand social and cultural life on the planet. Fieldwork must generally be supplemented with additional sources giving access to the wider context of the phenomena being explored through participant observation.

The 'Indigenisation of Modernity'?

As early as the 1960s, the media theorist Marshall McLuhan introduced the concept of 'the global village' (McLuhan 1964). This notion was intended to account for the new cultural situation in the world, following the spread of modern mass media. The world had become one place, McLuhan argued, and he called this place a global village.

An essential point in anthropological research on globalisation lies in the necessity to account for the relationship between the global on the one hand, and the village, or the localised environment, on the other. To an anthropologist, McLuhan's term therefore implies an unhealthy mix of two levels, the level of interaction and the anonymous level: micro and macro.

The central paradox of globalisation is, perhaps, that it has made the world both larger and smaller at the same time. It has become smaller in the sense that it is possible to travel anywhere in less than 24 hours, and that it is practically possible to have the same lifestyle anywhere in the world. On the other hand, it has become larger in the sense that we thereby know more about remote and 'exotic' places, and thus more easily recognise our mutual differences. Jonathan Friedman puts it like this: 'Ethnic and cultural fragmentation and modernist homogenisation are not two arguments, two opposing views on what is happening in the world today, but two constituent trends in global reality' (1990, p. 311). There is, in other words, a movement towards integration into ever larger systems – where a growing majority of the world's population takes part in a perfectly unlimited system of exchange – and a localising emphasis on cultural uniqueness. What needs to be studied ethnographically, Sahlins argues, is 'the indigenization of modernity' (1994). This, as noted in Chapters 16 and 17, frequently takes the form of 'traditionalist' movements, often presented as ethnic or nationalist ones. Remarking on the modernist, reflexive conception of culture and its global dissemination, Sahlins writes:

'Culture' – the word itself, or some local equivalent – is on everyone's lips. Tibetans and Hawaiians, Ojibway, Kwakiutl and Eskimo, Kazakhs and Mongols, native Australians, Balinese, Kashmiris and New Zealand Maoris: all now discover that they have a 'culture'. For centuries they may hardly have noticed it. But today, as the

The 'cultural implosions' typical of the late twentieth century are full of apparent paradoxes – formerly unknown mixtures of the old and the new, the local and the global. In Noida, a new industrial estate near New Delhi, the intermingling of sacred cows with computer engineers and capitalist entrepreneurs is a common sight. (Photo by the author)

New Guinean said to the anthropologist, 'If we didn't have *kastom*, we would be just like white men'. (1994, p. 378)

On a more specific note, Edvard Hviding (1994) shows how Solomon Islanders, whose kinship concepts and practices have strong cognatic leanings, have in recent years begun to emphasise patrilineal descent, which proves more efficient in the formation of corporations and the making of land claims. Whether this should be labelled 'indigenisation of modernity' or 'modernisation of indigenity' is an open question, but it is clear that the shift in kinship practices and concepts is related to sociocultural change and the spread of the idea of culture as a political resource.

Two Localising Strategies

Paris is one of the most important 'African' cities in the world, and it attracts thousands of musicians, students, labour migrants and refugees from the Francophone parts of Africa. Many Parisians have West African parents and a personal identity partly connected to Senegal, Cameroon or the Ivory Coast, and many West Africans travel to and fro between the city and the home country.

Friedman (1990; see also Gandoulou 1989) has described a particular category of labour migrants to Paris. They originate in Brazzaville (Congo), where they are collectively known as *les sapeurs* (literally, 'the underminers'). Most of them are of humble origins, but they manage to travel to Paris, where they work very hard and consume as little as possible, in order to buy expensive fashion clothes to display publicly in the streets of Brazzaville at a later stage. This kind of consumption strategy falls squarely into the general category described earlier as conspicuous consumption: it expresses rank and prestige. What is interesting about 'les sapeurs' is not only the fact that they are much poorer than they look, but also that most of them belong to an ethnic group no longer in power. Friedman thus interprets their conspicuous consumption as a local political strategy: as a way of challenging power by overcommunicating one's own superiority and success. 'La sape' thus appears as a local countercultural strategy drawing on local evaluations of prestige and power, which in turn draw on what is globally prestigious; that is, expensive fashion clothes. It would not have been possible to understand this phenomenon in its full context without knowledge of both the local and the non-local levels.

An example of a rather different kind is Katarina Sjöberg's (1993) study of the Ainu, a Japanese minority. Officially, the Ainu have no status as an ethnic minority, since the Japanese government does not recognise the existence of minorities. Instead, they are categorised as an 'underdeveloped group'. Like indigenous people elsewhere, the Ainu have been subjected to systematic discrimination (they look more or less like Europeans and are considered hairy, ugly people); they have lost their traditional right to land and suffer from high rates of alcoholism and unemployment. Until the 1970s, it seemed as though Ainu identity was about to disappear completely. The language was nearly extinct, and the Ainu seemed to be about to become a Japanese underclass instead of an ethnic group. Then an ethnic revitalisation movement emerged – as with many other indigenous peoples during the same period. In the 1970s and 1980s a very active movement developed, its aim being to make the Japanese state recognise the Ainu as an ethnic group with a right to its own customs and its own language. The strategy, however, largely consisted of presenting Ainu culture as a commodity. Old rituals, traditional dress, handicrafts and culinary specialities were revitalised and presented in a commercialised, 'touristified' way. In this way, Japanese tourists to the Ainu north might discover that the Ainu 'had a culture' worthy of their respect, but the language of that 'culture' first had to be translated into the global language of commodity exchange, so to speak.

Commenting on Sjöberg's work and his own, Friedman (1990) notes that the strategies of both 'les sapeurs' and the Ainu may look like recipes for cultural suicide, since they are based on cultural premises which are not indigenous. The Congolese express prestige and individuality through the appropriation of foreign symbols; the Ainu express (and create) their ethnic identity by turning it into a commodity; they adapt it to a commercial market. The anthropological point in this respect is nevertheless not whether the 'cultures' expressed 'as a matter of fact' are local, 'authentic', etc., but whether they are efficient in promoting the experience of identity and political interests among the groups in question.

A Seamless World: Homogenisation and Differentiation

Cultural identity and 'uniqueness' have since the 1960s gradually become legitimate political resources in large parts of the world. A growing number of groups 'discover' their cultural uniqueness and exploit it for political purposes. Why does this happen?

A simple explanation might be that social identities become important only from the moment they feel threatened, and that tendencies towards the globalisation of culture, threatening to eradicate important cultural differences, more or less automatically trigger counter-reactions in the shape of ethnic or traditionalist movements.

A related, but probably more accurate explanation – which is also consistent with the account of ethnicity and nationalism in the two previous chapters – might be that the demarcation of boundaries about social identities (i) is perceived by many as necessary as a result of intensified contact between groups, and (ii) becomes possible because of technological and cultural changes following modernisation.

Towards the end of the twentieth century, it is doubtless the case that both homogenisation and differentiation are strong trends. Indeed, as the examples of the Ainu and the Congolese 'sapeurs' indicate, people may in fact favour both at the same time, in the sense that localising strategies are framed in 'global' terms – in the languages of commodity exchange and individual rights.

One important point to be made here is that the interrelationship between culture and identity is subjective and intersubjective, not objective. A social identity, whether ethnic, national or something else, can be created in a variety of ways. Anthropologists, for example, have a shared identity wherever they are; they form a community of sorts. As with ethnicity, the double criterion for a social identity to be socially valid is 'self-ascription and ascription by others' (see Chapter 16).

Another important point is related to power. Economic dependence in poor countries and poor localities has largely been studied through a focus on underpaid labour, unequal exchange and unequal relations of production. A stronger focus on, and a critical view of, the notion of cultural dependence, coupled with analyses of economic dependence, would certainly give increased depth to studies of the globalisation of culture. For even if people may choose their strategies, they do not do so under circumstances of their own choosing – and these circumstances differ greatly, not only with respect to differential access to, say, CNN on TV, but also regarding personal autonomy.

In an interview Lévi-Strauss related the following anecdote. He was visiting South Korea, and his hosts eagerly took him around to show him the great advances made by this much publicised NIC (newly industrialised country). They showed him sports stadia, freeways, skyscrapers and factories. Lévi-Strauss was not particularly interested, and wandered off as often as he could to museums where he could study old masks. 'Professor Lévi-Strauss!', his hosts eventually exclaimed, 'you are only interested in things that no longer exist!' – 'Yes,' he replied sullenly, 'I am only interested in things that no longer exist.'

To Lévi-Strauss, the cultural variation within modernity was not sufficient to call for his attention; to him, Seoul appeared more or less identical with Paris.

Seen from this kind of perspective, it is clear that the cultural variation of the world has been radically narrowed. Fewer and fewer anthropologists today encounter radical otherness of the kind described by Lévi-Strauss in *Tristes tropiques* (1976 [1955]). In this beautiful, melancholic book, he describes a field trip to Amazonia, where he met natives who were so close that he could touch them, and yet they seemed infinitely far away: he could not understand them.

From a certain point of view, the world is becoming progressively disenchanted, to use Max Weber's expression about modernity (*Entzauberung*): it seems to hide fewer and fewer secrets. The white spots on the map are gone, and there are probably no peoples left who have not, to a greater or lesser degree, been in contact with the modern world. Halfway through the twenty-first century, there may be no matrilineal peoples left. A sense of loss is apparent not only among anthropologists, but among very many of the peoples of the world. Yet – and that has been the perspective of this chapter – new cultural forms and social projects are continuously developed in local settings all over the world, and the processes of change happen in unpredictable and frequently surprising ways. There will, in other words, always remain variations in world views, ways of life, power relations and life-projects that are certain to provide ample challenges to anyone who is committed to trying to understand the differences and similarities between humans in societies.

Suggestions for Further Reading

Mike Featherstone, ed.: *Global Culture: Nationalism, Globalization and Modernity*. London: Sage 1990.
Jonathan Friedman: *Cultural Identity and Global Process*. London: Sage 1994.
Anthony Giddens: *The Consequences of Modernity*. Cambridge: Polity 1990.
Ulf Hannerz: *Cultural Complexity*. New York: Columbia University Press 1992.

EPILOGUE: AND SO WHAT?

I ordered my servant to bring my horse from the stables. He did not understand me. I went out to the stables myself, saddled my horse and mounted it. Somewhere far away I heard a trumpet. I asked him what it meant. He knew nothing and had heard nothing. At the gate he halted me and asked: 'Where does the master ride to?' — 'I do not know,' I answered, 'but away from here, only away from here. All the time away from here, only thus can I reach my aims.' — 'So you know your aim?' he asked. — 'Yes,' I answered, 'I told you. Away from here – that is my aim.'
—Franz Kafka, 'The Departure' ('Der Aufbruch', Kafka 1970 [1922])

What is the ultimate point of social anthropology? One may, obviously, use the subject to collect academic distinctions and eventually get a job. On the other hand, in most cases there are faster and more rewarding methods, at least in a pecuniary sense, of acquiring a livelihood. Fortunately, there are also other reasons for becoming involved in the subject.

The single most important human insight to be gained from this way of comparing societies is perhaps the realisation that everything could have been different in our own society – that the way we live is only one among innumerable ways of life which humans have adopted. If we glance sideways and backwards, we will quickly discover that modern society, with its many possibilities and seducing offers, its dizzying complexity and its impressive technological advances, is a way of life which has not been tried out for long. Perhaps, psychologically speaking, we have just left the cave: in terms of the history of our species, we have but spent a moment in modern societies.

As well as offering wisdom and insights, anthropology has its problematic points too – at least if we try to make it a moral philosophy. Perhaps the most common professional neurosis among anthropologists consists in the tendency to turn cultural relativism into a moral doctrine: as long as one can justify some notion or other as 'cultural', one feels committed to defending it. The result, of course, is that one becomes unable to pass moral judgement on anything at all. It must therefore be said that it is possible to understand without liking; it is possible to understand the mass worship of private cars and the death penalty as expressions of certain variants of North American culture without approving of them; and it is certainly possible to understand the principles for the exchange of women among the Kachin, or the principles of political organisation among the Nuer, without regarding them as 'superior' or 'inferior' to our own.

It is also perfectly feasible to admire New Guinean garden magic without being against the mass production of CD players and potato chips. It is not even certain that one is doing a favour to one's chosen people by trying to protect them against the impact of modernity.

A related professional neurosis can be termed 'sociologism'. This means that absolutely everything about human existence is interpreted in a socio-logical or anthropological frame of understanding. Art and literature, love and aesthetic experiences may thus be understood purely as social products. If one prefers Beethoven to pop, this is allegedly due to one's upbringing and the need to maintain symbolic fences vis-à-vis the lower classes, not to the fact that Beethoven's music may happen to possess artistic qualities. When the attitude of sociologism is profoundly embedded in one's personality, the whole world may appear as a set of 'phenomena', possibly classified into 'interesting' and 'uninteresting' ones. One ends by turning everything into 'empirical material', ultimately even one's own life.

Anthropology deals with 'the Others', but it does also in crucial ways concern ourselves. Anthropological studies may provide us with a mirror, a window, a contrast which makes it possible to reflect on our own existence in a new way. Descriptions of life in the Trobriand Islands remind us that our own society is not the only conceivable one. The Ndembu, the Inuits and the Dogon may tell us that our whole life could have been very different, and thanks to anthropological analyses of their societies they may even tell us *how* it might have been different. They force us to ask fundamental questions about ourselves and our own society. Sometimes they may even force us to act accordingly.

Anthropology also teaches us something about the complexity of culture and social life. Sometimes, as in the analysis of rituals, it may indeed seem that there is no easy question to the answers provided by anthro-pological research. Our job, faced with ideological simplifications, prejudice, ignorance and bigotry, must be to make the world more complex rather than simplifying it.

Anthropology may not provide the answer to the question of the meaning of life, but at least it can tell us that there are many ways in which to make a life meaningful. If it does not provide answers, anthropology may at least give us the feeling of being very close to the questions.

BIBLIOGRAPHY

Alford, Richard D. 1988. *Naming and Identity: A Cross-cultural Study of Personal Naming Practices*. New York: Harper & Row.

Anderson, Benedict. 1991. *Imagined Communities. An Inquiry into the Origins and Spread of Nationalism*, 2nd edition. London: Verso.

Appadurai, Arjun. 1986. Introduction: Commodities and the Politics of Value. In Arjun Appadurai, ed., *The Social Life of Things. Commodities in Cultural Perspective*, pp. 3–63. Cambridge: Cambridge University Press.

——. 1990. Disjuncture and Difference in the Global Cultural Economy. In Mike Featherstone, ed., *Global Culture. Nationalism, Globalization, and Modernity*, pp. 295–310. London: Sage.

Archetti, Eduardo P. 1991 [1984]. De l'idéologie du pouvoir. Analyse culturelle comparative. In Arne Martin Klausen, ed., *Le Savoir-etre norvegien: regards anthropologiques sur la culture norvegienne*, pp. 243–62, trans. Marina-Christine Coidan and Evelyne Nomme. Paris: L'Harmattan.

——. 1992a. *El mundo social y simbólico del cuy*. Quito: CEPLAES.

——. 1992b. Cultural Globalization and Localization in the XVI Winter Olympic Games of Albertville. Paper presented at 2nd EASA (European Association of Social Anthropologists) Conference, Prague, 28–31 August.

——. 1994. Introduction. In Eduardo P. Archetti, ed., *Exploring the Written. Anthropology and the Multiplicity of Writing*, pp. 11–30. Oslo: Scandinavian University Press.

Ardener, Edwin. 1977. Belief and the Problem of Women. In Shirley Ardener, ed., *Perceiving Women*, pp. 1–17. London: J.M. Dent & Sons.

——. 1989. *The Voice of Prophecy and Other Essays*, ed. Malcolm Chapman. Oxford: Blackwell.

Arens, William. 1978. *The Man-eating Myth. Anthropology and Anthropophagy*. Oxford: Oxford University Press.

Aron, Raymond. 1964. *La Lutte des classes*. Paris: Gallimard.

Asad, Talal. 1972. Market Model, Class Structure and Consent: A Reconsideration of Swat Political Organisation. *Man* (n.s.), 7: 74–94.

Bailey, F.G. 1971. *Gifts and Poison*. Oxford: Blackwell.

——. 1968. Parapolitical Systems. In M.J. Swartz, ed., *Local-level Politics. Social and Cultural Perspectives*, pp. 281–93. Chicago: Aldine.

Balandier, Georges. 1967. *Anthropologie politique*. Paris: Presses Universitaires Françaises.

Balikci, Asen. 1968. The Netsilik Eskimos: Adaptive Processes. In Richard Lee and Irven deVore, eds, *Man the Hunter*, pp. 78–82. Chicago: Aldine.

Bamberger, Joan. 1974. The Myth of Matriarchy: Why Men Rule in Primitive Society. In Michelle Z. Rosaldo and Louise Lamphere, eds, *Woman, Culture, Society*, pp. 263–80. Stanford, CA: Stanford University Press.

Barnard, Alan and Anthony Good. 1984. *Research Practices in the Study of Kinship*. London: Academic Press.

Barnes, John A. 1990. *Models and Interpretations. Selected Essays*. Cambridge: Cambridge University Press.

Barth, Fredrik. 1959. *Political Leadership among Swat Pathans*. London: Athlone Press.

———. 1961. *Nomads of South Persia. The Basseri Tribe of the Khamseh Confederacy*. Oslo: Scandinavian University Press.

———. 1966. *Models of Social Organization*. London: Royal Anthropological Institute, Occasional Papers, **23**.

———. 1967. Economic Spheres in Darfur. In Raymond Firth, ed., *Themes in Economic Anthropology*, pp. 149–74. London: Tavistock

———. ed. 1969. *Ethnic Groups and Boundaries. The Social Organization of Culture Difference*. Oslo: Scandinavian University Press.

———. 1975. *Ritual and Knowledge among the Baktaman*. Oslo: Scandinavian University Press.

———. ed. 1978. *Scale and Social Organization*. Oslo: Scandinavian University Press.

———. 1981. *Features of Person and Society in Swat. Selected Essays of Fredrik Barth*, vol. 2. London: Routledge & Kegan Paul.

———. 1993. *Balinese Worlds*. Chicago: University of Chicago Press.

Barth, Theo. 1991. Agón. Unpublished thesis, Department and Museum of Anthropology, University of Oslo.

Bateson, Gregory. 1958 [1936]. *Naven*. Stanford, CA: Stanford University Press.

———. 1972. *Steps to an Ecology of Mind*. New York: Chandler.

———. 1979. *Mind and Nature*. Glasgow: Fontana.

Bauman, Zygmunt. 1992. *Intimations of Postmodernity*. London: Routledge.

Beaudoin, Gérard. 1984. *Les Dogons du Mali*. Paris: Armand Colin.

Beidelman, T.O. 1971. *The Kaguru. A Matrilineal People of East Africa*. New York: Holt, Rinehart & Winston.

Benedict, Ruth. 1970 [1934]. *Patterns of Culture*. Boston, MA: Houghton Mifflin.

———. 1974 [1946]. *The Chrysanthemum and the Sword*. Boston, MA: Houghton Mifflin.

Berger, Peter and Thomas Luckmann. 1967. *The Social Construction of Reality*. Harmondsworth: Penguin.

Bernard, H. Russell. 1994. *Research Methods in Anthropology. Qualitative and Quantitative Approaches*. London: Sage.

Bernstein, Basil. 1972. Social Class, Language and Socialization. In Pier Paolo Giglioli, ed., *Language and Social Context*, pp. 157–78. Harmondsworth: Penguin 1972.

Berreman, Gerald. 1962. *Behind Many Masks: Ethnography and Impression Management in a Himalayan Village*. Society for Applied Anthropology: Monograph no. 4.

———. 1971. Self, Situation and Escape from Stigmatized Ethnic Identity. Oslo: *Etnografisk Museums Årbok*, pp. 11–25. Oslo: Ethnographic Museum.

———. 1979. *Caste and Other Inequalities: Essays on Inequality*. Meerut: Folklore Institute.

Bloch, Maurice. 1971. *Placing the Dead: Tombs, Ancestral Villages and Kinship Organization in Madagascar*. London: Seminar.

———. ed. 1975. *Marxist Analyses and Social Anthropology*. London: Malaby.

———. 1986. *From Blessing to Violence*. Cambridge: Cambridge University Press.

———. 1991. Language, Anthropology and Cognitive Science. *Man*, **26**: 183–98.

Blom, Jan-Petter. 1969. Ethnic and Cultural Differentiation. In Fredrik Barth, ed., *Ethnic Groups and Boundaries. The Social Organization of Culture Difference*, pp. 75–85. Oslo: Scandinavian University Press.

Boas, Franz. 1969 [1925]. *Contributions to the Ethnology of the Kwakiutl*. New York: AMS Press.

Bohannan, Laura. 1952. A Genealogical Charter. *Africa*, **22**: 301–15.

—— and Paul Bohannan. 1953. *The Tiv of Central Nigeria*. London: Oxford University Press.

Bohannan, Paul. 1957. *Judgement and Justice among the Tiv*. London: Oxford University Press.

——. 1959. The Impact of Money on an African Subsistence Economy. *Journal of Economic History*, **19**: 491–503.

Borofsky, Robert. 1994. On the Knowledge and Knowing of Cultural Activities. In Robert Borofsky, ed., *Assessing Cultural Anthropology*, pp. 331–47. New York: McGraw-Hill.

Boserup, Ester. 1970. *Women's Role in Economic Development*. London: Allen & Unwin.

Bourdieu, Pierre. 1963. The Algerian Peasant's Attitude towards Time. In Julian Pitt-Rivers, ed., *Mediterranean Countrymen*, pp. 55–72. Paris: Mouton.

——. 1977 [1972]. *Outline of a Theory of Practice*, trans. Richard Nice. Cambridge: Cambridge University Press.

——. 1984 [1979]. *Distinction*, trans. Richard Nice. London: Routledge.

——. 1982. *Ce que parler veut dire*. Paris: Fayard.

——. 1988 [1984]. *Homo Academicus*, trans. Peter Collier. Cambridge: Polity.

——. 1990 [1980]. *The Logic of Practice*, trans. Richard Nice. Cambridge: Polity.

Brøgger, Jan. 1990. *Pre-bureaucratic Europeans*. Oslo: Scandinavian University Press.

Bulmer, Ralph. 1967. Why Is the Cassowary Not a Bird? A Problem of Zoological Taxonomy among the Karam of New Guinea. *Man* (n.s.), **2**: 5–25.

Burghart, Richard. 1990. Ethnographers and their Local Counterparts in India. In Richard Fardon, ed., *Localizing Strategies*, pp. 260–79. Edinburgh: Scottish Academic Press.

Burnham, P.C. and Roy F. Ellen, eds. 1979. *Social and Ecological Systems*. London: Academic Press.

Carrithers, Michael. 1992. *Why Humans Have Cultures. Explaining Anthropology and Social Diversity*. Oxford: Oxford University Press

——, Steven Collins and Steven Lukes, eds. 1985. *The Category of the Person. Anthropology, Philosophy, History*. Cambridge: Cambridge University Press.

Cavalli-Sforza, Luca, Paolo Menozzi and Alberto Piazza, eds. 1994. *The History and Geography of Human Genes*. Princeton, NJ: Princeton University Press.

Chagnon, Napoleon A. 1983. *Yanomamö. The Fierce People*, 3rd edition. New York: Holt, Rinehart & Winston.

Chapman, Malcolm. 1982. 'Semantics' and the 'Celt'. In David Parkin, ed., *Semantic Anthropology*, pp. 123–44. London: Academic Press.

Claessen, H.J. and Peter Skálnik, eds. 1974. *The Early State*. The Hague: Mouton.

Classen, Constance. 1993. *Worlds of Sense. Exploring the Senses in History and across Cultures*. London: Routledge.

Clastres, Pierre. 1977. *Society against the State*. Oxford: Mole.

Clifford, James and George Marcus, eds. 1986. *Writing Culture. The Poetics and Politics of Ethnography*. Berkeley: University of California Press.

Cohen, Abner. 1969. *Custom and Politics in Urban Africa*. London: Routledge.

——. 1974. *Two-dimensional Man*. London: Tavistock.

——. 1981. *The Politics of Elite Culture*. Berkeley: University of California Press.

——. 1993. *Masquerade Politics: Explorations in the Structure of Urban Cultural Movements*. Berkeley: University of California Press.

Cohen, Anthony P. 1985. *The Symbolic Construction of Community*. London: Routledge.

Cohen, David William and E.S. Atieno Odhiambo. 1989. *Siaya. The Historical Anthropology of a Landscape*. London: James Currey.

Collier, Jane and Sylvia Yanagisako. 1987. *Gender and Kinship: Essays toward an Unified Analysis*. Stanford, CA: Stanford University Press.

Connerton, Paul. 1989. *How Societies Remember*. Cambridge: Cambridge University Press.

Cresswell, Robert. 1991. Technologie. In Pierre Bonté and Michel Izard, eds, *Dictionnaire de l'ethnologie et de l'anthropologie*, pp. 698–701. Paris: Presses Universitaires Françaises.

Das, Veena. 1994. The Anthropological Discourse on India. In Robert Borofsky, ed., *Assessing Cultural Anthropology*, pp. 133–144. New York: McGraw-Hill.

Davis, John. 1992a. Tense in Ethnography: Some Practical Considerations. In Judith Okely and Helen Calloway, eds, *Anthropology and Autobiography*, pp. 205–20. London: Routledge.

——. 1992b. *Exchange*. Buckingham: Open University Press.

Dawkins, Richard. 1976. *The Selfish Gene*. Oxford: Oxford University Press.

Descola, Philippe and Michel Izard. 1992. Guerre. In Pierre Bonté and Michel Izard, eds, *Dictionnaire de l'ethnologie et de l'anthropologie*, pp. 313–16. Paris: Presses Universitaires Françaises.

Despres, Leo, ed. 1975. *Ethnicity and Resource Competition in Plural Societies*. The Hague: Mouton.

Douglas, Mary. 1966. *Purity and Danger*. London: Routledge & Kegan Paul.

——. 1970. *Natural Symbols*. London: Barrie & Rockliff.

——. 1975. *Implicit Meanings*. London: Routledge & Kegan Paul.

——. 1978. *Cultural Bias*. London: Royal Anthropological Institute.

——. 1987. *How Institutions Think*. London: Routledge.

—— and Baron Isherwood. 1978. *The World of Goods. Towards an Anthropology of Consumption*. New York: Basic Books.

Duerr, Hans Peter. 1985. *Satyricon: Essays und Interviews*. Frankfurt-am-Main: Suhrkamp.

Dumont, Louis. 1969 [1961]. Caste, Racism and 'Stratification': Reflections of a Social Anthropologist. In André Béteille, ed., *Inequality*, pp. 337–61. Harmondsworth: Penguin.

——. 1980. *Homo Hierarchicus. The Caste System and its Implications*, 2nd edition, trans. Mark Sainsbury, Louis Dumont and Basia Gulati. Chicago: University of Chicago Press.

——. 1986. *Essays on Individualism*: Modern Ideology in Anthropological Perspective. Chicago: University of Chicago Press.

Durkheim, Emile. 1951 [1897]. *Suicide: A Study in Sociology*, trans. John A. Spaulding and George Simpson. New York: Free Press.

——. 1960 [1893]. *De la division de travail social*. Paris: Presses Universitaires Françaises.

—— and Marcel Mauss. 1963 [1903]. *Primitive Classification*, trans. Rodney Needham. London: Cohen & West.

Eidheim, Harald. 1971. *Aspects of the Lappish Minority Situation*. Oslo: Scandinavian University Press.

Ellen, Roy F., ed. 1984. *Ethnographic Research*. London: Academic Press.

Epstein, A.L. 1978. *Ethos and Identity*. London: Tavistock.

Eriksen, Thomas Hylland. 1988. *Communicating Cultural Difference and Identity: Ethnicity and Nationalism in Mauritius*. Oslo: Occasional Papers in Social Anthropology, **16**.
———. 1990. Liming in Trinidad: The Art of Doing Nothing. *Folk*, **32**: 23–43.
———. 1992. *Us and Them in Modern Societies: Ethnicity and Nationalism in Mauritius, Trinidad and Beyond*. Oslo: Scandinavian University Press.
———. 1993. *Ethnicity & Nationalism: Anthropological Perspectives*. London: Pluto.
———. 1994. The Anthropologist as Author. Some West Indian Lessons about the Relevance of Fiction for Anthropology. In Eduardo P. Archetti, ed., *Exploring the Written. Anthropology and the Multiplicity of Writing*, pp. 167–96. Oslo: Scandinavian University Press.
Evans-Pritchard, E.E. 1940. *The Nuer*. Oxford: Clarendon.
———. 1951. *Social Anthropology*. Glencoe: Free Press.
———. 1956. *Nuer Religion*. Oxford: Clarendon.
———. 1962. *Social Anthropology and Other Essays*. New York: Free Press.
———. 1965. *Theories of Primitive Religion*. Oxford: Clarendon.
———. 1983 [1937]. *Witchcraft, Magic and Oracles among the Azande*, ed. Eva Gillies. Oxford: Oxford University Press.

Featherstone, Mike, ed. 1990. *Global Culture: Nationalism, Globalization and Modernity*. London: Sage.
Feld, Steven. 1982. *Sound and Sentiment. Birds, Weeping, Politics and Song in Kaluli Expression*. Philadelphia: University of Pennsylvania Press.
—. 1994. Notes on 'World Beat'. In Charles Keil and Steven Feld, *Music Grooves*, pp. 238–46. Chicago: University of Chicago Press.
Feldman, Allen. 1991. *Formations of Violence. The Narrative of the Body and Political Terror in Northern Ireland*. Chicago: University of Chicago Press 1991.
Feyerabend, Paul K. 1975. *Against Method*. London: Verso.
Finnegan, Ruth. 1988. *Literacy and Orality: Studies in the Technology of Communication*. Oxford: Blackwell.
Firth, Raymond. 1951. *Elements of Social Organization*. London: Watts.
———. ed. 1967. *Themes in Economic Anthropology*. London: Routledge.
———. 1985. Degrees of Intelligibility. In Joanna Overing, ed., *Reason and Morality*, pp. 29–46. London: Tavistock.
———. 1989. The Future of Social Anthropology. Lecture given at the University of Oslo, November 1989.
Fitzgerald, Thomas. 1993. *Metaphors of Identity. A Culture–Communication Dialogue*. New York: SUNY Press.
Fortes, Meyer. 1945. *The Dynamics of Clanship among the Tallensi*. London: Oxford University Press.
——— and E.E. Evans-Pritchard, eds. 1940. *African Political Systems*. Oxford: Oxford University Press.
Foucault, Michel. 1970. *The Order of Things*. London: Tavistock.
———. 1979. *Discipline and Punish: the Birth of the Prison*, trans. Alan Sheridan. New York: Vintage.
Fox, Richard G., ed. 1991. *Recapturing Anthropology: Working in the Present*. Santa Fe: School of American Research Press.
Fox, Robin. 1967. *Kinship and Marriage*. Harmondsworth: Penguin.
Frank, Andre Gunder. 1979. *Dependent Accumulation and Underdevelopment*. New York: Monthly Review Press.
Frazer, James. 1974 [1922]. *The Golden Bough* (abridged edition). London: Macmillan.
Freeman, Derek. 1983. *Margaret Mead and Samoa. The Making and Unmaking of an Anthropological Myth*. Cambridge, MA: Harvard University Press.

Friedman, Jonathan. 1975. Tribes, States, and Transformations. In Maurice Bloch, ed., *Marxist Analyses and Social Anthropology*, pp. 161–202. London: Malaby.
——. 1990. Being in the World: Globalization and Localization. In Mike Feather-stone, ed., *Global Culture. Nationalism, Globalization, and Modernity*, pp. 311–28. London: Sage.
——. 1994. *Cultural Identity and Global Process*. London: Sage.
Friedman, Kajsa Ekholm. 1991. *Catastrophe and Creation: The Formation of an African Culture*. London: Harwood.
——. 1994. *Den magiska världsbilden. Om statens frigörelse från folket i Folkrepubliken Kongo*. Stockholm: Carlssons.

Galey, Jean-Claude. 1992. Orientalisme et anthropologie. In Pierre Bonté and Michel Izard, eds, *Dictionnaire de l'ethnologie et de l'anthropologie*, pp. 529–32. Paris: Presses Universitaires Françaises.
Gandoulou, J.-D. 1989. *Dandies à Bacongo: Le Culte de l'élégance dans la société congolaise contemporaine*. Paris: L'Harmattan.
Geertz, Clifford. 1963. *Agricultural Involution: The Processes of Ecological Change in Indonesia*. Berkeley: University of California Press.
——. 1971. The Wet and the Dry: Traditional Irrigation in Bali and Morocco. *Human Ecology*, 1(1): 23–9.
——. 1973. *The Interpretation of Cultures*. New York: Basic Books.
——. 1983. *Local Knowledge: Further Essays in Interpretive Anthropology*. New York: Basic Books.
——. 1988. *Works and Lives. The Anthropologist as Author*. Cambridge: Polity.
——. 1994. The Uses of Diversity. In Robert Borofsky, ed., *Assessing Cultural Anthropology*. New York: McGraw-Hill.
Gell, Alfred. 1992. *The Anthropology of Time*. Oxford: Berg.
Gellner, Ernest. 1983. *Nations and Nationalism*. Oxford: Blackwell.
Georges, Eugenia. 1990. *The Making of a Transnational Community. Migration, Development and Cultural Change in the Dominican Republic*. New York: Columbia University Press.
Giddens, Anthony. 1979. *Central Problems in Social Theory*. London: Macmillan.
——. 1984. *The Constitution of Society*. Cambridge: Polity.
——. 1985. *The Nation-state and Violence*. Cambridge: Polity.
——. 1990. *The Consequences of Modernity*. Cambridge: Polity.
Gilmore, David D. 1989. *Manhood in the Making. Cultural Conceptions of Masculinity*. New Haven, CT: Yale University Press.
Gledhill, John. 1994. *Power and its Disguises: Perspectives on Political Anthropology*. London: Pluto.
Gluckman, Max. 1982 [1956]. *Custom and Conflict in Africa*. Oxford: Blackwell.
Godelier, Maurice. 1975. Infrastructures, Societies and History. *Current Anthropology*, 19(4): 763–71.
——. 1977. *Perspectives in Marxist Anthropology*. Cambridge: Cambridge University Press.
——. ed. 1991. *Transitions et subordinations au capitalisme*. Paris: Maison des Sciences de l'Homme.
Goffman, Erving. 1961. *Encounters. Two Studies in the Sociology of Interaction*. Indianapolis: Boobs-Merrill Educational Publishing.
——. 1978 [1959]. *The Presentation of Self in Everyday Life*. Harmondsworth: Penguin.
Goody, Jack. 1976. *From Production to Reproduction. A Comparative Study of the Domestic Domain*. Cambridge: Cambridge University Press.
——. 1977. *The Domestication of the Savage Mind*. Cambridge: Cambridge University Press.

——. 1982. *Cooking, Cuisine and Class*. Cambridge: Cambridge University Press.

——. 1986. *The Logic of Writing and the Organization of Society*. Cambridge: Cambridge University Press.

——. ed. 1968. *Literacy in Traditional Societies*. Cambridge: Cambridge University Press.

Gough, E. Kathleen. 1959. The Nayars and the Definition of Marriage. *Journal of the Royal Anthropological Institute*, **89**: 23–34.

Guha, Ranajit, ed. 1989. *Subaltern Studies VI. Writings on South Asian History and Society*. New Delhi: Oxford University Press.

Gullestad, Marianne. 1984. *Kitchen-table Society*. Oslo: Scandinavian University Press.

Haaland, Gunnar. 1969. Economic Determinants in Ethnic Processes. In Fredrik Barth, ed., *Ethnic Groups and Boundaries. The Social Organization of Culture Difference*, pp. 58–74. Oslo: Scandinavian University Press.

Habermas, Jürgen. 1967. *Wissenschaft und Technik als 'Ideologie'*. Frankfurt-am-Main: Suhrkamp.

Hall, Edward O. 1966. *The Hidden Dimension*. Garden City, NY: Doubleday.

Halverson, John. 1992. Goody and the Implosion of the Literacy Thesis. *Man*, **27**(2): 300–17.

Handelman, Don. 1977. The Organization of Ethnicity. *Ethnic Groups*, **1**: 269–74.

——. 1990. *Models and Mirrors. Towards an Anthropology of Public Events*. Cambridge: Cambridge University Press.

Handler, Richard. 1988. *Nationalism and the Politics of Culture in Quebec*. Madison: Wisconsin University Press.

——. and Daniel Segal. 1993. How European is Nationalism? *Social Analysis*, **32**(1): 1–15.

Hannerz, Ulf. 1980. *Exploring the City: Inquiries toward an Urban Anthropology*. New York: Columbia University Press.

——. 1990. Cosmopolitans and Locals in World Culture. In Mike Featherstone, ed., *Global Culture. Nationalism, Globalization, and Modernity*, pp. 237–52. London: Sage.

——. 1992. *Cultural Complexity*. New York: Columbia University Press.

Harris, Marvin. 1964. *The Nature of Cultural Things*. New York: Random House.

——. 1979. *Cultural Materialism: The Struggle for a Science of Culture*. New York: Random House.

Harris, Olivia. In press. Knowing the Past: The Antinomies of Loss in Highland Bolivia. In Richard Fardon, ed., *Counterwork: Managing Diverse Knowledges*. London: Routledge.

Hastrup, Kirsten. 1992. Writing Ethnography: State of the Art. In Helen Calloway and Judith Okely, eds, *Anthropology and Autobiography*, pp. 116–33. London: Routledge.

Holy, Ladislav. 1990. Strategies for Old Age among the Berti of the Sudan. In Paul Spencer, ed., *Anthropology and the Riddle of the Sphinx*, pp. 167–82. London: Routledge.

—— and Milan Stuchlik. 1983. *Actions, Norms and Representations*. Cambridge: Cambridge University Press.

Horowitz, Donald. 1985. *Ethnic Groups in Conflict*. Berkeley: University of California Press.

Horton, Robin. 1970. African Traditional Thought and Western Science. In Bryan R. Wilson, ed., *Rationality*, pp. 131–71. Oxford: Blackwell.

Howell, Signe. 1989. 'To Be Angry Is Not to Be Human, but to Be Fearful Is': Chewong Concepts of Human Nature. In Signe Howell and Roy Willis, eds, *Societies at Peace: Anthropological Perspectives*, pp. 45–59. London: Routledge.

—— and Marit Melhuus. 1993. The Study of Kinship; the Study of Person; a Study of Gender? In Teresa del Valle, ed., *Gendered Anthropology*, pp. 38–53. London: Routledge 1993.
—— and Roy Willis, eds. 1989. *Societies at Peace: Anthropological Perspectives*. London: Routledge.
Huntington, Ellsworth. 1945. *Mainsprings of Civilization*. London: Wiley.
Hviding, Edvard. 1994. Indigenous Essentialism? 'Simplifying' Customary Land Ownership in New Georgia, Solomon Islands. *Bijdragen*, 149: 802–24.

Inden, Ronald. 1990. *Imagining India*. Oxford: Blackwell.
Ingold, Tim. 1979. The Social and Ecological Relations of Culture-bearing Organisms: An Essay in Evolutionary Dynamics. In P.C. Burnham and Roy F. Ellen, eds, *Social and Ecological Systems*, pp. 271–92. London: Academic Press.
——. 1986. *Evolution and Social Life*. Cambridge: Cambridge University Press.
——. 1993. The Art of Translation in a Continuous World. In Gisli Pálsson, ed., *Beyond Boundaries: Understanding, Translation and Anthropological Discourse*, pp. 210–30. Oxford: Berg.
——. 1994a. Humanity and Animality. In Tim Ingold, ed., *Companion Encyclopedia of Anthropology: Humanity, Culture and Social Life*, pp. 14–32. London: Routledge.
——. 1994b. Introduction to Social Life. In Tim Ingold, ed., *Companion Encyclopedia of Anthropology: Humanity, Culture and Social Life*, pp. 735–37. London: Routledge.

Jarvie, Ian C. 1968. Limits to the Functionalism and Alternatives to it in Anthropology. In Robert A. Manners and David Kaplan, eds, *Theory in Anthropology – A Source Book*, pp. 196–203. Chicago: University of Chicago Press.
Jenkins, Richard. 1993. *Pierre Bourdieu*. Cambridge: Polity.

Kafka, Franz. 1970 [1922]. Der Aufbruch. In Franz Kafka, *Sämtliche Erzählungen*, p. 376. Frankfurt-am-Main: Fischer.
Kapferer, Bruce. 1984. The Ritual Process and the Problem of Reflexivity in Sinhalese Demon Exorcism. In John MacAloon, ed., *Rite, Drama, Festival, Spectacle*, pp. 179–207. Ithaca, NY: Cornell University Press.
——. 1988. *Legends of People; Myths of State*. Baltimore, MD: Smithsonian Institution Press.
Keesing, Roger M. 1981. *Cultural Anthropology – Contemporary Perspectives*. New York: Holt, Rinehart & Winston.
——. 1994. Theories of Culture Revisited. In Robert Borofsky, ed., *Assessing Cultural Anthropology*, pp. 301–9. New York: McGraw-Hill.
Kertzer, David I. 1988. *Ritual, Politics and Power*. New Haven, CT: Yale University Press.
Klass, Morton. 1991. *Singing with Sai Baba: The Politics of Revitalization in Trinidad*. Boulder, CO: Westview.
Kluckhohn, Clyde and Alfred E. Kroeber. 1952. *Culture: A Critical Review of Concepts and Definitions*. Cambridge, MA: Harvard University Press.
Knudsen, Anne. 1987. Silent Bodies and Singing Minds. *Folk*, 29: 239–56.
——. 1992. Dual Histories. In Kirsten Hastrup, ed., *Other Histories*, pp. 82–102. London: Routledge.
Kopytoff, Igor. 1971. Ancestors as Elders in Africa. *Africa*, 41: 129–41.
——. 1986. The Cultural Biography of Things: Commoditization as Process. In Arjun Appadurai, ed., *The Social Life of Things. Commodities in Cultural Perspective*, pp. 64–94. Cambridge: Cambridge University Press.

Kroeber, Alfred L. 1952 [1917]. *The Nature of Culture*. Chicago: University of Chicago Press.

Kuhn, Thomas. 1962. *The Structure of Scientific Revolutions*. Chicago: University of Chicago Press.

Kuper, Adam. 1983. *Anthropology and Anthropologists: The Modern British School*. London: Routledge & Kegan Paul.

—— 1988. *The Invention of Primitive Society. Transformations of an Illusion*. London: Routledge.

—— 1994. Anthropological Futures. In Robert Borofsky, ed., *Assessing Cultural Anthropology*, pp. 113–18. New York: McGraw-Hill.

Labov, William. 1972. The Logic of Nonstandard English. In Pier Paolo Giglioli, ed., *Language and Social Context*, pp. 179–216. Harmondsworth: Penguin.

Lakoff, George and Mark Johnson. 1980. *Metaphors We Live By*. Chicago: University of Chicago Press.

Lan, David. 1985. *Guns and Rain. Guerrillas and Spirit Mediums in Zimbabwe*. London: James Currey.

Lash, Scott and Jonathan Friedman, eds. 1991. *Modernity and Identity*. London: Routledge.

Leach, Edmund R. 1954. *Political Systems of Highland Burma*. London: Athlone.

——. 1968. Ritual. *Encyclopedia of the Social Sciences*. New York: Free Press.

——. 1970. *Lévi-Strauss*. Glasgow: Fontana.

——. 1976. *Culture and Communication. The Logic by which Symbols Are Connected*. Cambridge: Cambridge University Press.

——. 1982. *Social Anthropology*. Glasgow: Fontana.

Leach, Jerry W. and G. Kildea. 1974. *Trobriand Cricket: An Ingenious Response to Colonialism* (documentary film). Berkeley: University of California Extension Media Center.

—— and Edmund Leach, eds. 1983. *The Kula. New Perspectives on Massim Exchange*. Cambridge: Cambridge University Press.

Lee, Richard. 1968. What Hunters Do for a Living, or How to Make out on Scarce Resources. In Richard Lee and Irven deVore, eds, *Man the Hunter*, pp. 30–48. Chicago: Aldine.

Lévi-Strauss, Claude. 1963. *Totemism*, trans. Rodney Needham. Boston, MA: Beacon.

——. 1966 [1962]. *The Savage Mind*. Chicago: University of Chicago Press.

——. 1969 [1949]. *The Elementary Structures of Kinship*, trans. Rodney Needham. London: Tavistock.

——. 1976 [1955]. *Tristes tropiques*, trans. John and Doreen Weightman. Harmondsworth: Penguin.

——. 1983. *Le Regard éloigné*. Paris: Plon. (English edn.: *The View from Afar*. New York: Basic Books 1985)

Lewis, Gordon K. 1983. *Main Currents in Caribbean Thought*. Kingston: Heinemann.

Lieberman, Philip. 1994. The Origins and Evolution of Language. In Tim Ingold, ed., *Companion Encyclopedia of Anthropology: Humanity, Culture and Social Life*, pp. 108–32. London: Routledge.

Lien, Marianne. 1988. *Fra boknafesk til pizza* (From Boknafesk [dried and salted cod] to Pizza). Oslo: Department of Social Anthropology, Occasional papers no. 18.

Lienhardt, Godfrey. 1985. From Study to Field, and Back. *Times Literary Supplement*, 7 June.

——. 1987. Self, Public, Private: Some African Representations. In Michael Carrithers, Steven Collins and Steven Lukes, eds, *The Category of the Person: Anthropology, Philosophy, History*, pp. 141–45. Cambridge: Cambridge University Press.

Little, Kenneth. 1978. Countervailing Influences in African Ethnicity: A Less Apparent Factor. In Brian du Toit, ed., *Ethnicity in Modern Africa*, pp. 175–89. Boulder, CO: Sage.

Lock, Margaret. 1990. On Being Ethnic: The Politics of Identity Breaking and Making in Canada, or, *Nevra* on a Sunday. *Culture, Medicine and Psychiatry*, **14**: 237–54.

Lukács, György. 1971 [1923]. History and Class Consciousness: Studies in Marxist Dialectics, trans. Rodney Livingstone. London: Merlin.

Lukes, Steven. 1977. *Power: A Radical View*. London: Macmillan.

Lutz, Catherine. 1988. *Unnatural Emotions*. Chicago: University of Chicago Press.

Mach, Zdzislav. 1993. *Symbols, Conflict, and Identity. Essays in Political Anthropology*. New York: SUNY Press.

Macintyre, Alasdair. 1970. Is Understanding Religion Compatible with Believing? In Bryan R. Wilson, ed., *Rationality*, pp. 62–77. Oxford: Blackwell.

Malinowski, Bronislaw. 1966 [1935]. *Coral Gardens and their Magic*. London: Allen & Unwin.

———. 1967. *A Diary in the Strict Sense of the Term*. London: Routledge & Kegan Paul.

———. 1974 [1948]. *Magic, Science and Religion and Other Essays*. London: Souvenir.

———. 1984 [1922]. *Argonauts of the Western Pacific*. Prospect Heights, IL: Waveland.

Malthus, Thomas. 1982 [1798]. *An Essay on the Principle of Population*. Harmondsworth: Penguin.

Mandelbaum, David G. 1988. *Women's Seclusion and Men's Honour. Sex Roles in North India, Bangladesh, and Pakistan*. Tucson: University of Arizona Press.

Manganaro, Marc, ed. 1990. *Modernist Anthropology. From Fieldwork to Text*. Princeton, NJ: Princeton University Press.

Marcus, George and Michael Fischer. 1986. *Anthropology as a Cultural Critique. An Experimental Moment in the Human Sciences*. Chicago: University of Chicago Press.

Marx, Karl. 1906 [1867–1894]. *Capital: A Critique of Political Economy*. New York: Modern Library.

——— and Friedrich Engels. 1968 [1848]. *The Communist Manifesto*. New York: The Modern Reader.

Mauss, Marcel. 1954 [1924] *The Gift*, trans. Ian Cunnison. London: Cohen & West.

———. 1985 [1938]. A Category of the Human Mind: The Notion of the Self. In Michael Carrithers, Steven Collins and Steven Lukes, eds, *The Category of the Person. Anthropology, Philosophy, History*, pp. 1–26. Cambridge: Cambridge University Press.

McLuhan, Marshall. 1964. *Understanding Media*. New York: McGraw-Hill.

Mead, George Herbert. 1962 [1934]. *Mind, Self, & Society from the Standpoint of a Social Behaviorist*. Chicago: University of Chicago Press.

Mead, Margaret. 1978 [1928]. *Coming of Age in Samoa*. Harmondsworth: Penguin.

Meillassoux, Claude. 1967. Recherche d'un niveau de détermination dans la société cynégetique. *L'Homme et la société*, **6**: 95–105.

Melhuus, Marit. 1990. A Shame to Honour – A Shame to Suffer. *Ethnos*, **55**: 5–25.

Middleton, John and David Tait, eds. 1970 [1958]. *Tribes without Rulers*. London: Routledge & Kegan Paul.

Miller, Daniel. 1987. *Material Culture and Mass Consumption*. Oxford: Blackwell.

———. 1988. Appropriating the State on a Council Estate. *Man*, **26**: 323–41.

———. 1993a. The Young and the Restless in Trinidad: A Case of the Local and the Global in Mass Consumption. In R. Silverstone and E. Hirsch, eds, *Consuming Technologies*, pp. 163–82. London: Routledge.

———. 1993b. *Modernity – An Ethnographic Approach*. Oxford: Berg.

——. 1994. Artefacts and the Meaning of Things. In Tim Ingold, ed., *Companion Encyclopedia of Anthropology: Humanity, Culture and Social Life*, pp. 396–419. London: Routledge.

Miller, Solomon. 1965. Proletarianization of Indian Peasants in Northern Peru. In Dwight B. Heath, ed., *Contemporary Cultures and Societies of Latin America*, pp. 135–42. Prospect Heights, IL: Waveland.

Mills, C. Wright. 1959. *The Sociological Imagination*. Oxford: Oxford University Press.

Milton, Kay, ed. 1993. *Environmentalism*. London: Routledge.

Mintz, Sidney. 1974. *Caribbean Transformations*. Chicago: Aldine.

Mitchell, J. Clyde. 1956. *The Kalela Dance: Aspects of Social Relationships among Urban Africans in Northern Rhodesia*. Livingstone: Rhodes-Livingstone Papers, **27**.

——. 1966. Theoretical Orientations in African Urban Studies. In Michael Banton, ed., *The Social Anthropology of Complex Societies*, pp. 37–68. London: Tavistock.

Moerman, Michael. 1965. Who Are the Lue: Ethnic Identification in a Complex Civilization. *American Anthropologist*, **67**: 1215–29.

Morphy, Howard. 1994. The Anthropology of Art. In Tim Ingold, ed., *Companion Encyclopedia of Anthropology: Humanity, Culture and Social Life*, pp. 648–85. London: Routledge.

Morris, Brian. 1994. *Anthropology of the Self. The Individual in Cultural Perspective*. London: Pluto.

Murphy, Yolanda and Robert Murphy. 1985. *Women of the Forest*. New York: Columbia University Press.

Nadel, S.F. 1952. Witchcraft in Four African Societies: An Essay in Comparison. *American Anthropologist*, **54**: 18–29.

Nash, Manning. 1988. *The Cauldron of Ethnicity in the Modern World*. Chicago: University of Chicago Press.

Needham, Rodney. 1962. *Structure and Sentiment*. Chicago: University of Chicago Press.

——. 1971. Incest. In Rodney Needham, ed., *Rethinking Kinship and Marriage*, pp. 24–34. London: Tavistock.

——. ed. 1971. *Rethinking Kinship and Marriage*. London: Tavistock.

Newman, Katherine. 1988. *Falling from Grace. The Experience of Downward Mobility in the American Middle Class*. New York: Vintage.

Okely, Judith. 1983. *The Traveller-gypsies*. Cambridge: Cambridge University Press.

Olwig, Karen Fog. 1985. *Cultural Adaptation and Resistance on St. John. Three Centuries of Afro-Caribbean Life*. Gainesville: University of Florida Press.

——. 1993. *Global Culture, Island Identity*. Chur, Switzerland: Harwood Academic Publishers.

Ong, Walter J. 1969. World as View and World as Event. *American Anthropologist*, **71**(4): 634–47.

——. 1982. *Orality and Literacy: The Technologizing of the Word*. London: Methuen.

Ortner, Sherry B. 1974. Is Female to Male as Nature Is to Culture? In Michelle Z. Rosaldo and Louise Lamphere, eds, *Woman, Culture & Society*, pp. 67–87. Stanford, CA: Stanford University Press.

—— and Harriet Whitehead. 1981. Accounting for Sexual Meanings. In Sherry B. Ortner and Harriet Whitehead, eds, *Sexual Meanings*, pp. 1–27. Cambridge: Cambridge University Press.

Orwell, George. 1984 [1949]. *1984*. Oxford: Clarendon.

Overing, Joanna, ed. 1985. *Reason and Morality*. London: Tavistock.

Paine, Robert. 1985. Ethnodrama and the 'Fourth World': The Saami Action Group in Norway. Memorial University of Newfoundland: *Social and Economic Papers,* **14.**

——. 1992. The Claim of Aboriginality: Saami in Norway. In Reidar Grønhaug, Gunnar Haaland and Georg Henriksen, eds, *The Ecology of Choice and Symbol. Essays in Honour of Fredrik Barth,* pp. 388–407. Bergen: Alma Mater.

Pálsson, Gisli, ed. 1993. *Beyond Boundaries. Understanding, Translation and Anthropological Discourse.* Oxford: Berg.

Parkin, David. 1969. *Neighbours and Nationals in an African City Ward.* London: Routledge & Kegan Paul.

Parsons, Talcott. 1977. *The Evolution of Societies.* Englewood Cliffs, NJ: Prentice-Hall.

Pehrson, Robert N. 1964. *The Bilateral Networks of Social Relations in Könkämä Lapp District.* Oslo: Ethnographic Museum.

Pelto, Pertti J. and Gretel H. Pelto. 1970. *Anthropological Research.* Cambridge: Cambridge University Press.

Peristiany, J.G., ed. 1967. *Honour and Shame. The Values of Mediterranean Society.* London: Weidenfeld & Nicholson.

Pfaffenberger, Bryan. 1988. Fetishised Objects and Humanised Nature: Towards an Anthropology of Technology. *Man* (n.s.), **23**: 236–52.

Polanyi, Karl. 1957 [1941]. *The Great Transformation: The Political and Economic Origins of our Time.* Boston, MA: Beacon.

Popper, Karl. 1968 [1959]. *The Logic of Scientific Discovery.* New York: Harper & Row.

Pratt, Mary Louise. 1986. Fieldwork in Common Places. In James Clifford and George E. Marcus, eds, *Writing Culture. The Poetics and Politics of Ethnography,* pp. 27–50. Berkeley: University of California Press.

Radcliffe-Brown, A.R. 1951. The Comparative Method in Social Anthropology. *Journal of the Royal Anthropological Institute,* **81**: 15–22.

——. 1952. *Structure and Function in Primitive Society.* London: Cohen & West.

Rappaport, Roy A. 1968. *Pigs for the Ancestors. Ritual in the Ecology of a New Guinea People.* New Haven, CT: Yale University Press.

——. 1984. Epilogue, 1984. In Roy A. Rappaport: *Pigs for the Ancestors,* 2nd edition. New Haven, CT: Yale University Press.

Redfield, Robert. 1955. *The Little Community. Viewpoints for the Study of a Human Whole.* Chicago: University of Chicago Press.

Reining, Conrad C. 1966. *The Zande Scheme: An Anthropological Case Study of Economic Development in Africa.* Evanston, IL: North-Western University Press.

Renteln, Alison Dundes. 1990. *International Human Rights.* London: Sage.

Riches, David, ed. 1986. *The Anthropology of Violence.* Oxford: Blackwell.

Riegelhaupt, Joyce. 1967. Saloio Women: An Analysis of Informal and Formal Political and Economic Roles of Portuguese Peasant Women. *Anthropological Quarterly,* **40**: 109–36.

Rivers, W.H.R. 1924. *Social Organization.* London: Kegan Paul.

Rodman, Margaret C. 1992. Empowering Place: Multilocality and Multivocality. *American Anthropologist,* **94**: 640–56.

Roosens, Eugeen E. 1989. *Creating Ethnicity: The Process of Ethnogenesis.* London: Sage.

Rosaldo, Michelle Z. 1974. Woman, Culture and Society: A Theoretical Overview. In Michelle Z. Rosaldo and Louise Lamphere, eds, *Woman, Culture and Society,* pp. 17–43. Stanford, CA: Stanford University Press.

—— 1980. *Knowledge and Passion: Ilongot Notions of Self and Social Life.* Cambridge: Cambridge University Press.

——. 1984. Toward an Anthropology of Self and Feeling. In Richard Shweder and Robert A. LeVine, eds, *Culture Theory*, pp. 137–54. Cambridge: Cambridge University Press.

—— and Louise Lamphere, eds. 1974. *Woman, Culture and Society*. Stanford, CA: Stanford University Press.

Rostow, W.W. 1965. *The Stages of Economic Growth: A Non-Communist Manifesto.* Cambridge: Cambridge University Press.

Rubin, Gayle. 1975. The 'Traffic' in Women: Notes on the 'Political Economy of Sex'. In Rayna Reiter, ed., *Toward an Anthropology of Women*, pp. 157–200. New York: Monthly Review Press.

Rushdie, Salman. 1989. *The Satanic Verses*. London: Viking.

Sahlins, Marshall D. 1963. Poor Man, Rich Man, Big Man, Chief: Political Types in Melanesia and Polynesia. *Comparative Studies in Society and History.* 5: 285–303.

——. 1968. *Tribesmen*. New York: Prentice-Hall.

——. 1972. *Stone Age Economics*. Chicago: Aldine.

——. 1976. *Culture and Practical Reason*. Chicago: Aldine.

——. 1977. *The Use and Abuse of Biology*. Chicago: University of Chicago Press.

——. 1985. *Islands of History*. Chicago: University of Chicago Press.

——. 1994. Goodbye to Tristes Tropes: Ethnography in the Context of Modern World History. In Robert Borofsky, ed., *Assessing Cultural Anthropology*, pp. 377–94. New York: McGraw-Hill.

Said, Edward. 1978. *Orientalism*. New York: Pantheon.

Salmond, Anne. 1982. Theoretical Landscapes: On a Cross-cultural Conception of Knowledge. In David Parkin, ed., *Semantic Anthropology*, pp. 65–87. London: Academic Press.

Sartre, Jean-Paul. 1957 [1943]. *Being and Nothingness: An Essay on Phenomenological Ontology*. London: Methuen.

——. 1960. *Critique de la raison dialectique*. Paris: Gallimard.

Saussure, Ferdinand de. 1965 [1916]. *Course in General Linguistics*. New York: McGraw-Hill.

Schechner, Richard. 1994. Ritual and Performance. In Tim Ingold, ed., *Companion Encyclopedia of Anthropology: Humanity, Culture and Social Life*, pp. 613–47. London: Routledge.

Scheper-Hughes, Nancy. 1994. Embodied Knowledge: Thinking with the Body in Critical Medical Anthropology. In Robert Borofsky, ed., *Assessing Cultural Anthropology*, pp. 229–39. New York: McGraw-Hill.

—— and Margaret Lock. 1987. The Mindful Body: A Prolegomenon to Future Work in Medical Anthropology. *Medical Anthropology Quarterly*, 1(1): 6–41.

Schlegel, Alice. 1977. Male and Female in Hopi Thought and Action. In Alice Schlegel, ed., *Sexual Stratification*, pp. 186–210. New York: Columbia University Press.

Schneider, David M. 1984. *A Critique of the Study of Kinship*. Ann Arbor: University of Michigan Press.

Scott, James C. 1985. *Weapons of the Weak: Everyday Forms of Peasant Resistance*. New Haven, CT: Yale University Press.

Seeger, Anthony. 1994. Music and Dance. In Tim Ingold, ed., *Companion Encyclopedia of Anthropology: Humanity, Culture and Social Life*, pp. 686–705. London: Routledge.

Sharp, Lauriston. 1974 [1952]. Steel Axes for Stone Age Australians. In Yehudi A. Cohen, ed., *Man in Adaptation: The Cultural Present*. Chicago: Aldine.

Shore, Cris. 1993. Ethnicity as Revolutionary Strategy: Communist Identity Construction in Italy. In Sharon Macdonald, ed., *Inside European Identities*, pp. 27–53. Oxford: Berg.

Sigaut, François. 1994. Technology. In Tim Ingold, ed., *Companion Encyclopedia of Anthropology: Humanity, Culture and Social Life*, pp. 420–59. London: Routledge.

Sjöberg, Katarina. 1993. *The Return of the Ainu: Cultural Mobilization and the Practice of Ethnicity in Japan*. London: Harwood.

Skálnik, Peter. 1992. Etat. In Pierre Bonté and Michel Izard, eds, *Dictionnaire de l'ethnologie et de l'anthropologie*, pp. 239–42. Paris: Presses Universitaires Françaises.

Smith, Anthony D. 1986. *The Ethnic Origins of Nations*. Oxford: Blackwell.

——. 1991. *National Identity*. Harmondsworth: Penguin.

Smith, Raymond T. 1956. *The Negro Family of British Guiana*. London: Routledge & Kegan Paul.

Sørum, Arve. 1993. Personal communication.

Sperber, Dan. 1985. Anthropology and Psychology: Towards an Epidemiology of Representations. *Man*, **20**(1): 73–87.

——. 1989. L'Etude anthropologique des répresentations: problèmes et perspectives. In Denise Jodelet, ed., *Les Représentations sociales*, pp. 115–30. Paris: Presses Universitaires Françaises.

Srinivas, M.N. 1952. *Religion and Society among the Coorgs of South India*. Oxford: Clarendon.

Stenning, Derrick J. 1962. Household Viability among the Pastoral Fulani. In Jack Goody, ed., *The Developmental Cycle of Domestic Groups*, pp. 92–119. Cambridge: Cambridge University Press.

Steward, Julian. 1955. *The Theory of Culture Change: The Methodology of Multilinear Evolution*. Urbana: University of Illinois Press.

Strathern, Marilyn. 1988. *The Gender of the Gift. Problems with Women and Problems with Society in Melanesia*. Berkeley: University of California Press.

——. 1992. *After Nature. English Kinship in the Late Twentieth Century*. Cambridge: Cambridge University Press.

Street, Brian W. and Niko Besnier. 1994. Aspects of Literacy. In Tim Ingold, ed., *Companion Encyclopedia of Anthropology: Humanity, Culture and Social Life*, pp. 503–26. London: Routledge.

Sussman, Linda K. 1983. *Medical Pluralism on Mauritius: A Study of Medical Beliefs and Practices in a Polyethnic Society*. Ann Arbor: University Microfilms.

Talle, Aud. 1988. *Women at a Loss: Changes in Maasai Pastoralism and their Effects on Gender Relations*. Stockholm: Stockholm Studies in Social Anthropology, **19**.

Tambiah, Stanley J. 1989. The Politics of Ethnicity. *American Ethnologist*, **16**(2): 335–49.

Taussig, Michael. 1984. Culture of Terror – Space of Death. Roger Casement's Putamayo Report and the Explanation of Torture. *Comparative Studies in Society and History*, **26**(3): 467–97.

Taylor, Charles. 1992. *Multiculturalism and the Politics of Recognition*, ed. Amy Gutmann. Princeton, NJ: Princeton University Press.

Tempels, Placide. 1959. *Bantu Philosophy*. Paris: Présence Africaine.

Terray, Emmanuel. 1972. *Marxism and 'Primitive' Societies*. New York: Monthly Review Press.

Thaiss, Gustav. 1978. The Conceptualization of Social Change through Metaphors. *Journal of Asian and African Studies*, **13**(1): 1–15.

Thomas, Nicholas. 1991. *Entangled Objects. Exchange, Material Culture and Colonialism in the Pacific*. Cambridge, MA: Harvard University Press.

Tilly, Charles. 1984. *Big Structures, Large Processes, Huge Comparisons*. New York: Russel Sage.
Tinker, Hugh. 1974. *A New System of Slavery: The Export of Indian Labour Overseas, 1830–1920*. Oxford: Oxford University Press.
Todorov, Tzvetan. 1989. *Nous et les autres. La Réflexion française sur la diversité humaine*. Paris: Seuil.
Tonkin, Elizabeth, Maryon Mcdonald and Malcolm Chapman, eds. 1989. *History and Ethnicity*. London: Routledge.
Tönnies, Ferdinand. 1963 [1889]. *Community and Society*. New York: Harper & Row.
Turnbull, Colin. 1979 [1961]. *The Forest People*. London: Picador.
———. 1983. *The Mbuti Pygmies: Adaptation and Change*. New York: Holt, Rinehart & Winston.
———. 1985. *The Human Cycle*. New York: Simon & Schuster.
Turner, Victor. 1967. *The Forest of Symbols: Aspects of Ndembu Ritual*. Ithaca, NJ: Cornell University Press.
———. 1969. *The Ritual Process*. Chicago: Aldine.
———. 1974. *Dramas, Fields, and Metaphors*. Ithaca, NJ: Cornell University Press.
Tylor, Edward B. 1968 [1871]. The Science of Culture. In Morton Fried, ed., *Readings in Anthropology*, vol. II: *Cultural Anthropology*. New York: Crowell.

Van den Berghe, Pierre. 1975. Ethnicity and Class in Highland Peru. In Leo Despres, ed., *Ethnicity and Resource Competition in Plural Societies*. The Hague: Mouton.
Van der Veer, Peter. 1994. *Religious Nationalism: Hindus and Muslims in India*. Berkeley: University of California Press.
Van Gennep, Arnold. 1909. *Les Rites de passage*. Paris: Emile Nourry.
Veblen, Thorstein. 1953 [1899]. *The Theory of the Leisure Class. An Economic Study of Institutions*. New York: Mentor Books.
Vermeulen, Hans and Cora Govers, eds. 1994. *The Anthropology of Ethnicity. Beyond 'Ethnic Groups and Boundaries'*. Amsterdam: Het Spinhuis.
Vertovec, Steven. 1992. *Hindu Trinidad*. London: Macmillan.

Wallerstein, Immanuel. 1974–79. *The Modern World-System* (3 vols). New York: Academic Press.
———. 1979. *The Capitalist World Economy*. Cambridge: Cambridge University Press.
Wallman, Sandra. 1986. Ethnicity and the Boundary Process in Context. In David Mason and John Rex, eds, *Theories of Race and Ethnic Relations*. London: Macmillan.
Weber, Max. 1978 [1919] *Economy and Society: An Outline of Interpretive Sociology*, ed. Günther Roth and Claus Wittich. Berkeley: University of California Press.
Weiner, Annette B. 1988. *The Trobrianders of Papua New Guinea*. New York: Holt, Rinehart & Winston.
Welsh, Robert L. 1983. Traditional Medicine and Western Medical Options among the Ningerum of Papua New Guinea. In Lola Romanucci-Ross et al., *The Anthropology of Medicine*, pp. 32–51. New York: Praeger.
Werbner, Pnina. 1994. Diaspora and Millennium. British Pakistani Global-local Fabulations on the Gulf War. In Akbar S. Ahmed and Hastings Donnan, eds, *Islam, Globalization and Modernity*, pp. 213–35. London: Routledge.
Whorf, Benjamin Lee. 1956. *Language, Thought, and Reality*. New York: Wiley.
Wikan, Unni. 1977. Man Becomes Woman: Transsexualism in Oman as a Key to Gender Roles. *Man*, **12** (2): 304–19.
———. 1992. *Managing Turbulent Hearts*. Chicago: University of Chicago Press.
Williams, Raymond. 1981. *Keywords*. London: Flamingo.

Wilson, Edward O. 1975. *Sociobiology: The New Synthesis*. Cambridge, MA: Harvard University Press.

——. 1978. *On Human Nature*. Cambridge, MA: Harvard University Press.

Wilson, Godfrey. 1941–2. *An Essay on the Economics of Detribalization in Northern Rhodesia, Parts I–II*. Livingstone: Rhodes-Livingstone Institute.

Wilson, Peter J. 1978. *Crab Antics*, 2nd edition. New Haven, CT: Yale University Press.

Wilson, Richard. 1991. Machine Guns and Mountain Spirits: The Cultural Effects of State Repression among the Q'eqchi' of Guatemala. *Critique of Anthropology* **11**(1): 33–61.

Winch, Peter. 1970 [1964]. Understanding a Primitive Society. In Bryan Wilson, ed., *Rationality*, pp. 1–18. Oxford: Blackwell.

Wittfogel, Karl. 1959. *Oriental Despotism: A Comparative Study of Total Power*. New Haven, CT: Yale University Press.

Wittgenstein, Ludwig. 1983 [1958]. *Philosophical Investigations*, trans. G.E.M. Anscombe. Oxford: Blackwell.

Wolf, Eric. 1966. *Peasants*. Englewood Cliffs, NJ: Prentice-Hall.

——. 1969 [1956]. The Hacienda System and Agricultural Classes in San José, Puerto Rico. In André Béteille, ed., *Inequality*, pp. 172–92. Harmondsworth: Penguin.

——. 1982. *Europe and the People without History*. Berkeley: University of California Press.

Woodburn, James. 1982. Social Dimensions of Death in Four African Hunting and Gathering Societies. In Maurice Bloch and Jonathan Parry, eds, *Death and the Regeneration of Life*, pp. 187–210. Cambridge: Cambridge University Press.

Worsley, Peter. 1968. *The Trumpet Shall Sound*, 2nd edition. New York: Shocken Books.

——. 1984. *The Three Worlds. Culture & World Development*. London: Weidenfeld & Nicholson.

——. 1990. Models of the Modern World-system. In Mike Featherstone, ed., *Global Culture. Nationalism, Globalization and Modernity*, pp. 83–96. London: Sage.

INDEX

314